David Masson

The Collected Writings Of Thomas De Quincey Vol-Xiii

David Masson

The Collected Writings Of Thomas De Quincey Vol-Xiii

ISBN/EAN: 9783742848864

Manufactured in Europe, USA, Canada, Australia, Japa

Cover: Foto ©Andreas Hilbeck / pixelio.de

Manufactured and distributed by brebook publishing software (www.brebook.com)

David Masson

The Collected Writings Of Thomas De Quincey Vol-Xiii

DE QUINCEY'S COLLECTED WRITINGS

VOL. XIII

TALES AND PROSE PHANTASIES

CONTENTS OF VOL. XIII

	PAGE
EDITOR'S PREFACE	1
ON MURDER CONSIDERED AS ONE OF THE FINE ARTS—	
FIRST PAPER	9
SECOND PAPER	52
POSTSCRIPT IN 1854	70
EARLY MEMORIALS OF GRASMERE	125
THE SPANISH MILITARY NUN	159
AUTHOR'S POSTSCRIPT	238
APPENDED EDITORIAL NOTE	245
SORTILEGE AND ASTROLOGY	251
THE ENGLISH MAIL-COACH—	
SECTION I.—THE GLORY OF MOTION	270
SECTION II.—THE VISION OF SUDDEN DEATH	300
SECTION III.—DREAM-FUGUE; FOUNDED ON THE PRECEDING THEME OF SUDDEN DEATH	318
POSTSCRIPT	328
SUSPIRIA DE PROFUNDIS: BEING A SEQUEL TO THE CONFESSIONS OF AN ENGLISH OPIUM-EATER—	
DREAMING	333
THE PALIMPSEST OF THE HUMAN BRAIN	340
VISION OF LIFE	350
MEMORIAL SUSPIRIA	351

SUSPIRIA DE PROFUNDIS (*continued*):—   PAGE
    SAVANNAH-LA-MAR 359
    LEVANA AND OUR LADIES OF SORROW . . 362

MISCELLANEA

DANISH ORIGIN OF THE LAKE-COUNTRY DIALECT . . 373

HISTORICO-CRITICAL INQUIRY INTO THE ORIGIN OF THE ROSICRUCIANS AND FREE-MASONS . . . 384

EDITOR'S PREFACE

It may be the chief recommendation of the present volume to a considerable number of readers that it overtakes at last the famous set of papers,—begun by De Quincey in a "First Essay" in 1827, continued in a "Second Essay" in 1839, and completed by a "Postscript" in 1854,—which bears the still startling name of *Murder Considered as one of the Fine Arts.* But the papers that follow in the volume are not without claims to admiration, even in so trying a companionship. It needed the imagination of a De Quincey to weave out of the real incidents of the perishing of two peasants, husband and wife, in a snow-storm among the Westmorland hills, such a legend of pathetic beauty for ever as is enshrined in his *Memorials of Grasmere.* Then, what a change of key, and what a revelation of another kind of dexterity, in his romance of *The Spanish Military Nun*! Here, it is true, he worked on materials ready to his hands; but it was his own art that rescued those materials from the comparative coarseness of their previous handling, and brought it about that, wherever the strange Spanish adventuress of the seventeenth century should be remembered, she should pass as a creation of De Quincey's. The little paper which comes next, called *Sortilege and Astrology,* is a specimen of De Quincey's cleverness in the invention of a light and playful bit of phantasy for a passing social occasion. Of *The English Mail-Coach,* in its three consecutive sections, what need to say more than that this is one of the papers which, by the suffrage of De Quincey's admirers all the world over, would be selected for preservation if it were necessary to limit the choice to those that would best transmit to future times an impression of some of his finest characteristics? To this succeeds the little cluster of fragments called *Suspiria de Profundis*. As De Quincey did not live to carry out fully his project of a pretty numerous series of papers under this collective name, and indeed disposed of some papers he had actually written for the series by publishing them separately and independently, the half-dozen pieces so reproduced in this volume are all that he left in print under that express designation. Remarkable pieces they are, three of them especially; but the crowning distinction of the whole cluster is derived from one in particular. Absolutely, and by universal admission, the little piece called "Levana and Our Ladies of Sorrow," which we have put last among the *Suspiria*, is the finest thing that ever came from De Quincey's pen.

So large a portion of the contents of the volume being thus representative of De Quincey in some of the most intimate and peculiar qualities of his genius, one may dwell a little here on two of those qualities in particular.

While nearly all the chief writers in the long chronological list which summarises the literary history of the British Islands have been Humourists to some extent, only some have been wholly Humourists, or Humourists by such an overbalance in the general sum of their writings that one feels them to be sufficiently described all in all by that one name. Others have been Humourists only in the sense that portions of their writings have been of the humorous order, or that there has been an interfusion of the humorous here and there in their writings throughout. So far, therefore, as it may be desired to include De Quincey among the English Humourists, it must be in this modified, or non-exclusive, sense.

In that sense, most certainly, he *is* to be included among our English Humourists. Of the incidentally humorous in his miscellaneous writings there have been examples in abundance through the preceding volumes. It is in the present volume, however, that the peculiar humour of De Quincey may be studied in some of its best specimens. Take the story of *The Spanish Military Nun.* Not only is there in this story, as in so many others of De Quincey's papers, ample amusement in the form of playful wit in individual passages, and not only is there fun like that of the Spanish picaresque novels in the descriptions of the characters and situations; but it is because of the bathing of the whole from first to last in the spirit of that deeper kind of humour which suggests universal kindliness and tolerance, and can find the lovable and admirable even in the disreputable,— the humour of Shakespeare in his Falstaffs, Bardolphs, Nyms, and Pistols,—it is because of the importation by De Quincey of this kind of humour into the story that it is rescued, as we have said, from coarseness, and raised into poetry and romance. Though *Sortilege and Astrology* is a much slighter affair, he has contrived to exhibit in it two varieties of his skill in humorous effect. To the frolicsome gaiety of the first part there succeeds a satirical and murky kind of grotesque in the second; and one hardly knows which is the more De Quinceyish. But, as the world everywhere knows, it is by the two essays on *Murder considered as one of the Fine Arts* that De Quincey has most of all established his reputation for originality among English Humourists. True, the instrument of his humour throughout those two celebrated essays is the old Swiftian instrument of outrageous and sustained irony; but, apart from the pleasure derived from the curiously compacted erudition of the essays and from the artist-like finish of their style, what a difference between the serpentine exquisiteness of De Quincey's irony, the oily quietude of his assumed gravity, and the rough directness, the broadside strength, of the irony of Swift! And then the horrible gruesomeness of the total result! In the first of the essays the revel in ghastly fancies is already so various that one thinks it can go no farther; but in the second essay it breaks into sheer rollick and limitless delirium. In both, and indeed in the very conception of the papers, De Quincey's achievement was one of those feats of which only great writers are capable. Every great writer requires now and then what may be bluntly called "more elbow-room," and, on a sudden inspiration, will burst conventional bounds. Hence those occasional "extravaganzas" by a happy succession of which English Literature has been saved from all risk of stagnancy. So conscious was De Quincey of the unusually daring character of the "extravaganza" which *he* had perpetrated in his two Murder essays that he tried to safeguard himself by an attached apology. For some readers even yet the apology may not suffice ; but there the essays are,—irrevocably De Quincey's, and regarded now by conclusive opinion in the highest quarters as among the things likeliest to be permanent in English Prose. And this distinction they owe to the fact that they *were* extravaganzas, that they *did* burst bounds.

Besides the interest of the contents of the present volume as illustrating in a special manner De Quincey's faculty of humour, they have a further interest as illustrating also certain notions of his as to the undeveloped capabilities of English Prose.

One has to remember here those paragraphs in De Quincey's General Preface in 1853 to the Collective Edinburgh Edition of his writings, then just begun, in which, taking for his basis the twelve already-published volumes of the American Collective Edition, he ventured to indicate how his writings might be classified. (See *ante*, Vol. I, pp. 8-15.) After speaking, first, of that numerous class of his papers the chief purpose of which was general amusement combined with useful information (viz. his descriptive, biographical, and historical papers), and after having distinguished another class as consisting of essays properly so called (viz. speculative and critical discussions, with investigations of abstruse problems), he called attention to a third class. "Finally, as a third class," he said, "and, in "virtue of their aim, as a far higher class, of compositions "included in the American Edition, I rank *The Confessions* "*of an Opium-Eater*, and also (but more emphatically) the "*Suspiria de Profundis*. On these, as modes of impassioned "prose ranging under no precedents that I am aware of in any "literature, it is much more difficult to speak justly, whether "in a hostile or a friendly character." In some further sentences he emphasised his remark on the novelty of his literary attempts in this kind by asking his readers "to con- "sider the utter sterility of universal literature in this one "department of impassioned prose." His meaning in these expressions by themselves is far from clear; but I think it may be elucidated by bringing together the sense of various dispersed passages in his writings.

De Quincey, I find, recognised three kinds of prose as worthy of the name of literary art, in distinction from the ordinary jog-trot prose which suffices for business-documents, books of information, &c. :—1 RHETORICAL PROSE. His exposition of the characteristics of this kind of prose will be found best in his essay on *Rhetoric* (*ante*, Vol. X, pp. 81-133). The term which he had selected, as I had occasion to remark in connexion with the essay, an unhappy misnomer, inasmuch as it proceeded from a conception of Rhetoric utterly astray from all previous tradition. But, though the name was capricious, it did point to a special kind of literary practice for which a name is required. What De Quincey meant by "rhetoric" or a "rhetorical" style of writing was, as I ventured to explain (Vol. X, p. 3), "the art of rich or " ornate style, the art of conscious playing with a subject " intellectually and inventively, and of never leaving it till " it has been brocaded with the utmost possible amount of " subsidiary thought, humour, fancy, ornamentation, and " anecdote." De Quincey gave a list of eminent English representatives of this " rich " kind of English style, beginning with Donne, Jeremy Taylor, and Sir Thomas Browne; and, if he had stretched the list into his own time, he would have had to include himself! De Quincey's writings generally are among the best illustrations that could be cited of the " rich " style in English prose. Of this, of course, he was aware; but it was not this that he had in view when he referred to certain of his writings as examples of a mode of prose in which there had been no precedents.—II. ELOQUENT PROSE, or PROSE ELOQUENCE. In the same essay De Quincey distinguished " Eloquence " from what he wanted to call " Rhetoric," and, though hinting that examples of what he would regard specifically as " eloquence " might be found in the writings of some of his " rhetorical " favourites, evidently desired to wall off " eloquent writing " as a species by itself. In fact, what he proposed thus to distinguish as a distinct species of literary practice was Oratory, the literature of fervid and powerfully moved feeling of any sort,—indignation, pity, scorn, patriotic enthusiasm, earnestness of religious or moral conviction. As, however, there had been no deficiency of such "eloquent prose" in the course of English Literature, but, on the contrary, an abundance of most splendid examples, the "impassioned prose" of which De Quincey conceived himself to be the first exemplar must have been something of a very special nature. Our interpretation of his meaning is that, while he was willing to take his chance of being reputed capable of eloquent or impassioned writing in the general sense, what he reserved as the "mode of impassioned prose" in which he could claim to be singular was a kind of new lyrical prose that could undertake the expression of feelings till then supposed unutterable except in verse. Oratory in some of its extremes—as when the feeling to be expressed is peculiarly keen and ecstatic—does tend to pass into song or metrical lyric; and De Quincey, in order to extend the powers of prose in this extreme and difficult direction, proposed to institute, we may say, a new form of prose-literature nameable as the prose-lyric. III. PROSE PHANTASY or PROSE POETRY. Despite the prevalence still of the vulgar and disastrous misconception which has made Poetry a mere synonym for Verse-Literature of any sort, all sound theorists are agreed in some variety or other of that definition of Poetry which makes it to consist essentially in a particular kind of matter or mental product,—viz. the matter or product of the faculty or mood of mind called Imagination or Phantasy. Hence, in all sound theory, the novel, the romance, the prose-drama, and all other prose-works of the imaginative order,—*i.e.* of "feigned history," as Bacon called it,—are regarded as so many forms of Poetry, having their metrical equivalents in the verse-epic, the verse-drama, &c. Fielding, for example, expressly vindicated the right of the novel to be considered as simply the prose epic. At the same time, not only is it certain that even such solid matter of phantasy or "feigned history" as may be undertaken in prose receives incalculable modifications when it is lifted into verse; but it is also certain that there are peculiar kinds of phantasy for which Prose in all ages has felt itself incompetent, or which it has been too shamefaced to attempt. Such, in especial, are the visionary phantasies that form themselves in the poetic mind in its most profound fits of solitary self-musing, its hours of inventive day-dream in some sequestered nook of rocky sea-shore, or of long nocturnal reverie within-doors over the embers of a dying fire. Now, as De Quincey had been a dreamer all his life, with an abnormal faculty of dreaming at work in him constitutionally from his earliest infancy, and with the qualification moreover that he had unlocked the terrific potencies of opium for the generation of dreams beyond the human, his idea seems to have been that, if prose would but exert itself, it could compass, almost equally with verse, or even better, the representation of some forms at least of dream-experience and dream-phantasmagory. Add this idea to that other of the possibility of a prose-lyric that should rival the verse-lyric in ability to express the keenest and rarest forms of human feeling, or suppose the two ideas combined, and De Quincey's conception of the exact nature of his service towards the extension of the liberties and powers of English prose will be fully apprehended.

Examples of De Quincey's use of a twofold agency of dreamy prose-phantasy and impassioned prose-lyric are scattered through his writings generally. He refers, however, to his *Confessions of an Opium-Eater* as more largely representative in this respect; and those who have read the *Confessions* in the enlarged edition of them in 1856 will remember passages enough in illustration. He purposely bedded in the text of that enlarged edition passages of this sort which he had penned independently; and he annexed to the edition, by way of overplus and appendage, the fine prose-phantasy called *The Daughter of Lebanon*. His *Autobiographic Sketches* were similarly used, in various places, as a receptacle for independently-written pieces of prose-lyric. But it is in the present volume that there will be found those specimens of De Quincey's genius in his peculiar art of prose-phantasy from which his conceptions of the art itself may be best inferred, and the amount of his success in it most surely appraised. *The English Mail-Coach* and the *Suspiria de Profundis* have a certain interconnexion, and possess between them the supreme interest in the class to which they belong. The first two sections of *The English Mail-Coach* are noble pieces of prose-poetry, and more successful, all in all, I think, than the appended "Dream Fugue." Though that is an extraordinary piece of writing too, and gains on one perhaps by repeated reading, the prefixed direction "*Tumultuosissimamente*" rather repels one, as too suggestive of artificiality and the flourished baton of the leader of an orchestra; and the total effect does not seem equal to the exertion expended. The first three fragments of the *Suspiria*, besides being but a kind of wreckage from prior materials, are somewhat didactic in their tenor, and only prepare the way, and that rather raggedly, for the "Memorial Suspiria" and the fragments called "Savannah-la-Mar" and "Levana and Our Ladies of Sorrow." Most memorable pieces of impassioned prose-phantasy are all these three; but it is the last that is transcendent. Even alone, *that* would have made De Quincey immortal.

Some space having been left after the conclusion of the series of De Quincey's papers classed in this edition as his "Tales, Romances, and Prose-Phantasies," we commence in this volume the publication of those surplus papers of his, pretty numerous and of different sorts, which may be thrown together as *Miscellanea*. The bulk of these will follow in our next and final volume; and, as the arrangement *there* is to be as nearly chronological as possible, the precedence in the entire series is due to the two that appear in the present. *The Danish Origin of the Lake-Country Dialect* is of date 1819-20, and is taken from an interesting recent pamphlet by Mr. Pollitt of Kendal, telling the story of De Quincey's strange editorship of the "Westmorland Gazette." The long paper on the *Origin of the Rosicrucians and Free-masons* is a De Quinceyfied compilation from the German, done in 1824. Though it is unpromising at the outset, and rather haggard in form, the reader who may persist will find it full of ingenious and curious matter.

D. M.

ON MURDER

CONSIDERED AS ONE OF THE FINE ARTS

FIRST PAPER[1]

I. ADVERTISEMENT OF A MAN MORBIDLY VIRTUOUS[2]

MOST of us who read books have probably heard of a Society for the Promotion of Vice, of the Hell-Fire Club founded in the last century by Sir Francis Dashwood, &c.[3] At Brighton I think it was that a Society was formed for the Suppression of Virtue. That society was itself suppressed; but I am sorry to say that another exists in London, of a character still more atrocious. In tendency, it may be denominated a Society for the Encouragement of Murder; but, according to their own delicate εὐφημισμός, it is styled, the Society of Connoisseurs in Murder. They profess to be curious in

---

[1] This First Paper of the composite series now bearing the general title "On Murder Considered as one of the Fine Arts," appeared originally in *Blackwood's Magazine* for February 1827,—the same number which contained De Quincey's article on the Last Days of Kant. He reprinted it, with modifications, in 1854, in vol. iv of the Collective Edition of his Writings, along with the Second or Supplementary Paper, which had meanwhile appeared in *Blackwood* for November 1839,—at the same time completing the Murder Series by the addition of the long "Postscript."—M.

[2] This sub-title for the introductory paragraph was invented by De Quincey when he reprinted the paper in 1854. As originally printed in *Blackwood*, the paper opened thus:—"*To the Editor of Blackwood's Magazine.*—Sir, We have all heard of a Society for the Promotion of Vice," &c.—M.

[3] Convivial fraternities under the outrageous name of *Hell-Fire Clubs*,—because founded on a principle of ostentatious contempt and

homicide, amateurs and dilettanti in the various modes of carnage, and, in short, Murder-Fanciers. Every fresh atrocity of that class which the police annals of Europe bring up, they meet and criticise as they would a picture, statue, or other work of art. But I need not trouble myself with any attempt to describe the spirit of their proceedings, as the reader will collect *that* much better from one of the Monthly Lectures read before the society last year. This has fallen into my hands accidentally, in spite of all the vigilance exercised to keep their transactions from the public eye. The publication of it will alarm them; and my purpose is that it should. For I would much rather put them down quietly, by an appeal to public opinion, than by such an exposure of names as would follow an appeal to Bow Street; which last appeal, however, if this should fail, I must really resort to. For my intense virtue will not put up with such things in a Christian land. Even in a heathen land the toleration of murder—viz. in the dreadful shows of the amphitheatre—was felt by a Christian writer to be the most crying reproach of the public morals. This writer was Lactantius[1]; and with his words, as singularly applicable to the present occasion, I shall conclude:—"Quid tam horribile," says he, "tam tetrum, quam hominis trucidatio? Ideo
" severissimis legibus vita nostra munitur; ideo bella execra-
" bilia sunt. Invenit tamen consuetudo quatenus homicidium
" sine bello ac sine legibus faciat; et hoc sibi voluptas quod
" scelus vindicavit. Quod, si interesse homicidio sceleris
" conscientia est, et eidem facinori spectator obstrictus est

ridicule of the established religion and of all ordinary morality, and indulging, it was supposed, in blasphemous and profligate orgies,—came into being in the early part of the eighteenth century, and spread like an epidemic through the British Islands during the next fifty or sixty years. The particular club of this kind which De Quincey here mentions was the famous fraternity of the *Monks of St. Francis*, called also *The Medmenham Club*, whose usual place of meeting was the mansion-house of Medmenham in Buckinghamshire, originally a Cistercian monastery. The most notorious members of the club were Sir Francis Dashwood, baronet (known from 1763 onwards as Lord Le Despencer), and John Wilkes; but it included the poet Churchill, the less-known poets Lloyd and Whitehead, Sir John Dashwood King, Bubb Doddington, and others.—M.

[1] Latin Christian writer of the fourth century.—M.

"cui et admissor, ergo et in his gladiatorum cædibus non minus cruore profunditur qui spectat quam ille qui facit: nec potest esse immunis a sanguine qui voluit effundi, aut videri non interfecisse qui interfectori et favit et præmium postulavit."—"What is so dreadful," says Lactantius, "what so dismal and revolting, as the murder of a human creature? Therefore it is that life for us is protected by laws the most rigorous; therefore it is that wars are objects of execration. And yet the traditional usage of Rome has devised a mode of authorising murder apart from war, and in defiance of law; and the demands of taste (voluptas) are now become the same as those of abandoned guilt." Let the Society of Gentlemen Amateurs consider this; and let me call their especial attention to the last sentence, which is so weighty, that I shall attempt to convey it in English: "Now, if merely to be present at a murder fastens on a man the character of an accomplice; if barely to be a spectator involves us in one common guilt with the perpetrator: it follows, of necessity, that, in these murders of the amphitheatre, the hand which inflicts the fatal blow is not more deeply imbrued in blood than his who passively looks on; neither can *he* be clear of blood who has countenanced its shedding; nor that man seem other than a participator in murder who gives his applause to the murderer and calls for prizes on his behalf." The "*præmia postulavit*" I have not yet heard charged upon the Gentlemen Amateurs of London, though undoubtedly their proceedings tend to that; but the "*interfectori favit*" is implied in the very title of this association, and expressed in every line of the lecture which follows.   X. Y. Z.[1]

[1] To this introductory paragraph as it originally appeared in *Blackwood* there was subjoined the following, probably from the pen of De Quincey's friend Christopher North, the reputed editor of the magazine:—"[*Note of the Editor*:—We thank our correspondent for his "communication, and also for the quotation from Lactantius, which is "very pertinent to *his* view of the case; our own, we confess, is differ-"ent. We cannot suppose the lecturer to be in earnest, any more than "Erasmus in his Praise of Folly, or Dean Swift in his Proposal for "Eating Children. However, either on his own view or on ours, it "is equally fit that the lecture should be made public.]"—Wilson, it would seem, was a little dubious as to the reception of a paper in such a ghastly strain and with such a ghastly title. The words "our

II. THE LECTURE

GENTLEMEN:—I have had the honour to be appointed by your committee to the trying task of reading the Williams Lecture on Murder Considered as One of the Fine Arts,—a task which might be easy enough three or four centuries ago, when the art was little understood, and few great models had been exhibited; but in this age, when masterpieces of excellence have been executed by professional men, it must be evident that in the style of criticism applied to them the public will look for something of a corresponding improvement. Practice and theory must advance *pari passu*. People begin to see that something more goes to the composition of a fine murder than two blockheads to kill and be killed, a knife, a purse, and a dark lane. Design, gentlemen, grouping, light and shade, poetry, sentiment, are now deemed indispensable to attempts of this nature. Mr. Williams has exalted the ideal of murder to all of us,[1] and to me, therefore, in particular, has deepened the arduousness of my task. Like Æschylus or Milton in poetry, like Michael Angelo in painting, he has carried his art to a point of colossal sublimity, and, as Mr. Wordsworth observes, has in a manner "created the taste by which he is to be enjoyed." To sketch the history of the art, and to examine its principles critically, now remains as a duty for the connoisseur, and for judges of quite another stamp from his Majesty's Judges of Assize.

Before I begin, let me say a word or two to certain prigs, who affect to speak of our society as if it were in some degree immoral in its tendency. Immoral! Jupiter protect me, gentlemen![2] what is it that people mean? I am for morality, and always shall be, and for virtue, and all that; and I do affirm, and always shall (let what will come of it), that murder is an improper line of conduct, highly improper; and I do not stick to assert that any man who deals in murder must have very incorrect ways of thinking,

correspondent" seem to imply that the paper was sent by De Quincey from Grasmere.—M.

[1] John Williams, the London murderer of 1811. The story of his murders is told in the *Postscript*.—M.

[2] The original phrase in *Blackwood* was "Immoral! God bless my soul, gentlemen!"—M.

and truly inaccurate principles; and, so far from aiding and abetting him by pointing out his victim's hiding-place, as a great moralist of Germany declared it to be every good man's duty to do,[1] I would subscribe one shilling and sixpence to have him apprehended,—which is more by eighteen-pence than the most eminent moralists have hitherto subscribed for that purpose. But what then? Everything in this world has two handles. Murder, for instance, may be laid hold of by its moral handle (as it generally is in the pulpit and at the Old Bailey), and *that*, I confess, is its weak side; or it may also be treated *æsthetically*, as the Germans call it—that is, in relation to good taste.

To illustrate this, I will urge the authority of three eminent persons: viz. S. T. Coleridge, Aristotle, and Mr. Howship the surgeon.

To begin with S. T. C..—One night, many years ago, I was drinking tea with him in Berners Street (which, by the way, for a short street, has been uncommonly fruitful in men of genius).[2] Others were there besides myself; and, amidst

[1] Kant—who carried his demands of unconditional veracity to so extravagant a length as to affirm that, if a man were to see an innocent person escape from a murderer, it would be his duty, on being questioned by the murderer, to tell the truth, and to point out the retreat of the innocent person, under any certainty of causing murder. Lest this doctrine should be supposed to have escaped him in any heat of dispute, on being taxed with it by a celebrated French writer, he solemnly re-affirmed it, with his reasons.

[2] In Cunningham's *Handbook of London* (1850) the street is thus described:—"A street chiefly inhabited by artists. Sir William "Chambers was living in it in 1773, Fuseli in 1804, and Opie from "1792 to 1808. No. 8 was Opie's; No. 13 Fuseli's; and No. 15 "Bone the enameler's; No. 6 was the Banking House of Marsh, "Stracey, Fauntleroy, and Graham. The loss to the Bank of Eng-"land by Fauntleroy's forgeries amounted to the sum of £360,000. "No. 54 was (26th November 1810) the scene of the famous Berners "Street Hoax,—a trick of Theodore Hook's when a young man "(described at length in the *Quarterly Review*, No. 143, p. 62). The "lady on whom the hoax was played was Mrs. Tottingham, and the "trick itself (since frequently imitated) consisted in sending out two "hundred orders to different tradespeople to deliver goods, both "bulky and small, at the same house, to the same person, at the "same hour."—De Quincey may have had all this in his mind, as well as the fact that Coleridge had at one time lodged in the street. The phrase "many years ago," used in 1827, may imply that the time was between 1810 and 1812.—M.

some carnal considerations of tea and toast, we were all imbibing a dissertation on Plotinus from the Attic lips of S. T. C. Suddenly a cry arose of "*Fire—fire!*" upon which all of us, master and disciples, Plato and οἱ περὶ τον Πλατωνα, rushed out, eager for the spectacle. The fire was in Oxford Street, at a pianoforte-maker's; and, as it promised to be a conflagration of merit, I was sorry that my engagements forced me away from Mr. Coleridge's party before matters had come to a crisis. Some days after, meeting with my Platonic host, I reminded him of the case, and begged to know how that very promising exhibition had terminated. "Oh, sir," said he, "it turned out so ill that we damned it unanimously." Now, does any man suppose that Mr. Coleridge—who, for all he is too fat to be a person of active virtue, is undoubtedly a worthy Christian—that this good S. T. C., I say, was an incendiary, or capable of wishing any ill to the poor man and his pianofortes (many of them, doubtless, with the additional keys)? On the contrary, I know him to be that sort of man that I durst stake my life upon it he would have worked an engine in a case of necessity, although rather of the fattest for such fiery trials of his virtue. But how stood the case? Virtue was in no request. On the arrival of the fire engines, morality had devolved wholly on the insurance office. This being the case, he had a right to gratify his taste. He had left his tea. Was he to have nothing in return?

I contend that the most virtuous man, under the premises stated, was entitled to make a luxury of the fire, and to hiss it, as he would any other performance that raised expectations in the public mind which afterwards it disappointed. Again, to cite another great authority, what says the Stagirite? He (in the Fifth Book, I think it is, of his Metaphysics) describes what he calls κλεπτὴν τέλειον—i.e. *a perfect thief*[1]; and, as to Mr. Howship, in a work of his on

---

[1] It is in the Fourth Book, chap. xvi, and stands thus:—"A perfect or finished physician, and a perfect or finished musician, are such when they are in no wise deficient as far as regards the species of excellence that is proper to their professions so also, transferring our remarks to the case of evil things, we say a perfect or finished sycophant, and a *finished thief*."—M.

Indigestion [1] he makes no scruple to talk with admiration of a certain ulcer which he had seen, and which he styles "a beautiful ulcer." Now, will any man pretend that, abstractly considered, a thief could appear to Aristotle a perfect character, or that Mr. Howship could be enamoured of an ulcer? Aristotle, it is well known, was himself so very moral a character that, not content with writing his Nicomachean Ethics in one volume octavo, he also wrote another system, called *Magna Moralia*, or Big Ethics. Now, it is impossible that a man who composes any ethics at all, big or little, should admire a thief *per se*; and, as to Mr. Howship, it is well known that he makes war upon all ulcers, and, without suffering himself to be seduced by their charms, endeavours to banish them from the county of Middlesex. But the truth is that, however objectionable *per se*, yet, relatively to others of their class, both a thief and an ulcer may have infinite degrees of merit. They are both imperfections, it is true; but, to be imperfect being their essence, the very greatness of their imperfection becomes their perfection. *Spartam nactus es, hanc exorna.* A thief like Autolycus or the once famous George Barrington,[2] and a grim phagedænic ulcer,[3] superbly defined, and running regularly through all its natural stages, may no less justly be regarded as ideals after *their* kind than the most faultless moss-rose amongst flowers, in its progress from bud to "bright consummate flower," or, amongst human flowers, the most magnificent young female, apparelled in the pomp of womanhood. And thus not only the ideal of an inkstand may be imagined, as Mr. Coleridge illustrated in his celebrated correspondence with Mr. Blackwood,[4]—in which, by

[1] Howship, John: *Practical Remarks upon Indigestion*, 8vo, London, 1825.—M.

[2] George Waldron *alias* Barrington, the most famous gentleman-pickpocket of his time, was transported to Botany Bay in 1790, and died there in 1804, in respectable employment and with the reputation of a reformed character.—M.

[3] *Phagedænic*, Greek for "eating" or "corrosive": the word, whether in the form of the noun *phagedæna*, or of the adjective *phagedænic* or *phagedænous*, is a surgical definition of a special kind of ulcer.—M.

[4] Refers to certain whimsical letters of Coleridge in *Blackwood* for October 1821, in one of which are enumerated the requisites for a perfect or ideal inkstand.—M.

the way, there is not so much, because an inkstand is a laudable sort of thing, and a valuable member of society,—but even imperfection itself may have its ideal or perfect state.

Really, gentlemen, I beg pardon for so much philosophy at one time; and now let me apply it. When a murder is in the paulo-post-futurum tense—not done, not even (according to modern purism) *being* done, but only going to be done—and a rumour of it comes to our ears, by all means let us treat it morally. But suppose it over and done, and that you can say of it, Τετέλεσται, It is finished, or (in that adamantine molossus[1] of *Medea*) Εἴργασται, Done it is, it is â *fait accompli*; suppose the poor murdered man to be out of his pain, and the rascal that did it off like a shot nobody knows whither; suppose, lastly, that we have done our best, by putting out our legs, to trip up the fellow in his flight, but all to no purpose—"abiit, evasit, excessit, erupit," etc.—why, then, I say, what's the use of any more virtue? Enough has been given to morality; now comes the turn of Taste and the Fine Arts. A sad thing it was, no doubt, very sad; but *we* can't mend it. Therefore let us make the best of a bad matter; and, as it is impossible to hammer anything out of it for moral purposes, let us treat it æsthetically, and see if it will turn to account in that way. Such is the logic of a sensible man; and what follows? We dry up our tears, and have the satisfaction, perhaps, to discover that a transaction which, morally considered, was shocking, and without a leg to stand upon, when tried by principles of Taste, turns out to be a very meritorious performance. Thus all the world is pleased; the old proverb is justified, that it is an ill wind which blows nobody good; the amateur, from looking bilious and sulky by too close an attention to virtue, begins to pick up his crumbs; and general hilarity prevails. Virtue has had her day; and henceforward, *Virtù*, so nearly the same thing as to differ only by a single letter (which surely is not worth haggling or higgling about)—*Virtù*, I repeat, and

---

[1] *Molossus* is the name in Greek prosody for a word or foot of three consecutive long syllables. The particular molossus which De Quincey goes on to quote,—the word εἴργασται,—occurs in line 293 of the *Medea* of Euripides.—M.

Connoisseurship, have leave to provide for themselves. Upon this principle, gentlemen, I propose to guide your studies from Cain to Mr. Thurtell. Through this great gallery of murder, therefore, together let us wander hand in hand, in delighted admiration; while I endeavour to point your attention to the objects of profitable criticism.

The first murder is familiar to you all. As the inventor of murder, and the father of the art, Cain must have been a man of first-rate genius. All the Cains were men of genius. Tubal Cain invented tubes, I think, or some such thing. But, whatever might be the originality and genius of the artist, every art was then in its infancy; and the works turned out from each several *studio* must be criticised with a recollection of that fact. Even Tubal's work would probably be little approved at this day in Sheffield; and therefore of Cain (Cain senior, I mean) it is no disparagement to say that his performance was but so-so. Milton, however, is supposed to have thought differently. By his way of relating the case, it should seem to have been rather a pet murder with him, for he retouches it with an apparent anxiety for its picturesque effect :—

> " Whereat he inly raged, and, as they talked,
> Smote him into the midriff with a stone
> That beat out life : he fell, and, deadly pale,
> Groaned out his soul, *with gushing blood effused*."
> *Par. Lost*, Bk. XI.

Upon this Richardson the painter, who had an eye for effect, remarks as follows in his " Notes on Paradise Lost," p. 497 : —" It has been thought," says he, " that Cain beat (as the " common saying is) the breath out of his brother's body with " a great stone : Milton gives in to this, with the addition, " however, of a large wound." In this place it was a judicious addition; for the rudeness of the weapon, unless raised and enriched by a warm, sanguinary colouring, has too much of the naked air of the savage school; as if the deed were perpetrated by a Polypheme, without science, premeditation, or anything but a mutton-bone. However, I am chiefly pleased with the improvement, as it implies that Milton was an amateur. As to Shakspere, there never was a better;

witness his description of the murdered Duncan, Banquo, &c.; and above all witness his incomparable miniature, in "Henry VI," of the murdered Gloucester.[1]

The foundation of the art having been once laid, it is pitiable to see how it slumbered without improvement for ages. In fact, I shall now be obliged to leap over all murders, sacred and profane, as utterly unworthy of notice until long after the Christian era. Greece, even in the age of Pericles, produced no murder, or at least none is recorded, of the

---

[1] The passage occurs in the *second* part (act 3) of "Henry VI," and is doubly remarkable: first, for its critical fidelity to nature, were the description meant only for *poetic* effect; but, secondly, for the *judicial* value impressed upon it when offered (as here it *is* offered) in silent corroboration legally of a dreadful whisper, all at once arising, that foul play had been dealing with a great prince, clothed with an official state character. It is the Duke of Gloucester, faithful guardian and loving uncle of the simple and imbecile king, who has been found dead in his bed. How shall this event be interpreted? Had he died under some natural visitation of Providence, or by violence from his enemies? The two court factions read the circumstantial indications of the case into opposite constructions. The affectionate and afflicted young king, whose position almost pledges him to neutrality, cannot, nevertheless, disguise his overwhelming suspicions of hellish conspiracy in the background. Upon this, a leader of the opposite faction endeavours to break the force of this royal frankness, countersigned and echoed most impressively by Lord Warwick. "What *instance*," he asks—meaning by *instance* not example or illustration, as thoughtless commentators have constantly supposed, but, in the common scholastic sense, what *instantia*, what pressure of argument, what urgent plea, can Lord Warwick put forward in support of his "dreadful oath"—an oath, namely, that, as surely as he hopes for the life eternal, so surely

"I do believe that violent hands were laid
Upon the life of this thrice famèd duke."

Ostensibly the challenge is to Warwick, but substantially it is meant for the King. And the reply of Warwick, the argument on which he builds, lies in a solemn array of all the changes worked in the duke's features by death, as irreconcilable with any other hypothesis than that this death had been a violent one. What argument have I that Gloucester died under the hands of murderers? Why, the following roll-call of awful changes, affecting head, face, nostrils, eyes, hands, &c., which do not belong indifferently to *any* mode of death, but exclusively to a death by violence:—

"But see, his face is black and full of blood,
His eyeballs further out than when he lived,
Staring full ghastly like a strangled man;
His hair uprear'd, his nostrils stretched with struggling;

slightest merit; and Rome had too little originality of genius in any of the arts to succeed where her model failed her.[1] In fact, the Latin language sinks under the very idea of murder. "The man was murdered;"—how will this sound in Latin? *Interfectus est, interemptus est*—which simply expresses a homicide; and hence the Christian Latinity of the middle ages was obliged to introduce a new word, such as the feebleness of classic conceptions never ascended to. *Murdratus est*, says the sublimer dialect of Gothic ages.[2] Meantime,

> His hands abroad display'd, as one that gasp'd
> And tugg'd for life, and was by strength subdued.
> Look, on the sheets, his hair, you see, is sticking;
> His well-proportion'd beard made rough and rugged,
> Like to the summer's corn by tempest lodged.
> It cannot be but he was murder'd here;
> The least of all these things were probable"

As the logic of the case, let us not for a moment forget that, to be of any value, the signs and indications pleaded must be sternly *diagnostic*. The discrimination sought for is between death that is natural and death that is violent. All indications, therefore, that belong equally and indifferently to either are equivocal, useless, and alien from the very purpose of the signs here registered by Shakspere.

[1] At the time of writing this [1827] I held the common opinion upon that subject. Mere inconsideration it was that led to so erroneous a judgment. Since then, on closer reflection, I have seen ample reason to retract it: satisfied I now [1854] am that the Romans, in every art which allowed to them any parity of advantages, had merits as racy, native, and characteristic, as the best of the Greeks. Elsewhere I shall plead this cause circumstantially, with the hope of converting the reader. In the meantime, I was anxious to lodge my protest against this ancient error,—an error which commenced in the time-serving sycophancy of Virgil the court-poet. With the base purpose of gratifying Augustus in his vindictive spite against Cicero, and by way of introducing, therefore, the little clause *orabunt causas melius* as applying to all Athenian against all Roman orators, Virgil did not scruple to sacrifice by wholesale the just pretensions of his compatriots collectively. [Compare *ante*, vol. x, pp. 54-59.—M.]

[2] De Quincey is here characteristically correct. The word *Murder* (though the same at ultimate root with the Latin *mori*, "to die," and *mors-mortis*, "death," and so with the Sanskrit *mri*, "to die") did come into the Christian Latinity of the Middle Ages, and so into the Romance tongues of Europe, by importation from the Gothic. "Wasuh than sa haitana Barabbas, mith thaim mith imma drobyandam gabundans, thaiei in auhyodau *maurthr* gatawidedun": so runs the verse, Mark xv. 7, in the Mœso-Gothic of Ulphilas; and, though it is a bit of the speech of the Goths of the Danube as old as 360 A.D., we

the Jewish school of murder kept alive whatever was yet known in the art, and gradually transferred it to the Western World. Indeed, the Jewish school was always respectable, even in its mediæval stages, as the case of Hugh of Lincoln shows, which was honoured with the approbation of Chaucer, on occasion of another performance from the same school, which, in his Canterbury Tales, he puts into the mouth of the Lady Abbess.[1]

Recurring, however, for one moment, to classical antiquity, I cannot but think that Catiline, Clodius, and some of that coterie, would have made first-rate artists; and it is on all accounts to be regretted that the priggism of Cicero robbed

can recognise its kinship with our own English in the same passage, "And there was one named Barabbas, which lay bound with them that had made insurrection with him, who had committed murder in the insurrection." I do not suppose that an older example can be produced of the Gothic noun *maurthr* (*murther*, *murder*); and I do not find it referred to in the article on the word *Murder* in even the latest edition of Du Cange's great Dictionary of Mediæval Latin. The essentially Gothic origin of the word is there recognised, however, in the general statement that it is from the "Saxon" *morth*, meaning death or slaughter (*ex Saxonico morth*); and, in five columns of copious learning, it is shown how the Mediæval Latinists appropriated this *morth* or *moroth*,—at first bedding it in that uncouth form in their own Latin texts, but at length boldly Latinising it into *murdrum* or *murtrum*, and so providing themselves with a train of requisite cognates in *multricium*, *murdificatio*, *murdredum*, *murdrare*, *murdrire*, *murdrator*, *murdritor*, &c. &c. From the Latin the word passed easily, of course, into the vernacular Romance tongues: *e.g.* the French *meurtre*, *meurtrir*. As the various Teutonic nations had conserved the Gothic word, in one form or another, in their own vernaculars,—*e.g.* in Anglo-Saxon, *morth* (death), *morthor* (violent death), and in German *mord* (murder), *morden* (to murder), *morder* (murderer),—their claim to it may be regarded as aboriginal. It may be doubted, however, whether the word *murder*, so common in early English after the Conquest in the alternative forms *morthre* and *mordre* (which alternative was kept up in much later English in the forms *murther* and *murder*), was only the native old Anglo-Saxon word *morth* or *morthor* conserved, or was a recovery from the Mediæval Latin directly or through the Norman-French. *Murther*, with the *th* sound, looks the more native English form; and in the First Folio Shakespeare the prevailing spelling of the word is, I think, *murther*, though the modern editors substitute *murder*.—M.

[1] Chaucer's *Prioresses Tale* in his Canterbury Pilgrimage is the story of a little Christian boy in a city in Asia, supposed to have been murdered by the Jews of the city because of the offence he gave

his country of the only chance she had for distinction in this line. As the *subject* of a murder, no person could have answered better than himself. Oh Gemini![1] how he would have howled with panic, if he had heard Cethegus under his bed. It would have been truly diverting to have listened to him; and satisfied I am, gentlemen, that he would have preferred the *utile* of creeping into a closet, or even into a *cloaca*, to the *honestum* of facing the bold artist.

To come now to the Dark Ages—(by which we that speak with precision mean, *par excellence*, the tenth century as a meridian line, and the two centuries immediately before and after, full midnight being from A.D. 888 to A.D. 1111)—those ages ought naturally to be favourable to the art of murder, as they were to church architecture, to stained glass, &c.; and, accordingly, about the latter end of this period, there arose a great character in our art,—I mean the Old Man of the Mountains. He was a shining light indeed, and I need not tell you that the very word "assassin" is deduced from him.[2] So keen an amateur was he that on one occasion,

them by always singing the Christian hymn *O Alma Redemptoris Mater* through the streets as he went to school. The Prioress concludes the story by referring to a specially English legend of a like character,— that of young "Hugh of Lincoln," whom some Jews of that town were said to have put to death for similar reasons by a horrible crucifixion. The historian Matthew Paris, who relates the thing as a fact that happened in his own lifetime, dates it in the year 1255, and adds that a number of Jews were executed for the crime in London in the following year. This explains the wording of the reference to it by the Prioress:—

"O yonge Hugh of Lincoln, sleyn also
With cursed Jewes, as it is notable,
For it nis but a little whyle ago."—M.

[1] "*Oh Gemini!*" This is a softening in 1854 from the original exclamation of 1827; which was "*Lord!*" Taste in such matters had become less robust in the interval.—M.

[2] The name "Old Man of the Mountains" does not designate any individual person, but was the title,—in Arabic *Sheikh-al-jebal*, "Prince of the Mountain,"—of a series of chiefs who presided from 1090 to 1258 over a community or military order of fanatical Mohammedan sectaries, called *The Assassins*, distributed through Persia and Syria, but with certain mountain-ranges for their headquarters. But, though there is no doubt that the words *assassin* and *assassination*, as terms for secret murder, and especially for secret murder by stabbing, are a recollection of the reputed habits of this old Persian and Syrian

when his own life was attempted by a favourite assassin, he was so much pleased with the talent shown that, notwithstanding the failure of the artist, he created him a duke upon the spot, with remainder to the female line, and settled a pension on him for three lives. Assassination is a branch of the art which demands a separate notice; and it is possible that I may devote an entire lecture to it. Meantime, I shall only observe how odd it is that this branch of the art has flourished by intermitting fits. It never rains but it pours. Our own age can boast of some fine specimens, such, for instance, as Bellingham's affair with the prime minister Perceval, the Duc de Berri's case at the Parisian Opera House, the Maréchal Bessières's case at Avignon[1]; and about two and a half centuries ago, there was a most brilliant constellation of murders in this class. I need hardly say that I allude especially to those seven splendid works: the assassinations of William I. of Orange; of the three French Henries, viz. of Henri, Duke of Guise, that had a fancy for the throne of France, of Henri III, last prince of the line of Valois,

community, the original etymology of the word *Assassins* itself, as the name of the community, is not so certain. Skeat sets it down as simply the Arabic *hashishin*, "hashish-drinkers," from the fact or on the supposition that the agents of the Old Man of the Mountains, when they were detached on their murderous errands, went forth nerved for the task by the intoxication of *hashish*, or Indian hemp.

[1] These three assassinations are an insertion in 1854. Spencer Perceval, whose Premiership began in 1809, was assassinated, by a pistol-shot in the lobby of the House of Commons, on the 11th May 1812, by a bankrupt Liverpool merchant named John Bellingham. The Duc de Berri, who was the second son of the Count d'Artois, heir-apparent to Louis XVIII, and afterwards that king's successor on the throne of France by the title of Charles X, had, by the death of his elder brother, the Duke of Orleans, become his father's prospective heir, when, on Sunday the 13th February 1820, he was stabbed by a Republican fanatic as he was leaving the opera-house in Paris, and handing his wife to her carriage. Jean-Baptiste Bessières, born 1768, one of Napoleon's ablest generals, and made marshal in 1804 and Duke of Istria in 1809, fell by a chance bullet in a skirmish with the Germans, 1st May 1813, the day before the battle of Lutzen; and his name is a misrecollection by De Quincey here for that of another of Napoleon's generals,—Guillaume Marie Anne Brune, born 1763, made a marshal in 1804, and assassinated by the populace at Avignon, 2d August 1815, just after the collapse of Napoleon's fortunes at Waterloo.—M.

who then occupied that throne, and finally of Henri IV, his brother-in-law, who succeeded to that throne as first prince in the line of Bourbon: not eighteen years later came the 5th on the roll, viz. that of our Duke of Buckingham (which you will find excellently described in the letters published by Sir Henry Ellis, of the British Museum), 6thly of Gustavus Adolphus, and 7thly of Wallenstein. What a glorious Pleiad of Murders! And it increases one's admiration that this bright constellation of artistic displays, comprehending 3 Majesties, 3 Serene Highnesses, and 1 Excellency, all lay within so narrow a field of time as between A.D. 1588 and 1635.[1] The King of Sweden's assassination, by the bye, is doubted by many writers, Harte amongst others; but they are wrong. He *was* murdered; and I consider his murder unique in its excellence; for he was murdered at noon-day, and on the field of battle—a feature of original conception which occurs in no other work of art that I remember. To conceive the idea of a secret murder on private account as enclosed within a little parenthesis on a vast stage of public battle-carnage is like Hamlet's subtle device of a tragedy within a tragedy. Indeed, all of these assassinations may be

[1] The chronology of the seven famous assassinations here grouped together by De Quincey is, more exactly, as follows:—(1) William of Orange, called "William the Silent," the first stadtholder of the United Dutch Provinces, assassinated at Delft, 10th July 1584, by Balthazar Gerard; (2) Henri, Duke of Guise, the head of the Guise faction, and of their design for dethroning Henry III of France, but assassinated by that king's contrivance in the royal apartments at Blois, 23d December 1588; (3) the said Henry III of France, assassinated by Jacques Clement, a fanatical Dominican friar, 2d August 1589; (4) Henry IV of France, the great and good Henry of Navarre, who came to the throne as a Huguenot, assassinated, 14th May 1610, by Francis Ravaillac; (5) the resplendent George Villiers, Duke of Buckingham, favourite of James I. and Charles I., and supreme minister of England in the end of James's reign and the beginning of Charles's, assassinated at Portsmouth, 23d August 1628, by the knife of John Felton; (6) Gustavus Adolphus, the heroic King of Sweden, champion of European Protestantism through one of the stages of the great Thirty Years' War, shot on his horse in the battle-field of Lutzen, as he was leading a charge, and in the moment of victory, 6th November 1632; (7) Waldstein, or Wallenstein, the great captain on the other, or Catholic, side in the same stage of the Thirty Years' War, assassinated, in the interest of the Emperor Ferdinand, by some Irish soldiers, in the Castle of Eger, 25th February 1634.—M.

studied with profit by the advanced connoisseur. They are all of them *exemplaria*, model murders, pattern murders, of which one may say

"Nocturna versate manu, versate diurna"—

especially *nocturna*.

In these assassinations of princes and statesmen there is nothing to excite our wonder. Important changes often depend on their deaths; and, from the eminence on which they stand, they are peculiarly exposed to the aim of every artist who happens to be possessed by the craving for scenical effect. But there is another class of assassinations, which has prevailed from an early period of the seventeenth century, that really *does* surprise me: I mean the assassination of philosophers. For, gentlemen, it is a fact that every philosopher of eminence for the two last centuries has either been murdered, or at the least been very near it,—insomuch that, if a man calls himself a philosopher and never had his life attempted, rest assured there is nothing in him; and against Locke's Philosophy in particular I think it an unanswerable objection (if we needed any) that, although he carried his throat about with him in this world for seventy-two years, no man ever condescended to cut it.[1] As these cases of philosophers are not much known, and are generally good and well composed in their circumstances, I shall here read an excursus on that subject, chiefly by way of showing my own learning.

The first great philosopher of the seventeenth century (if we except Bacon and Galileo) was Des Cartes; and, if ever one could say of a man that he was all *but* murdered—murdered within an inch—one must say it of him. The case was this, as reported by Baillet in his *Vie de M. Des Cartes*, tom. i. pp. 102-3:—In the year 1621, when Des Cartes might be about twenty-six years old, he was touring about as usual (for he was as restless as a hyena); and, coming to the Elbe, either at Gluckstadt or at Hamburgh, he took shipping for East Friezland. What he could want in East Friezland no man has ever discovered; and perhaps he took this into

[1] Locke, born 1632, died 1704. This is not the only place in De Quincey's writings in which he shows his dislike of Locke and Locke's philosophy.—M.

consideration himself: for, on reaching Emblden, he resolved to sail instantly for *West* Friezland; and, being very impatient of delay, he hired a bark, with a few mariners to navigate it. No sooner had he got out to sea than he made a pleasing discovery, viz. that he had shut himself up in a den of murderers. His crew, says M. Baillet, he soon found out to be "des scélérats"—not *amateurs*, gentlemen, as we are, but professional men, the height of whose ambition at that moment was to cut his individual throat. But the story is too pleasing to be abridged; I shall give it, therefore, accurately from the French of his biographer: " M. Des " Cartes had no company but that of his servant, with whom " he was conversing in French. The sailors, who took him for " a foreign merchant, rather than a cavalier, concluded that " he must have money about him. Accordingly, they came " to a resolution by no means advantageous to his purse. " There is this difference, however, between sea-robbers and " the robbers in forests, that the latter may without hazard " spare the lives of their victims, whereas the others cannot " put a passenger on shore in such a case without running the " risk of being apprehended. The crew of M. Des Cartes " arranged their measures with a view to evade any danger " of that sort. They observed that he was a stranger from a " distance, without acquaintance in the country, and that " nobody would take any trouble to inquire about him, in " case he should never come to hand (*quand il viendroit à* " *manquer*)." Think, gentlemen, of these Friezland dogs discussing a philosopher as if he were a puncheon of rum consigned to some shipbroker. " His temper, they remarked, " was very mild and patient; and, judging from the gentle- " ness of his deportment, and the courtesy with which he " treated themselves, that he could be nothing more than " some green young man, without station or root in the " world, they concluded that they should have all the easier " task in disposing of his life. They made no scruple to " discuss the whole matter in his presence, as not supposing " that he understood any other language than that in which " he conversed with his servant; and the amount of their " deliberation was—to murder him, then to throw him into " the sea, and to divide his spoils."

Excuse my laughing, gentlemen; but the fact is I always *do* laugh when I think of this case—two things about it seem so droll. One is the horrid panic or "funk" (as the men of Eton call it) in which Des Cartes must have found himself upon hearing this regular drama sketched for his own death, funeral, succession and administration to his effects. But another thing which seems to me still more funny about this affair is that, if these Friezland hounds had been "game," we should have no Cartesian philosophy; and how we could have done without *that*, considering the world of books it has produced, I leave to any respectable trunk-maker to declare.

However, to go on spite of his enormous funk, Des Cartes showed fight, and by that means awed these Anti-Cartesian rascals. "Finding," says M. Baillet, "that the matter was no "joke, M. Des Cartes leaped upon his feet in a trice, assumed a "stern countenance that these cravens had never looked for, "and, addressing them in their own language, threatened to "run them through on the spot if they dared to give him any "insult." Certainly, gentlemen, this would have been an honour far above the merits of such inconsiderable rascals— to be spitted like larks upon a Cartesian sword; and therefore I am glad M. Des Cartes did not rob the gallows by executing his threat, especially as he could not possibly have brought his vessel to port after he had murdered his crew; so that he must have continued to cruise for ever in the Zuyder Zee, and would probably have been mistaken by sailors for the *Flying Dutchman* homeward bound. "The spirit which M. "Des Cartes manifested," says his biographer, "had the effect "of magic on these wretches. The suddenness of their con- "sternation struck their minds with a confusion which "blinded them to their advantage, and they conveyed him "to his destination as peaceably as he could desire."

Possibly, gentlemen, you may fancy that, on the model of Cæsar's address to his poor ferryman—"*Cæsarem vehis et fortunas ejus*"—M. Des Cartes needed only to have said, "Dogs, you cannot cut my throat, for you carry Des Cartes and his philosophy," and might safely have defied them to do their worst. A German emperor had the same notion when, being cautioned to keep out of the way of a cannonading, he replied, "Tut! man. Did you ever hear of a cannon-ball that killed an emperor"?[1] As to an emperor I cannot say, but a less thing has sufficed to smash a philosopher; and the next great philosopher of Europe undoubtedly *was* murdered. This was Spinoza.

I know very well the common opinion about him is that he died in his bed. Perhaps he did, but he was murdered for all that; and this I shall prove by a book published at Brussels in the year 1731, entitled "La Vie de Spinoza, par M. Jean Colerus," with many additions from a MS. life by one of his friends. Spinoza died on the 21st February 1677, being then little more than forty-four years old. This, of itself, looks suspicious; and M. Jean admits that a certain expression in the MS. life of him would warrant the conclusion "que sa mort n'a pas été tout-à-fait naturelle." Living in a damp country, and a sailor's country, like Holland, he may be thought to have indulged a good deal in grog, especially in punch,[2] which was then newly discovered. Undoubtedly he might have done so; but the fact is that he did not. M. Jean calls him "extrêmement sobre en son boire et en son manger." And, though some wild stories were afloat about his using the juice of mandragora (p. 140) and opium (p. 144), yet neither of these articles is found in his druggist's bill. Living, therefore, with such sobriety, how was it possible that he should die a natural death at forty-four? Hear his biographer's account:—" Sunday "morning, the 21st of February, before it was church time, "Spinoza came downstairs, and conversed with the master

---

[1] This same argument has been employed at least once too often. Some centuries back a dauphin of France, when admonished of his risk from small-pox, made the same demand as the emperor—"Had any gentleman heard of a dauphin killed by small-pox?" No; not any gentleman *had* heard of such a case. And yet, for all that, this dauphin died of that same small-pox.

[2] "June 1, 1675.—Drinke part of three boules of punch (a liquor very strainge to me)," says the Rev. Mr. Henry Teonge, in his Diary published by C. Knight. In a note on this passage, a reference is made to Fryer's Travels to the East Indies, 1672, who speaks of "that enervating liquor called *paunch* (which is Hindostanee for five), from five ingredients." Made thus, it seems the medical men called it diapente; if with four only, diatessaron. No doubt, it was this evangelical name that recommended it to the Rev. Mr. Teonge.

" and mistress of the house." At this time, therefore, perhaps ten o'clock on Sunday morning, you see that Spinoza was alive, and pretty well. But it seems " he had summoned from Amsterdam a certain physician, whom," says the biographer, " I shall not otherwise point out to notice than by these two letters, L. M." This L. M. had directed the people of the house to purchase " an ancient cock," and to have him boiled forthwith, in order that Spinoza might take some broth about noon ; which in fact he did, and ate some of the *old cock* with a good appetite, after the landlord and his wife had returned from church.

"In the afternoon, L. M. staid alone with Spinoza, the
" people of the house having returned to church ; on coming
" out from which, they learned, with much surprise, that
" Spinoza had died about three o'clock, in the presence of L.
" M., who took his departure for Amsterdam that same even-
" ing, by the night-boat, without paying the least attention
" to the deceased,"—and probably without paying very much attention to the payment of his own little account. "No
" doubt, he was the readier to dispense with these duties as
" he had possessed himself of a ducatoon, and a small quantity
" of silver, together with a silver-hafted knife, and had
" absconded with his pillage." Here you see, gentlemen, the murder is plain, and the manner of it. It was L. M. who murdered Spinoza for his money. Poor Spinoza was an invalid, meagre and weak : as no blood was observed, L. M. no doubt threw him down, and smothered him with pillows —the poor man being already half suffocated by his infernal dinner. After masticating that "ancient cock," which I take to mean a cock of the preceding century, in what condition could the poor invalid find himself for a stand-up fight with L. M. ? But who was L. M. ? It surely never could be Lindley Murray, for I saw him at York in 1825 ; and, besides, I do not think he would do such a thing—at least, not to a brother-grammarian : for you know, gentlemen, that Spinoza wrote a very respectable Hebrew grammar.

Hobbes—but why, or on what principle, I never could understand—was not murdered. This was a capital oversight of the professional men in the seventeenth century ; because in every light he was a fine subject for murder, except, indeed, that he was lean and skinny; for I can prove that he had money, and (what was very funny) he had no right to make the least resistance; since, according to himself, irresistible power creates the very highest species of right, so that it is rebellion of the blackest dye to refuse to be murdered when a competent force appears to murder you. However, gentlemen, though he was not murdered, I am happy to assure you that (by his own account) he was three times very near being murdered,—which is consolatory. The first time was in the spring of 1640, when he pretends to have circulated a little MS. on the King's behalf against the Parliament.[1] He never could produce this MS., by the bye; but he says that, "had not His Majesty dissolved the Parliament" (in May), "it had brought him into danger of his life." Dissolving the Parliament, however, was of no use; for in November of the same year the Long Parliament assembled,[2] and Hobbes, a second time fearing he should be murdered, ran away to France. This looks like the madness of John Dennis,[3] who thought that Louis XIV would never make peace with Queen Anne unless he (Dennis to wit) were given up to French vengeance, and actually ran away from the sea-coast under that belief. In France, Hobbes managed to take care of his throat pretty well for ten years; but at the end of that time, by way of paying court to Cromwell, he published his "Leviathan." The old coward now began to "funk" horribly for the third time; he fancied the swords of the Cavaliers were constantly at his throat, recollecting how they had served the Parliament ambassadors at the Hague and Madrid. "*Tum*," says he, in his dog-Latin life of himself,—

"'Tum venit in mentem mihi Dorislaus et Ascham;
Tanquam proscripto terror ubique aderat."[4]

---

[1] The English Parliament which Charles I., after there had been complete disuse of parliaments in England for eleven years, called together on 13th April 1640, to assist him out of his difficulties with the Scottish Covenanters. As it proved refractory, it sat but about three weeks, being dissolved on the 5th May; and hence it is known in English History as "The Short Parliament."—M.

[2] 3d November 1640.—M.

[3] John Dennis, literary critic, born 1657, died 1734.—M.

[4] "Then there came into my mind Dorislaus and Ascham; fear attended me everywhere as one proscribed." The quotation is from

And, accordingly, he ran home to England. Now, certainly, it is very true that a man deserved a cudgelling for writing "Leviathan," and two or three cudgellings for writing a pentameter ending so villainously as "*terror ubique aderat*"! But no man ever thought him worthy of anything beyond cudgelling. And, in fact, the whole story is a bounce of his own. For, in a most abusive letter which he wrote "to a learned person" (meaning Wallis the mathematician), he gives quite another account of the matter, and says (p. 8), he ran home "because he would not trust his safety with the French clergy"; insinuating that he was likely to be murdered for his religion; which would have been a high joke indeed —Tom's being brought to the stake for religion !

Bounce or not bounce, however, certain it is that Hobbes, to the end of his life, feared that somebody would murder him. This is proved by the story I am going to tell you: it is not from a manuscript, but (as Mr. Coleridge says) it is as good as manuscript; for it comes from a book now entirely forgotten, viz. "The Creed of Mr. Hobbes Examined: in a Conference between him and a Student in Divinity" (published about ten years before Hobbes's death). The book is anonymous; but it was written by Tenison,— the same who, about thirty years after, succeeded Tillotson as Archbishop of Canterbury.[1] The introductory anecdote is as follows :—"A certain divine" (no doubt Tenison himself) "took an annual tour of one month to different parts of the island." In one of these excursions (1670), he visited the Peak in Derbyshire, partly in consequence of Hobbes's description of it.[2] Being in that neighbourhood, he could

Hobbes's Life of himself in Latin elegiac verse, first published in December 1679, about three weeks after his death.—Dr. Isaac Dorislaus, a Dutchman naturalised in England, and who had acted as one of the counsel for the prosecution at the trial of Charles I., was sent to the Hague as envoy for the English Commonwealth in the first year of its existence, but had no sooner arrived than he was assassinated in his inn (3d May 1649) by some Royalist exiles. Anthony Ascham, sent to Spain in the following year as envoy for the Commonwealth, had a similar fate, being assassinated in Madrid by English Royalist refugees, 27th May 1650.—M.

[1] Thomas Tenison, born 1636, became Archbishop of Canterbury 1694, died 1715.—M.

[2] One of Hobbes's earliest publications was a Latin poem *De Mira-*

not but pay a visit to Buxton; and at the very moment of
his arrival he was fortunate enough to find a party of gentlemen dismounting at the inn-door, amongst whom was a long
thin fellow, who turned out to be no less a person than Mr.
Hobbes, who probably had ridden over from Chatsworth.[1]
Meeting so great a lion, a tourist in search of the picturesque
could do no less than present himself in the character of
bore. And, luckily for this scheme, two of Mr. Hobbes's
companions were suddenly summoned away by express; so
that, for the rest of his stay at Buxton, he had Leviathan
entirely to himself, and had the honour of boozing with him
in the evening. Hobbes, it seems, at first showed a good
deal of stiffness, for he was shy of divines; but this wore off,
and he became very sociable and funny, and they agreed to
go into the bath together. How Tenison could venture to
gambol in the same water with Leviathan I cannot explain;
but so it was: they frolicked about like two dolphins,
though Hobbes must have been as old as the hills; and "in
" those intervals wherein they abstained from swimming and
" plunging themselves" (*i.e.* diving) "they discoursed of
" many things relating to the baths of the Ancients, and
" the Origine of Springs. When they had in this manner
" passed away an hour, they stepped out of the bath; and,
" having dried and cloathed themselves, they sate down in
" expectation of such a supper as the place afforded; design-
" ing to refresh themselves like the *Deipnosophistæ*, and rather
" to reason than to drink profoundly. But in this innocent
" intention they were interrupted by the disturbance arising
" from a little quarrel in which some of the ruder people in
" the house were for a short time engaged. At this Mr.

bilibus Pecci ("On the Wonders of the Peak.") It was first printed
in London in 1636, when the author was in his forty-eighth year; and
there was a second edition in 1666.—M.

[1] Chatsworth was then, as now, the superb seat of the Cavendishes
in their highest branch—in those days Earl, at present Duke, of
Devonshire. It is to the honour of this family that, through two
generations, they gave an asylum to Hobbes. It is noticeable that
Hobbes was born in the year of the Spanish Armada, *i.e.* in 1588:
such, at least, is my belief [5th April 1588, the day being the Good
Friday of that year.—M.] And, therefore, at this meeting with Tenison in 1670 he must have been about eighty-two years old.

"Hobbes seemed much concerned, though he was at some distance from the persons." And why was he concerned, gentlemen? No doubt, you fancy, from some benign and disinterested love of peace, worthy of an old man and a philosopher. But listen—"For a while he was not composed, but related it once or twice, as to himself, with a low and careful, *i.e.* anxious, tone, how Sextus Roscius was murthered after supper by the Balneæ Palatinæ.[1] Of such general extent is that remark of Cicero in relation to Epicurus the Atheist, of whom he observed that he of all men dreaded most those things which he contemned— Death and the Gods." Merely because it was supper-time, and in the neighbourhood of a bath, Mr. Hobbes must have the fate of Sextus Roscius! He must be murthered, because Sextus Roscius was murthered! What logic was there in this, unless to a man who was always dreaming of murder? Here was Leviathan, no longer afraid of the daggers of English cavaliers or French clergy, but "frightened from his propriety" by a row in an alehouse between some honest clodhoppers of Derbyshire, whom his own gaunt scarecrow of a person, that belonged to quite another century, would have frightened out of their wits.

Malebranche, it will give you pleasure to hear, *was* murdered. The man who murdered him is well known: it was Bishop Berkeley. The story is familiar, though hitherto not put in a proper light. Berkeley, when a young man, went to Paris, and called on Père Malebranche. He found him in his cell cooking. Cooks have ever been a *genus irritabile*; authors still more so. Malebranche was both: a dispute arose; the old father, warm already, became warmer; culinary and metaphysical irritations united to derange his liver: he took to his bed, and died. Such is the common version of the story: "so the whole ear of Denmark is abused." The fact is that the matter was hushed up, out of

---

[1] Sextus Roscius, a wealthy citizen of Ameria, who often visited Rome, was assassinated there on one of his visits (B C. 80) near the Palatine Baths, as he was returning from a banquet. The assassins were two of his relatives; who, to shield themselves and secure his property, accused his son, also called Sextus Roscius, of the crime. Cicero's first speech in a criminal case was in defence of this Sextus; and he was acquitted.—M.

consideration for Berkeley, who (as Pope justly observes) had "every virtue under heaven": else it was well known that Berkeley, feeling himself nettled by the waspishness of the old Frenchman, squared at him; a *turn-up* was the consequence: Malebranche was floored in the first round; the conceit was wholly taken out of him, and he would perhaps have given in; but Berkeley's blood was now up, and he insisted on the old Frenchman's retracting his doctrine of Occasional Causes. The vanity of the man was too great for this; and he fell a sacrifice to the impetuosity of Irish youth, combined with his own absurd obstinacy.[1]

Leibnitz being every way superior to Malebranche, one might, *a fortiori*, have counted on *his* being murdered; which, however, was not the case. I believe he was nettled at this neglect, and felt himself insulted by the security in which he passed his days. In no other way can I explain his conduct at the latter end of his life, when he chose to grow very avaricious, and to hoard up large sums of gold, which he kept in his own house. This was at Vienna,

---

[1] Berkeley was certainly in Paris on a visit in 1713, when he was twenty-eight years of age, and a Junior Fellow of Trinity College, Dublin. In a letter of his dated "Paris, November 25, 1713, N.S." he says "To-morrow I intend. to visit Father Malebranche, and discourse him on certain points." Whether he made out this visit is unknown; and, if he did, it is not to this visit in 1713 that De Quincey refers, but to a second one in October 1715. .On the 13th of that month Malebranche died, in the 77th year of his age; and the story, as told in Stock's Life of Berkeley, published in 1776, is that it was Berkeley's visit that had caused his death. "He found the "ingenious Father in a cell, cooking, in a small pipkin, a medicine "for a disorder with which he was then troubled,—an inflammation "on the lungs. The conversation naturally turned on Berkeley's "system, of which he had received some knowledge from a translation "just published. But the issue of the debate proved tragical to poor "Malebranche. In the heat of the disputation he raised his voice "too high, and gave way so freely to the natural impetuosity of a man "of parts and a Frenchman, that he brought on himself a violent in- "crease of his disorder, which carried him off in a few days." This quotation from Stock is from Professor Campbell Fraser's *Life and Letters of Berkeley* (1871); where the authenticity of the story is carefully discussed. "It is unfortunate," says Professor Fraser, "that we have "no authentic account of the meeting, especially one by Berkeley "himself, nor any authority that I can find, except the biographer's, "for its having occurred at all."—M.

where he died; and letters are still in existence describing the immeasurable anxiety which he entertained for his throat. Still, his ambition for being *attempted* at least was so great that he would not forgo the danger. A late English pedagogue of Birmingham manufacture—viz. Dr. Parr [1]—took a more selfish course under the same circumstances. He had amassed a considerable quantity of gold and silver plate, which was for some time deposited in his bedroom at his parsonage-house, Hatton. But, growing every day more afraid of being murdered,—which he knew that he could not stand (and to which, indeed, he never had the slightest pretensions),—he transferred the whole to the Hatton blacksmith; conceiving, no doubt, that the murder of a blacksmith would fall more lightly on the *salus reipublicæ* than that of a pedagogue. But I have heard this greatly disputed; and it seems now generally agreed that one good horseshoe is worth about two and a quarter Spital sermons.[2]

As Leibnitz, though not murdered, may be said to have died partly of the fear that he should be murdered, and partly of vexation that he was not, Kant, on the other hand —who manifested no ambition in that way—had a narrower escape from a murderer than any man we read of except Des Cartes. So absurdly does fortune throw about her favours! The case is told, I think, in an anonymous life of this very great man. For health's sake, Kant imposed upon himself, at one time, a walk of six miles every day along a high-road. This fact becoming known to a man who had his private reasons for committing murder, at the third milestone from Konigsberg he waited for his "intended," who came up to time as duly as a mail-coach. But for an accident, Kant was a dead man. This accident lay in the

---

[1] Dr. Samuel Parr, born 1747, died 1825. See *ante*, Vol. V, for De Quincey's long paper entitled *Dr. Samuel Parr; or, Whiggism in its relations to Literature.*—M.

[2] "*Spital Sermons*":—Dr. Parr's chief public appearances as an author, after his original appearance in the famous Latin preface to Bellendënus (don't say Bellendĕnus), occurred in certain sermons at periodic intervals, delivered on behalf of some hospital (I really forget what) which retained for its official designation the old word *Spital*; and thus it happened that the sermons themselves were generally known by the title of *Spital* Sermons.

scrupulous, or what Mrs. Quickly would have called the *peevish*, morality of the murderer. An old professor, he fancied, might be laden with sins. Not so a young child. On this consideration, he turned away from Kant at the critical moment, and soon after murdered a child of five years old. Such is the German account of the matter; but my opinion is that the murderer was an amateur, who felt how little would be gained to the cause of good taste by murdering an old, arid, and adust metaphysician. there was no room for display, as the man could not possibly look more like a mummy when dead than he had done alive.

Thus, gentlemen, I have traced the connexion between Philosophy and our Art, until insensibly I find that I have wandered into our own era. This I shall not take any pains to characterise apart from that which preceded it; for, in fact, they have no distinct character. The seventeenth and eighteenth centuries, together with so much of the nineteenth as we have yet seen, jointly compose the Augustan age of Murder. The finest work of the seventeenth century is, unquestionably, the murder of Sir Edmundbury Godfrey,[1]— which has my entire approbation. In the grand feature of *mystery*, which in some shape or other ought to colour every judicious attempt at murder, it is excellent; for the mystery is not yet dispersed. The attempt to fasten the murder upon the Papists, which would injure it as much as some well-known Correggios have been injured by the professional picture-cleaners, or would even ruin it by translating it

[1] On the 17th of October 1678 a dead body, with a sword run through it, the face bruised, and marks of strangulation round the neck, was found in a ditch at the foot of Primrose Hill, in the fields north of London. It turned out to be that of Sir Edmundbury Godfrey, a Westminster magistrate, who had been missing for several days from his house in Green's Lane, in the Strand. The conclusion, from the appearances, was that he had been strangled in London, somewhere about the Strand, and that his body had been removed to the place where it was found. As it chanced that he was the magistrate before whom Titus Oates had made his first deposition, on the 27th of the preceding month, as to the existence of a great Popish plot for the ruin of London and the whole nation, the rumour immediately ran about that his assassination was the work of the Catholics; and, during the long and mad "No Popery" excitement which followed, the murder of Sir Edmundbury Godfrey was used as a goad to the popular fury, and be continued to be spoken of as "The Protestant Martyr."—M.

into the spurious class of mere political or partisan murders, thoroughly wanting in the murderous *animus*, I exhort the society to discountenance. In fact, this notion is altogether baseless, and arose in pure Protestant fanaticism. Sir Edmundbury had not distinguished himself amongst the London magistrates by any severity against the Papists, or in favouring the attempts of zealots to enforce the penal laws against individuals. He had not armed against himself the animosities of any religious sect whatever. And, as to the droppings of wax-lights upon the dress of the corpse when first discovered in a ditch, from which it was inferred at the time that the priests attached to the Popish Queen's Chapel had been concerned in the murder, either these were mere fraudulent artifices devised by those who wished to fix the suspicion upon the Papists, or else the whole allegation—wax-droppings and the suggested cause of the droppings—might be a bounce or fib of Bishop Burnet; who, as the Duchess of Portsmouth used to say, was the one great master of fibbing and romancing in the seventeenth century. At the same time, it must be observed that the quantity of murder was not great in Sir Edmundbury's century, at least amongst our own artists; which, perhaps, is attributable to the want of enlightened patronage. *Sint Mæcenates, non deerunt, Flacce, Marones.*[1] Consulting Grant's *Observations on the Bills of Mortality* (4th edition, Oxford, 1665), I find that, out of 229,250 who died in London during one period of twenty years in the seventeenth century, not more than eighty-six were murdered; that is, about four and three-tenths per annum. A small number this, gentlemen, to found an academy upon; and, certainly, where the quantity is so small, we have a right to expect that the quality should be first-rate. Perhaps it was; yet still I am of opinion that the best artist in this century was not equal to the best in that which followed. For instance, however praiseworthy the case of Sir Edmundbury Godfrey may be (and nobody can be more sensible of its merits than I am), still I cannot consent to place it on a level with that of Mrs. Ruscombe of Bristol, either as to originality of design, or boldness and breadth of style. This good lady's murder took place early

[1] This may be translated: "*Let Mæcenases come, and Virgils will not be wanting.*"—M.

in the reign of George III—a reign which was notoriously favourable to the arts generally. She lived in College Green, with a single maid-servant, neither of them having any pretension to the notice of History but what they derived from the great artist whose workmanship I am recording. One fine morning, when all Bristol was alive and in motion, some suspicion arising, the neighbours forced an entrance into the house, and found Mrs. Ruscombe murdered in her bedroom, and the servant murdered on the stairs: this was at noon; and, not more than two hours before, both mistress and servant had been seen alive. To the best of my remembrance, this was in 1764; upwards of sixty years, therefore, have now elapsed, and yet the artist is still undiscovered. The suspicions of posterity have settled upon two pretenders —a baker and a chimney-sweeper. But posterity is wrong; no unpractised artist could have conceived so bold an idea as that of a noonday murder in the heart of a great city. It was no obscure baker, gentlemen, or anonymous chimney-sweeper, be assured, that executed this work. I know who it was. (*Here there was a general buzz, which at length broke out into open applause; upon which the lecturer blushed, and went on with much earnestness.*) For heaven's sake, gentlemen, do not mistake me; it was not *I* that did it. I have not the vanity to think myself equal to any such achievement; be assured that you greatly overrate my poor talents; Mrs. Ruscombe's affair was far beyond my slender abilities. But I came to know who the artist was from a celebrated surgeon who assisted at his dissection. This gentleman had a private museum in the way of his profession, one corner of which was occupied by a cast from a man of remarkably fine proportions.

"That," said the surgeon, "is a cast from the celebrated "Lancashire highwayman who concealed his profession for "some time from his neighbours by drawing woollen stock- "ings over his horse's legs, and in that way muffling the "clatter which he must else have made in riding up a flagged "alley that led to his stable. At the time of his execution "for highway robbery I was studying under Cruickshank; and "the man's figure was so uncommonly fine that no money or "exertion was spared to get into possession of him with the "least possible delay. By the connivance of the under-

"sheriff, he was cut down within the legal time, and instantly
"put into a chaise-and-four; so that, when he reached
"Cruickshank's, he was positively not dead. Mr. ——, a
"young student at that time, had the honour of giving him
"the *coup de grace*, and finishing the sentence of the law."

This remarkable anecdote, which seemed to imply that all the gentlemen in the dissecting-room were amateurs of our class, struck me a good deal; and I was repeating it one day to a Lancashire lady, who thereupon informed me that she had herself lived in the neighbourhood of that highwayman, and well remembered two circumstances which combined, in the opinion of all his neighbours, to fix upon him the credit of Mrs. Ruscombe's affair. One was the fact of his absence for a whole fortnight at the period of that murder; the other, that within a very little time after the neighbourhood of this highwayman was deluged with dollars: now Mrs Ruscombe was known to have hoarded about two thousand of that coin. Be the artist, however, who he might, the affair remains a durable monument of his genius; for such was the impression of awe and the sense of power left behind by the strength of conception manifested in this murder that no tenant (as I was told in 1810) had been found up to that time for Mrs Ruscombe's house.[1]

But, whilst I thus eulogise the Ruscombian case, let me not be supposed to overlook the many other specimens of extraordinary merit spread over the face of this century. Such cases, indeed, as that of Miss Bland,[2] or of Captain Donnellan and Sir Theophilus Boughton,[3] shall never have

[1] This is not the only time of De Quincey's telling the story of the famous Bristol murder. See a longer account of it in one of the chapters of his Autobiography, *ante*, Vol. I. pp. 386-393 —M.

[2] This must be Mary Blandy, who was executed, 6th April 1752, for poisoning her father, a respectable attorney of Henley-on-Thames, with powders that had been furnished her by a scamp of a lover.—M.

[3] Captain Donnellan and Sir Theodosius (not Theophilus) Boughton make but one case between them.—Donnellan having been the murderer and Boughton the victim. Donnellan, an ex-military man, had married in 1777 an only sister of Sir Theodosius, a young Warwickshire baronet; and, as the property was to come to her in case of her brother's death, Donnellan, while staying in the house of the young man, poisoned him by putting "laurel-water" into some medicine he was taking. Tried for the crime in March 1781, Donnellan was hanged at Warwick on the 2d of April in that year.—M.

any countenance from me. Fie on these dealers in poison, say I: can they not keep to the old honest way of cutting throats, without introducing such abominable innovations from Italy? I consider all these poisoning cases, compared with the legitimate style, as no better than waxwork by the side of sculpture, or a lithographic print by the side of a fine Volpato. But, dismissing these, there remain many excellent works of art in a pure style, such as nobody need be ashamed to own; and this every candid connoisseur will admit. *Candid*, observe, I say; for great allowances must be made in these cases; no artist can ever be sure of carrying through his own fine preconception. Awkward disturbances will arise; people will not submit to have their throats cut quietly; they will run, they will kick, they will bite; and, whilst the portrait-painter often has to complain of too much torpor in his subject, the artist in our line is generally embarrassed by too much animation. At the same time, however disagreeable to the artist, this tendency in murder to excite and irritate the subject is certainly one of its advantages to the world in general which we ought not to overlook, since it favours the development of latent talent. Jeremy Taylor notices with admiration the extraordinary leaps which people will take under the influence of fear. There was a striking instance of this in the recent case of the M'Keans[1]: the boy cleared a height such as he will never clear again to his dying day. Talents also of the most brilliant description for thumping, and, indeed, for all the gymnastic exercises, have sometimes been developed by the panic which accompanies our artists,—talents else buried and hid under a bushel, to the possessors, as much as to their friends. I remember an interesting illustration of this fact in a case of which I learned in Germany.

Riding one day in the neighbourhood of Munich, I overtook a distinguished amateur of our society, whose name, for obvious reasons, I shall conceal. This gentleman informed me that, finding himself wearied with the frigid pleasures (such he esteemed them) of mere amateurship, he had quitted England for the Continent—meaning to practise a little professionally. For this purpose he resorted to Germany,

[1] See account of this case in the *Postscript*.—M.

conceiving the police in that part of Europe to be more heavy and drowsy than elsewhere. His *début* as a practitioner took place at Mannheim ; and, knowing me to be a brother amateur, he freely communicated the whole of his maiden adventure. "Opposite to my lodging," said he, "lived a baker: he was somewhat of a miser, and lived quite alone. Whether it were his great expanse of chalky face, or what else, I know not, but the fact was, I 'fancied' him, and resolved to commence business upon his throat; which, by the way, he always carried bare—a fashion which is very irritating to my desires. Precisely at eight o'clock in the evening, I observed that he regularly shut up his windows. One night I watched him when thus engaged—bolted in after him—locked the door—and, addressing him with great suavity, acquainted him with the nature of my errand ; at the same time advising him to make no resistance, which would be mutually unpleasant. So saying, I drew out my tools, and was proceeding to operate. But at this spectacle the baker, who seemed to have been struck by catalepsy at my first announcement, awoke into tremendous agitation. 'I will *not* be murdered!' he shrieked aloud ; 'what for will I' (meaning *shall* I) 'lose my precious throat?'—'What for?' said I ; 'if for no other reason, for this—that you put alum into your bread. But no matter ; alum or no alum (for I was resolved to forestall any argument on that point), know that I am a virtuoso in the art of murder—am desirous of improving myself in its details—and am enamoured of your vast surface of throat, to which I am determined to be a customer.'— 'Is it so?' said he ; 'but I'll find you a customer in another line' ; and, so saying, he threw himself into a boxing attitude. The very idea of his boxing struck me as ludicrous. It is true, a London baker had distinguished himself in the ring, and became known to fame under the title of The Master of the Rolls, but he was young and unspoiled ; whereas this man was a monstrous feather-bed in person, fifty years old, and totally out of condition. Spite of all this, however, and contending against *me*, who am a master in the art, he made so desperate a defence that many times I feared he might turn the tables upon me, and that I, an amateur, might be murdered by a rascally baker

What a situation! Minds of sensibility will sympathise with my anxiety. How severe it was you may understand by this, that for the first thirteen rounds the baker positively had the advantage. Round the 14th, I received a blow on the right eye, which closed it up; in the end, I believe, this was my salvation; for the anger it roused in me was so great that in the next, and every one of the three following rounds, I floored the baker.

"Round 19th. The baker came up piping, and manifestly the worse for wear. His geometrical exploits in the four last rounds had done him no good. However, he showed some skill in stopping a message which I was sending to his cadaverous mug; in delivering which my foot slipped, and I went down.

"Round 20th. Surveying the baker, I became ashamed of having been so much bothered by a shapeless mass of dough; and I went in fiercely, and administered some severe punishment. A rally took place—both went down—baker undermost—ten to three on amateur.

"Round 21st. The baker jumped up with surprising agility; indeed, he managed his pins capitally, and fought wonderfully, considering that he was drenched in perspiration; but the shine was now taken out of him, and his game was the mere effect of panic. It was now clear that he could not last much longer. In the course of this round we tried the weaving system, in which I had greatly the advantage, and hit him repeatedly on the conk. My reason for this was that his conk was covered with carbuncles, and I thought I should vex him by taking such liberties with his conk,—which in fact I did.

"The three next rounds, the master of the rolls staggered about like a cow on the ice. Seeing how matters stood, in round 24th I whispered something into his ear which sent him down like a shot. It was nothing more than my private opinion of the value of his throat at an annuity office. This little confidential whisper affected him greatly; the very perspiration was frozen on his face, and for the next two rounds I had it all my own way. And, when I called *time* for the 27th round, he lay like a log on the floor."

After which, said I to the amateur, "It may be presumed that you accomplished your purpose." — "You are right," said he mildly; "I did; and a great satisfaction, you know, it was to my mind, for by this means I killed two birds with one stone"; meaning that he had both thumped the baker and murdered him. Now, for the life of me, I could not see *that*; for, on the contrary, to my mind it appeared that he had taken two stones to kill one bird, having been obliged to take the conceit out of him first with his fist, and then with his tools. But no matter for his logic. The moral of his story was good, for it showed what an astonishing stimulus to latent talent is contained in any reasonable prospect of being murdered. A pursy, unwieldy, half-cataleptic baker of Mannheim had absolutely fought seven-and-twenty rounds with an accomplished English boxer, merely upon this inspiration; so greatly was natural genius exalted and sublimed by the genial presence of his murderer.

Really, gentlemen, when one hears of such things as these, it becomes a duty, perhaps, a little to soften that extreme asperity with which most men speak of murder. To hear people talk, you would suppose that all the disadvantages and inconveniences were on the side of being murdered, and that there were none at all in *not* being murdered. But considerate men think otherwise. "Certainly," says Jeremy Taylor, "it is a less temporal evil to fall by the rudeness of " a sword than the violence of a fever: and the axe" (to which he might have added the ship-carpenter's mallet and the crowbar) "a much less affliction than a strangury." Very true; the bishop talks like a wise man and an amateur, as I am sure he was; and another great philosopher, Marcus Aurelius, was equally above the vulgar prejudices on this subject. He declares it to be one of "the noblest functions of reason to know whether it is time to walk out of the world or not" (Book III, Collers's Translation). No sort of knowledge being rarer than this, surely *that* man must be a most philanthropic character who undertakes to instruct people in this branch of knowledge gratis, and at no little hazard to himself. All this, however, I throw out only in the way of speculation to future moralists; declaring in the meantime my own private conviction that very few men commit murder upon philanthropic or patriotic principles, and repeating what I have already said once at least—that, as to the majority of murderers, they are very incorrect characters.

With respect to the Williams murders, the sublimest and most entire in their excellence that ever were committed, I shall not allow myself to speak incidentally. Nothing less than an entire lecture, or even an entire course of lectures, would suffice to expound their merits.[1] But one curious fact connected with his case I shall mention, because it seems to imply that the blaze of his genius absolutely dazzled the eye of criminal justice. You all remember, I doubt not, that the instruments with which he executed his first great work (the murder of the Marrs) were a ship-carpenter's mallet and a knife. Now, the mallet belonged to an old Swede, one John Peterson, and bore his initials. This instrument Williams left behind him in Marr's house, and it fell into the hands of the magistrates. But, gentlemen, it is a fact that the publication of this circumstance of the initials led immediately to the apprehension of Williams, and, if made earlier, would have prevented his second great work (the murder of the Williamsons), which took place precisely twelve days after. Yet the magistrates kept back this fact from the public for the entire twelve days, and until that second work was accomplished. That finished, they published it, apparently feeling that Williams had now done enough for his fame, and that his glory was at length placed beyond the reach of accident.

As to Mr. Thurtell's case,[2] I know not what to say.

---

[1] For a full account of the Williams Murders see Postscript.—M.

[2] On Friday, October 24, 1823, at about eight o'clock in the evening, a farmer at Butler's Green, in the south of Hertfordshire, heard the noise of a vehicle going down a country-lane in his neighbourhood, called Gill's-Hill Lane, "and, shortly after, the report of a pistol, followed by deep groans." The next morning, a pistol was found under the hedge of the lane by two labourers, who reported that they had seen two persons come down the lane at daybreak, and "grabble" about the spot, as if looking for something. In consequence of further inquiries and of information received, search was made, two or three days after, in a marshy pond, some miles off; and there a dead body was found, the legs tied together, and the upper part, with the throat cut and the skull fractured, thrust into a sack, weighted with

Naturally, I have every disposition to think highly of my predecessor in the chair of this society; and I acknowledge that his lectures were unexceptionable. But, speaking ingenuously, I do really think that his principal performance as an artist has been much overrated. I admit that at first I was myself carried away by the general enthusiasm. On the morning when the murder was made known in London there was the fullest meeting of amateurs that I have ever known since the days of Williams; old bedridden connoisseurs, who had got into a peevish way of sneering and complaining "that there was nothing doing," now hobbled down

stones. The body, as had been expected, was that of Mr. William Weare, a gentleman of gambling propensities, whose residence was in Lyon's Inn, off the Strand, London. The person arrested as the murderer-in-chief was John Thurtell, owner of a gambling-house in Manchester Buildings, Westminster, but of a respectable Norwich family; and there were arrested also a London vocalist and coffee-house keeper called Joseph Hunt, who was a friend of Thurtell's, and a man named William Probert, also a friend of Thurtell's, who had been insolvent in the London wine-trade, and had retired into Hertfordshire, where he rented a cottage near the scene of the murder. At the Hertford assizes, where Thurtell, Hunt, and Probert were tried for the murder,—Thurtell as principal and the other two as accessories,—Thurtell and Hunt were sentenced to death, Probert having got off by turning king's evidence. The capital sentence was carried into execution only in the case of Thurtell, who was hanged at Hertford on the 8th of January 1824. Never did a murderer go out of the world encircled with such praise and popularity. Not only had the circumstances of the crime, and the legends connected with it, taken a peculiarly strong effect upon the public fancy; but the impressive defence which Thurtell had made for himself at his trial, and his whole subsequent demeanour in prison under his death-sentence, as it was reported by the jailers and turnkeys, had won him golden opinions. —What is most memorable of all now is the peculiar literary celebrity which Thurtell and his Hertfordshire murder of 1824 have chanced to obtain. In a contemporary street-ballad, attributed to Theodore Hook, there is this immortal summary of the facts:—

> "They cut his throat from ear to ear,
> His brains they battered in.
> His name was Mr. William Weare,
> He dwelt in Lyon's Inn."

The naked strength of this stanza so recommended it to Sir Walter Scott that he delighted in quoting it; nor, in all Sir Walter's many readings in murder-literature, does he seem to have come upon any murder that more fascinated him than that which Theodore Hook had to our club-room: such hilarity, such benign expression of general satisfaction, I have rarely witnessed. On every side you saw people shaking hands, congratulating each other, and forming dinner parties for the evening; and nothing was to be heard but triumphant challenges of—"Well! will *this* do?" "Is *this* the right thing?" "Are you satisfied at last?" But, in the middle of the row, I remember, we all grew silent, on hearing the old cynical amateur L. S—— stumping along with his wooden leg. He entered the room with his usual scowl; and, as he advanced, he continued to growl and stutter the whole way—"Mere plagiarism—base

thus celebrated. Here is an extract from Scott's diary at Abbotsford in those sad months of 1826 when his commercial ruin had come upon him, and he lay stunned and broken-hearted for the time under the great misfortune —"July 16.—Sleepy, stupid, indolent,—finished "arranging the books, and after that was totally useless,—unless it "can be called study that I slumbered for three or four hours over a "variorum edition of the Gill's Hill Tragedy. Admirable escape for "low spirits,—for, not to mention the brutality of so extraordinary a "murder, it led John Bull into one of his most uncommon fits of "gambols, until at last he became so maudlin as to weep for the "pitiless assassin Thurtell, and treasure up the leaves and twigs of the "hedge and shrubs in the fatal garden as valuable relics,—nay, "thronged the minor theatres to see the roan horse and yellow gig in "which his victim was transported from one house to the other. I "have not stept over the threshold to-day, so very stupid have I been." Nearly two years afterwards, when on a return journey to Scotland from a visit to London, Scott could not resist going out of his way to visit Gill's-Hill and the remains of Probert's cottage. In his Diary, under date 28th May 1828, there is a description of the place and of the impressions it made upon him, summed up in this quotation from Wordsworth:—

"A merry spot, 'tis said, in days of yore; But something ails it now,—the place is cursed."

Carlyle also had read the contemporary accounts of Thurtell's trial; and one incident of it furnished him with one of the best-known and most persistent of his Carlylisms. "What sort of person was Mr. Weare?" one of the witnesses had been asked at the trial. "He was always a respectable person," was the answer. "What do you mean by respectable?" asked the counsel. "He kept a gig," said the witness. Mr. Weare's "gig" became from that moment Carlyle's pet symbol for respectability; and the world was never to hear the last of it from him, whether in the simple form of the mere "gig" or in the generalised forms of "gigmanity," "gigmanity disgigged," and other compounds.—M.

plagiarism from hints that I threw out! Besides, his style is as harsh as Albert Durer, and as coarse as Fuseli." Many thought that this was mere jealousy and general waspishness; but I confess that, when the first glow of enthusiasm had subsided, I have found most judicious critics to agree that there was something *falsetto* in the style of Thurtell. The fact is, he was a member of our society, which naturally gave a friendly bias to our judgments; and his person was universally familiar to the "fancy",—which gave him, with the whole London public, a temporary popularity that his pretensions are not capable of supporting; for *opinionum commenta delet dies, naturae judicia confirmat*. There was, however, an unfinished design of Thurtell's for the murder of a man with a pair of dumb-bells, which I admired greatly; it was a mere outline that he never filled in; but to my mind it seemed every way superior to his chief work. I remember that there was great regret expressed by some amateurs that this sketch should have been left in an unfinished state; but there I cannot agree with them; for the fragments and first bold outlines of original artists have often a felicity about them which is apt to vanish in the management of the details.

The case of the M'Keans[1] I consider far beyond the vaunted performance of Thurtell—indeed, above all praise; and bearing that relation, in fact, to the immortal works of Williams which the "Æneid" bears to the "Iliad."

But it is now time that I should say a few words about the principles of murder, not with a view to regulate your practice, but your judgment. As to old women, and the mob of newspaper readers, they are pleased with anything, provided it is bloody enough. But the mind of sensibility requires something more. *First*, then, let us speak of the kind of person who is adapted to the purpose of the murderer; *secondly*, of the place where; *thirdly*, of the time when, and other little circumstances.

As to the person, I suppose it is evident that he ought to be a good man, because, if he were not, he might himself, by possibility, be contemplating murder at the very time; and such "diamond-cut-diamond" tussles, though pleasant enough

[1] See the Postscript.

where nothing better is stirring, are really not what a critic can allow himself to call murders. I could mention some people (I name no names) who have been murdered by other people in a dark lane; and so far all seemed correct enough; but, on looking further into the matter, the public have become aware that the murdered party was himself, at the moment, planning to rob his murderer, at the least, and possibly to murder him, if he had been strong enough. Whenever that is the case, or may be thought to be the case, farewell to all the genuine effects of the art. For the final purpose of murder, considered as a fine art, is precisely the same as that of tragedy in Aristotle's account of it; viz. "to cleanse the heart by means of pity and terror." Now, terror there may be, but how can there be any pity for one tiger destroyed by another tiger?

It is also evident that the person selected ought not to be a public character. For instance, no judicious artist would have attempted to murder Abraham Newland.[1] For the case was this: everybody read so much about Abraham Newland, and so few people ever saw him, that to the general belief he was a mere abstract idea. And I remember that once, when I happened to mention that I had dined at a coffee-house in company with Abraham Newland, everybody looked scornfully at me, as though I had pretended to have played at billiards with Prester John, or to have had an affair of honour with the Pope. And, by the way, the Pope would be a very improper person to murder; for he has such a virtual ubiquity as the father of Christendom, and, like the cuckoo, is so often heard but never seen, that I suspect most people regard *him* also as an abstract idea. Where, indeed, a public man is in the habit of giving dinners, "with every delicacy of the season," the case is very different: every person is satisfied that *he* is no abstract idea; and, therefore, there can

[1] Abraham Newland [chief cashier of the Bank of England, who died 1807—M] is now utterly forgotten. But, when this was written [1827], his name had not ceased to ring in British ears, as the most familiar and most significant that perhaps has ever existed. It was the name which appeared on the face of all Bank of England notes, great or small; and had been, for more than a quarter of a century (especially through the whole career of the French Revolution), a shorthand expression for paper money in its safest form.

be no impropriety in murdering him; only that his murder will fall into the class of assassinations, which I have not yet treated.

Thirdly. The subject chosen ought to be in good health; for it is absolutely barbarous to murder a sick person, who is usually quite unable to bear it. On this principle, no tailor ought to be chosen who is above twenty-five, for after that age he is sure to be dyspeptic. Or, at least, if a man will hunt in that warren, he will of course think it his duty, on the old established equation, to murder some multiple of 9—say 18, 27, or 36. And here, in this benign attention to the comfort of sick people, you will observe the usual effect of a fine art to soften and refine the feelings. The world in general, gentlemen, are very bloody-minded; and all they want in a murder is a copious effusion of blood; gaudy display in this point is enough for *them*. But the enlightened connoisseur is more refined in his taste; and from our art, as from all the other liberal arts when thoroughly mastered, the result is, to humanise the heart; so true is it that

"Ingenuas didicisse fideliter artes
Emollit mores, nec sinit esse feros."

A philosophic friend, well known for his philanthropy and general benignity, suggests that the subject chosen ought also to have a family of young children wholly dependent on his exertions, by way of deepening the pathos. And, undoubtedly, this is a judicious caution. Yet I would not insist too keenly on such a condition. Severe good taste unquestionably suggests it; but still, where the man was otherwise unobjectionable in point of morals and health, I would not look with too curious a jealousy to a restriction which might have the effect of narrowing the artist's sphere.

So much for the person. As to the time, the place, and the tools, I have many things to say which at present I have no room for. The good sense of the practitioner has usually directed him to night and privacy. Yet there have not been wanting cases where this rule was departed from with excellent effect. In respect to time, Mrs Ruscombe's case is a beautiful exception which I have already noticed; and in respect both to time and place there is a fine exception in the annals of Edinburgh (year 1805), familiar to every child in Edinburgh, but which has unaccountably been defrauded of its due portion of fame amongst English amateurs. The case I mean is that of a porter to one of the banks, who was murdered whilst carrying a bag of money, in broad daylight, on turning out of the High Street, one of the most public streets in Europe; and the murderer is to this hour undiscovered.[1]

"Sed fugit interea, fugit irreparabile tempus,
Singula dum capti circumvectamur amore"

And now, gentlemen, in conclusion, let me again solemnly disclaim all pretensions on my own part to the character of a professional man. I never attempted any murder in my life, except in the year 1801,—upon the body of a tom-cat; and *that* turned out differently from my intention. My purpose,

[1] Had De Quincey been better acquainted with Edinburgh in 1827, his allusion to this famous murder would probably have been less slight and more accurate. The circumstances, as narrated in Robert Chambers's *Traditions of Edinburgh*, are these:—On the 13th November 1806, about five o'clock in the evening, there was found in Tweeddale Court,—a narrow court off the High Street of Edinburgh, leading to a small square, where there were then the chief premises of the British Linen Company's Bank,—the dead body of William Begbie, a porter of the Bank, who had that afternoon, in the course of a customary duty, left a branch office of the Bank in Leith, in charge of a package of bank-notes, to the amount of £4392, to be deposited in the Edinburgh Head Office. He had been stabbed to the heart in the narrow court, just after he had entered it from the main street, and probably while there was still a glimmering in the court of the fading light of a late November afternoon. The knife with which the deed had been done remained in the body, struck up to the wooden haft; and, in proof that the murder had been deliberately premeditated, it was found that the blade, which was broad and thin, had been ground at the end to a sharp point, and that a bunch of soft paper had been wrapped round the haft, whether to give a better hold or to prevent the sputtering back of the blood on the murderer. The package of bank-notes was gone. There was an immediate hue and cry, with offers of reward, &c., and several arrests were made on suspicion. But all that came out was that some people thought they had seen a man accompanying or dogging Begbie on his way from Leith, and that others thought they had seen a man running out of Tweeddale Court across the High Street, and disappearing into a wynd on the other side of the street, leading in the direction of Leith. Months passed, and the quest after the murderer of Begbie had not ceased, when, on

I own, was downright murder. "Semper ego auditor tantum?" said I, "nunquamne reponam?" And I went downstairs in search of Tom at one o'clock on a dark night, with the "animus," and no doubt with the fiendish looks, of a murderer. But, when I found him, he was in the act of plundering the pantry of bread and other things. Now this gave a new turn to the affair; for, the time being one of general scarcity, when even Christians were reduced to the use of potato-bread, rice-bread, and all sorts of things, it was downright treason in a tom-cat to be wasting good wheaten-bread in the way he was doing. It instantly became a patriotic duty to put him to death; and, as I raised aloft and shook the glittering steel, I fancied myself rising, like Brutus, effulgent from a crowd of patriots, and, as I stabbed him, I

> "Called aloud on Tully's name,
> And bade the father of his country hail!"

---

the 10th of August 1807, a parcel of the missing notes was accidentally found by some workmen in a hole in a stone wall in what was then a vacant ground in the northern neighbourhood of the town. The murderer had kept the smaller notes, and had stuffed the larger ones, to the amount of about £3000 altogether, into this hole. Even this did not furnish any further clue; years rolled on; and, though public suspicion fastened capriciously on one person or another from time to time, the Begbie murder became a legend of the past. To this day, when the murderer of Begbie, however long he lived, must have been lying in his grave somewhere for many years, people passing Tweeddale Court in the High Street of Edinburgh remember what happened there, and the phrase "The Begbie Murder" is in Edinburgh parlance a synonym for any typical mystery or unsolved problem.—It was on the 23d of February 1827, the very month of the appearance of this paper of De Quincey in *Blackwood*, that there took place in Edinburgh that famous Theatrical Fund Dinner at which Sir Walter Scott presided, and at which he was led, by the manner in which his health was proposed by his friend Lord Meadowbank, to drop the mask he had worn so long, and announce himself as the real and sole author of the Waverley Novels. The raptures of applause which greeted the announcement were still filling the hall, and Sir Walter had resumed his seat, when, as Lockhart tells the story, he sent on a slip of paper to one of the guests at some distance from him,—the well-known Mr. Patrick Robertson, *alias* "Peter of the Paunch," then the witty Falstaff of the Scottish Bar, as he was afterwards of the Scottish Bench. Peter was to be one of the speakers; and the message to him was "Confess something too,—why not the murder of Begbie?"—M.

Since then, what wandering thoughts I may have had of attempting the life of an ancient ewe, of a superannuated hen, and such "small deer," are locked up in the secrets of my own breast; but for the higher departments of the art I confess myself to be utterly unfit. My ambition does not rise so high. No, gentlemen: in the words of Horace,

> "Fungar vice cotis, acutum
> Reddere quæ ferrum valet, exsors ipsa secandi."

SECOND PAPER[1]

A GOOD many years ago, the reader may remember that I came forward in the character of a *dilettante* in murder.[2] Perhaps *dilettante* is too strong a word. *Connoisseur* is better suited to the scruples and infirmity of public taste. I suppose there is no harm in *that*, at least. A man is not bound to put his eyes, ears, and understanding into his breeches pocket when he meets with a murder. If he is not in a downright comatose state, I suppose he must see that one murder is better or worse than another, in point of good taste. Murders have their little differences and shades of merit, as well as statues, pictures, oratorios, cameos, intaglios, or what not. You may be angry with the man for talking too much, or too publicly (as to the too much, that I deny—a man can never cultivate his taste too highly); but you

---

[1] Appeared originally in *Blackwood's Magazine* for November 1839, nearly thirteen years after the publication of the First Paper.—M.

[2] In the original article in *Blackwood* there was this opening paragraph:—"DOCTOR NORTH—You are a liberal man: liberal in the true classical sense, not in the slang sense of modern politicians and education-mongers. Being so, I am sure that you will sympathise with my case. I am an ill-used man, Dr. North—particularly ill-used; and, with your permission, I will briefly explain how. A black scene of calumny will be laid open; but you, Doctor, will make all things square again. One frown from you, directed to the proper quarter, or a warning shake of the crutch, will set me right in public opinion; which at present, I am sorry to say, is rather hostile to me and mine—all owing to the wicked acts of slanderers. But you shall hear." The article then proceeds with the sentence "A good many years ago," &c. as now, save that "the reader may remember" is substituted for "you [i.e. Dr. North] may remember." That touch of alteration recurs throughout.—M.

must allow him to think, at any rate. Well, would you believe it? all my neighbours came to hear of that little æsthetic essay which I had published; and, unfortunately, hearing at the very same time of a club that I was connected with, and a dinner at which I presided—both tending to the same little object as the essay, viz. the diffusion of a just taste among Her Majesty's subjects [1]—they got up the most barbarous calumnies against me. In particular, they said that I, or that the club (which comes to the same thing), had offered bounties on well-conducted homicides—with a scale of drawbacks, in case of any one defect or flaw, according to a table issued to private friends. Now, let me tell the whole truth about the dinner and the club, and it will be seen how malicious the world is. But, first, confidentially, allow me to say what my real principles are upon the matter in question.

As to murder, I never committed one in my life. It's a well-known thing amongst all my friends. I can get a paper to certify as much, signed by lots of people. Indeed, if you come to that, I doubt whether many people could produce as strong a certificate. Mine would be as big as a breakfast tablecloth. There is indeed one member of the club who pretends to say he caught me once making too free with his throat on a club night, after everybody else had retired. But, observe, he shuffles in his story according to his state of civilation.[2] When not far gone, he contents himself with saying that he caught me ogling his throat, and that I was melancholy for some weeks after, and that my voice sounded in a way expressing, to the nice ear of a connoisseur, *the sense of opportunities lost;* but the club all know that he is a disappointed man himself, and that he speaks querulously at times about the fatal neglect of a man's coming abroad without his tools. Besides, all this is an affair between two amateurs, and everybody makes allowances for little asperities and fibs in such a case. "But," say you, "if no murderer,

---

[1] *Her* Majesty: In the lecture, having occasion to refer to the reigning sovereign, I said "*His* Majesty"; for at that time [1827] William IV was on the throne [no: George IV.—M.]; but between the lecture and this supplement had occurred the accession of our present Queen. [This note was added in 1854.—M.]

[2] De Quincey elsewhere explains this word *civilation*. It is *civilization* as pronounced by an after-dinner speaker.—M.

you may have encouraged, or even have bespoken, a murder." No, upon my honour—no. And that was the very point I wished to argue for your satisfaction. The truth is, I am a very particular man in everything relating to murder; and perhaps I carry my delicacy too far. The Stagirite most justly, and possibly with a view to my case, placed virtue in the τὸ μέσον, or middle point between two extremes. A golden mean is certainly what every man should aim at. But it is easier talking than doing; and, my infirmity being notoriously too much milkiness of heart, I find it difficult to maintain that steady equatorial line between the two poles of too much murder on the one hand and too little on the other. I am too soft; and people get excused through me—nay, go through life without an attempt made upon them—that ought *not* to be excused. I believe, if I had the management of things, there would hardly be a murder from year's end to year's end. In fact, I'm for peace, and quietness, and fawningness, and what may be styled *knocking-underness*.[1] A man came to me as a can-

---

[1] The phrase in the original *Blackwood* article was "I'm for virtue, and goodness, and all that sort of thing." Not only is this phrase altered and amplified; but there is total omission of a longish passage which followed it. The passage is worth reproducing, and ran as follows:—"And two instances I'll give you to what an extremity I "carry my virtue. The first may seem a trifle; but not if you knew "my nephew, who was certainly born to be hanged, and would have "been so long ago, but for my restraining voice. He is horribly am- "bitious, and thinks himself a man of cultivated taste in most "branches of murder, whereas, in fact, he has not one idea on the "subject but such as he has stolen from me. This is so well known "that the Club has twice blackballed him, though every indulgence "was shown to him as my relative. People came to me and said— "'Now really, President, we would do much to serve a relative of "yours. But still, what can be said? You know yourself that he'll "disgrace us. If we were to elect him, why, the next thing we "should hear of would be some vile butcherly murder, by way of "justifying our choice. And what sort of a concern would it be? "You know, as well as we do, that it would be a disgraceful affair, "more worthy of the shambles than of an artist's *atelier*. He would "fall upon some great big man, some huge farmer returning drunk "from a fair. There would be plenty of blood, and *that* he would "expect us to take in lieu of taste, finish, scenical grouping. Then, "again, how would he tool? Why, most probably with a cleaver "and a couple of paving stones: so that the whole *coup d'œil* would

didate for the place of my servant, just then vacant. He had the reputation of having dabbled a little in our art; some said, not without merit. What startled me, however, was, that he supposed this art to be part of his regular duties in my service, and talked of having it considered in his wages. Now, that was a thing I would not allow; so I said at once, "Richard (or James, as the case might be), you misunderstand my character. If a man will and must practise this difficult (and, allow me to add, dangerous) branch of art—if he has an overruling genius for it—why, in that case, all I say is that he might as well pursue his studies whilst living in my service as in another's. And also I may observe that it can do no harm either to himself or to the subject on whom he operates that he should be guided by men of more taste than himself. Genius may do much, but long study of the art must always entitle a man to offer advice. So far I will go—general principles I will suggest. But, as to any particular case, once for all I will have

"remind you rather of some hideous Ogre or Cyclops than of the "delicate operator of the 19th century.' The picture was drawn with "the hand of truth; *that* I could not but allow, and, as to personal "feelings in the matter, I dismissed them from the first. The next "morning I spoke to my nephew: I was delicately situated, as you "see, but I determined that no consideration should induce me to "flinch from my duty. 'John,' said I, 'you seem to me to have "taken an erroneous view of life and its duties. Pushed on by am- "bition, you are dreaming rather of what it might be glorious to "attempt than what it would be possible for you to accomplish. "Believe me, it is not necessary to a man's respectability that he "should commit a murder. Many a man has passed through life "most respectably without attempting any species of homicide— "good, bad, or indifferent. It is your first duty to ask yourself, *quid "valeant humeri, quid ferre recusent?* We cannot all be brilliant "men in this life. And it is for your interest to be contented rather "with a humble station well filled than to shock everybody with "failures, the more conspicuous by contrast with the ostentation of "their promises.' John made no answer; he looked very sulky at the "moment, and I am in high hopes that I have saved a near relative "from making a fool of himself by attempting what is as much be- "yond his capacity as an epic poem. Others, however, tell me that "he is meditating a revenge upon me and the whole Club. But, let "this be as it may, *liberavi animam meam*; and, as you see, have "run some risk with a wish to diminish the amount of homicide."— De Quincey's reason for omitting this passage in 1854 does not appear.—M.

nothing to do with it. Never tell me of any special work of art you are meditating—I set my face against it *in toto*. For, if once a man indulges himself in murder, very soon he comes to think little of robbing, and from robbing he comes next to drinking and Sabbath-breaking, and from that to incivility and procrastination. Once begin upon this downward path, you never know where you are to stop. Many a man dated his ruin from some murder or other that perhaps he thought little of at the time. *Principiis obsta*— that's my rule." Such was my speech, and I have always acted up to it; so, if that is not being virtuous, I should be glad to know what is.

But now about the dinner and the club. The club was not particularly of my creation; it arose,—pretty much as other similar associations for the propagation of truth and the communication of new ideas,—rather from the necessities of things than upon any one man's suggestion. As to the dinner, if any man more than another could be held responsible for that, it was a member known amongst us by the name of *Toad-in-the-hole*. He was so called from his gloomy misanthropical disposition, which led him into constant disparagements of all modern murders as vicious abortions, belonging to no authentic school of art. The finest performances of our own age he snarled at cynically; and at length this querulous humour grew upon him so much, and he became so notorious as a *laudator temporis acti*, that few people cared to seek his society. This made him still more fierce and truculent. He went about muttering and growling; wherever you met him, he was soliloquising, and saying "Despicable pretender—without grouping—without two ideas upon handling—without——"; and there you lost him. At length existence seemed to be painful to him; he rarely spoke; he seemed conversing with phantoms in the air; his housekeeper informed us that his reading was nearly confined to "God's Revenge upon Murder" by Reynolds,[1] and a more ancient book of the same title, noticed by Sir

---

[1] *The Triumphs of God's Revenge against the Crying and Execrable Sin of Murder*, London, 1621. There were five subsequent parts; all six were printed together in folio in 1635; and there was a reprint, with additions, in 1679.—M.

Walter Scott in his "Fortunes of Nigel."[1] Sometimes, perhaps, he might read in the "Newgate Calendar" down to the year 1788; but he never looked into a book more recent. In fact, he had a theory with regard to the French Revolution, as having been the great cause of degeneration in murder. "Very soon, sir," he used to say, "men will have lost the art of killing poultry: the very rudiments of the art will have perished!" In the year 1811 he retired from general society. Toad-in-the-hole was no more seen in any public resort. We missed him from his wonted haunts· "Nor up the lawn, nor at the wood was he." By the side of the main conduit his listless length at noontide he would stretch, and pore upon the filth that muddled by.[2] "Even dogs," this pensive moralist would say, "are not what they were, sir—not what they should be. I remember in my grandfather's time that some dogs had an idea of murder. I have known a mastiff, sir, that lay in ambush for a rival,—yes, sir, and finally murdered him, with pleasing circumstances of good taste. I also was on intimate terms of acquaintance with a tom-cat that was an assassin. But now——"; and then, the subject growing too painful, he dashed his hand to his forehead, and went off abruptly in a homeward direction towards his favourite conduit; where he was seen by an amateur in such a state that he thought

---

[1] The terrible book which Nigel is represented as reading late at night in his room in the house of the old miser Trapbois when he hears the shriek of Martha Trapbois announcing that her father had been murdered.—Scott describes it thus:—"The book was entitled *God's Revenge against Murder*, not, as the bibliomaniacal reader may easily conjecture, the work which Reynolds published under that imposing name, but one of a much earlier date, printed and sold by old Wolfe." Yet an early copy of Reynolds's book would have almost suited the date of the story.—M.

[2] Having quoted a line from one of the closing stanzas of Gray's *Elegy*,
"Nor up the lawn, nor at the wood was he,"
De Quincey keeps up the metrical tune in his mischievous parody of this other stanza of the passage describing the solitary poet—

"There at the foot of yonder nodding beech
That wreathes its old fantastic roots so high
His listless length at noontide he would stretch,
And pore upon the brook that bubbles by."—M.

it dangerous to address him. Soon after Toad shut himself entirely up; it was understood that he had resigned himself to melancholy; and at length the prevailing notion was that Toad-in-the-hole had hanged himself.

The world was wrong *there*, as it had been on some other questions. Toad-in-the-hole might be sleeping, but dead he was not; and of that we soon had ocular proof. One morning in 1812, an amateur surprised us with the news that he had seen Toad-in-the-hole brushing with hasty steps the dews away, to meet the postman by the conduit side. Even that was something: how much more, to hear that he had shaved his beard—had laid aside[1] his sad-coloured clothes, and was adorned like a bridegroom of ancient days. What could be the meaning of all this? Was Toad-in-the-hole mad? or how? Soon after the secret was explained: in more than a figurative sense "the murder was out." For in came the London morning papers, by which it appeared that, but three days before, a murder the most superb of the century by many degrees had occurred in the heart of London. I need hardly say that this was the great exterminating *chef-d'œuvre* of Williams at Mr. Marr's, No. 29 Ratcliffe Highway. That was the *début* of the artist; at least for anything the public knew. What occurred at Mr. Williamson's twelve nights afterwards—the second work turned out from the same chisel—some people pronounced even superior. But Toad-in-the-hole always "reclaimed," he was even angry, at such comparisons. "This vulgar *goût de comparaison*, as La Bruyère calls it," he would often remark, "will be our ruin; each work has its own separate characteristics—each in and for itself is incomparable. One, perhaps, might suggest the

---

[1] This also falls into verse: *e.g.*—

"Brushing with hasty steps the dews away,
To meet the postman by the conduit side.
Even that was something · how much more, to hear
That he had shaved his beard—had laid aside";

which is a kind of parody of Gray's stanza:—

"Haply some hoary-headed swain may say,
Oft have I seen him at the peep of dawn
Brushing with hasty steps the dews away,
To meet the sun upon the upland lawn."—M.

Iliad—the other the *Odyssey*: but what do you get by such comparisons? Neither ever was or will be surpassed; and, when you've talked for hours, you must still come back to that." Vain, however, as all criticism might be, he often said that volumes might be written on each case for itself; and he even proposed to publish a quarto on the subject.

Meantime, how had Toad-in-the-hole happened to hear of this great work of art so early in the morning? He had received an account by express, despatched by a correspondent in London who watched the progress of art on *Toad's* behalf, with a general commission to send off a special express, at whatever cost, in the event of any estimable works appearing. The express arrived in the night-time; Toad-in-the-hole was then gone to bed; he had been muttering and grumbling for hours; but of course he was called up. On reading the account, he threw his arms round the express, declared him his brother and his preserver, and expressed his regret at not having it in his power to knight him. We, amateurs, having heard that he was abroad, and therefore had *not* hanged himself, made sure of soon seeing him amongst us. Accordingly he soon arrived; seized every man's hand as he passed him—wrung it almost frantically, and kept ejaculating, "Why, now, here's something like a murder!—this is the real thing—this is genuine—this is what you can approve, can recommend to a friend: this—says every man, on reflection—this is the thing that ought to be! Such works are enough to make us all young." And in fact the general opinion is that Toad-in-the-hole would have died but for this regeneration of art, which he called a second age of Leo the Tenth; and it was our duty, he said, solemnly to commemorate it. At present, and *en attendant*, he proposed that the club should meet and dine together. A dinner, therefore, was given by the club; to which all amateurs were invited from a distance of one hundred miles.

Of this dinner there are ample shorthand notes amongst the archives of the club. But they are not "extended," to speak diplomatically; and the reporter who only could give the whole report *in extenso* is missing—I believe, murdered. Meantime, in years long after that day, and on an occasion perhaps equally interesting, viz. the turning up of Thugs and

Thuggism,[1] another dinner was given. Of this I myself kept notes, for fear of another accident to the shorthand reporter. And I here subjoin them.

Toad-in-the-hole, I must mention, was present at this dinner. In fact, it was one of its sentimental incidents. Being as old as the valleys at the dinner of 1812, naturally he was as old as the hills at the Thug dinner of 1838. He had taken to wearing his beard again; why, or with what view, it passes my persimmon to tell you. But so it was. And his appearance was most benign and venerable. Nothing could equal the angelic radiance of his smile as he inquired after the unfortunate reporter (whom, as a piece of private scandal, I should tell you that he was himself supposed to have murdered in a rapture of creative art). The answer was, with roars of laughter, from the under-sheriff of our county—"Non est inventus." Toad-in-the-hole laughed outrageously at this: in fact, we all thought he was choking; and, at the earnest request of the company, a musical composer furnished a most beautiful glee upon the occasion, which was sung five times after dinner, with universal applause and inextinguishable laughter, the words being these (and the chorus so contrived, as most beautifully to mimic the peculiar laughter of Toad-in-the-hole):—

"Et interrogatum est a Toad-in-the-hole—Ubi est ille reporter?
Et responsum est cum cachinno—*Non est inventus.*"

Chorus.

"Deinde iteratum est ab omnibus, cum cachinnatione undulante, trepidante—*Non est inventus.*"

——— Toad-in-the-hole, I ought to mention, about nine years before, when an express from Edinburgh brought him the earliest intelligence of the Burke-and-Hare revolution in the art,[2] went mad upon the spot, and, instead of a pension to

---

[1] It was about the year 1831 that the British authorities in India began really energetic measures for the suppression of the Thugs,—the sect or fraternity in Northern India whose practice it was, under the sanction of hereditary custom and religion, to waylay and murder travellers, carefully burying the bodies, and dividing the spoil. One of the first books on Thugs and Thuggism was Thornton's *Illustrations of the History and Practices of the Thugs*, published in 1837.—M.

[2] In 1828 Edinburgh was horrified by the discovery that two Irish-

the express for even one life, or a knighthood, endeavoured to Burke *him*; in consequence of which he was put into a strait-waistcoat. And that was the reason we had no dinner then. But now all of us were alive and kicking, strait-waistcoaters and others; in fact, not one absentee was reported upon the entire roll. There were also many foreign amateurs present —— Dinner being over, and the cloth drawn, there was a general call made for the new glee of *Non est inventus*; but, as this would have interfered with the requisite gravity of the company during the earlier toasts, I overruled the call. After the national toasts had been given,

men, William Burke and William Hare, with one or more accomplices, had been carrying on a traffic in murder for the hideous purpose of selling the dead bodies as subjects for anatomical use. Their method was to lure wayfaring strangers, beggar-women, idiots, and such other poor creatures as were not likely to be missed, into the dens where they lived, especially into Burke's house in a court off the West Port, and there to make them drunk, and then smother or strangle them. It is computed that as many as sixteen victims had been thus disposed of before the horror was found out. Condemned for one of the murders, Burke was hanged on the 28th of January 1829, his colleague Hare having, greatly to the disgust of the public, escaped the same doom by acting as king's evidence on the trial.—There is no more striking instance of the coining of a metonymy than in the immediate conversion of the name of the Edinburgh murderer of 1828 into a new word in the English language. People at once began to use the word *burk* (the final *e* dropped) as a verb for *suffocate*, whether in the literal sense of killing by suffocation (in which sense an anatomical lecture-room in a northern Scottish town was for a while popularly known as "The Burking-House," from the notion that subjects were obtained for it, or actually manufactured within its walls, by Burke's method), or in a more figurative sense in such phrases as "His speech was *burked*," *i.e.* choked off or suppressed by the impatient audience.— Hare, whom the Edinburgh mob would have torn to pieces if they could have clutched him, disappeared from public view, and lived on, no one knows where, or in how many different places, under another name. There is a legend that, as he was working somewhere as a plasterer's labourer, his fellow-workmen, finding out who he was, rolled him in lime or pelted him with lime, with the result of the total destruction of his eyesight. An old gray-haired man who used to sit begging by the railings of the National Gallery in Trafalgar Square, London, was pointed out to myself, more than twenty years ago, as no other than the murderer Hare. I was sceptical at the time, the rather because the look of the old man was not unvenerable; and I have heard since of the supposed identification of Hare with this or that similarly conspicuous blind mendicant in other localities.—M.

the first official toast of the day was *The Old Man of the Mountains*[1]—drunk in solemn silence.

Toad-in-the-hole returned thanks in a neat speech. He likened himself to the Old Man of the Mountains in a few brief allusions that made the company yell with laughter; and he concluded with giving the health of

Mr. von Hammer, with many thanks to him for his learned History of the Old Man and his subjects the Assassins.[2]

Upon this I rose and said that doubtless most of the company were aware of the distinguished place assigned by Orientalists to the very learned Turkish scholar, Von Hammer the Austrian; that he had made the profoundest researches into our art, as connected with those early and eminent artists, the Syrian assassins in the period of the Crusaders; that his work had been for several years deposited, as a rare treasure of art, in the library of the club. Even the author's name, gentlemen, pointed him out as the historian of our art—Von Hammer——

"Yes, yes," interrupted Toad-in-the-hole, "Von Hammer —he's the man for a *malleus hæreticorum*. You all know what consideration Williams bestowed on the hammer, or the ship-carpenter's mallet, which is the same thing. Gentlemen, I give you another great hammer—Charles the Hammer, the Marteau, or, in old French, the Martel: he hammered the Saracens till they were all as dead as doornails."

"*Charles the Hammer*, with all the honours."

But the explosion of Toad-in-the-hole, together with the uproarious cheers for the grandpapa of Charlemagne, had now made the company unmanageable. The orchestra was

---

[1] See footnote, *ante*, p. 21.—M.

[2] Von Hammer's *Geschichte der Assassinen* was published in 1818. In a note to Gibbon's account of the Assassins and the Old Man of the Mountains, he had acknowledged his authority thus:—"All that can be known of the Assassins of Persia and Syria is procured from the copious, and even profuse, erudition of M. Falconet in two *Mémoires* read before the Academy of Inscriptions"; to which this note by Milman is added in the 1839 edition of Gibbon:—"Von Hammer's History of the Assassins has now thrown Falconet's Dissertation into the shade."—M.

again challenged with shouts the stormiest for the new glee. I foresaw a tempestuous evening; and I ordered myself to be strengthened with three waiters on each side,—the vice-president with as many. Symptoms of unruly enthusiasm were beginning to show out; and I own that I myself was considerably excited as the orchestra opened with its storm of music and the impassioned glee began—" Et interrogatum est a Toad-in-the-hole—Ubi est ille Reporter?" And the frenzy of the passion became absolutely convulsing as the full chorus fell in—" Et iteratum est ab omnibus—*Non est inventus.*"

The next toast was—*The Jewish Sicarii.*

Upon which I made the following explanation to the company:—" Gentlemen, I am sure it will interest you all to hear that the Assassins, ancient as they were, had a race of predecessors in the very same country. All over Syria, but particularly in Palestine, during the early years of the Emperor Nero, there was a band of murderers, who prosecuted their studies in a very novel manner. They did not practise in the night-time, or in lonely places; but, justly considering that great crowds are in themselves a sort of darkness by means of the dense pressure, and the impossibility of finding out who it was that gave the blow, they mingled with mobs everywhere; particularly at the great paschal feast in Jerusalem; where they actually had the audacity, as Josephus assures us, to press into the temple —and whom should they choose for operating upon but Jonathan himself, the Pontifex Maximus? They murdered him, gentlemen, as beautifully as if they had had him alone on a moonless night in a dark lane. And, when it was asked who was the murderer, and where he was——"

" Why, then, it was answered," interrupted Toad-in-the-hole, "'*Non est inventus.*'" And then, in spite of all I could do or say, the orchestra opened, and the whole company began—" Et interrogatum est a Toad-in-the-hole— Ubi est ille Sicarius? Et responsum est ab omnibus—*Non est inventus.*"

When the tempestuous chorus had subsided, I began again:—" Gentlemen, you will find a very circumstantial account of the Sicarii in at least three different parts of

Josephus: once in Book XX, sec. v, c. viii, of his 'Antiquities'; once in Book I. of his 'Wars': but in sec. x of the chapter first cited you will find a particular description of their tooling. This is what he says:—'They tooled with small scimitars not much different from the Persian *acinacæ*, but more curved, and for all the world most like the Roman semi-lunar *sicæ*.' It is perfectly magnificent, gentlemen, to hear the sequel of their history. Perhaps the only case on record where a regular army of murderers was assembled, a *justus exercitus*, was in the case of these *Sicarii*. They mustered in such strength in the wilderness that Festus himself was obliged to march against them with the Roman legionary force. A pitched battle ensued; and this army of amateurs was all cut to pieces in the desert. Heavens, gentlemen, what a sublime picture! The Roman legions—the wilderness—Jerusalem in the distance—an army of murderers in the foreground!"

The next toast was—"To the further improvement of Tooling, and thanks to the Committee for their services."

Mr. L., on behalf of the Committee who had reported on that subject, returned thanks. He made an interesting extract from the report, by which it appeared how very much stress had been laid formerly on the mode of tooling by the Fathers, both Greek and Latin. In confirmation of this pleasing fact, he made a very striking statement in reference to the earliest work of antediluvian art. Father Mersenne, that learned French Roman Catholic, in page one thousand four hundred and thirty-one[1] of his operose Commentary on Genesis, mentions, on the authority of several rabbis, that the quarrel of Cain with Abel was about

[1] "Page one thousand four hundred and thirty-one"—*literally*, good reader, and no joke at all. [Marin Mersenne, a monk of a convent near Paris, was born 1588 and died 1648. Among his works is a Commentary on Genesis, published at Paris in 1623 under the title *P. Marini Mersenni, ordinis minorum S. Francisci de Paula Quæstiones celeberrimæ in Genesim, cum accurata Textus explicatione.* It is a large folio, each page divided into two columns, and with the columns numbered, and not the pages. De Quincey, with all his exactness, had not observed this, and is consequently wrong in his twice emphasised joke that the passage he cites is on "page one thousand four hundred and thirty-one." It is in *column* 1431, which would be *page* 716 only.—M]

a young woman; that, according to various accounts, Cain had tooled with his teeth (Abelem fuisse *morsibus* dilaceratum a Cain); according to many others, with the jawbone of an ass,—which is the tooling adopted by most painters. But it is pleasing to the mind of sensibility to know that, as science expanded, sounder views were adopted. One author contends for a pitchfork, St. Chrysostom for a sword, Irenæus for a scythe, and Prudentius, the Christian poet of the fourth century, for a hedging-bill. This last writer delivers his opinion thus:—

> "Frater, probatæ sanctitatis æmulus,
> Germana curvo colla frangit sarculo:"

i.e. his brother, jealous of his attested sanctity, fractures his fraternal throat with a curved hedging-bill. "All which is respectfully submitted by your committee, not so much as decisive of the question (for it is not), but in order to impress upon the youthful mind the importance which has ever been attached to the quality of the tooling by such men as Chrysostom and Irenæus."

"Irenæus be hanged!" said Toad-in-the-hole, who now rose impatiently to give the next toast:—"Our Irish friends; wishing them a speedy revolution in their mode of tooling, as well as in everything else connected with the art!"

"Gentlemen, I'll tell you the plain truth. Every day of the year when we take up a paper we read the opening of a murder. We say, This is good, this is charming, this is excellent! But, behold you! scarcely have we read a little farther before the word Tipperary or Ballina-something betrays the Irish manufacture. Instantly we loathe it; we call to the waiter; we say, 'Waiter, take away this paper; send it out of the house; it is absolutely a scandal in the nostrils of all just taste.' I appeal to every man whether, on finding a murder (otherwise perhaps promising enough) to be Irish, he does not feel himself as much insulted as when, Madeira being ordered, he finds it to be Cape, or when, taking up what he takes to be a mushroom, it turns out what children call a toad-stool? Tithes, politics, something wrong in principle, vitiate every Irish murder.

Gentlemen, this must be reformed, or Ireland will not be a land to live in; at least, if we do live there, we must import all our murders, that's clear." Toad-in-the-hole sat down, growling with suppressed wrath; and the uproarious "Hear, hear!" clamorously expressed the general concurrence.

The next toast was—"The sublime epoch of Burkism and Harism!"

This was drunk with enthusiasm; and one of the members who spoke to the question made a very curious communication to the company:—"Gentlemen, we fancy Burkism to be a pure invention of our own times; and in fact no Pancirollus has ever enumerated this branch of art when writing *de rebus deperditis*.[1] Still, I have ascertained that the essential principle of this variety in the art *was* known to the ancients; although, like the art of painting upon glass, of making the myrrhine cups, &c., it was lost in the dark ages for want of encouragement. In the famous collection of Greek epigrams made by Planudes[2] is one upon a very fascinating case of Burkism: it is a perfect little gem of art. The epigram itself I cannot lay my hand upon at this moment; but the following is an abstract of it by Salmasius, as I find it in his notes on Vopiscus[3]: 'Est et elegans epigramma Lucilii,[4] ubi medicus et pollinctor de compacto sic egerunt ut medicus ægros omnes curæ suæ commissos occideret.' This was the basis of the contract, you see,—that on the one part the doctor, for himself and

---

[1] Guido Panciroli, Italian jurist (born 1523, died 1599), author of a work on lost arts and inventions.—M.

[2] This collection of Greek epigrams by Planudes Maximus, a Byzantine monk of the fourteenth century, was first printed at Florence in 1594.—M.

[3] Flavius Vopiscus, of the fourth century, was the author of some of those lives of Roman Emperors which are known collectively as the *Augusta Historia*. His annotator Salmasius, or Claude de Saumaise, thought the most learned man of his age (born 1588, died 1653), is perhaps best remembered now from Milton's assault on him in the *Defensio pro Populo Anglicano*.—M

[4] The epigram, which had been preserved by Planudes in its Greek form, is here attributed by Salmasius to the Latin satirical poet, Caius Lucilius, who was born about B.C. 148, and died about B.C. 103. It is not found, however, among the preserved fragments of Lucilius; and the Greek form of the epigram is anonymous.

his assigns, doth undertake and contract duly and truly to murder all the patients committed to his charge: but why? There lies the beauty of the case—'Et ut pollinctori 'amico suo traderet pollingendos.' The *pollinctor*, you are aware, was a person whose business it was to dress and prepare dead bodies for burial. The original ground of the transaction appears to have been sentimental: 'He was my friend,' says the murderous doctor,—'he was dear to me,'— in speaking of the pollinctor. But the law, gentlemen, is stern and harsh: the law will not hear of these tender motives: to sustain a contract of this nature in law, it is essential that a 'consideration' should be given. Now, what *was* the consideration? For thus far all is on the side of the pollinctor: he will be well paid for his services; but meantime the generous, the noble-minded doctor gets nothing. What *was* the equivalent, again I ask, which the law would insist on the doctor's taking, in order to establish that 'con- 'sideration' without which the contract had no force? You shall hear: 'Et ut pollinctor vicissim τελαμῶνας quos fura- 'batur de pollinctione mortuorum medico mitteret donis ad 'alliganda vulnera eorum quos curabat'; *i.e.* and that reciprocally the pollinctor should transmit to the physician, as free gifts for the binding up of wounds in those whom he treated medically, the belts or trusses (τελαμῶνας) which he had succeeded in purloining in the course of his functions about the corpses.

"Now the case is clear: the whole went on a principle of reciprocity which would have kept up the trade for ever. The doctor was also a surgeon: he could not murder *all* his patients: some of the patients must be retained intact. For these he wanted linen bandages. But, unhappily, the Romans wore woollen; on which account it was that they bathed so often. Meantime, there *was* linen to be had in Rome; but it was monstrously dear; and the τελαμῶνες, or linen swathing bandages, in which superstition obliged them to bind up corpses, would answer capitally for the surgeon. The doctor, therefore, contracts to furnish his friend with a constant succession of corpses,—provided, and be it understood always, that his said friend, in return, should supply him with one-half of the articles he would receive from the friends of the parties murdered or to be murdered. The doctor invariably recommended his invaluable friend the pollinctor (whom let us call the undertaker); the undertaker, with equal regard to the sacred rights of friendship, uniformly recommended the doctor. Like Pylades and Orestes, they were models of a perfect friendship: in their lives they were lovely; and on the gallows, it is to be hoped, they were not divided.

"Gentlemen, it makes me laugh horribly when I think of those two friends drawing and re-drawing on each other: 'Pollinctor in account with Doctor, debtor by sixteen corpses: creditor by forty-five bandages, two of which damaged.' Their names unfortunately are lost[1]; but I conceive they must have been Quintus Burkius and Publius Harius. By the way, gentlemen, has anybody heard lately of Hare? I understand he is comfortably settled in Ireland, considerably to the west, and does a little business now and then; but, as he observes with a sigh, only as a retailer—nothing like the fine thriving wholesale concern so carelessly blown up at Edinburgh. 'You see what comes of neglecting business'—is the chief moral, the ἐπιμύθιον, as Æsop would say, which Hare draws from his past experience."[2]

At length came the toast of the day—*Thugdom in all its branches.*

The speeches *attempted* at this crisis of the dinner were past all counting. But the applause was so furious, the music so stormy, and the crashing of glasses so incessant, from the general resolution never again to drink an inferior

---

[1] In the Greek form of the epigram the Doctor figures as *Krateas* and the Pollinctor as *Damon*. So the readers of the original article in *Blackwood* were informed in an editorial note which Wilson took the trouble to subjoin to De Quincey's text. The note was in these words:—"Here is the Greek epigram—with a version. C. N. [*i.e.* Christopher North]. We need not give the Greek here: Wilson's version (or was it his?) is as follows:—

"Damon, who plied the undertaker's trade,
  With Doctor Krateas an agreement made.
What graveclothes Damon from the dead could seize
  He to the Doctor sent for bandages;
While the good Doctor—here no bargain-breaker—
  Sent all his patients to the Undertaker."—M.

[2] See footnote, *ante*, p. 61.—M.

toast from the same glass, that I am unequal to the task of reporting. Besides which, Toad-in-the-hole now became ungovernable. He kept firing pistols in every direction; sent his servant for a blunderbuss, and talked of loading with ball-cartridge. We conceived that his former madness had returned at the mention of Burke and Hare; or that, being again weary of life, he had resolved to go off in a general massacre. This we could not think of allowing; it became indispensable, therefore, to kick him out; which we did with universal consent, the whole company lending their toes *uno pede*, as I may say, though pitying his gray hairs and his angelic smile During the operation the orchestra poured in their old chorus. The universal company sang, and (what surprised us most of all) Toad-in-the-hole joined us furiously in singing—

"Et interrogatum est ab omnibus—Ubi est ille Toad-in-the-Hole?
Et responsum est ab omnibus—*Non est inventus.*"

POSTSCRIPT in 1854

WITH AN ACCOUNT OF THE WILLIAMS AND M'KEAN MURDERS [1]

It is impossible to conciliate readers of so saturnine and gloomy a class that they cannot enter with genial sympathy into any gaiety whatever, but, least of all, when the gaiety trespasses a little into the province of the extravagant. In such a case, not to sympathise is not to understand; and the playfulness which is not relished becomes flat and insipid, or absolutely without meaning. Fortunately, after all such churls have withdrawn from my audience in high displeasure, there remains a large majority who are loud in acknowledging the amusement which they have derived from this little paper [2]; at the same time proving the sincerity of their praise by one hesitating expression of censure. Repeatedly they have suggested to me that perhaps the extravagance, though clearly intentional, and forming one element in the general gaiety of the conception, went too far. I am not myself of that opinion; and I beg to remind these friendly censors that it is amongst the direct purposes and efforts of this *bagatelle* to graze the brink of horror, and of all that would in actual realisation be most repulsive. The very

---

[1] This was an addition by De Quincey in 1854, when he reprinted the two foregoing papers in vol. IV of his Collected Writings. He entitled it simply "POSTSCRIPT"; but the extended title here given is now more convenient.—M.

[2] The use of the word "paper" in the singular suggests that the Postscript *may* have been in manuscript shortly after the publication of the "First Paper" and before the "Second" had been written.—M.

excess of the extravagance, in fact, by suggesting to the reader continually the mere aeriality of the entire speculation, furnishes the surest means of disenchanting him from the horror which might else gather from his feelings. Let me remind such objectors, once for all, of Dean Swift's proposal for turning to account the supernumerary infants of the three kingdoms,—which, in those days, both at Dublin and at London, were provided for in foundling hospitals,—by cooking and eating them. This was an extravaganza, though really bolder and more coarsely practical than mine, which did not provoke any reproaches even to a dignitary of the supreme Irish Church; its own monstrosity was its excuse; mere extravagance was left to license and accredit the little *jeu d'esprit*, precisely as the blank impossibilities of Lilliput, of Laputa, of the Yahoos, &c., had licensed those.[1] If, therefore, any man thinks it worth his while to tilt against so mere a foam-bubble of gaiety as this lecture on the æsthetics of murder, I shelter myself for the moment under the Telamonian shield of the Dean. But, in reality,—which (to say the truth) formed one motive for detaining the reader by this

---

[1] The paper of Swift's referred to was published in 1729, and bears the title *A Modest Proposal for preventing the Children of Poor People in Ireland from being a Burden to their Parents or Country, and for making them beneficial to the Publick.* The grimness of its irony will appear from a selected sentence or two:—"I have been assured by a "very knowing American of my acquaintance in London that a young "healthy child, well nursed, is at a year old a most delicious, "nourishing and wholesome food, whether stewed, roasted, baked, or "boiled; and I make no doubt that it will equally serve in a *fricassé* "or *ragoust*. I do therefore humbly offer it to publick considera- "tion that of the hundred and twenty thousand children already "computed [as born every year in Ireland] twenty thousand may be "reserved for breed, whereof only one-fourth part to be males; which "is more than we allow to sheep, black cattle, or swine; ... that "the remaining hundred thousand may, at a year old, be offered in "sale to the persons of quality and fortune through the kingdom; "always advising the mother to let them suck plentifully in the last "month, so as to render them plump, and fit for a good table. A "child will make two dishes at an entertainment for friends; and, "when the family dines alone, the fore or hind quarter will make a "reasonable dish, and, seasoned with a little pepper or salt, will be "very good boiled on the fourth day, especially in winter."—No wonder that De Quincey brought this precedent into his Apology. Christopher North had already done it for him. See note, p 11.— M.

Postscript,—my own little paper may plead a privileged excuse for its extravagance, such as is altogether wanting to the Dean's. Nobody can pretend, for a moment, on behalf of the Dean, that there is any ordinary and natural tendency in human thoughts which could ever turn to infants as articles of diet; under any conceivable circumstances, this would be felt as the most aggravated form of cannibalism—cannibalism applying itself to the most defenceless part of the species. But, on the other hand, the tendency to a critical or æsthetic valuation of fires and murders is universal. If you are summoned to the spectacle of a great fire, undoubtedly the first impulse is—to assist in putting it out. But that field of exertion is very limited, and is soon filled by regular professional people, trained and equipped for the service. In the case of a fire which is operating upon *private* property, pity for a neighbour's calamity checks us at first in treating the affair as a scenic spectacle. But perhaps the fire may be confined to public buildings. And in any case, after we have paid our tribute of regret to the affair considered as a calamity, inevitably, and without restraint, we go on to consider it as a stage spectacle. Exclamations of—How grand! how magnificent! arise in a sort of rapture from the crowd. For instance, when Drury Lane was burned down in the first decennium of this century,[1] the falling in of the roof was signalised by a mimic suicide of the protecting Apollo that surmounted and crested the centre of this roof. The god was stationary with his lyre, and seemed looking down upon the fiery ruins that were so rapidly approaching him. Suddenly the supporting timbers below him gave way; a convulsive heave of the billowing flames seemed for a moment to raise the statue; and then, as if by some impulse of despair, the presiding deity appeared not to fall, but to throw himself into the fiery deluge, for he went down head foremost, and in all respects the descent had the air of a voluntary act. What followed? From every one of the bridges over the river, and from other open areas which commanded the spectacle, there arose a sustained uproar of admiration and sympathy. Some few years before this event, a prodigious fire occurred at Liverpool: the *Goree*, a vast pile

[1] 24th February 1809.—M.

of warehouses close to one of the docks, was burned to the ground. The huge edifice, eight or nine storeys high, and laden with most combustible goods,—many thousand bales of cotton, wheat and oats in thousands of quarters, tar, turpentine, rum, gunpowder, &c.,—continued through many hours of darkness to feed this tremendous fire. To aggravate the calamity, it blew a regular gale of wind; luckily for the shipping, it blew inland,—that is, to the east; and all the way down to Warrington, eighteen miles distant to the eastward, the whole air was illuminated by flakes of cotton, often saturated with rum, and by what seemed absolute worlds of blazing sparks, that lighted up all the upper chambers of the air. All the cattle lying abroad in the fields through a breadth of eighteen miles were thrown into terror and agitation. Men, of course, read in this hurrying overhead of scintillating and blazing vortices the annunciation of some gigantic calamity going on in Liverpool; and the lamentation on that account was universal. But that mood of public sympathy did not at all interfere to suppress or even to check the momentary bursts of rapturous admiration, as this arrowy sleet of many-coloured fire rode on the wings of hurricane, alternately through open depths of air or through dark clouds overhead.

Precisely the same treatment is applied to murders. After the first tribute of sorrow to those who have perished, but, at all events, after the personal interests have been tranquillised by time, inevitably the scenical features (what æsthetically may be called the comparative *advantages*) of the several murders are reviewed and valued. One murder is compared with another; and the circumstances of superiority,—as, for example, in the incidence and effects of surprise, of mystery, &c.,—are collated and appraised. I, therefore, for *my* extravagance, claim an inevitable and perpetual ground in the spontaneous tendencies of the human mind when left to itself. But no one will pretend that any corresponding plea can be advanced on behalf of Swift.

In this important distinction between myself and the Dean lies one reason which prompted the present Postscript. A second purpose of the Postscript is to make the reader acquainted circumstantially with three memorable cases of murder which long ago the voice of amateurs has crowned with laurel, but especially with the two earliest of the three, viz. the immortal Williams murders of 1812.[1] The act and the actor are each separately in the highest degree interesting; and, as forty-two years have elapsed since 1812, it cannot be supposed that either is known circumstantially to the men of the current generation.

Never, throughout the annals of universal Christendom, has there indeed been any act of one solitary insulated individual armed with power so appalling over the hearts of men as that exterminating murder by which, during the winter of 1812, John Williams, in one hour, smote two houses with emptiness, exterminated all but two entire households, and asserted his own supremacy above all the children of Cain. It would be absolutely impossible adequately to describe the frenzy of feelings which, throughout the next fortnight, mastered the popular heart,—the mere delirium of indignant horror in some, the mere delirium of panic in others. For twelve succeeding days, under some groundless notion that the unknown murderer had quitted London, the panic which had convulsed the mighty metropolis diffused itself all over the island. I was myself at that time nearly three hundred miles from London; but there, and everywhere, the panic was indescribable. One lady, my next neighbour, whom personally I knew, living at the moment, during the absence of her husband, with a few servants in a very solitary house, never rested until she had placed eighteen doors (so she told me, and, indeed, satisfied me by ocular proof), each secured by ponderous bolts, and bars, and chains, between her own bedroom and any intruder of human build. To reach her, even in her drawing-room, was like going as a flag of truce into a beleaguered fortress; at every sixth step one was stopped by a sort of portcullis. The panic was not confined to the rich; women in the humblest ranks more than once died upon the spot from the

---

[1] Strange that De Quincey should have forgotten the exact date of those Williams murders of which he makes so much! They were in December 1811. He wrote perhaps from memory; and the panic caused by the murders did extend into 1812.—M.

shock attending some suspicious attempts at intrusion upon the part of vagrants meditating probably nothing worse than a robbery, but whom the poor women, misled by the London newspapers, had fancied to be the dreadful London murderer. Meantime this solitary artist, that rested in the centre of London, self-supported by his own conscious grandeur, as a domestic Attila, or "Scourge of God,"—this man that walked in darkness, and relied upon murder (as afterwards transpired) for bread, for clothes, for promotion in life,—was silently preparing an effectual answer to the public journals; and on the twelfth day after his inaugural murder he advertised his presence in London, and published to all men the absurdity of ascribing to *him* any ruralising propensities, by striking a second blow and accomplishing a second family extermination. Somewhat lightened was the *provincial* panic by this proof that the murderer had not condescended to sneak into the country, or to abandon for a moment, under any motive of caution or fear, the great metropolitan *castra stativa* of gigantic crime seated for ever on the Thames. In fact, the great artist disdained a provincial reputation; and he must have felt, as a case of ludicrous disproportion, the contrast between a country town or village, on the one hand, and, on the other, a work more lasting than brass—a κτῆμα ἐς ἀεί—a murder such in quality as any murder that *he* would condescend to own for a work turned out from his own *studio*.

Coleridge, whom I saw some months after these terrific murders, told me that, for *his* part, though at the time resident in London, he had not shared in the prevailing panic; *him* they affected only as a philosopher, and threw him into a profound reverie upon the tremendous power which is laid open in a moment to any man who can reconcile himself to the abjuration of all conscientious restraints, if at the same time thoroughly without fear. Not sharing in the public panic, however, Coleridge did not consider that panic at all unreasonable; for, as he said most truly, in that vast metropolis there are many thousands of households composed exclusively of women and children; many other thousands there are who necessarily confide their safety, in the long evenings, to the discretion of a young servant girl;

and, if she suffers herself to be beguiled by the pretence of a message from her mother, sister, or sweetheart, into opening the door, there, in one second of time, goes to wreck the security of the house. However, at that time, and for many months afterwards, the practice of steadily putting the chain upon the door before it was opened prevailed generally, and for a long time served as a record of that deep impression left upon London by Mr. Williams. Southey, I may add, entered deeply into the public feeling on this occasion, and said to me, within a week or two of the first murder, that it was a private event of that order which rose to the dignity of a national event.[1] But now, having prepared the reader to appreciate on its true scale this dreadful tissue of murder (which, as a record belonging to an era that is now left forty-two years behind us, not one person in four of this generation can be expected to know correctly), let me pass to the circumstantial details of the affair.

Yet, first of all, one word as to the local scene of the murders. Ratcliffe Highway is a public thoroughfare in a most chaotic quarter of eastern or nautical London; and at this time (viz. in 1812), when no adequate police existed except the *detective* police of Bow Street,—admirable for its own peculiar purposes, but utterly incommensurate to the general service of the capital,—it was a most dangerous quarter. Every third man at the least might be set down as a foreigner. Lascars, Chinese, Moors, Negroes, were met at every step. And, apart from the manifold ruffianism shrouded impenetrably under the mixed hats and turbans of men whose past was untraceable to any European eye, it is well known that the navy (especially, in time of war, the commercial navy) of Christendom is the sure receptacle of all the murderers and ruffians whose crimes have given them a motive for withdrawing themselves for a season from the public eye. It is true that few of this class are qualified to act as "able" seamen; but at all times, and especially during war, only a small proportion (or *nucleus*) of each ship's com-

---

[1] I am not sure whether Southey held at this time his appointment to the editorship of the "Edinburgh Annual Register." If he did, no doubt in the domestic section of that chronicle will be found an excellent account of the whole.

pany consists of such men,—the large majority being mere untutored landsmen. John Williams, however, who had been occasionally rated as a seaman on board of various Indiamen, &c., was probably a very accomplished seaman. Pretty generally, in fact, he was a ready and adroit man, fertile in resources under all sudden difficulties, and most flexibly adapting himself to all varieties of social life. Williams was a man of middle stature (five feet seven and a half to five feet eight inches high), slenderly built, rather thin, but wiry, tolerably muscular, and clear of all superfluous flesh. A lady who saw him under examination (I think at the Thames Police Office) assured me that his hair was of the most extraordinary and vivid colour,—viz. bright yellow, something between an orange and a lemon colour. Williams had been in India; chiefly in Bengal and Madras, but he had also been upon the Indus. Now, it is notorious that in the Punjaub horses of a high caste are often painted—crimson, blue, green, purple; and it struck me that Williams might, for some casual purpose of disguise, have taken a hint from this practice of Scinde and Lahore, so that the colour might not have been natural. In other respects his appearance was natural enough, and,—judging by a plaster cast of him which I purchased in London,—I should say mean as regarded his facial structure. One fact, however, was striking, and fell in with the impression of his natural tiger character,—that his face wore at all times a bloodless ghastly pallor. "You might imagine," said my informant, "that in his veins circulated not red life-blood, such as could kindle into the blush of shame, of wrath, of pity—but a green sap that welled from no human heart." His eyes seemed frozen and glazed, as if their light were all converged upon some victim lurking in the far background. So far his appearance might have repelled; but, on the other hand, the concurrent testimony of many witnesses, and also the silent testimony of facts, showed that the oiliness and snaky insinuation of his demeanour counteracted the repulsiveness of his ghastly face, and amongst inexperienced young women won for him a very favourable reception. In particular, one gentle-mannered girl, whom Williams had undoubtedly designed to murder, gave in evidence that once, when sitting alone with her, he had said, "Now, Miss R., supposing that I should appear about midnight at your bedside armed with a carving knife, what would you say?" To which the confiding girl had replied, "Oh, Mr. Williams, if it was anybody else, I should be frightened. But, as soon as I heard *your* voice, I should be tranquil." Poor girl! had this outline sketch of Mr. Williams been filled in and realised, she would have seen something in the corpselike face, and heard something in the sinister voice, that would have unsettled her tranquillity for ever. But nothing short of such dreadful experiences could avail to unmask Mr. John Williams.

Into this perilous region it was that, on a Saturday night in December,[1] Mr. Williams, whom we must suppose to have long since made his *coup d'essai*, forced his way through the crowded streets, bound on business. To say was to do. And this night he had said to himself secretly that he would execute a design which he had already sketched, and which, when finished, was destined on the following day to strike consternation into "all that mighty heart" of London, from centre to circumference. It was afterwards remembered that he had quitted his lodgings on this dark errand about eleven o'clock P.M. , not that he meant to begin so soon; but he needed to reconnoitre. He carried his tools closely buttoned up under his loose roomy coat. It was in harmony with the general subtlety of his character, and his polished hatred of brutality, that by universal agreement his manners were distinguished for exquisite suavity; the tiger's heart was masked by the most insinuating and snaky refinement. All his acquaintances afterwards described his dissimulation as so ready and so perfect that, if, in making his way through the streets, always so crowded on Saturday night in neighbourhoods so poor, he had accidentally jostled any person, he would (as they were all satisfied) have stopped to offer the most gentlemanly apologies: with his devilish heart brooding over the most hellish of purposes, he would yet have paused to express a benign hope that the huge mallet buttoned up under his elegant surtout, with a view to the little business that awaited him about ninety minutes further on, had not inflicted any pain on the stranger with whom he had come

[1] Saturday, 7th December 1811.—M.

into collision. Titian, I believe, but certainly Rubens, and perhaps Vandyke, made it a rule never to practise their art but in full dress—point-ruffles, bag-wig, and diamond-hilted sword; and Mr. Williams, there is reason to believe, when he went out for a grand compound massacre (in another sense, one might have applied to it the Oxford phrase of *going out as Grand Compounder*), always assumed black silk stockings and pumps; nor would he on any account have degraded his position as an artist by wearing a morning gown. In his second great performance, it was particularly noticed and recorded, by the one sole trembling man who under killing agonies of fear was compelled (as the reader will find) from a secret stand to become the solitary spectator of his atrocities, that Mr. Williams wore a long blue frock, of the very finest cloth, and richly lined with silk. Amongst the anecdotes which circulated about him, it was also said at the time that Mr. Williams employed the first of dentists and also the first of chiropodists. On no account would he patronise any second-rate skill. And, beyond a doubt, in that perilous little branch of business which was practised by himself he might be regarded as the most aristocratic and fastidious of artists.

But who meantime was the victim to whose abode he was hurrying? For surely he never could be so indiscreet as to be sailing about on a roving cruise in search of some chance person to murder? Oh no; he had suited himself with a victim some time before, viz. an old and very intimate friend. For he seems to have laid it down as a maxim that the best person to murder was a friend, and, in default of a friend, which is an article one cannot always command, an acquaintance: because, in either case, on first approaching his subject, suspicion would be disarmed, whereas a stranger might take alarm, and find in the very countenance of his murderer elect a warning summons to place himself on guard. However, in the present case, his destined victim was supposed to unite both characters: originally he had been a friend; but subsequently, on good cause arising, he had become an enemy. Or more probably, as others said, the feelings had long since languished which gave life to either relation of friendship or of enmity. Marr was the name of that unhappy man who (whether in the character of friend or enemy) had been selected for the subject of this present Saturday night's performance. And the story current at that time about the connexion between Williams and Marr,—having (whether true or not true) never been contradicted upon authority,—was that they sailed in the same Indiaman to Calcutta, and that they had quarrelled when at sea. But another version of the story said—No: they had quarrelled after returning from sea; and the subject of their quarrel was Mrs. Marr, a very pretty young woman, for whose favour they had been rival candidates, and at one time with most bitter enmity towards each other. Some circumstances give a colour of probability to this story. Otherwise it has sometimes happened, on occasion of a murder not sufficiently accounted for, that, from pure goodness of heart intolerant of a mere sordid motive for a striking murder, some person has forged, and the public has accredited, a story representing the murderer as having moved under some loftier excitement: and in this case the public, too much shocked at the idea of Williams having on the single motive of gain consummated so complex a tragedy, welcomed the tale which represented him as governed by deadly malice, growing out of the more impassioned and noble rivalry for the favour of a woman. The case remains in some degree doubtful; but, certainly, the probability is that Mrs. Marr had been the true cause, the *causa teterrima*, of the feud between the men. Meantime the minutes are numbered, the sands of the hour-glass are running out, that measure the duration of this feud upon earth. This night it shall cease. To-morrow is the day which in England they call Sunday, which in Scotland they call by the Judaic name of "Sabbath." To both nations, under different names, the day has the same functions; to both it is a day of rest. For thee also, Marr, it shall be a day of rest; so is it written; thou, too, young Marr, shalt find rest—thou, and thy household, and the stranger that is within thy gates. But that rest must be in the world which lies beyond the grave. On this side the grave ye have all slept your final sleep.

The night was one of exceeding darkness; and in this humble quarter of London, whatever the night happened to be, light or dark, quiet or stormy, all shops were kept open on Saturday nights until twelve o'clock at the least, and many for half an hour longer. There was no rigorous and pedantic Jewish superstition about the exact limits of Sunday. At the very worst, the Sunday stretched over from one o'clock A.M. of one day up to eight o'clock A.M. of the next, making a clear circuit of thirty-one hours. This, surely, was long enough. Marr, on this particular Saturday night, would be content if it were even shorter, provided it would come more quickly; for he has been toiling through sixteen hours behind his counter. Marr's position in life was this:—He kept a little hosier's shop, and had invested in his stock and the fittings of his shop about £180. Like all men engaged in trade, he suffered some anxieties. He was a new beginner; but already bad debts had alarmed him, and bills were coming to maturity that were not likely to be met by commensurate sales. Yet, constitutionally, he was a sanguine hoper. At this time he was a stout, fresh-coloured young man of twenty-seven; in some slight degree uneasy from his commercial prospects; but still cheerful, and anticipating—(how vainly!)—that for this night, and the next night, at least, he will rest his wearied head and his cares upon the faithful bosom of his sweet, lovely young wife. The household of Marr, consisting of five persons, is as follows:—First, there is himself, who, if he should happen to be ruined in a limited commercial sense, has energy enough to jump up again, like a pyramid of fire, and soar high above ruin many times repeated. Yes, poor Marr, so it might be if thou wert left to thy native energies unmolested; but even now there stands on the other side of the street one born of hell who puts his peremptory negative on all these flattering prospects. Second in the list of this household stands his pretty and amiable wife; who is happy after the fashion of youthful wives, for she is only twenty-two, and anxious (if at all) only on account of her darling infant. For, thirdly, there is in a cradle, not quite nine feet below the street, viz. in a warm, cosy kitchen, and rocked at intervals by the young mother, a baby eight months old. Nineteen months have Marr and herself been married; and this is their first-born child. Grieve not for this child, that it must keep the deep rest of

Sunday in some other world; for wherefore should an orphan, steeped to the lips in poverty when once bereaved of father and mother, linger upon an alien and a murderous earth? Fourthly, there is a stoutish boy, an apprentice, say thirteen years old,—a Devonshire boy, with handsome features, such as most Devonshire youths have [1]; satisfied with his place; not overworked; treated kindly, and aware that he was treated kindly, by his master and mistress. Fifthly, and lastly, bringing up the rear of this quiet household, is a servant girl, a grown-up young woman; and she, being particularly kind-hearted, occupied (as often happens in families of humble pretensions as to rank) a sort of sisterly place in her relation to her mistress. A great democratic change is at this very time (1854), and has been for twenty years, passing over British society. Multitudes of persons are becoming ashamed of saying "my master" or "my mistress": the term now in the slow process of superseding it is "my employer." Now, in the United States, such an expression of democratic hauteur, though disagreeable as a needless proclamation of independence which nobody is disputing, leaves, however, no lasting bad effect. For the domestic "helps" are pretty generally in a state of transition so sure and so rapid to the headship of domestic establishments belonging to themselves that in effect they are but ignoring, for the present moment, a relation which would at any rate dissolve itself in a year or two. But in England, where no such resources exist of everlasting surplus lands, the tendency of the change is painful. It carries with it a sullen and a coarse expression of immunity from a yoke which was in any case a light one, and often a benign one. In some other place I will illustrate my meaning. Here, apparently, in Mrs. Marr's service, the principle concerned illustrated itself practically. Mary, the female servant, felt a sincere and unaffected respect for a mistress whom she saw so steadily occupied with her domestic duties, and who,

---

[1] An artist told me in this year, 1812, that, having accidentally seen a native Devonshire regiment (either volunteers or militia), nine hundred strong, marching past a station at which he had posted himself, he did not observe a dozen men that would not have been described in common parlance as "good-looking."

though so young, and invested with some slight authority, never exerted it capriciously, or even showed it at all conspicuously. According to the testimony of all the neighbours, she treated her mistress with a shade of unobtrusive respect on the one hand, and yet was eager to relieve her, whenever that was possible, from the weight of her maternal duties, with the cheerful voluntary service of a sister.

To this young woman it was that, suddenly, within three or four minutes of midnight, Marr called aloud from the head of the stairs—directing her to go out and purchase some oysters for the family supper. Upon what slender accidents hang oftentimes solemn life-long results! Marr, occupied in the concerns of his shop, Mrs. Marr, occupied with some little ailment and restlessness of her baby, had both forgotten the affair of supper; the time was now narrowing every moment as regarded any variety of choice; and oysters were perhaps ordered as the likeliest article to be had at all after twelve o'clock should have struck. And yet upon this trivial circumstance depended Mary's life. Had she been sent abroad for supper at the ordinary time of ten or eleven o'clock, it is almost certain that she, the solitary member of the household who escaped from the exterminating tragedy, would *not* have escaped; too surely she would have shared the general fate. It had now become necessary to be quick. Hastily, therefore, receiving money from Marr, with a basket in her hand, but unbonneted, Mary tripped out of the shop. It became afterwards, on recollection, a heart-chilling remembrance to herself that, precisely as she emerged from the shop-door, she noticed, on the opposite side of the street, by the light of the lamps, a man's figure; stationary at the instant, but in the next instant slowly moving. This was Williams, as a little incident, either just before or just after (at present it is impossible to say which), sufficiently proved. Now, when one considers the inevitable hurry and trepidation of Mary under the circumstances stated, time barely sufficing for any chance of executing her errand, it becomes evident that she must have connected some deep feeling of mysterious uneasiness with the movements of this unknown man; else, assuredly, she would not have found her attention disposable for such a case. Thus far she herself threw some little light upon what it might be that, semi-consciously, was then passing through her mind: she said that, notwithstanding the darkness, which would not permit her to trace the man's features, or to ascertain the exact direction of his eyes, it yet struck her that, from his carriage when in motion, and from the apparent inclination of his person, he must be looking at No. 29. The little incident which I have alluded to as confirming Mary's belief was that, at some period not very far from midnight, the watchman had specially noticed this stranger; he had observed him continually peeping into the window of Marr's shop, and had thought this act, connected with the man's appearance, so suspicious that he stepped into Marr's shop and communicated what he had seen. This fact he afterwards stated before the magistrates; and he added that subsequently, viz. a few minutes after twelve (eight or ten minutes, probably, after the departure of Mary), he (the watchman), when re-entering upon his ordinary half-hourly beat, was requested by Marr to assist him in closing the shutters. Here they had a final communication with each other; and the watchman mentioned to Marr that the mysterious stranger had now apparently taken himself off; for that he had not been visible since the first communication made to Marr by the watchman. There is little doubt that Williams had observed the watchman's visit to Marr, and had thus had his attention seasonably drawn to the indiscretion of his own demeanour; so that the warning, given unavailingly to Marr, had been turned to account by Williams. There can be still less doubt that the bloodhound had commenced his work within one minute of the watchman's assisting Marr to put up his shutters; and on the following consideration:—That which prevented Williams from commencing even earlier was the exposure of the shop's whole interior to the gaze of street passengers. It was indispensable that the shutters should be accurately closed before Williams could safely get to work. But, as soon as ever this preliminary precaution had been completed, once having secured that concealment from the public eye, it then became of still greater importance not to lose a moment by delay than previously it had been not to hazard anything by precipitance. For all depended upon going in before Marr should have locked the door. On any other mode of effecting an entrance (as, for instance, by waiting for the return of Mary, and making his entrance simultaneously with her) it will be seen that Williams must have forfeited that particular advantage which mute facts, when read into their true construction, will soon show the reader that he must have employed. Williams waited, of necessity, for the sound of the watchman's retreating steps; waited, perhaps, for thirty seconds; but, when that danger was past, the next danger was lest Marr should lock the door: one turn of the key, and the murderer would have been locked out. In, therefore, he bolted, and by a dexterous movement of his left hand, no doubt, turned the key, without letting Marr perceive this fatal stratagem. It is really wonderful and most interesting to pursue the successive steps of this monster, and to notice the absolute certainty with which the silent hieroglyphics of the case betray to us the whole process and movements of the bloody drama, not less surely and fully than if we had been ourselves hidden in Marr's shop, or had looked down from the heavens of mercy upon this hell-kite that knew not what mercy meant. That he had concealed from Marr his trick, secret and rapid, upon the lock, is evident; because else Marr would instantly have taken the alarm, especially after what the watchman had communicated. But it will soon be seen that Marr had *not* been alarmed. In reality, towards the full success of Williams it was important, in the last degree, to intercept and forestall any yell or shout of agony from Marr. Such an outcry, and in a situation so slenderly fenced off from the street, viz. by walls the very thinnest, makes itself heard outside pretty nearly as well as if it were uttered in the street. Such an outcry it was indispensable to stifle. It *was* stifled; and the reader will soon understand *how*. Meantime, at this point, let us leave the murderer alone with his victims. For fifty minutes let him work his pleasure. The front-door, as we know, is now fastened against all help. Help there is none. Let us, therefore, in vision, attach ourselves to Mary; and, when all is over, let us come back with *her*, again raise the curtain, and read the dreadful record of all that has passed in her absence.

The poor girl, uneasy in her mind to an extent that she could but half understand, roamed up and down in search of an oyster shop; and, finding none that was still open within any circuit that her ordinary experience had made her acquainted with, she fancied it best to try the chances of some remoter district. Lights she saw gleaming or twinkling at a distance, that still tempted her onwards; and thus, amongst unknown streets poorly lighted,[1] and on a night of peculiar darkness, and in a region of London where ferocious tumults were continually turning her out of what seemed to be the direct course, naturally she got bewildered. The purpose with which she started had by this time become hopeless. Nothing remained for her now but to retrace her steps. But this was difficult; for she was afraid to ask directions from chance passengers whose appearance the darkness prevented her from reconnoitring. At length by his lantern she recognised a watchman; through him she was guided into the right road; and in ten minutes more she found herself back at the door of No. 29, in Ratcliffe Highway. But by this time she felt satisfied that she must have been absent for fifty or sixty minutes; indeed, she had heard, at a distance, the cry of *past one o'clock*, which, commencing a few seconds after one, lasted intermittingly for ten or thirteen minutes.

In the tumult of agonising thoughts that very soon surprised her, naturally it became hard for her to recall distinctly the whole succession of doubts, and jealousies, and shadowy misgivings that soon opened upon her. But, so far as could be collected, she had not in the first moment of reaching home noticed anything decisively alarming. In very many cities bells are the main instruments for communicating between the street and the interior of houses; but in London knockers prevail. At Marr's there was both a knocker and a bell. Mary rang, and at the same time very gently knocked. She had no fear of disturbing her

[1] I do not remember, chronologically, the history of gas-lights. But in London, long after Mr. Winsor [a German] had shown the value of gas-lighting, and its applicability to street purposes [which he did by lighting up Pall Mall with gas, 28th January 1807—M.], various districts were prevented, for many years, from resorting to the new system, in consequence of old contracts with oil-dealers, subsisting through long terms of years.

master or mistress; *them* she made sure of finding still up.
Her anxiety was for the baby, who, being disturbed, might
again rob her mistress of a night's rest. And she well knew
that, with three people all anxiously awaiting her return, and
by this time, perhaps, seriously uneasy at her delay, the least
audible whisper from herself would in a moment bring one
of them to the door. Yet how is this? To her astonishment,—but with the astonishment came creeping over her an
icy horror,—no stir nor murmur was heard ascending from
the kitchen. At this moment came back upon her, with
shuddering anguish, the indistinct image of the stranger in
the loose dark coat whom she had seen stealing along under
the shadowy lamp-light, and too certainly watching her
master's motions: keenly she now reproached herself that,
under whatever stress of hurry, she had not acquainted Mr.
Marr with the suspicious appearances. Poor girl! she did
not then know that, if this communication could have availed
to put Marr upon his guard, it had reached him from another
quarter; so that her own omission, which had in reality
arisen under her hurry to execute her master's commission,
could not be charged with any bad consequences. But all
such reflections this way or that were swallowed up at this
point in overmastering panic. That her double summons
could have been unnoticed—this solitary fact in one moment
made a revelation of horror. One person might have fallen
asleep, but two—but three—*that* was a mere impossibility.
And, even supposing all three together with the baby locked
in sleep, still how unaccountable was this utter — utter
silence! Most naturally at this moment something like
hysterical horror overshadowed the poor girl, and now at last
she rang the bell with the violence that belongs to sickening
terror. This done, she paused: self-command enough she
still retained, though fast and fast it was slipping away from
her, to bethink herself that, if any overwhelming accident
had compelled both Marr and his apprentice-boy to leave the
house in order to summon surgical aid from opposite quarters
—a thing barely supposable—still, even in that case Mrs.
Marr and her infant would be left, and some murmuring
reply, under any extremity, would be elicited from the poor
mother. To pause, therefore, to impose stern silence upon

herself, so as to leave room for the possible answer to this final appeal, became a duty of spasmodic effort. Listen, therefore, poor trembling heart; listen, and for twenty seconds be still as death! Still as death she was; and during that dreadful stillness, when she hushed her breath that she might listen, occurred an incident of killing fear, that to her dying day would never cease to renew its echoes in her ear. She, Mary, the poor trembling girl, checking and overruling herself by a final effort, that she might leave full opening for her dear young mistress's answer to her own last frantic appeal, heard at last and most distinctly a sound within the house. Yes, now beyond a doubt there is coming an answer to her summons. What was it? On the stairs,— not the stairs that led downwards to the kitchen, but the stairs that led upwards to the single storey of bedchambers above,—was heard a creaking sound. Next was heard most distinctly a footfall: one, two, three, four, five stairs were slowly and distinctly descended. Then the dreadful footsteps were heard advancing along the little narrow passage to the door. The steps — oh heavens! *whose* steps? — have paused at the door. The very breathing can be heard of that dreadful being who has silenced all breathing except his own in the house. There is but a door between him and Mary. What is he doing on the other side of the door? A cautious step, a stealthy step it was that came down the stairs, then paced along the little narrow passage—narrow as a coffin— till at last the step pauses at the door. How hard the fellow breathes! He, the solitary murderer, is on one side the door; Mary is on the other side. Now, suppose that he should suddenly open the door, and that incautiously in the dark Mary should rush in, and find herself in the arms of the murderer. Thus far the case is a possible one—that to a certainty, had this little trick been tried immediately upon Mary's return, it would have succeeded; had the door been opened suddenly upon her first tingle-tingle, headlong she would have tumbled in, and perished. But now Mary is upon her guard. The unknown murderer and she have both their lips upon the door, listening, breathing hard; but luckily they are on different sides of the door; and upon the least indication of unlocking or unlatching she would have recoiled into the asylum of general darkness.

What was the murderer's meaning in coming along the passage to the front-door? The meaning was this:—Separately, as an individual, Mary was worth nothing at all to him. But, considered as a member of a household, she had this value, viz. that she, if caught and murdered, perfected and rounded the desolation of the house. The case being reported, as reported it would be all over Christendom, led the imagination captive. The whole covey of victims was thus netted; the household ruin was thus full and orbicular; and in that proportion the tendency of men and women, flutter as they might, would be helplessly and hopelessly to sink into the all-conquering hands of the mighty murderer. He had but to say 'My testimonials are dated from No. 29 Ratcliffe Highway,' and the poor vanquished imagination sank powerless before the fascinating rattlesnake eye of the murderer. There is not a doubt that the motive of the murderer for standing on the inner side of Marr's front-door whilst Mary stood on the outside was a hope that, if he quietly opened the door, whisperingly counterfeiting Marr's voice, and saying, What made you stay so long? possibly she might have been inveigled. He was wrong; the time was past for that; Mary was now maniacally awake; she began now to ring the bell and to ply the knocker with unintermitting violence. And the natural consequence was that the next-door neighbour, who had recently gone to bed and instantly fallen asleep, was roused; and by the incessant violence of the ringing and the knocking, which now obeyed a delirious and uncontrollable impulse in Mary, he became sensible that some very dreadful event must be at the root of so clamorous an uproar. To rise, to throw up the sash, to demand angrily the cause of this unseasonable tumult, was the work of a moment. The poor girl remained sufficiently mistress of herself rapidly to explain the circumstance of her own absence for an hour, her belief that Mr. and Mrs. Marr's family had all been murdered in the interval, and that at this very moment the murderer was in the house.

The person to whom she addressed this statement was a

pawnbroker; and a thoroughly brave man he must have been; for it was a perilous undertaking, merely as a trial of physical strength, singly to face a mysterious assassin, who had apparently signalised his prowess by a triumph so comprehensive. But, again, for the imagination it required an effort of self-conquest to rush headlong into the presence of one invested with a cloud of mystery, whose nation, age, motives, were all alike unknown. Rarely on any field of battle has a soldier been called upon to face so complex a danger. For, if the entire family of his neighbour Marr had been exterminated,—were this indeed true,—such a scale of bloodshed would seem to argue that there must have been two persons as the perpetrators; or, if one singly had accomplished such a ruin, in that case how colossal must have been his audacity! probably, also, his skill and animal power! Moreover, the unknown enemy (whether single or double) would, doubtless, be elaborately armed. Yet, under all these disadvantages, did this fearless man rush at once to the field of butchery in his neighbour's house. Waiting only to draw on his trousers, and to arm himself with the kitchen poker, he went down into his own little back-yard. On this mode of approach, he would have a chance of intercepting the murderer; whereas from the front there would be no such chance, and there would also be considerable delay in the process of breaking open the door. A brick wall, 9 or 10 feet high, divided his own back premises from those of Marr. Over this he vaulted; and, at the moment when he was recalling himself to the necessity of going back for a candle, he suddenly perceived a feeble ray of light already glimmering on some part of Marr's premises. Marr's back-door stood wide open. Probably the murderer had passed through it one half-minute before. Rapidly the brave man passed onwards to the shop, and there beheld the carnage of the night stretched out on the floor, and the narrow premises so floated with gore that it was hardly possible to escape the pollution of blood in picking out a path to the front-door. In the lock of the door still remained the key which had given to the unknown murderer so fatal an advantage over his victims. By this time the heart-shaking news involved in the outcries of Mary (to whom it occurred that by possibility some one out of so many victims might still be within the reach of medical aid, but that all would depend upon speed) had availed, even at that late hour, to gather a small mob about the house. The pawnbroker threw open the door. One or two watchmen headed the crowd; but the soul-harrowing spectacle checked them, and impressed sudden silence upon their voices, previously so loud. The tragic drama read aloud its own history, and the succession of its several steps—few and summary. The murderer was as yet altogether unknown; not even suspected. But there were reasons for thinking that he must have been a person familiarly known to Marr. He had entered the shop by opening the door after it had been closed by Marr. But it was justly argued that, after the caution conveyed to Marr by the watchman, the appearance of any stranger in the shop at that hour, and in so dangerous a neighbourhood, and entering by so irregular and suspicious a course (*i.e.* walking in after the door had been closed, and after the closing of the shutters had cut off all open communication with the street), would naturally have roused Marr to an attitude of vigilance and self-defence. Any indication, therefore, that Marr had *not* been so roused would argue to a certainty that *something* had occurred to neutralise this alarm, and fatally to disarm the prudent jealousies of Marr. But this "something" could only have lain in one simple fact, viz. that the person of the murderer was familiarly known to Marr as that of an ordinary and unsuspected acquaintance. This being presupposed as the key to all the rest, the whole course and evolution of the subsequent drama becomes clear as daylight:—The murderer, it is evident, had opened gently, and again closed behind him with equal gentleness, the street-door. He had then advanced to the little counter, all the while exchanging the ordinary salutation of an old acquaintance with the unsuspecting Marr. Having reached the counter, he would then ask Marr for a pair of unbleached cotton socks. In a shop so small as Marr's there could be no great latitude of choice for disposing of the different commodities. The arrangement of these had no doubt become familiar to the murderer; and he had already ascertained that, in order to reach down the particular parcel wanted at present, Marr would find it requisite to face round to the rear, and at the same moment to raise his eyes and his hands to a level eighteen inches above his own head. This movement placed him in the most disadvantageous possible position with regard to the murderer; who now, at the instant when Marr's hands and eyes were embarrassed, and the back of his head fully exposed, suddenly from below his large surtout had unslung a heavy ship-carpenter's mallet, and with one solitary blow had so thoroughly stunned his victim as to leave him incapable of resistance. The whole position of Marr told its own tale. He had collapsed naturally behind the counter, with his hands so occupied as to confirm the whole outline of the affair as I have here suggested it. Probable enough it is that the very first blow, the first indication of treachery that reached Marr, would also be the last blow as regarded the abolition of consciousness. The murderer's plan and *rationale* of murder started systematically from this infliction of apoplexy, or at least of a stunning sufficient to insure a long loss of consciousness. This opening step placed the murderer at his ease. But still, as returning sense might constantly have led to the fullest exposures, it was his settled practice, by way of consummation, to cut the throat. To one invariable type all the murders on this occasion conformed: the skull was first shattered; this step secured the murderer from instant retaliation; and then, by way of locking up all into eternal silence, uniformly the throat was cut. The rest of the circumstances, as self-revealed, were these:—The fall of Marr might, probably enough, cause a dull confused sound of a scuffle, and the more so as it could not now be confounded with any street uproar—the shop-door being shut. It is more probable, however, that the signal for the alarm passing down to the kitchen would arise when the murderer proceeded to cut Marr's throat. The very confined situation behind the counter would render it impossible, under the critical hurry of the case, to expose the throat broadly; the horrid scene would proceed by partial and interrupted cuts; deep groans would arise; and then would come the rush upstairs. Against this, as the only dangerous stage in the transaction, the murderer would have specially prepared. Mrs. Marr and the apprentice-boy, both young and active, would make, of course, for the street-door; had Mary been at home, and three persons at once had combined to distract the purposes of the murderer, it is barely possible that one of them would have succeeded in reaching the street. But the dreadful swing of the heavy mallet intercepted both the boy and his mistress before they could reach the door. Each of them lay stretched out on the centre of the shop floor; and the very moment that this disabling was accomplished the accursed hound was down upon their throats with his razor. The fact is that, in the mere blindness of pity for poor Marr on hearing his groans, Mrs. Marr had lost sight of her obvious policy: she and the boy ought to have made for the back-door; the alarm would thus have been given in the open air; which, of itself, was a great point; and several means of distracting the murderer's attention offered upon that course which the extreme limitation of the shop denied to them upon the other.

Vain would be all attempts to convey the horror which thrilled the gathering spectators of this piteous tragedy. It was known to the crowd that one person had, by some accident, escaped the general massacre; but she was now speechless, and probably delirious; so that, in compassion for her pitiable situation, one female neighbour had carried her away, and put her to bed. Hence it had happened, for a longer space of time than could else have been possible, that no person present was sufficiently acquainted with the Marrs to be aware of the little infant; for the bold pawn-broker had gone off to make a communication to the coroner, and another neighbour to lodge some evidence which he thought urgent at a neighbouring police-office. Suddenly some person appeared amongst the crowd who was aware that the murdered parents had a young infant; this would be found either below-stairs, or in one of the bedrooms above. Immediately a stream of people poured down into the kitchen, where at once they saw the cradle—but with the bedclothes in a state of indescribable confusion. On disentangling these, pools of blood became visible; and the next ominous sign was that the hood of the cradle had been smashed to pieces. It became evident that the wretch had found himself doubly embarrassed—first, by the arched hood at the head of the cradle, which accordingly he had beat into a ruin with his mallet, and, secondly, by the gathering of the blankets and pillows about the baby's head. The free play of his blows had thus been baffled. And he had therefore finished the scene by applying his razor to the throat of the little innocent; after which, with no apparent purpose, as though he had become confused by the spectacle of his own atrocities, he had busied himself in piling the clothes elaborately over the child's corpse. This incident undeniably gave the character of a vindictive proceeding to the whole affair, and so far confirmed the current rumour that the quarrel between Williams and Marr had originated in rivalship. One writer, indeed, alleged that the murderer might have found it necessary for his own safety to extinguish the crying of the child; but it was justly replied that a child only eight months old could not have cried under any sense of the tragedy proceeding, but simply in its ordinary way for the absence of its mother; and such a cry, even if audible at all out of the house, must have been precisely what the neighbours were hearing constantly, so that it could have drawn no special attention, nor suggested any reasonable alarm to the murderer. No one incident, indeed, throughout the whole tissue of atrocities, so much envenomed the popular fury against the unknown ruffian as this useless butchery of the infant.

Naturally, on the Sunday morning that dawned four or five hours later, the case was too full of horror not to diffuse itself in all directions; but I have no reason to think that it crept into any one of the numerous Sunday papers. In the regular course, any ordinary occurrence, not occurring or not transpiring[1] until 15 minutes after 1 A.M. on a Sunday morning, would first reach the public ear through the Monday editions of the Sunday papers, and the regular morning papers of the Monday. But, if such were the course pursued on this occasion, never can there have been a more signal oversight. For it is certain that to have met the public demand for details on the Sunday, which might so

[1] There could not be a neater example than this of the difference between *occur* and *transpire*, or a neater rebuke of the vulgar use of *transpire* in the sense of *occur*.—M.

easily have been done by cancelling a couple of dull columns, and substituting a circumstantial narrative, for which the pawnbroker and the watchman could have furnished the materials, would have made a small fortune. By proper handbills dispersed through all quarters of the infinite metropolis, 250,000 extra copies might have been sold,— that is, by any journal that should have collected *exclusive* materials, meeting the public excitement, everywhere stirred to the centre by flying rumours, and everywhere burning for ampler information.[1]—On the Sunday se'ennight (Sunday the *octave* from the event) took place the funeral of the Marrs: in the first coffin was placed Marr; in the second Mrs. Marr, and the baby in her arms; in the third the apprentice-boy. They were buried side by side; and 30,000 labouring people followed the funeral procession, with horror and grief written in their countenances.

[1] An interesting pamphlet just published by Mr. Charles Pollitt of Kendal, under the title *De Quincey's Editorship of the Westmorland Gazette*, informs us that, during the whole period of his editorship of that provincial Tory journal (which extended, it now appears, exactly from 11th July 1818 to 5th November 1819), he was notably fond of filling its columns with assize reports and murder trials. "During the whole of his connexion with the paper," says Mr. Pollitt, "assize news formed not only a prominent, but frequently "an all-absorbing, portion of the available space." In illustration, Mr. Pollitt quotes the following editorial notice from the paper for 8th August 1818:—"This week it will be observed that our columns "are occupied almost exclusively with assize reports. We have "thought it right to allow them precedency of all other news, whether "domestic or foreign, for the three following reasons:—(1) Because to "all ranks alike they possess a powerful and commanding interest. "(2) Because to the more uneducated classes they yield a singular "benefit, by teaching them their social duties in the most impressive "shape: that is to say, not in a state of abstraction from all that may "explain, illustrate, and enforce them (as in the naked terms of the "Statute), but exemplified (and, as the logicians say, *concreted*) in the "actual circumstances of an interesting case, and in connexion with "the penalties that accompany their neglect or their violation. (3) "Because they present the best indications of the moral condition "of society." What the Westmorland people thought of this perpetual provision of horrors for them by the editor of the *Gazette* does not quite appear; but it seems to have been one of the causes of that dissatisfaction on the part of the proprietors of the paper which led, according to Mr. Pollitt, to the termination of De Quincey's editorship.—M.

As yet no whisper was astir that indicated, even conjecturally, the hideous author of those ruins—this patron of gravediggers. Had as much been known on this Sunday of the funeral concerning that person as became known universally six days later, the people would have gone right from the churchyard to the murderer's lodgings, and (brooking no delay) would have torn him limb from limb. As yet, however, in mere default of any object on whom reasonable suspicion could settle, the public wrath was compelled to suspend itself. Else, far indeed from showing any tendency to subside, the public emotion strengthened every day conspicuously, as the reverberation of the shock began to travel back from the provinces to the capital. On every great road in the kingdom continual arrests were made of vagrants and "trampers" who could give no satisfactory account of themselves, or whose appearance in any respect answered to the imperfect description of Williams furnished by the watchman.

With this mighty tide of pity and indignation pointing backwards to the dreadful past there mingled also in the thoughts of reflecting persons an under-current of fearful expectation for the immediate future. "The earthquake," to quote a fragment from a striking passage in Wordsworth—

"The earthquake is not satisfied at once."

All perils, specially malignant, are recurrent. A murderer who is such by passion and by a wolfish craving for bloodshed as a mode of unnatural luxury cannot relapse into *inertia*. Such a man, even more than the Alpine chamois-hunter, comes to crave the dangers and the hairbreadth escapes of his trade, as a condiment for seasoning the insipid monotonies of daily life. But, apart from the hellish instincts that might too surely be relied on for renewed atrocities, it was clear that the murderer of the Marrs, wheresoever lurking, must be a needy man, and a needy man of that class least likely to seek or to find resources in honourable modes of industry; for which, equally by haughty disgust and by disuse of the appropriate habits, men of violence are specially disqualified. Were it, therefore, merely for a livelihood, the murderer, whom all hearts were yearning to decipher, might be expected to make his resurrection on some stage of horror, after a reasonable interval. Even in the Marr murder, granting that it had been governed chiefly by cruel and vindictive impulses, it was still clear that the desire of booty had co-operated with such feelings. Equally clear it was that this desire must have been disappointed : excepting the trivial sum reserved by Marr for the week's expenditure, the murderer found, doubtless, little or nothing that he could turn to account. Two guineas, perhaps, would be the outside of what he had obtained in the way of booty. A week or so would see the end of that. The conviction, therefore, of all people was that in a month or two, when the fever of excitement might a little have cooled down, or have been superseded by other topics of fresher interest, so that the new-born vigilance of household life would have had time to relax, some new murder, equally appalling, might be counted upon.

Such was the public expectation. Let the reader then figure to himself the pure frenzy of horror when in this hush of expectation, looking, indeed, and waiting for the unknown arm to strike once more, but not believing that any audacity could be equal to such an attempt as yet,—whilst all eyes were watching,—suddenly, on the twelfth night from the Marr murder, a second case of the same mysterious nature, a murder on the same exterminating plan, was perpetrated in the very same neighbourhood. It was on the Thursday next but one succeeding to the Marr murder that this second atrocity took place [1]; and many people thought at the time that in its dramatic features of thrilling interest this second case even went beyond the first. The family which suffered in this instance was that of a Mr. Williamson ; and the house was situated, if not absolutely in Ratcliffe Highway, at any rate immediately round the corner of some secondary street, running at right angles to this public thoroughfare. Mr. Williamson was a well-known and respectable man, long settled in that district ; he was supposed to be rich ; and, more with a view to the employment furnished by such a calling than with much anxiety for further accumulations, he kept a sort of tavern which, in this respect, might be considered on an old patriarchal footing—that, although people

[1] On Thursday night, 19th December 1811.—M.

of considerable property resorted to the house in the evenings, no kind of anxious separation was maintained between them and the other visitors from the class of artisans or common labourers. Anybody who conducted himself with propriety was free to take a seat and call for any liquor that he might prefer. And thus the society was pretty miscellaneous; in part stationary, but in some proportion fluctuating. The household consisted of the following five persons:—1, Mr. Williamson, its head, who was an old man above seventy, and was well fitted for his situation, being civil, and not at all morose, but at the same time firm in maintaining order; 2, Mrs. Williamson, his wife, about ten years younger than himself; 3, a little grand-daughter, about nine years old; 4, a housemaid, who was nearly forty years old; 5, a young journeyman, aged about twenty-six, belonging to some manufacturing establishment (of what class I have forgotten; neither do I remember of what nation he was). It was the established rule at Mr. Williamson's that exactly as the clock struck eleven all the company, without favour or exception, moved off. That was one of the customs by which, in so stormy a district, Mr. Williamson had found it possible to keep his house free from brawls. On the present Thursday night everything had gone on as usual, except for one slight shadow of suspicion, which had caught the attention of more persons than one. Perhaps at a less agitating time it would hardly have been noticed; but now, when the first question and the last in all social meetings turned upon the Marrs and their unknown murderer, it was a circumstance naturally fitted to cause some uneasiness that a stranger, of sinister appearance, in a wide surtout, had flitted in and out of the room at intervals during the evening, had sometimes retired from the light into obscure corners, and by more than one person had been observed stealing into the private passages of the house. It was presumed in general that the man must be known to Williamson. And, in some slight degree, as an occasional customer of the house, it is not impossible that he *was*. But afterwards this repulsive stranger, with his cadaverous ghastliness, extraordinary hair, and glazed eyes, showing himself intermittingly through the hours from 8 to 11 P.M., revolved upon the memory of all who had steadily observed him with something of the same freezing effect as belongs to the two assassins in "Macbeth" who present themselves reeking from the murder of Banquo, and gleaming dimly, with dreadful faces, from the misty background, athwart the pomps of the regal banquet.

Meantime the clock struck eleven; the company broke up; the door of entrance was nearly closed; and at this moment of general dispersion the situation of the five inmates left upon the premises was precisely this:—The three elders, viz. Williamson, his wife, and his female servant, were all occupied on the ground-floor. Williamson himself was drawing ale, porter, &c., for those neighbours in whose favour the house-door had been left ajar until the hour of twelve should strike; Mrs. Williamson and her servant were moving to and fro between the back-kitchen and a little parlour; the little grand-daughter, whose sleeping-room was on the *first* floor (which term in London means always the floor raised by one flight of stairs above the level of the street), had been fast asleep since nine o'clock; lastly, the journeyman artisan had retired to rest for some time. He was a regular lodger in the house; and his bed-room was on the second floor. For some time he had been undressed, and had lain down in bed. Being, as a working man, bound to habits of early rising, he was naturally anxious to fall asleep as soon as possible. But, on this particular night, his uneasiness, arising from the recent murders at No. 29, rose to a paroxysm of nervous excitement which kept him awake. It is possible that from somebody he had heard of the suspicious-looking stranger or might even personally have observed him slinking about. But, were it otherwise, he was aware of several circumstances dangerously affecting this house: for instance, the ruffianism of this whole neighbourhood, and the disagreeable fact that the Marrs had lived within a few doors of this very house, which again argued that the murderer also lived at no great distance. These were matters of *general* alarm. But there were others peculiar to this house: in particular, the notoriety of Williamson's opulence,—the belief, whether well or ill founded, that he accumulated in desks and drawers the money continually flowing into his hands; and, lastly, the danger so ostentatiously courted by that habit of leaving the house-door ajar through one entire hour,—and that hour loaded with extra danger by the well-advertised assurance that no collision need be feared with chance convivial visitors, since all such people were banished at eleven. A regulation which had hitherto operated beneficially for the character and comfort of the house now, on the contrary, under altered circumstances, became a positive proclamation of exposure and defencelessness through one entire period of an hour. Williamson himself, it was said generally, being a large unwieldy man, past seventy, and signally inactive, ought, in prudence, to make the locking of his door coincident with the dismissal of his evening party.

Upon these and other grounds of alarm (particularly this, that Mrs. Williamson was reported to possess a considerable quantity of plate), the journeyman was musing painfully, and the time might be within twenty-eight or twenty-five minutes of twelve, when all at once, with a crash, proclaiming some hand of hideous violence, the house-door was suddenly shut and locked. Here, then, beyond all doubt, was the diabolic man, clothed in mystery, from No. 29 Ratcliffe Highway. Yes, that dreadful being, who for twelve days had employed all thoughts and all tongues, was now, too certainly, in this defenceless house, and would, in a few minutes, be face to face with every one of its inmates. A question still lingered in the public mind—whether at Marr's there might not have been *two* men at work. If so, there would be two at present; and one of the two would be immediately disposable for the upstairs work; since no danger could obviously be more immediately fatal to such an attack than any alarm given from an upper window to the passengers in the street. Through one half-minute the poor panic-stricken man sat up motionless in bed. But then he rose, his first movement being towards the door of his room. Not for any purpose of securing it against intrusion—too well he knew that there was no fastening of any sort— neither lock nor bolt; nor was there any such moveable furniture in the room as might have availed to barricade the door, even if time could be counted on for such an attempt.

It was no effect of prudence, merely the fascination of killing fear it was, that drove him to open the door. One step brought him to the head of the stairs; he lowered his head over the balustrade in order to listen; and at that moment ascended from the little parlour this agonising cry from the woman-servant, "Lord Jesus Christ! we shall all be murdered!" What a Medusa's head must have lurked in those dreadful bloodless features, and those glazed rigid eyes, that seemed rightfully belonging to a corpse, when one glance at them sufficed to proclaim a death-warrant.

Three separate death-struggles were by this time over; and the poor petrified journeyman, quite unconscious of what he was doing, in blind, passive, self-surrender to panic, absolutely descended both flights of stairs. Infinite terror inspired him with the same impulse as might have been inspired by headlong courage. In his shirt, and upon old decaying stairs, that at times creaked under his feet, he continued to descend, until he had reached the lowest step but four. The situation was tremendous beyond any that is on record. A sneeze, a cough, almost a breathing, and the young man would be a corpse, without a chance or a struggle for his life. The murderer was at that time in the little parlour—the door of which parlour faced you in descending the stairs; and this door stood ajar; indeed, much more considerably open than what is understood by the term "ajar." Of that quadrant, or 90 degrees, which the door would describe in swinging so far open as to stand at right angles to the lobby, or to itself in a closed position, 55 degrees at the least were exposed. Consequently, two out of three corpses were exposed to the young man's gaze. Where was the third? And the murderer—where was he? As to the murderer, he was walking rapidly backwards and forwards in the parlour, audible but not visible at first, being engaged with something or other in that part of the room which the door still concealed. What the something might be the sound soon explained; he was applying keys tentatively to a cupboard, a closet, and a scrutoire, in the hidden part of the room. Very soon, however, he came into view; but, fortunately for the young man, at this critical moment the murderer's purpose too entirely absorbed him to allow of

his throwing a glance to the staircase, on which else the
white figure of the journeyman, standing in motionless
horror, would have been detected in one instant, and seasoned
for the grave in the second. As to the third corpse, the
missing corpse, viz. Mr. Williamson's, *that* is in the cellar;
and how its local position can be accounted for remains as a
separate question, much discussed at the time, but never
satisfactorily cleared up. Meantime, that Williamson was
dead became evident to the young man; since else he would
have been heard stirring or groaning. Three friends, therefore, out of four whom the young man had parted with forty
minutes ago, were now extinguished; remained, therefore,
40 per cent (a large percentage for Williams to leave);
remained, in fact, himself and his pretty young friend, the
little grand-daughter, whose childish innocence was still
slumbering, without fear for herself, or grief for her aged
grand-parents. If *they* are gone for ever, happily one friend
(for such he will prove himself indeed, if from such a danger
he can save this child) is pretty near to her. But alas! he
is still nearer to a murderer. At this moment he is unnerved
for any exertion whatever; he has changed into a pillar of
ice; for the objects before him, separated by just thirteen
feet, are these :—The housemaid had been caught by the
murderer on her knees; she was kneeling before the fire-
grate, which she had been polishing with black lead. That
part of her task was finished; and she had passed on to
another task,—viz. the filling of the grate with wood and
coals, not for kindling at this moment, but so as to have it
ready for kindling on the next day. The appearances all
showed that she must have been engaged in this labour at
the very moment when the murderer entered; and perhaps
the succession of the incidents arranged itself as follows :—
From the awful ejaculation and loud outcry to Christ, as
overheard by the journeyman, it was clear that then first she
had been alarmed; yet this was at least one and a half or
even two minutes after the door-slamming. Consequently
the alarm which had so fearfully and seasonably alarmed the
young man must, in some unaccountable way, have been
misinterpreted by the two women. It was said, at the time,
that Mrs. Williamson laboured under some dulness of hear-

ing; and it was conjectured that the servant, having her ears filled with the noise of her own scrubbing, and her head half under the grate, might have confounded it with the street noises, or else might have imputed this violent closure to some mischievous boys. But, howsoever explained, the fact was evident that, until the words of appeal to Christ, the servant had noticed nothing suspicious, nothing which interrupted her labours. If so, it followed that neither had Mrs. Williamson noticed anything; for, in that case, she would have communicated her own alarm to the servant, since both were in the same small room. Apparently the course of things after the murderer had entered the room was this :—Mrs. Williamson had probably not seen him, from the accident of standing with her back to the door. Her, therefore, before he was himself observed at all, he had stunned and prostrated by a shattering blow on the back of her head; this blow, inflicted by a crowbar, had smashed in the hinder part of the skull. She fell; and by the noise of her fall (for all was the work of a moment) had first roused the attention of the servant, who then uttered the cry which had reached the young man; but before she could repeat it the murderer had descended with his uplifted instrument upon *her* head, crushing the skull inwards upon the brain. Both the women were irrecoverably destroyed, so that further outrages were needless; and, moreover, the murderer was conscious of the imminent danger from delay; and yet, in spite of his hurry, so fully did he appreciate the fatal consequences to himself, if any of his victims should so far revive into consciousness as to make circumstantial depositions, that, by way of making this impossible, he had proceeded instantly to cut the throats of each. All this tallied with the appearances as now presenting themselves. Mrs. Williamson had fallen backwards with her head to the door; the servant, from her kneeling posture, had been incapable of rising, and had presented her head passively to blows; after which, the miscreant had but to bend her head backwards so as to expose her throat, and the murder was finished. It is remarkable that the young artisan, paralysed as he had been by fear, and evidently fascinated for a time so as to walk right towards the lion's mouth, yet found himself able to notice everything important. The reader must suppose him at this point watching the murderer whilst hanging over the body of Mrs. Williamson, and whilst renewing his search for certain important keys. Doubtless it was an anxious situation for the murderer; for, unless he speedily found the keys wanted, all this hideous tragedy would end in nothing but a prodigious increase of the public horror, in tenfold precautions therefore, and redoubled obstacles interposed between himself and his future game. Nay, there was even a nearer interest at stake; his own immediate safety might, by a probable accident, be compromised. Most of those who came to the house for liquor were giddy girls or children, who, on finding this house closed, would go off carelessly to some other; but, let any thoughtful woman or man come to the door now, a full quarter of an hour before the established time of closing, in that case suspicion would arise too powerful to be checked. There would be a sudden alarm given; after which, mere luck would decide the event. For it is a remarkable fact, and one that illustrates the singular inconsistency of this villain,—who, being often so superfluously subtle, was in other directions so reckless and improvident,—that at this very moment, standing amongst corpses that had deluged the little parlour with blood, Williams must have been in considerable doubt whether he had any sure means of egress. There were windows, he knew, to the back; but upon what ground they opened he seems to have had no certain information; and in a neighbourhood so dangerous the windows of the lower storey would not improbably be nailed down; those in the upper might be free, but then came the necessity of a leap too formidable. From all this, however, the sole practical inference was to hurry forward with the trial of further keys, and to detect the hidden treasure. This it was, this intense absorption in one overmastering pursuit, that dulled the murderer's perceptions as to all around him; otherwise he must have heard the breathing of the young man, which to himself at times became fearfully audible. As the murderer stood once more over the body of Mrs. Williamson, and searched her pockets more narrowly, he pulled out various clusters of keys,—one of which, dropping, gave a harsh jingling sound upon the floor. At this time it was that the secret witness, from his secret stand, noticed the fact of Williams's surtout being lined with silk of the finest quality. One other fact he noticed, which eventually became more immediately important than many stronger circumstances of incrimination: this was that the shoes of the murderer, apparently new, and bought probably with poor Marr's money, creaked as he walked, harshly and frequently. With the new clusters of keys, the murderer walked off to the hidden section of the parlour. And here, at last, was suggested to the journeyman the sudden opening for an escape. Some minutes would be lost to a certainty in trying all these keys, and subsequently in searching the drawers, supposing that the keys answered—or in violently forcing them, supposing that they did *not*. He might thus count upon a brief interval of leisure, whilst the rattling of the keys might obscure to the murderer the creaking of the stairs under the reascending journeyman. His plan was now formed. On regaining his bedroom, he placed the bed against the door by way of a transient retardation to the enemy, that might give him a short warning, and, in the worst extremity, might give him a chance for life by means of a desperate leap. This change made as quietly as was possible, he tore the sheets, pillowcases, and blankets into broad ribbons, and, after plaiting them into ropes, spliced the different lengths together. But at the very first he descries this ugly addition to his labours. Where shall he look for any staple, hook, bar, or other fixture, from which his rope, when twisted, may safely depend? Measured from the window-*sill*—*i.e* the lowest part of the window architrave—there count but twenty-two or twenty-three feet to the ground. Of this length ten or twelve feet may be looked upon as cancelled, because to that extent he might drop without danger. So much being deducted, there would remain, say, a dozen feet of rope to prepare. But, unhappily, there is no stout iron fixture anywhere about his window. The nearest, indeed the sole, fixture of that sort is not near to the window at all; it is a spike fixed (for no reason at all that is apparent) in the bed-tester. Now, the bed being shifted, the spike is shifted; and its distance from the window, having always been four feet, is now seven.

Seven entire feet, therefore, must be added to that which would have sufficed if measured from the window. But courage! God, by the proverb of all nations in Christendom, helps those that help themselves. This our young man thankfully acknowledges; he reads already, in the very fact of any spike at all being found where hitherto it has been useless, an earnest of providential aid. Were it only for himself that he worked, he could not feel himself meritoriously employed; but this is not so. In deep sincerity he is now agitated for the poor child, whom he knows and loves; every minute, he feels, brings ruin nearer to *her*; and, as he passed her door, his first thought had been to take her out of bed in his arms, and to carry her where she might share his chances. But, on consideration, he felt that this sudden awaking of her, and the impossibility of even whispering any explanation, would cause her to cry audibly; and the inevitable indiscretion of one would be fatal to the two. As the Alpine avalanches, when suspended above the traveller's head, oftentimes (we are told) come down through the stirring of the air by a simple whisper, precisely on such a tenure of a whisper was now suspended the murderous malice of the man below. No; there is but one way to save the child; towards *her* deliverance the first step is through his own. And he has made an excellent beginning; for the spike, which too fearfully he had expected to see torn away by any strain upon it from the half-carious wood, stands firmly when tried against the pressure of his own weight. He has rapidly fastened on to it three lengths of his new rope, measuring eleven feet. He plaits it roughly; so that only three feet have been lost in the intertwisting; he has spliced on a second length equal to the first; so that, already, sixteen feet are ready to throw out of the window; and thus, let the worst come to the worst, it will not be absolute ruin to swarm down the rope so far as it will reach, and then to drop boldly. All this has been accomplished in about six minutes; and the hot contest between above and below is still steadily, but fervently, proceeding. Murderer is working hard in the parlour; journeyman is working hard in the bedroom. Miscreant is getting on famously downstairs; one batch of bank-notes he has already bagged, and is hard upon

the scent of a second. He has also sprung a covey of
golden coins. Sovereigns as yet were not; but guineas at
this period fetched thirty shillings apiece; and he has
worked his way into a little quarry of these. Murderer is
almost joyous; and, if any creature is still living in this
house, as shrewdly he suspects and very soon means to know,
with that creature he would be happy, before cutting the
creature's throat, to drink a glass of something. Instead of
the glass, might he not make a present to the poor creature
of his throat? Oh no! impossible! Throats are a sort of
thing that he never makes presents of; business—business
must be attended to. Really the two men, considered simply
as men of business, are both meritorious. Like chorus and
semi-chorus, strophe and anti-strophe, they work each against
the other. Pull journeyman, pull murderer! Pull baker,
pull devil! As regards the journeyman, he is now safe. To his
sixteen feet, of which seven are neutralised by the distance
of the bed, he has at last added six feet more; which will be
short of reaching the ground by perhaps ten feet—a trifle
which man or boy may drop without injury. All is safe,
therefore, for him; which is more than one can be sure of
for miscreant in the parlour. Miscreant, however, takes it
coolly enough: the reason being that, with all his cleverness,
for once in his life miscreant has been overreached. The
reader and I know, but miscreant does not in the least
suspect, a little fact of some importance, viz. that just now
through a space of full three minutes he has been overlooked
and studied by one who (though reading in a dreadful book and
suffering under mortal panic) took accurate notes of so much as
his limited opportunities allowed him to see, and will assuredly
report the creaking shoes and the silk-mounted surtout in
quarters where such little facts will tell very little to his
advantage. But, although it is true that Mr. Williams,
unaware of the journeyman's having "assisted" at the
examination of Mrs. Williamson's pockets, could not connect
any anxiety with that person's subsequent proceedings, nor
specially therefore with his having embarked in the rope-
weaving line, assuredly he knew of reasons enough for not
loitering. And yet he *did* loiter. Reading his acts by the
light of such mute traces as he left behind him, the police

became aware that latterly he must have loitered. And the reason which governed him is striking; because at once it records that murder was not pursued by him simply as a means to an end, but also as an end for itself. Mr. Williams had now been upon the premises for perhaps fifteen or twenty minutes; and in that space of time he had despatched, in a style satisfactory to himself, a considerable amount of business. He had done, in commercial language, "a good stroke of business." Upon two floors, viz. the cellar-floor and the ground-floor, he has "accounted for" all the population. But there remained at least two floors more; and it now occurred to Mr. Williams that, although the landlord's somewhat chilling manner had shut him out from any familiar knowledge of the household arrangements, too probably on one or other of those floors there must be some throats. As to plunder, he has already bagged the whole. And it was next to impossible that any arrear, the most trivial, should still remain for a gleaner. But the throats—the throats—there it was that arrears and gleanings might perhaps be counted on. And thus it appeared that, in his wolfish thirst for blood, Mr. Williams put to hazard the whole fruits of his night's work, and his life into the bargain. At this moment, if the murderer knew all,—could he see the open window above stairs ready for the descent of the journeyman, could he witness the life-and-death rapidity with which that journeyman is working, could he guess at the almighty uproar which within ninety seconds will be maddening the population of this populous district,—no picture of a maniac in flight of panic or in pursuit of vengeance would adequately represent the agony of haste with which he would himself be hurrying to the street-door for final evasion. That mode of escape was still free. Even at this moment there yet remained time sufficient for a successful flight, and, therefore, for the following revolution in the romance of his own abominable life:—He had in his pockets above a hundred pounds of booty,—means, therefore, for a full disguise. This very night, if he will shave off his yellow hair, and blacken his eyebrows, buying, when morning light returns, a dark-coloured wig, and clothes such as may co-operate in personating the character of a grave professional man, he may elude all suspicions of impertinent policemen—may sail by any one of a hundred vessels bound for any port along the huge line of seaboard (stretching through 2400 miles) of the American United States; may enjoy fifty years for leisurely repentance; and may even die in the odour of sanctity. On the other hand, if he prefer active life, it is not impossible that, with *his* subtlety, hardihood, and unscrupulousness, in a land where the simple process of naturalisation converts the alien at once into a child of the family, he might rise to the President's chair; might have a statue at his death; and afterwards a life in three volumes quarto, with no hint glancing towards No. 29 Ratcliffe Highway. But all depends on the next ninety seconds. Within that time there is a sharp turn to be taken; there is a wrong turn, and a right turn. Should his better angel guide him to the right one, all may yet go well as regards this world's prosperity. But behold! in two minutes from this point we shall see him take the wrong one; and then Nemesis will be at his heels with ruin perfect and sudden.

Meantime, if the murderer allows himself to loiter, the ropemaker overhead does *not*. Well he knows that the poor child's fate is on the edge of a razor; for all turns upon the alarm being raised before the murderer reaches her bedside.

And at this very moment, whilst desperate agitation is nearly paralysing his fingers, he hears the sullen stealthy step of the murderer creeping up through the darkness. It had been the expectation of the journeyman (founded on the clamorous uproar with which the street-door was slammed) that Williams, when disposable for his upstairs work, would come racing at a long jubilant gallop, and with a tiger roar; and perhaps, on his natural instincts, he would have done so. But this mode of approach, which was of dreadful effect when applied to a case of surprise, became dangerous in the case of people who might by this time have been placed fully upon their guard. The step which he had heard was on the staircase—but upon which stair? He fancied upon the lowest; and, in a movement so slow and cautious, even this might make all the difference; yet might it not have been the tenth, twelfth, or fourteenth stair? Never, perhaps, in this world did any man feel his own responsibility so cruelly loaded and strained as at this moment did the poor journeyman on behalf of the slumbering child. Lose but two seconds, through awkwardness or through the self-counteractions of panic, and for *her* the total difference arose between life and death. Still there is a hope; and nothing can so frightfully expound the hellish nature of him whose baleful shadow, to speak astrologically, at this moment darkens the house of life, as the simple expression of the ground on which this hope rested. The journeyman felt sure that the murderer would not be satisfied to kill the poor child whilst unconscious. This would be to defeat his whole purpose in murdering her at all. To an epicure in murder such as Williams, it would be taking away the very sting of the enjoyment if the poor child should be suffered to drink off the bitter cup of death without fully apprehending the misery of the situation. But this luckily would require time: the double confusion of mind,—first, from being roused up at so unusual an hour, and, secondly, from the horror of the occasion when explained to her,—would at first produce fainting, or some mode of insensibility or distraction, such as must occupy a considerable time. The logic of the case, in short, all rested upon the *ultra* fiendishness of Williams. Were he likely to be content with the mere fact of the child's death, apart from the process and leisurely expansion of its mental agony—in that case there would be no hope. But, because our present murderer is fastidiously finical in his exactions—a sort of martinet in the scenical grouping and draping of the circumstances in his murders—therefore it is that hope becomes reasonable, since all such refinements of preparation demand time. Murders of mere necessity Williams was obliged to hurry: but in a murder of pure voluptuousness, entirely disinterested, where no hostile witness was to be removed, no extra booty to be gained, and no revenge to be gratified, it is clear that to hurry would be altogether to ruin. If this child, therefore, is to be saved, it will be on pure æsthetical considerations.[1]

---

[1] Let the reader who is disposed to regard as exaggerated or romantic the pure fiendishness imputed to Williams recollect that, except for the luxurious purpose of basking and revelling in the anguish of dying despair, he had no motive at all, small or great, for

But all considerations whatever are at this moment suddenly cut short. A second step is heard on the stairs, but still stealthy and cautious; a third—and then the child's doom seems fixed. But just at that moment all is ready. The window is wide open; the rope is swinging free; the journeyman has launched himself; and already he is in the first stage of his descent. Simply by the weight of his person he descended, and by the resistance of his hands he retarded the descent. The danger was that the rope should run too smoothly through his hands, and that by too rapid an acceleration of pace he should come violently to the ground. Happily he was able to resist the descending impetus; the knots of the splicings furnished a succession of retardations. But the rope proved shorter by four or five feet than he had calculated: ten or eleven feet from the ground he hung suspended in the air; speechless for the present through long-continued agitation, and not daring to drop boldly on the rough carriage pavement, lest he should fracture his legs. But the night was not dark, as it had been on occasion of the Marr murders. And yet, for purposes of criminal police, it was by accident worse than the darkest night that ever hid a murder or baffled a pursuit. London, from east to west, was covered with a deep pall (rising from the river) of universal fog. Hence it happened that for twenty or thirty seconds the young man hanging in the air was not observed. His white shirt at length attracted notice. Three or four people ran up, and received him in their arms, all anticipating some dreadful annunciation. To what house did he belong? Even *that* was not instantly apparent; but he pointed with his finger to Williamson's door, and said in a half-choking whisper—"*Marr's murderer, now at work!*"

All explained itself in a moment: the silent language of the fact made its own eloquent revelation. The mysterious exterminator of No. 29 Ratcliffe Highway had visited another house; and, behold! one man only had escaped through the

attempting the murder of this young girl. She had seen nothing, heard nothing—was fast asleep, and her door was closed; so that, as a witness against him, he knew that she was as useless as any one of the three corpses. And yet he *was* making preparations for her murder when the alarm in the street interrupted him.

air, and in his night-dress, to tell the tale. Superstitiously, there was something to check the pursuit of this unintelligible criminal. Morally, and in the interests of vindictive justice, there was everything to rouse, quicken, and sustain it.

Yes, Marr's murderer—the man of mystery—was again at work; at this moment perhaps extinguishing some lamp of life, and not at any remote place, but here—in the very house which the listeners to this dreadful announcement were actually touching. The chaos and blind uproar of the scene which followed, measured by the crowded reports in the journals of many subsequent days, and in one feature of that case, has never to my knowledge had its parallel; or, if a parallel, only in one case—what followed, I mean, on the acquittal of the seven bishops at Westminster in 1688. At present there was more than passionate enthusiasm. The frenzied movement of mixed horror and exultation—the ululation of vengeance which ascended instantaneously from the individual street, and then by a sublime sort of magnetic contagion from all the adjacent streets—can be adequately expressed only by a rapturous passage in Shelley:—

> "The transport of a fierce and monstrous gladness
>   Spread through the multitudinous streets, fast flying
> Upon the wings of fear:—From his dull madness
>   The starveling waked, and died in joy: the dying,
>   Among the corpses in stark agony lying,
>   Just heard the happy tidings, and in hope
> Closed their faint eyes: from house to house replying
>   With loud acclaim, the living shook heaven's cope
> And filled the startled earth with echoes."[1]

There was something, indeed, half inexplicable in the instantaneous interpretation of the gathering shout according to its true meaning. In fact, the deadly roar of vengeance, and its sublime unity, *could* point in this district only to the one demon whose idea had brooded and tyrannised, for twelve days, over the general heart; every door, every window in the neighbourhood, flew open as if at a word of command; multitudes, without waiting for the regular means of egress, leaped down at once from the windows on the lower storey; sick men rose from their beds; in one instance, as if expressly

[1] *Revolt of Islam*, canto xii.

to verify the image of Shelley (in v. 4, 5, 6, 7), a man whose death had been looked for through some days, and who actually *did* die on the following day, rose, armed himself with a sword, and descended in his shirt into the street. The chance was a good one, and the mob were made aware of it, for catching the wolfish dog in the high noon and carnival of his bloody revels—in the very centre of his own shambles. For a moment the mob was self-baffled by its own numbers and its own fury. But even that fury felt the call for self-control. It was evident that the massy street-door must be driven in, since there was no longer any living person to co-operate with their efforts from within, excepting only a female child. Crowbars dexterously applied in one minute threw the door out of hangings, and the people entered like a torrent. It may be guessed with what fret and irritation to their consuming fury a signal of pause and absolute silence was made by a person of local importance. In the hope of receiving some useful communication, the mob became silent. "Now, listen," said the man of authority, "and we shall learn whether he is above-stairs or below." Immediately a noise was heard as if of some one forcing windows, and clearly the sound came from a bedroom above. Yes, the fact was apparent that the murderer was even yet in the house: he had been caught in a trap. Not having made himself familiar with the details of Williamson's house, to all appearance he had suddenly become a prisoner in one of the upper rooms. Towards this the crowd now rushed impetuously. The door, however, was found to be slightly fastened; and, at the moment when this was forced, a loud crash of the window, both glass and frame, announced that the wretch had made his escape. He had leaped down; and several persons in the crowd, who burned with the general fury, leaped after him. These persons had not troubled themselves about the nature of the ground; but now, on making an examination of it with torches, they reported it to be an inclined plane, or embankment of clay, very wet and adhesive. The prints of the man's footsteps were deeply impressed upon the clay, and therefore easily traced up to the summit of the embankment; but it was perceived at once that pursuit would be useless, from the density of the mist. Two feet ahead of you a man was entirely withdrawn from your power of identification; and, on overtaking him, you could not venture to challenge him as the same whom you had lost sight of. Never, through the course of a whole century, could there be a night expected more propitious to an escaping criminal: means of disguise Williams now had in excess; and the dens were innumerable in the neighbourhood of the river that could have sheltered him for years from troublesome inquiries. But favours are thrown away upon the reckless and the thankless. That night, when the turning-point offered itself for his whole future career, Williams took the wrong turn; for, out of mere indolence, he took the turn to his old lodgings—that place which, in all England, he had just now the most reason to shun.

Meantime the crowd had thoroughly searched the premises of Williamson. The first inquiry was for the young grand-daughter. Williams, it was evident, had gone into her room; but in this room apparently it was that the sudden uproar in the streets had surprised him; after which his undivided attention had been directed to the windows, since through these only any retreat had been left open to him. Even this retreat he owed only to the fog, and to the hurry of the moment, and to the difficulty of approaching the premises by the rear. The little girl was naturally agitated by the influx of strangers at that hour; but otherwise, through the humane precautions of the neighbours, she was preserved from all knowledge of the dreadful events that had occurred whilst she herself was sleeping. Her poor old grandfather was still missing, until the crowd descended into the cellar; he was then found lying prostrate on the cellar floor: apparently he had been thrown down from the top of the cellar stairs, and with so much violence that one leg was broken. After he had been thus disabled, Williams had gone down to him, and cut his throat. There was much discussion at the time, in some of the public journals, upon the possibility of reconciling these incidents with other circumstantialities of the case, supposing that only one man had been concerned in the affair. That there *was* only one man concerned seems to be certain. One only was seen or heard at Marr's; one only, and beyond all

doubt the same man, was seen by the young journeyman in
Mrs. Williamson's parlour; and one only was traced by his
footmarks on the clay embankment Apparently the course
which he had pursued was this:—He had introduced himself
to Williamson by ordering some beer. This order would
oblige the old man to go down into the cellar; Williams
would wait until he had reached it, and would then "slam"
and lock the street door in the violent way described.
Williamson would come up in agitation upon hearing this
violence. The murderer, aware that he would do so, met
him, no doubt, at the head of the cellar stairs, and threw
him down; after which he would go down to consummate
the murder in his ordinary way. All this would occupy a
minute, or a minute and a half; and in that way the
interval would be accounted for that elapsed between the
alarming sound of the street-door as heard by the journeyman and the lamentable outcry of the female servant. It
is evident also that the reason why no cry whatsoever had
been heard from the lips of Mrs. Williamson is due to the
positions of the parties as I have sketched them. Coming
behind Mrs. Williamson,—unseen therefore, and from her
deafness unheard, — the murderer would inflict entire
abolition of consciousness while she was yet unaware of his
presence. But with the servant, who had unavoidably witnessed the attack upon her mistress, the murderer could not
obtain the same fulness of advantage; and *she* therefore had
time for making an agonising ejaculation.

It has been mentioned that the murderer of the Marrs
was not for nearly a fortnight so much as suspected,—meaning that, previously to the Williamson murder, no vestige of
any ground for suspicion in any direction whatever had
occurred either to the general public or to the police. But
there were two very limited exceptions to this state of absolute ignorance. Some of the magistrates had in their possession something which, when closely examined, offered a very
probable means for tracing the criminal. But as yet they had
not traced him. Until the Friday morning next after the
destruction of the Williamsons, they had not published the
important fact that upon the ship-carpenter's mallet (with
which, as regarded the stunning or disabling process, the

murders had been achieved) were inscribed the letters
"J. P." This mallet had, by a strange oversight on the
part of the murderer, been left behind in Marr's shop; and
it is an interesting fact, therefore, that, had the villain been
intercepted by the brave pawnbroker, he would have been
met virtually disarmed. This public notification was made
officially on the Friday, viz. on the thirteenth day after the
first murder. And it was instantly followed (as will be
seen) by a most important result. Meantime, within the
secrecy of one single bedroom in all London, it is a fact that
Williams had been whisperingly the object of very deep suspicion from the very first—that is, within that same hour
which witnessed the Marr tragedy. And singular it is that
the suspicion was due entirely to his own folly. Williams
lodged, in company with other men of various nations, at a
public-house. In a large dormitory there were arranged five
or six beds. These were occupied by artisans, generally of
respectable character. One or two Englishmen there were,
one or two Scotchmen, three or four Germans, and Williams,
whose birthplace was not certainly known. On the fatal
Saturday night, about half-past one o'clock, when Williams
returned from his dreadful labours, he found the English
and Scotch party asleep, but the Germans awake: one of
them was sitting up with a lighted candle in his hands, and
reading aloud to the other two. Upon this, Williams said,
in an angry and very peremptory tone, "Oh, put that candle
out; put it out directly: we shall all be burned in our
beds." Had the British party in the room been awake, Mr.
Williams would have roused a mutinous protest against this
arrogant mandate. But Germans are generally mild and
facile in their tempers; so the light was complaisantly extinguished. Yet, as there were no curtains, it struck the
Germans that the danger was really none at all; for bedclothes, massed upon each other, will no more burn than the
leaves of a closed book. Privately, therefore, the Germans
drew an inference that Mr. Williams must have had some
urgent motive for withdrawing his own person and dress
from observation. What this motive might be the next
day's news diffused all over London, and of course at this
house, not two furlongs from Marr's shop, made awfully

evident; and, as may well be supposed, the suspicion was communicated to the other members of the dormitory. All of them, however, were aware of the legal danger attaching, under English law, to insinuations against a man, even if true, which might not admit of proof. In reality, had Williams used the most obvious precautions, had he simply walked down to the Thames (not a stone's-throw distant) and flung two of his implements into the river, no conclusive proof could have been adduced against him. And he might have realised the scheme of Courvoisier (the murderer of Lord William Russell) — viz. have sought each separate month's support in a separate well-concerted murder. The party in the dormitory, meantime, were satisfied themselves, but waited for evidences that might satisfy others. No sooner, therefore, had the official notice been published as to the initials J. P. on the mallet than every man in the house recognised at once the well-known initials of an honest Norwegian ship-carpenter, John Petersen, who had worked in the English dockyards until the present year, but, having occasion to revisit his native land, had left his box of tools in the garrets of this inn. These garrets were now searched. Petersen's tool-chest was found, but wanting the mallet; and, on further examination, another overwhelming discovery was made. The surgeon who examined the corpses at Williamson's had given it as his opinion that the throats were not cut by means of a razor, but of some implement differently shaped. It was now remembered that Williams had recently borrowed a large French knife of peculiar construction; and, accordingly, from a heap of old lumber and rags, there was soon extricated a waistcoat, which the whole house could swear to as recently worn by Williams. In this waistcoat, and glued by gore to the lining of its pockets, was found the French knife. Next, it was matter of notoriety to everybody in the inn that Williams ordinarily wore at present a pair of creaking shoes, and a brown surtout lined with silk. Many other presumptions seemed scarcely called for. Williams was immediately apprehended, and briefly examined. This was on the Friday. On the Saturday morning (viz. fourteen days from the Marr murders) he was again brought up. The circumstantial evidence was overwhelming.

Williams watched its course, but said very little. At the close, he was fully committed for trial at the next sessions; and it is needless to say that, on his road to prison, he was pursued by mobs so fierce that, under ordinary circumstances, there would have been small hope of escaping summary vengeance. But upon this occasion a powerful escort had been provided; so that he was safely lodged in jail. In this particular jail at this time the regulation was that at five o'clock P.M. all the prisoners on the criminal side should be finally locked up for the night, and without candles. For fourteen hours (that is, until seven o'clock on the next morning) they were left unvisited, and in total darkness. Time, therefore, Williams had for committing suicide. The means in other respects were small. One iron bar there was, meant (if I remember) for the suspension of a lamp; upon this he had hanged himself by his braces. At what hour was uncertain: some people fancied at midnight. And in that case, precisely at the hour when, fourteen days before, he had been spreading horror and desolation through the quiet family of poor Marr, now was he forced into drinking of the same cup, presented to his lips by the same accursed hands.

The case of the M'Keans, which has been specially alluded to, merits also a slight rehearsal for the dreadful picturesqueness of some two or three amongst its circumstances. The scene of this murder was at a rustic inn, some few miles (I think) from Manchester; and the advantageous situation of this inn it was out of which arose the twofold temptations of the case. Generally speaking, an inn argues, of course, a close cincture of neighbours, as the original motive for opening such an establishment. But in this case the house individually was solitary, so that no interruption was to be looked for from any persons living within reach of screams; and yet, on the other hand, the circumjacent vicinity was eminently populous; as one consequence of which, a benefit club had established its weekly rendezvous in this inn, and left the pecuniary accumulations in their club-room, under the custody of the landlord. This fund arose often to a considerable amount, fifty or seventy pounds, before it was transferred to the hands of a banker. Here, therefore, was a treasure worth some little risk, and a situation that promised next to none. These attractive circumstances had, by accident, become accurately known to one or both of the two M'Keans; and, unfortunately, at a moment of overwhelming misfortune to themselves. They were hawkers, and until lately had borne most respectable characters; but some mercantile crash had overtaken them with utter ruin, in which their joint capital had been swallowed up to the last shilling. This sudden prostration had made them desperate: their own little property had been swallowed up in a large *social* catastrophe, and society at large they looked upon as accountable to them for a robbery. In preying, therefore, upon society, they considered themselves as pursuing a wild natural justice of retaliation. The money aimed at did certainly assume the character of public money, being the product of many separate subscriptions. They forgot, however, that in the murderous acts which too certainly they meditated as preliminaries to the robbery they could plead no such imaginary social precedent. In dealing with a family that seemed almost helpless, if all went smoothly, they relied entirely upon their own bodily strength. They were stout young men, twenty-eight to thirty-two years old: somewhat undersized as to height; but squarely built, deep-chested, broad-shouldered, and so beautifully formed, as regarded the symmetry of their limbs and their articulations, that, after their execution, the bodies were privately exhibited by the surgeons of the Manchester Infirmary as objects of statuesque interest. On the other hand, the household which they proposed to attack consisted of the following four persons:—1, the landlord, a stoutish farmer—but *him* they intended to disable by a trick then newly introduced amongst robbers, and termed *hocussing*, *i.e.* clandestinely drugging the liquor of the victim with laudanum; 2, the landlord's wife; 3, a young servant-woman; 4, a boy, twelve or fourteen years old. The danger was that out of four persons, scattered by possibility over a house which had two separate exits, one at least might escape, and, by better acquaintance with the adjacent paths, might succeed in giving an alarm to some of the houses a furlong distant. Their final resolution was—to be guided by circumstances as to the mode of conducting the affair; and yet, as it seemed essential to success that they should assume the air of strangers to each other, it was necessary that they should preconcert some general outline of their plan; since it would on this scheme be impossible, without awaking violent suspicions, to make any communications under the eyes of the family. This outline included, at the least, one murder: so much was settled; but otherwise their subsequent proceedings make it evident that they wished to have as little bloodshed as was consistent with their final object. On the appointed day they presented themselves separately at the rustic inn, and at different hours. One came as early as four o'clock in the afternoon; the other not until half-past seven. They saluted each other distantly and shyly; and, though occasionally exchanging a few words in the character of strangers, did not seem disposed to any familiar intercourse. With the landlord, however, on his return about eight o'clock from Manchester, one of the brothers entered into a lively conversation, invited him to take a tumbler of punch; and, at a moment when the landlord's absence from the room allowed it, poured into the punch a spoonful of laudanum. Some time after this the clock struck ten; upon which the elder M'Kean, professing to be weary, asked to be shown up to his bedroom: for each brother, immediately on arriving, had engaged a bed. On this, the poor servant-girl presented herself with a bed-candle to light him upstairs. At this critical moment the family were distributed thus:—The landlord, stupefied with the horrid narcotic which he had drunk, had retired to a private room adjoining the public room, for the purpose of reclining upon a sofa; and *he*, luckily for his own safety, was looked upon as entirely incapacitated for action. The landlady was occupied with her husband. And thus the younger M'Kean was left alone in the public room. He rose, therefore, softly, and placed himself at the foot of the stairs which his brother had just ascended, so as to be sure of intercepting any fugitive from the bedroom above. Into that room the elder M'Kean was ushered by the servant, who pointed to two beds —one of which was already half occupied by the boy, and the other empty: in these she intimated that the two strangers must dispose of themselves for the night, according to any arrangement that they might agree upon. Saying this, she presented him with the candle; which he in a moment placed upon the table, and, intercepting her retreat from the room, threw his arms around her neck with a gesture as though he meant to kiss her. This was evidently what she herself anticipated, and endeavoured to prevent. Her horror may be imagined when she felt the perfidious hand that clasped her neck armed with a razor, and violently cutting her throat. She was hardly able to utter one scream before she sank powerless upon the floor. This dreadful spectacle was witnessed by the boy; who was not asleep, but had presence of mind enough instantly to close his eyes. The murderer advanced hastily to the bed, and anxiously examined the expression of the boy's features: satisfied he was not, and he then placed his hand upon the boy's heart, in order to judge by its beatings whether he were agitated or not. This was a dreadful trial; and no doubt the counterfeit sleep would immediately have been detected, when suddenly a dreadful spectacle drew off the attention of the murderer. Solemnly, and in ghostly silence, uprose in her dying delirium the murdered girl; she stood upright, she walked steadily for a moment or two, she bent her steps towards the door. The murderer turned away to pursue her; and at that moment the boy, feeling that his one solitary chance was to fly whilst this scene was in progress, bounded out of bed. On the landing at the head of the stairs was one murderer; at the foot of the stairs was the other: who could believe that the boy had the shadow of a chance for escaping? And yet, in the most natural way, he surmounted all hindrances. In the boy's horror, he laid his left hand on the balustrade, and took a flying leap over it, which landed him at the bottom of the stairs, without having touched a single stair. He had thus effectually passed one of the murderers: the other, it is true, was still to be passed; and this would have been impossible but for a sudden accident. The landlady had been alarmed by the faint scream of the young woman; had hurried from her private room to the girl's assistance; but at the foot of the stairs had been intercepted by the younger brother, and was at this moment struggling with *him*. The confusion of this life-and-death conflict had allowed the boy to whirl past them. Luckily he took a turn into a kitchen out of which was a back-door, fastened by a single bolt that ran freely at a touch; and through this door he rushed into the open fields. But at this moment the elder brother was set free for pursuit by the death of the poor girl. There is no doubt that in her delirium the image moving through her thoughts was that of the club, which met once a-week. She fancied it no doubt sitting; and to this room, for help and for safety, she staggered along; she entered it, and within the doorway once more she dropped down and instantly expired. Her murderer, who had followed her closely, now saw himself set at liberty for the pursuit of the boy. At this critical moment all was at stake; unless the boy were caught the enterprise was ruined. He passed his brother, therefore, and the landlady, without pausing, and rushed through the open door into the fields. By a single second perhaps, he was too late. The boy was keenly aware that, if he continued in sight, he would have no chance of escaping from a powerful young man. He made, therefore, at once for a ditch; into which he tumbled headlong. Had the murderer ventured to make a leisurely examination of the nearest ditch, he would easily have found the boy — made so conspicuous by his white shirt. But he lost all heart, upon failing at once to arrest the boy's flight. And every succeeding second made his despair the greater. If the boy had really effected his escape to the neighbouring farm-houses, a party of men might be gathered within five minutes; and already it might have become difficult for himself and his brother, unacquainted with the field paths, to evade being intercepted. Nothing remained, therefore, but to summon his brother away. Thus it happened that the landlady, though mangled, escaped with life, and eventually recovered. The landlord owed his safety to the stupefying potion. And the baffled murderers had the misery of knowing that their dreadful crime had been altogether profitless. The road, indeed, was now open to the club-room; and, probably, forty seconds would have sufficed to carry off the box of treasure, which afterwards might have been burst open and pillaged at leisure. But the fear of intercepting enemies was too strongly upon them; and they fled rapidly by a road which carried them actually within six feet of the lurking boy. That night they passed through Manchester. When daylight returned, they slept in a thicket twenty miles distant from the scene of their guilty attempt. On the second and third nights, they pursued their march on foot, resting again during the day. About sunrise on the fourth morning they were entering some village near Kirby Lonsdale, in Westmorland. They must have designedly quitted the direct line of route; for their object was Ayrshire, of which county they were natives, and the regular road would have led them through Shap, Penrith, Carlisle. Probably they were seeking to elude the persecution of the stage-coaches, which, for the last thirty hours, had been scattering at all the inns and road-side *cabarets* hand-bills describing their persons and dress. It happened (perhaps through design) that on this fourth morning they had separated, so as to enter the village ten minutes apart from each other. They were exhausted and footsore. In this condition it was easy to stop them. A blacksmith had silently reconnoitred them, and compared their appearance with the descriptions of the hand-bills. They were then easily overtaken, and separately arrested. Their trial and condemnation speedily followed at Lancaster; and in those days it followed, of course, that they were executed. Otherwise, their case fell so far within the sheltering limits of what would *now* be regarded as extenuating circumstances that, whilst a murder more or less was not to repel them from their object, very evidently they were anxious to economise the bloodshed as much as possible. Immeasurable, therefore, was the interval which divided them from the monster Williams.[1]

They perished on the scaffold: Williams, as I have said,

---

[1] While De Quincey has told the story of the M'Kean murder in such detail, he has left it undated. The criminals, however, were two brothers, Alexander and Michael Mackean (spelt also M'Keand), who were tried and condemned at Lancaster on the 18th of August 1826 for the murder, on the preceding 22d of May, of Elizabeth Bates, servant to Joseph Blears, keeper of a public-house at Winton, near Manchester. Though only this servant had been actually murdered, Blears himself had been drugged, his wife nearly murdered, and a boy in the house (Michael Higgins) chased for his life, — much in the manner described by De Quincey.—M.

by his own hand ; and, in obedience to the law as it then stood, he was buried in the centre of a *quadrivium*, or conflux of four roads (in this case four streets), with a stake driven through his heart. And over him drives for ever the uproar of unresting London !

[The following appeared among the "Explanatory Notices" prefixed to the volume of De Quincey's Collected Writings which contained his completed revision of *Murder considered as one of the Fine Arts*:—"The paper on 'Murder as one of the Fine Arts' seemed to
" exact from me some account of Williams, the dreadful London
" murderer of the last generation,—not only because the amateurs had
" so much insisted on his merit as the supreme of artists for grandeur
" of design and breadth of style, and because, apart from this
" momentary connexion with my paper, the man himself merited a
" record for his matchless audacity, combined with so much of snaky
" subtlety and even insinuating amiableness in his demeanour,—but
" also because, apart from the man himself, the *works* of the man
" (those two of them especially which so profoundly impressed the
" nation in 1812) were in themselves, for dramatic effect, the most
" impressive on record. Southey pronounced their pre-eminence
" when he said to me that they ranked amongst the few domestic
" events which, by the depth and expansion of horror attending them,
" had risen to the dignity of a *national* interest. I may add that
" this interest benefited also by the mystery which invested the
" murders ; mystery as to various points, but especially as respected
" one important question, Had the murderer any accomplice ?[1] There
" was, therefore, reason enough, both in the man's hellish character
" and in the mystery which surrounded him, for this Postscript to the
" original paper ; since, in the lapse of forty-two years, both the man
" and his deeds had faded away from the knowledge of the present
" generation. But still I am sensible that my record is far too diffuse.
" Feeling this at the very time of writing, I was yet unable to correct
" it ; so little self-control was I able to exercise under the afflicting agita-
" tions and the unconquerable impatience of my nervous malady."]

[1] Upon a large overbalance of probabilities, it was, however, definitively agreed amongst amateurs that Williams must have been alone in these atrocities Meantime, amongst the colourable presumptions on the other side was this :—Some hours after the last murder, a man was apprehended at Barnet (the first stage from London on a principal north road), encumbered with a quantity of plate. How he came by it, or whither he was going, he steadfastly refused to say In the daily journals, which he was allowed to see, he read with eagerness the police examinations of Williams ; and, on the same day which announced the catastrophe of Williams, he also committed suicide in his cell.

EARLY MEMORIALS OF GRASMERE[1]

SOON after my return to Oxford in 1807-8,[2] I received a letter from Miss Wordsworth, asking for any subscriptions I might succeed in obtaining amongst my college friends in

---

[1] Appeared originally, with the title *Recollections of Grasmere*, in *Tait's Edinburgh Magazine* for September 1839, as one of the series of articles which De Quincey had begun to contribute to that periodical in 1834 under the title of "Sketches of Life and Manners from the Autobiography of an English Opium-Eater," with the alternative title of "Lake Reminiscences from 1807 to 1830" for a portion of them. When De Quincey reprinted the paper in 1854, in vol. II of the Collective Edition of his Writings, it was under its new title of *Early Memorials of Grasmere*, but still as one of the series of his Autobiographic Sketches—with its place in that series altered, however, so as to make it the first of his papers of "Lake Reminiscences," preceding and introducing those on Coleridge, Wordsworth, and Southey. This arrangement was retained in Messrs. Black's sixteen-volume reissue of the Collective Writings. But, though thus originally interjected into the series of De Quincey's Autobiographic Sketches, the paper is really independent, and quite different in kind from the rest of that series. Accordingly, it is best presented by itself as a specimen of De Quincey's descriptive and narrative art in commemorating a tragic incident of real English life which happened in the Lake District about the time of his own first acquaintance with that district. The words "Early Memorials of Grasmere," as the reader soon finds, do not mean "Memoirs of Grasmere in Early Times," or "Antiquities of Grasmere," or anything of that kind. It is to De Quincey himself, as associated with Grasmere, that the word "Early" has reference; and *A Tale of Grasmere when I first knew it* would be a more exact title. —On comparing De Quincey's reprint of 1854 with the original in *Tait's Magazine* for September 1839, I have found that he bestowed great pains on the revision, and made considerable changes. These, I think, were all improvements.—M.

[2] After one week of what he calls "delightful intercourse" with the poet and the poet's admirable sister Dorothy Wordsworth, he had

aid of the funds then raising on behalf of an orphan family, who had become such by an affecting tragedy that had occurred within a few weeks from my visit to Grasmere.

Miss Wordsworth's simple but fervid memoir not being within my reach at this moment,[1] I must trust to my own recollections and my own impressions to retrace the story; which, after all, is not much of a story to excite or to impress, unless for those who can find a sufficient interest in the trials and calamities of hard-working peasants, and can reverence the fortitude which, being lodged in so frail a tenement as the person of a little girl, not much, if anything, above nine years old, could face an occasion of sudden mysterious abandonment, and could tower up, during one night, into the perfect energies of womanhood, under the mere pressure of difficulty, and under the sense of new-born responsibilities awfully bequeathed to her, and in the most lonely, perhaps, of English habitations.

The little valley of Easedale,—which, and the neighbourhood of which, were the scenes of these interesting events,—is on its own account one of the most impressive solitudes amongst the mountains of the Lake district; and I must pause to describe it. Easedale is impressive *as* a solitude; for the depth of the seclusion is brought out and forced more pointedly upon the feelings by the thin scattering of houses over its sides, and over the surface of what may be called its floor. These are not above six at the most; and one, the remotest of the whole, was untenanted for all the thirty years of my acquaintance with the place. *Secondly*, it is impressive from the excessive loveliness which adorns its little area. This is broken up into small fields and miniature meadows, separated, not—as too often happens, with sad injury to the beauty of the Lake country—by stone walls,

---

left Grasmere "about the 12th of November 1807," to return to Oxford, where he had been a student in Worcester College since 1803. He was then twenty-two years of age.—M.

[1] From some sentences of the original paper of 1839, omitted in the reprint, it appears that the "memoir" here spoken of was one which Dorothy Wordsworth had drawn up by way of a circular appeal to charitable persons, but with a special view of its coming into the hands of Queen Charlotte and the other ladies of the royal family. —M.

but sometimes by little hedgerows, sometimes by little sparkling, pebbly "becks," lustrous to the very bottom, and not too broad for a child's flying leap, and sometimes by wild self-sown woodlands of birch, alder, holly, mountain ash, and hazel, that meander through the valley, intervening the different estates with natural sylvan marches, and giving cheerfulness in winter by the bright scarlet of their berries. It is the character of all the northern English valleys, as I have already remarked,—and it is a character first noticed by Wordsworth—that they assume, in their bottom areas, the level, floor-like shape, making everywhere a direct angle with the surrounding hills, and definitely marking out the margin of their outlines; whereas the Welsh valleys have too often the glaring imperfection of the basin shape, which allows no sense of any flat area or valley surface: the hills are already commencing at the very centre of what is called the level area. The little valley of Easedale is, in this respect, as highly finished as in every other; and in the Westmorland spring, which may be considered May and the earlier half of June, whilst the grass in the meadows is yet short from the habit of keeping the sheep on it until a much later period than elsewhere (viz. until the mountains are so far cleared of snow and the probability of storms as to make it safe to send them out on their summer migration), it follows naturally that the little fields in Easedale have the most lawny appearance, and, from the humidity of the Westmorland[1] climate, the most verdant that it is possible to imagine. But there is a third advantage possessed by this Easedale, above other rival valleys, in the sublimity of its mountain barriers. In one of its many rocky recesses is seen a "force" (such is the local name for a cataract), white with foam, descending at all seasons with considerable strength, and, after the melting of snows, with an Alpine violence. Follow the leading of this "force" for three

[1] It is pretty generally known, perhaps, that Westmorland and Devonshire are the two rainiest counties in England. At Kirby Lonsdale, lying just on the outer margin of the Lake district, one-fifth more rain is computed to fall than in the adjacent counties on the same western side of England. But it is also notorious that the western side of the island universally is more rainy than the east. Collins called it the showery west.

quarters of a mile, and you come to a little mountain lake, locally termed a "tarn,"[1] the very finest and most gloomily sublime of its class. From this tarn it was, I doubt not, though applying it to another, that Wordsworth drew the circumstances of his general description. And far beyond this "enormous barrier," that thus imprisons the very winds, tower upwards the aspiring heads (usually enveloped in cloud and mist) of Glaramara, Bow Fell, and the other fells of Langdale Head and Borrowdale. Easedale, in its relation to Grasmere, is a chamber within a chamber, or rather a closet within a chamber—a chapel within a cathedral—a little private oratory within a chapel. The sole approach, as I have mentioned, is from Grasmere; and some *one* outlet there must inevitably be in every vale that can be interesting to a human occupant, since without water it would not be habitable, and running water must force an egress for itself, and, consequently, an ingress for the reader and myself. But, properly speaking, there is no other. For, when you explore the remoter end of the vale, at which you suspect some communication with the world outside, you find before you a most formidable amount of climbing, the extent of which can hardly be measured where there is no solitary object of human workmanship or vestige of animal life,—not a sheep-track, not a shepherd's hovel, but rock and heath, heath and rock, tossed about in monotonous confusion. And, after the ascent is mastered, you descend into a second vale—long, narrow, sterile—known by the name of "Far Easedale": from which point, if you could drive a tunnel *under* the everlasting hills, perhaps six or seven miles might bring you to the nearest habitation of man, in Borrowdale; but, going *over* the mountains, the road cannot be less than twelve or fourteen, and, in point of fatigue, at the least twenty. This long valley, which is really terrific at noonday, from its utter

[1] A *tarn* is a lake, generally (perhaps always) a small one, and always, as I think (but this I have heard disputed), lying above the level of the inhabited valleys and the large lakes; and subject to this farther restriction, first noticed by Wordsworth, that it has no main feeder. Now, this latter accident of the *thing* at once explains and authenticates my account of the *word*, viz. that it is the Danish word *taaren* (*a trickling of tears*), a deposit of waters from the weeping of rain down the smooth faces of the rocks.

loneliness and desolation, completes the defences of little sylvan Easedale. There is one door into it from the Grasmere side; but that door is obscure; and on every other quarter there is no door at all; not any, the roughest, access, but such as would demand a day's walking.

Such is the solitude—so deep and so rich in miniature beauty—of Easedale; and in this solitude it was that George and Sarah Green, two poor and hard-working peasants, dwelt, with a numerous family of small children. Poor as they were, they had won the general respect of the neighbourhood, from the uncomplaining firmness with which they bore the hardships of their lot, and from the decent attire in which the good mother of the family contrived to send out her children to the Grasmere parish-school. It is a custom, and a very ancient one, in Westmorland—the same custom (resting on the same causes) I have witnessed also in southern Scotland—that any sale by auction of household furniture (and seldom a month passes without something of the sort) forms an excuse for the good women, throughout the whole circumference of perhaps four or five valleys, to assemble at the place of sale, with the nominal purpose of buying something they may happen to want. A sale, except it were of the sort exclusively interesting to farming *men*, is a kind of general intimation to the country, from the owner of the property, that he will, on that afternoon, be "at home" to all comers, and hopes to see as large an attendance as possible. Accordingly, it was the almost invariable custom—and often, too, when the parties were far too poor for such an effort of hospitality—to make ample provision, not of eatables, but of liquor, for all who came. Even a gentleman who should happen to present himself on such a festal occasion, by way of seeing the "humours" of the scene, was certain of meeting the most cordial welcome. The good woman of the house more particularly testified her sense of the honour done to her, and was sure to seek out some cherished and solitary article of china—a wreck from a century back—in order that he, being a porcelain man among so many delf men and women, might have a porcelain cup to drink from.

The main secret of attraction at these sales—many of which I have attended—was the social rendezvous thus effected between parties so remote from each other (either by real distance or by virtual distance resulting from the separation effected by mountains 3000 feet high) that, in fact, without some such common object, they would not be likely to hear of each other for months, or actually to meet for years. This principal charm of the "gathering," seasoned, doubtless, to many by the certain anticipation that the whole budget of rural gossip would then and there be opened, was not assuredly diminished to the men by the anticipation of excellent ale (usually brewed six or seven weeks before, in preparation for the event), and possibly of still more excellent *powsowdy* (a combination of ale, spirits, and spices); nor to the women by some prospect, not so inevitably fulfilled, but pretty certain in a liberal house, of communicating their news over excellent tea. Even the auctioneer was always a character in the drama: he was always a rustic old humourist, and a jovial drunkard, privileged in certain good-humoured liberties and jokes with all bidders, gentle or simple, and furnished with an ancient inheritance of jests appropriate to the articles offered for sale, —jests that had, doubtless, done their office from Elizabeth's golden days, but no more, on that account, failing of their expected effect, with either man or woman of this nineteenth century, than the sun fails to gladden the heart because it is that same old superannuated sun that has gladdened it for thousands of years.

One thing, however, in mere justice to the Dalesmen of Westmorland and Cumberland, I am bound in this place to record. Often as I have been at these sales, and years before even a scattering of gentry began to attend, yet so true to the natural standard of politeness was the decorum uniformly maintained that even the old buffoon of an auctioneer never forgot himself so far as to found upon any article of furniture a jest fitted to call up a painful blush in any woman's face. He might, perhaps, go so far as to awaken a little rosy confusion upon some young bride's countenance, when pressing a cradle upon her attention; but never did I hear him utter, nor would he have been tolerated in uttering, a scurrilous or disgusting jest, such as might easily have been suggested by something offered at a household sale. Such jests as these I heard for the first time at a sale in Grasmere in 1814; and, I am ashamed to say it, from some "gentlemen" of a great city. And it grieved me to see the effect, as it expressed itself upon the manly faces of the grave Dalesmen—a sense of insult offered to their women, who met in confiding reliance upon the forbearance of the men, and upon their regard for the dignity of the female sex; this feeling struggling with the habitual respect they are inclined to show towards what they suppose gentle blood and superior education. Taken generally, however, these were the most picturesque and festal meetings which the manners of the country produced. There you saw all ages and both sexes assembled; there you saw old men whose heads would have been studies for Guido; there you saw the most colossal and stately figures amongst the young men that England has to show; there the most beautiful young women. There it was that the social benevolence, the innocent mirth, and the neighbourly kindness of the people, most delightfully expanded, and expressed themselves with the least reserve.

To such a scene it was,—to a sale of domestic furniture at the house of some proprietor in Langdale,—that George and Sarah Green set forward in the forenoon of a day fated to be their last on earth. The sale was to take place in Langdalehead; to which, from their own cottage in Easedale, it was possible in daylight, and supposing no mist upon the hills, to find out a short cut of not more than five or six miles. By this route they went; and, notwithstanding the snow lay on the ground, they reached their destination in safety. The attendance at the sale must have been diminished by the rigorous state of the weather; but still the scene was a gay one as usual. Sarah Green, though a good and worthy woman in her maturer years, had been imprudent, and—as the merciful judgment of the country is apt to express it—"unfortunate" in her youth. She had an elder daughter, who was illegitimate; and I believe the father of this girl was dead. The girl herself was grown up; and the peculiar solicitude of poor Sarah's maternal heart was at this time called forth on *her* behalf: she wished to see her placed in a very respectable house, where the mistress was distinguished for her notable qualities, and for success in forming good servants. This object,—as important to Sarah Green in the narrow range of her cares as, in a more exalted family, it might be to obtain a ship for a lieutenant that had passed as master and commander, or to get him "posted,"— occupied her almost throughout the sale. A doubtful answer had been given to her application; and Sarah was going about the crowd, and weaving her person in and out, in order to lay hold of this or that intercessor who might have, or might seem to have, some weight with the principal person concerned.

This I think it interesting to notice, as the last occupation which is known to have stirred the pulses of her heart. An illegitimate child is everywhere, even in the indulgent society of Westmorland Dalesmen, under some cloud of discountenance[1]; so that Sarah Green might consider her duty to be the stronger towards this child of her "misfortune." And she probably had another reason for her anxiety—as some words dropped by her on this evening led people to presume—in her conscientious desire to introduce her daughter into a situation less perilous than that which had compassed her own youthful steps with snares. If so, it is painful to know that the virtuous wish, whose

> "Vital warmth
> Gave the last human motion to her heart,"

should not have been fulfilled. She was a woman of ardent and affectionate spirit; of which Miss Wordsworth gave me some circumstantial and affecting instances. This ardour it was, and her impassioned manner, that drew attention to what she did; for, otherwise, she was too poor a person to be important in the estimation of strangers, and, of all possible situations, to be important at a sale, where the public attention was naturally fixed upon the chief pur-

---

[1] But still nothing at all in England by comparison with its gloomy excess in Scotland. In the present generation the raucorous bigotry of this feeling has been considerably mitigated. But, if the reader wishes to view it in its ancient strength, I advise him to look into the "Life of Alexander Alexander" (2 vols. 1830). He was a poor outcast, whose latter days were sheltered from ruin by the munificence of the late Mr. Blackwood, senior.

chasers, and the attention of the purchasers fixed upon the chief competitors. Hence it happened that, after she ceased to challenge notice by the emphasis of her solicitations for her daughter, she ceased to be noticed at all; and nothing was recollected of her subsequent behaviour until the time arrived for general separation. This time was considerably after sunset; and the final recollections of the crowd with respect to George and Sarah Green were that, upon their intention being understood to retrace their morning path, and to attempt the perilous task of dropping down into Easedale from the mountains above Langdalehead, a sound of remonstrance arose from many quarters. However, at such a moment, when everybody was in the hurry of departure, and to such persons (persons, I mean, so mature in years and in local knowledge), the opposition could not be very obstinate: party after party rode off; the meeting melted away, or, as the northern phrase is, *scaled*[1]; and at length nobody was left of any weight that could pretend to influence the decision of elderly people. They quitted the scene, professing to obey some advice or other upon the choice of roads; but, at as early a point as they could do so unobserved, began to ascend the hills everywhere open from the rude carriage-way. After this they were seen no more. They had disappeared into the cloud of death. Voices were heard, some hours afterwards, from the mountains—voices, as some thought, of alarm: others said, No,—that it was only the voices of jovial people, carried by the wind into uncertain regions. The result was that no attention was paid to the sounds.

[1] "*Scaled*":—*Scale* is a verb both active and neuter. I use it here as a neuter verb, in the sense (a Cumberland sense) of separating to all the points of the compass. But by Shakspere it is used in an active or transitive sense. Speaking of some secret news, he says, "We'll scale it a little more"—*i.e.* spread it in all directions, and disentangle its complexities. [Not quite correct. The passage is in *Coriolanus* I. 1, where Menenius Agrippa, when about to tell the citizens the story of the rebellion of the Belly against the other members of the body, says they may have heard it already, but he will *scale't a little more*. Another reading of the phrase, however, is *stale't*; and the Cambridge editors adopt this reading.—*Scale* in the sense of *disperse* is one of the commonest of Scottish words: *e.g.* "*the kirk was scalin'*" for "the service was over and the congregation was dispersing itself."—M.]

That night, in little peaceful Easedale, six children sat by a peat fire, expecting the return of their parents, upon whom they depended for their daily bread. Let a day pass, and they were starving. Every sound was heard with anxiety; for all this was reported many hundred times to Miss Wordsworth, and to those who, like myself, were never wearied of hearing the details. Every sound, every echo amongst the hills, was listened to for five hours, from seven to twelve. At length the eldest girl of the family—about nine years old—told her little brothers and sisters to go to bed. They had been trained to obedience; and all of them, at the voice of their eldest sister, went off fearfully to their beds. What could be *their* fears it is difficult to say; they had no knowledge to instruct them in the dangers of the hills; but the eldest sister always averred that they had as deep a solicitude as she herself had about their parents. Doubtless she had communicated her fears to *them*. Some time in the course of the evening—but it was late, and after midnight—the moon arose, and shed a torrent of light upon the Langdale fells, which had already, long hours before, witnessed in darkness the death of their parents.

That night, and the following morning, came a further and a heavier fall of snow; in consequence of which the poor children were completely imprisoned, and cut off from all possibility of communicating with their next neighbours. The brook was too much for them to leap; and the little, crazy wooden bridge could not be crossed, or even approached with safety, from the drifting of the snow having made it impossible to ascertain the exact situation of some treacherous hole in its timbers, which, if trod upon, would have let a small child drop through into the rapid waters. Their parents did not return. For some hours of the morning the children clung to the hope that the extreme severity of the night had tempted them to sleep in Langdale; but this hope forsook them as the day wore away. Their father, George Green, had served as a soldier, and was an active man, of ready resources, who would not, under any circumstances, have failed to force a road back to his family, had he been still living; and this reflection, or rather semi-conscious feeling, which the awfulness of their situation forced upon the

minds of all but the mere infants, awakened them to the
whole extent of their calamity. Wonderful it is to see the
effect of sudden misery, sudden grief, or sudden fear, in
sharpening (where they do not utterly upset) the intellectual
perceptions. Instances must have fallen in the way of most
of us. And I have noticed frequently that even sudden and
intense bodily pain forms part of the machinery employed by
nature for quickening the development of the mind. The
perceptions of infants are not, in fact, excited by graduated
steps and continuously, but *per saltum*, and by unequal starts.
At least, within the whole range of my own experience, I
have remarked that, after any very severe fit of those peculiar
pains to which the delicate digestive organs of most infants
are liable, there always became apparent on the following day
a very considerable increase of vital energy and of quickened
attention to the objects around them. The poor desolate
children of Blentarn Ghyll,[1] hourly becoming more pathetically convinced that they were orphans, gave many evidences
of this awaking power as lodged, by a providential arrangement, in situations of trial that most require it. They
huddled together, in the evening, round their hearth-fire of
peats, and held their little family councils upon what was to
be done towards any chance—if chance remained—of yet
giving aid to their parents; for a slender hope had sprung
up that some hovel or sheepfold might have furnished them
a screen (or, in Westmorland phrase, a *bield*[2]) against the

---

[1] Wordsworth's conjecture as to the origin of the name is probably
the true one. There is, at a little elevation above the place, a small
concave tract of ground, shaped like the bed of a tarn. Some causes
having diverted the supplies of water, at some remote period, from the
little reservoir, the tarn has probably disappeared; but, the bed, and
other indications of a tarn (particularly a little ghyll, or steep rocky
cleft for discharging the water), having remained as memorials that it
once existed, the country people have called it the Blind Tarn—the
tarn which wants its eye, in wanting the luminous sparkle of the
waters of right belonging to it.

[2] Another instance of a word common to the vocabulary of the
English Lake district and that of Scotland. *Bield* in Scotch means
"a shelter," and is a word of fine and tender associations in that
sense. "*Better a wee buss than nae bield*" ("Better a small bush than
no shelter at all") is an old Scottish proverb, of which Burns was
particularly fond.—M.

weather quarter of the storm, in which hovel they might even now be lying snowed up; and, secondly, as regarded themselves, in what way they were to make known their situation, in case the snow should continue or should increase; for starvation stared them in the face if they should be confined for many days to their house.

Meantime, the eldest sister, little Agnes, though sadly alarmed, and feeling the sensation of *eeriness* as twilight came on and she looked out from the cottage-door to the dreadful fells on which, too probably, her parents were lying corpses (and possibly not many hundred yards from their own threshold), yet exerted herself to take all the measures which their own prospects made prudent. And she told Miss Wordsworth that, in the midst of the oppression on her little spirit from vague ghostly terrors, she did not fail, however, to draw some comfort from the consideration that the very same causes which produced their danger in one direction sheltered them from danger of another kind,—such dangers as she knew, from books that she had read, would have threatened a little desolate flock of children in other parts of England; for she considered thankfully that, if *they* could not get out into Grasmere, on the other hand bad men, and wild seafaring foreigners, who sometimes passsed along the high road even in that vale, could not get to *them*; and that, as to their neighbours, so far from having anything to fear in that quarter, their greatest apprehension was lest they might not be able to acquaint them with their situation; but that, if this could be accomplished, the very sternest amongst them were kind-hearted people, that would contend with each other for the privilege of assisting them. Somewhat cheered with these thoughts, and having caused all her brothers and sisters—except the two little things, not yet of a fit age—to kneel down and say the prayers which they had been taught, this admirable little maiden turned herself to every household task that could have proved useful to them in a long captivity. First of all, upon some recollection that the clock was nearly going down, she wound it up. Next, she took all the milk which remained from what her mother had provided for the children's consumption during her absence and for the breakfast of the following morning,—this luckily was still in sufficient plenty for two days' consumption (skimmed or "blue" milk being only one halfpenny a quart, and the quart a most redundant one, in Grasmere),—this she took and scalded, so as to save it from turning sour. That done, she next examined the meal chest; made the common oatmeal porridge of the country (the "burgoo" of the Royal Navy); but put all of the children, except the two youngest, on short allowance; and, by way of reconciling them in some measure to this stinted meal, she found out a little hoard of flour, part of which she baked for them upon the hearth into little cakes; and this unusual delicacy persuaded them to think that they had been celebrating a feast. Next, before night coming on should make it too trying to her own feelings, or before fresh snow coming on might make it impossible, she issued out of doors. There her first task was, with the assistance of two younger brothers, to carry in from the peat-stack as many peats as might serve them for a week's consumption. That done, in the second place she examined the potatoes, buried in "brackens" (that is, withered fern): these were not many; and she thought it better to leave them where they were, excepting as many as would make a single meal, under a fear that the heat of their cottage would spoil them if removed.

Having thus made all the provision in her power for supporting their own lives, she turned her attention to the cow. Her she milked; but, unfortunately, the milk she gave, either from being badly fed, or from some other cause, was too trifling to be of much consideration towards the wants of a large family. Here, however, her chief anxiety was to get down the hay for the cow's food from a loft above the outhouse; and in this she succeeded but imperfectly, from want of strength and size to cope with the difficulties of the case,—besides that the increasing darkness by this time, together with the gloom of the place, made it a matter of great self-conquest for her to work at all; but, as respected one night at any rate, she placed the cow in a situation of luxurious warmth and comfort. Then, retreating into the warm house, and "barring" the door, she sat down to undress the two youngest of the children; them she laid carefully and cosily in their little nests upstairs, and sang them to sleep. The rest she kept up to bear her company until the clock should tell them it was midnight; up to which time she had still a lingering hope that some welcome shout from the hills above, which they were all to strain their ears to catch, might yet assure them that they were not wholly orphans, even though one parent should have perished. No shout, it may be supposed, was ever heard; nor could a shout, in any case, *have* been heard, for the night was one of tumultuous wind. And, though, amidst its ravings, sometimes they fancied a sound of voices, still, in the dead lulls that now and then succeeded, they heard nothing to confirm their hopes. As last services to what she might now have called her own little family, Agnes took precautions against the drifting of the snow *within* the door and *within* the imperfect window, which had caused them some discomfort on the preceding day; and, finally, she adopted the most systematic and elaborate plans for preventing the possibility of their fire being extinguished,— which, in the event of their being thrown upon the ultimate resource of their potatoes, would be absolutely indispensable to their existence, and in any case a main element of their comfort.

The night slipped away, and morning came, bringing with it no better hopes of any kind. Change there had been none but for the worse. The snow had greatly increased in quantity; and the drifts seemed far more formidable. A second day passed like the first,—little Agnes still keeping her young flock quiet, and tolerably comfortable, and still calling on all the elders in succession to say their prayers, morning and night.

A third day came; and, whether on that or on the fourth I do not now recollect, but on one or other, there came a welcome gleam of hope. The arrangement of the snow-drifts had shifted during the night; and, though the wooden bridge was still impracticable, a low wall had been exposed, over which, by a circuit which evaded the brook, it seemed possible that a road might be found into Grasmere. In some walls it was necessary to force gaps; but this was effected without much difficulty, even by children; for the Westmorland field walls are "open,"—that is, uncemented with mortar; and the push of a stick will generally detach so much from the upper part of any old crazy fence as to lower it sufficiently for female, or even for childish, steps to pass. The little boys accompanied their sister until she came to the other side of the hill ; which, lying more sheltered from the weather, offered a path onwards comparatively easy. Here they parted ; and little Agnes pursued her solitary mission to the nearest house she could find accessible in Grasmere.

No house could have proved a wrong one in such a case. Miss Wordsworth and I often heard the description renewed of the horror which, in an instant, displaced the smile of hospitable greeting, when little weeping Agnes told her sad tale. No tongue can express the fervid sympathy which travelled through the vale, like fire in an American forest, when it was learned that neither George nor Sarah Green had been seen by their children since the day of the Langdale sale. Within half an hour, or little more, from the remotest parts of the valley—some of them distant nearly two miles from the point of rendezvous—all the men of Grasmere had assembled at the little cluster of cottages called "Kirktown," from its adjacency to the venerable parish-church of St. Oswald. There were at the time I settled in Grasmere—viz. in the spring of 1809, and, therefore, I suppose, in 1807-8, fifteen months previously—about sixty-three households in the vale : and the total number of souls was about 265 to 270 ; so that the number of fighting men would be about sixty or sixty-six, according to the common way of computing the proportion ; and the majority were athletic and powerfully built. Sixty, at least, after a short consultation as to the plan of operations, and for arranging the kind of signals by which they were to communicate from great distances, and in the perilous events of mists or snow-storms, set off with the speed of Alpine hunters to the hills. The dangers of the undertaking were considerable, under the uneasy and agitated state of the weather ; and all the women of the vale were in the greatest anxiety until night brought them back, in a body, unsuccessful. Three days at the least, and I rather think five, the search was ineffectual : which arose partly from the great extent of the ground to be examined, and partly from the natural mistake made of ranging almost exclusively during the earlier days on that part of the hills over which the path of Easedale might be presumed to have been selected under any reasonable latitude of circuitousness. But the fact is, when the fatal accident (for such it has often proved) of a permanent mist surprises a man on the hills, if he turns and loses his direction, he is a lost man; and, without doing this so as to lose the power of *s'orienter* [1] all at once, it is yet well known how difficult it is to avoid losing it insensibly and by degrees. Baffling snow-showers are the worst kind of mists. And the poor Greens had, under that kind of confusion, wandered many a mile out of their proper track; so that to search for them upon any line indicated by the ordinary probabilities would perhaps offer the slenderest chance for finding them.

The zeal of the people, meantime, was not in the least abated, but rather quickened, by the wearisome disappointments; every hour of daylight was turned to account; no man of the valley ever came home to meals; and the reply of a young shoemaker, on the fourth night's return, speaks sufficiently for the unabated spirit of the vale. Miss Wordsworth asked what he would do on the next morning. "Go up again, of course," was his answer. But what if to-morrow also should turn out like all the rest? "Why, go up in stronger force on the day after." Yet this man was sacrificing his own daily earnings, without a chance of recompense. At length sagacious dogs were taken up; and, about noonday, a shout from an aerial height, amongst thick volumes of cloudy vapour, propagated through repeating bands of men from a distance of many miles, conveyed as by telegraph into Grasmere the news that the bodies were found. George Green was lying at the bottom of a precipice from which he had fallen. Sarah Green was found on the summit of the precipice; and, by laying together all the indications of what had passed, and reading into coherency the sad hieroglyphics of their last agonies, it was conjectured that the husband had desired his wife to pause for a few minutes, wrapping her, meantime, in his own greatcoat, whilst he

---

[1] *S'orienter*, *i.e.* originally setting oneself by the east as one of the cardinal points of the compass; hence "steering one's course properly," "discovering where one is," or even "knowing what one is about."—M.

should go forward and reconnoitre the ground, in order to catch a sight of some object (rocky peak, or tarn, or peat-field) which might ascertain their real situation. Either the snow above, already lying in drifts, or the blinding snow-storms driving into his eyes, must have misled him as to the nature of the circumjacent ground; for the precipice over which he had fallen was but a few yards from the spot in which he had quitted his wife. The depth of the descent and the fury of the wind (almost always violent on these cloudy altitudes) would prevent any distinct communication between the dying husband below and his despairing wife above; but it was believed by the shepherds best acquainted with the ground, and the range of sound as regarded the capacities of the human ear under the probable circumstances of the storm, that Sarah might have caught, at intervals, the groans of her unhappy partner, supposing that his death were at all a lingering one. Others, on the contrary, supposed her to have gathered this catastrophe rather from the *want* of any sounds, and from his continued absence, than from any one distinct or positive expression of it; both because the smooth and unruffled surface of the snow where he lay seemed to argue that he had died without a struggle, perhaps without a groan, and because that tremendous sound of "hurtling" in the upper chambers of the air which often accompanies a snow-storm, when combined with heavy gales of wind, would utterly suppress and stifle (as they conceived) any sounds so feeble as those from a dying man. In any case, and by whatever sad language of sounds or signs, positive or negative, she might have learned or guessed her loss, it was generally agreed that the wild shrieks heard towards midnight in Langdalehead[1] announced

---

[1] I once heard, also, in talking with a Langdale family upon this tragic tale, that the sounds had penetrated into the valley of Little Langdale; which is possible enough. For, although this interesting recess of the entire Langdale basin (which bears somewhat of the same relation to the Great Langdale that Easedale bears to Grasmere) does, in fact, lie beyond Langdalehead by the entire breadth of that dale, yet, from the singular accident of having its area raised far above the level of the adjacent vales, one most solitary section of Little Langdale (in which lies a tiny lake, and on the banks of that lake dwells one solitary family), being exactly at right angles both to

the agonizing moment which brought to her now widowed heart the conviction of utter desolation and of final abandonment to her own solitary and fast-fleeting energies. It seemed probable that the *sudden* disappearance of her husband from her pursuing eyes would teach her to understand his fate, and that the consequent indefinite apprehension of instant death lying all around the point on which she sat had kept her stationary to the very attitude in which her husband left her, until her failing powers, and the increasing bitterness of the cold to one no longer in motion, would soon make those changes of place impossible which too awfully had made themselves known as dangerous. The footsteps in some places, wherever drifting had not obliterated them, yet traceable as to the outline, though partially filled up with later falls of snow, satisfactorily showed that, however much they might have rambled, after crossing and doubling upon their own tracks, and many a mile astray from their right path, they must have kept together to the very plateau or shelf of rock at which (*i.e. on* which, and *below* which) their wanderings had terminated; for there were evidently no steps from this plateau in the retrograde order.

By the time they had reached this final stage of their erroneous course, all possibility of escape must have been long over for both alike; because their exhaustion must have been excessive before they could have reached a point so remote and high; and, unfortunately, the direct result of all this exhaustion had been to throw them farther off their home, or from "*any* dwelling-place of man," than they were at starting. Here, therefore, at this rocky pinnacle, hope was extinct for the wedded couple, but not perhaps for the husband. It was the impression of the vale that perhaps, within half-an-hour before reaching this fatal point, George Green might, had his conscience or his heart allowed him in so base a desertion, have saved himself singly, without any very great difficulty. It is to be hoped, however—and, for my part, I think too well of human nature to hesitate in believing—that not many, even amongst the meaner-minded

Langdalehead and to the other complementary section of the Lesser Langdale, is brought into a position and an elevation virtually much nearer to objects (especially to audible objects) on the Easedale Fells.

and the least generous of men, could have reconciled themselves to the abandonment of a poor fainting female companion in such circumstances. Still, though not more than a most imperative duty, it was such a duty as most of his associates believed to have cost him (perhaps consciously) his life. It is an impressive truth that sometimes in the very lowest forms of duty, less than which would rank a man as a villain, there is, nevertheless, the sublimest ascent of self-sacrifice. To do *less* would class you as an object of eternal scorn: to do so much presumes the grandeur of heroism. For his wife not only must have disabled him greatly by clinging to his arm for support; but it was known, from her peculiar character and manner, that she would be likely to rob him of his coolness and presence of mind, by too painfully fixing his thoughts, where her own would be busiest, upon their helpless little family. "*Stung* with the thoughts of home"—to borrow the fine expression of Thomson in describing a similar case [1]—alternately thinking of the blessedness of that warm fireside at Blentarn Ghyll which was not again to spread its genial glow through her freezing limbs, and of those darling little faces which, in this world, she was to see no more; unintentionally, and without being aware even of that result, she would rob the brave man (for such he was) of his fortitude, and the strong man of his *animal* resources. And yet (such, in the very opposite direction, was equally the impression universally through Grasmere), had Sarah Green foreseen, could her affectionate heart have guessed, even the tenth part of that love and neighbourly respect for herself which soon afterwards expressed themselves in showers of bounty to her children; could she have

---

[1] In his *Winter*, where there is a description of a cottager lost in a snow-storm:—

>"The swain
>Disastered stands; sees other hills ascend,
>Of unknown, joyless brow; and other scenes,
>Of horrid prospect, shag the trackless plain;
>Nor finds the river, nor the forest, hid
>Beneath the formless wild; but wanders on
>From hill to dale, still more and more astray,
>Impatient flouncing through the drifted heaps,
>Stung with the thoughts of home."—M.

looked behind the curtain of destiny sufficiently to learn that the very desolation of these poor children which wrung her maternal heart, and doubtless constituted to her the sting of death, would prove the signal and the pledge of such anxious guardianship as not many rich men's children receive, and that this overflowing offering to her own memory would not be a hasty or decaying tribute of the first sorrowing sensibilities, but would pursue her children steadily until their hopeful settlement in life : anything approaching this, known or guessed, would have caused her (so said all who knew her) to welcome the bitter end by which such privileges were to be purchased, and solemnly to breathe out into the ear of that holy angel who gathers the whispers of dying mothers torn asunder from their infants a thankful *Nunc dimittis* (Lord, now lettest thou thy servant depart in peace), as the farewell ejaculation rightfully belonging to the occasion.

The funeral of the ill-fated Greens was, it may be supposed, attended by all the Vale : it took place about eight days after they were found ; and the day happened to be in the most perfect contrast to the sort of weather which prevailed at the time of their misfortune. Some snow still remained here and there upon the ground ; but the azure of the sky was unstained by a cloud ; and a golden sunlight seemed to sleep, so balmy and tranquil was the season, upon the very hills where the pair had wandered,—then a howling wilderness, but now a green pastoral lawn in its lower ranges, and a glittering expanse of virgin snow in its higher. George Green had, I believe, an elder family by a former wife; and it was for some of these children, who lived at a distance, and who wished to give their attendance at the grave, that the funeral was delayed. At this point, because really suggested by the contrast of the funeral tranquillity with the howling tempest of the fatal night, it may be proper to remind the reader of Wordsworth's memorial stanzas :—

> "Who weeps for strangers ? Many wept
> For George and Sarah Green ;
> Wept for that pair's unhappy fate
> Whose graves may here be seen.

"By night upon these stormy fells
  Did wife and husband roam;
Six little ones at home had left,
  And could not find that home.

"For *any* dwelling-place of man
  As vainly did they seek:
He perished; and a voice was heard—
  The widow's lonely shriek.

"Not many steps, and she was left
  A body without life—
A few short steps were the chain that bound
  The husband to the wife.

"*Now* do these sternly-featured hills
  Look gently on this grave;
And quiet *now* are the depths of air,
  As a sea without a wave.

"But deeper lies the heart of peace,
  In quiet more profound;
The heart of quietness is here
  Within this churchyard bound.

"And from all agony of mind
  It keeps them safe, and far
From fear and grief, and from all need
  Of sun or guiding star.

"O darkness of the grave! how deep,
  After that living night—
That last and dreary living one
  Of sorrow and affright!

"O sacred marriage-bed of death!
  That keeps them side by side
In bond of peace, in bond of love,
  That may not be untied!"

After this solemn ceremony of the funeral was over—at which, by the way, I heard Miss Wordsworth declare that the grief of Sarah's illegitimate daughter was the most overwhelming she had ever witnessed—a regular distribution of the children was made amongst the wealthier families of the Vale. There had already, and before the funeral, been a perfect struggle to obtain one of the children amongst all who had any facilities for discharging the duties of such a trust; and even the poorest had put in their claim to bear some part in the expenses of the case. But it was judiciously decided that none of the children should be intrusted to any persons who seemed likely, either from old age or from slender means, or from nearer and more personal responsibilities, to be under the necessity of devolving the trust, sooner or later, upon strangers who might have none of that interest in the children which attached, in the minds of the Grasmere people, to the circumstances that made them orphans. Two twins, who had naturally played together and slept together from their birth, passed into the same family: the others were dispersed; but into such kind-hearted and intelligent families, with continued opportunities of meeting each other on errands, or at church, or at sales, that it was hard to say which had the more comfortable home. And thus, in so brief a period as one fortnight, a household that, by health and strength, by the humility of poverty and by innocence of life, seemed sheltered from all attacks but those of time, came to be utterly broken up. George and Sarah Green slept in Grasmere churchyard, never more to know the want of "sun or guiding star." Their children were scattered over wealthier houses than those of their poor parents, through the Vales of Grasmere or Rydal; and Blentarn Ghyll, after being shut up for a season, and ceasing for months to send up its little slender column of smoke at morning and evening, finally passed into the hands of a stranger.

The Wordsworths, meantime, acknowledged a peculiar interest in the future fortunes and education of the children. They had taken by much the foremost place in pushing the subscriptions on behalf of the family,—feeling, no doubt, that, when both parents, in any little sequestered community like that of Grasmere, are suddenly cut off by a tragical death, the children in such a case devolve by a sort of natural right and providential bequest on the other members of this community. They energetically applied themselves to the task of raising funds by subscription; most of which, it is true, might not be wanted until future years should carry one after another of the children successively into different trades or occupations; but they well understood that more by tenfold would be raised under an immediate appeal to the sympathies of men whilst yet burning fervently towards the sufferers in this calamity than if the application were delayed until the money should be needed. The Royal Family were made acquainted with the details of the case[1]; they were powerfully affected by the story, especially by the account of little Agnes, and her premature assumption of the maternal character; and they contributed most munificently. Her Majesty, and three at least of her august daughters, were amongst the subscribers to the fund. For my part, I could have obtained a good deal from the careless liberality of Oxonian friends towards such a fund. But, knowing previously how little, in such an application, it would aid me to plead the name of Wordsworth as the founder of the subscription (a name that *now* would stand good for some thousands of pounds in that same Oxford: so passes the injustice, as well as the glory, of this world!)—knowing this, I did not choose to trouble anybody; and the more so as Miss Wordsworth, upon my proposal to write to various ladies upon whom I could have relied for their several contributions, wrote back to me desiring that I would not, and upon this satisfactory reason—that the fund had already swelled, under the Royal patronage, and the interest excited by so much of the circumstances as could be reported in hurried letters, to an amount beyond what was likely to be wanted for persons whom there was no good reason for pushing out of the sphere to which their birth had called them. The parish even was liable to give aid; and, in the midst of Royal bounty, this aid was not declined. Perhaps this was so far a solitary and unique case that it might be the only one in which some parochial Mr. Bumble found himself pulling in joint harness with the denizens of Windsor Castle, and a coadjutor of "Majesties" and "Royal Highnesses." Finally, to complete their own large share in the charity, the Wordsworths took into their own family one of the children, a girl: the least amiable, I believe, of the whole; slothful and sensual; so, at least, I imagined; for this girl it was, that in years to come caused by her criminal negligence the death of little Kate Wordsworth.[2]

---

[1] See footnote *ante*, p. 126.—M.
[2] In the original paper in *Tait's Magazine* the words were:—"a

From a gathering of years far ahead of the events, looking back by accident to this whole little cottage romance of Blentarn Ghyll, with its ups and downs, its lights and shadows, and its fitful alternations of grandeur derived from mountain solitude and of humility derived from the very lowliest poverty,—its little faithful Agnes keeping up her records of time in harmony with the mighty world outside, and feeding the single cow, the total "estate" of the new-made orphans,—I thought of that beautiful Persian apologue where some slender drop or crystallizing filament within the shell of an oyster fancies itself called upon to bewail its own obscure lot, consigned apparently and irretrievably to the gloomiest depths of the Persian Gulf. But changes happen, good and bad luck will fall out, even in the darkest depths of the Persian Gulf; and messages of joy can reach those that wait in silence, even where no post-horn has ever sounded. Behold! the slender filament has ripened into the most glorious of pearls. In a happy hour for himself, some diver from the blossoming forests of Ceylon brings up to heavenly light the matchless pearl; and very soon that solitary crystal drop, that had bemoaned its own obscure lot, finds itself glorifying the central cluster in the tiara bound upon the brow of him who signed himself "King of Kings," the Shah of Persia, and that shook all Asia from the Indus to the Euphrates. Not otherwise was the lot of little Agnes: faithful to duties so suddenly revealed amidst terrors ghostly as well as earthly; paying down her first tribute of tears to an affliction that seemed past all relief, and such that at first she, with her brothers and sisters, seemed foundering simultaneously with her parents in one mighty darkness. And yet, because, under the strange responsibilities which had suddenly surprised her, she sought counsel and strength from

---

"girl; Sarah by name; the least amiable, I believe, of the whole; "so at least I imagined; for this girl it was, and her criminal negli- "gence, that in years to come inflicted the first heavy wound that I "sustained in my affections, and first caused me to drink deeply from "the cup of grief."—Little Kate Wordsworth, the poet's daughter, was a special favourite of De Quincey, whom she used in her childish prattle to call "Kinsey"; and her death, on the 4th June 1812, when De Quincey was on a visit to London, affected him greatly. See the circumstances more in detail, *ante*, Vol. II, pp. 440-445.—M.

God, teaching her brothers and sisters to do the same, and seemed (when alone at midnight) to hear her mother's voice calling to her from the hills above, one moon had scarcely finished its circuit before the most august ladies on our planet were reading, with sympathizing tears, of Agnes Green, and from the towers of Windsor Castle came gracious messages of inquiry to little, lowly Blentarn Ghyll.[1]

In taking leave of this subject I may mention, by the way, that accidents of this nature are not by any means so uncommon in the mountainous districts of Cumberland and Westmorland as the reader might infer from the intensity of the excitement which waited on the catastrophe of the Greens. In that instance it was not the simple death by cold upon the hills, but the surrounding circumstances, which invested the case with its agitating power. The fellowship in death of a wife and husband; the general impression that the husband had perished in his generous devotion to his wife (a duty, certainly, and no more than a duty, but still, under the instincts of self-preservation, a generous duty); sympathy with their long agony, as expressed by their long ramblings, and the earnestness of their efforts to recover their home; awe for the long concealment which rested upon their fate; and pity for the helpless condition of the children, —so young and so instantaneously made desolate, and so nearly perishing through the loneliness of their situation, co-operating with stress of weather, had they not been saved by the prudence and timely exertions of a little girl not much above eight years old;—these were the circumstances and necessary adjuncts of the story which pointed and sharpened the public feelings on that occasion. Else the mere general case of perishing upon the mountains is not, unfortunately, so rare, in *any* season of the year, as for itself alone to command a powerful tribute of sorrow from the public mind. Natives as well as strangers, shepherds as well as tourists, have fallen victims, even in summer, to the misleading and confounding effects of deep mists. Sometimes they have continued to wander unconsciously in a small circle of two or three miles, never coming within hail of a human dwelling until ex-

[1] The whole of this paragraph is an addition in the reprint.—M.

haustion has forced them into a sleep which has proved their last. Sometimes a sprain or injury, that disabled a foot or leg, has destined them to die by the shocking death of hunger.[1] Sometimes a fall from the summit of awful precipices has dismissed them from the anguish of perplexity in

---

[1] The case of Mr. Gough, who perished in the bosom of Helvellyn [1805], and was supposed by some to have been disabled by a sprain of the ankle, whilst others believed him to have received that injury and his death simultaneously in a fall from the lower shelf of a precipice, became well known to the public, in all its details, through the accident of having been recorded in verse by two writers nearly at the same time, viz. Sir Walter Scott and Wordsworth [by Scott in stanzas entitled "Helvellyn" and by Wordsworth in lines called "Fidelity" —M.] But here, again, as in the case of the Greens, it was not the naked fact of his death amongst the solitudes of the mountains that would have won the public attention, or have obtained the honour of a metrical commemoration. Indeed, to say the truth, the general sympathy with this tragic event was not derived chiefly from the unhappy tourist's melancholy end; for that was too shocking to be even hinted at by either of the two writers (in fact, there was too much reason to fear that it had been the lingering death of famine). Not the personal sufferings of the principal figure in the little drama, but the sublime and mysterious fidelity of the secondary figure, his dog: this it was which won the imperishable remembrance of the vales, and which accounted for the profound interest that immediately gathered round the incidents—an interest that still continues to hallow the memory of the dog. Not the dog of Athens, nor the dog of Pompeii, so well deserve the immortality of history or verse.——Mr. Gough was a young man, belonging to the Society of Friends, who took an interest in the mountain scenery of the Lake district, both as a lover of the picturesque and as a man of science. It was in this latter character, I believe, that he had ascended Helvellyn at the time when he met his melancholy end. From his familiarity with the ground—for he had been an annual visitant to the Lakes—he slighted the usual precaution of taking a guide. Mist, unfortunately, impenetrable volumes of mist, came floating over (as so often they do) from the gloomy fells that compose a common centre for Easedale, Langdale, Eskdale, Borrowdale, Wastdale, Gatesgarthdale (pronounced Keskadale), and Ennerdale. Ten or fifteen minutes afford ample time for this aerial navigation: within that short interval, sunlight, moonlight, starlight, alike disappear; all paths are lost; vast precipices are concealed, or filled up by treacherous draperies of vapour; the points of the compass are irrecoverably confounded; and one vast cloud, too often the cloud of death even to the experienced shepherd, sits like a vast pavilion upon the summits and gloomy coves of Helvellyn. Mr. Gough ought to have allowed for this not unfrequent accident, and for its bewildering effects; under which all local knowledge (even that of shepherds)

the extreme, from the conflicts of hope and fear, by dismissing them at once from life. Sometimes, also, the mountainous solitudes have been made the scenes of remarkable suicides.

In particular, there was a case, a little before I came into the country, of a studious and meditative young boy, who found no pleasure but in books and the search after knowledge. He becomes in an instant unavailing. What was the course and succession of his dismal adventures after he became hidden from the world by the vapoury screen could not be fully deciphered even by the most sagacious of mountaineers, although in most cases they manifest an Indian truth of eye, together with an Indian felicity of weaving all the signs that the eye can gather into a significant tale by connecting links of judgment and natural inference, especially where the whole case ranges within certain known limits of time and of space. But in this case two accidents forbade the application of their customary skill to the circumstances. One was the want of snow at the time to receive the impression of his feet; the other, the unusual length of time through which his remains lay undiscovered. He had made the ascent at the latter end of October,—a season when the final garment of snow which clothes Helvellyn from the setting in of winter to the sunny days of June has frequently not made its appearance. He was not discovered until the following spring, when a shepherd, traversing the coves of Helvellyn or of Fairfield in quest of a stray sheep, was struck by the unusual sound (and its echo from the neighbouring rocks) of a short quick bark, or cry of distress, as if from a dog or young fox. Mr. Gough had not been missed; for those who saw or knew of his ascent from the Wyburn side of the mountain took it for granted that he had fulfilled his intention of descending in the opposite direction into the valley of Patterdale, or into the Duke of Norfolk's deer-park on Ullswater, or possibly into Matterdale, and that he had finally quitted the country by way of Penrith. Having no reason, therefore, to expect a domestic animal in a region so far from human habitations, the shepherd was the more surprised at the sound and its continued iteration. He followed its guiding, and came to a deep hollow, near the awful curtain of rock called *Striding-Edge* There, at the foot of a tremendous precipice, lay the body of the unfortunate tourist; and, watching by his side, a meagre shadow, literally reduced to a skin and to bones that could be counted (for it is a matter of absolute demonstration that he never could have obtained either food or shelter through his long winter's imprisonment), sat this most faithful of servants—mounting guard upon his master's honoured body, and protecting it (as he *had* done effectually) from all violation by the birds of prey which haunt the central solitudes of Helvellyn :—

" How nourished through that length of time
He knows who gave that love sublime
And sense of loyal duty—great
Beyond all human estimate "

languished with a sort of despairing nympholepsy after intellectual pleasures—for which he felt too well assured that his term of allotted time, the short period of years through which his relatives had been willing to support him at St. Bees,[1] was rapidly drawing to an end. In fact, it was just at hand; and he was sternly required to take a long farewell of the poets and geometricians for whose sublime contemplations he hungered and thirsted. One week was to have transferred him to some huckstering concern, which not in any spirit of pride he ever affected to despise, but which in utter alienation of heart he loathed, as one whom nature, and his own diligent cultivation of the opportunities recently opened to him for a brief season, had dedicated to a far different service. He mused—revolved his situation in his own mind—computed his power to liberate himself from the bondage of dependency—calculated the chances of his ever obtaining this liberation, from change in the position of his family, or revolution in his own fortunes—and, finally, attempted conjecturally to determine the amount of effect which his new and illiberal employments might have upon his own mind in weaning him from his present elevated tasks, and unfitting him for their enjoyment in distant years, when circumstances might again place it in his power to indulge them.

These meditations were in part communicated to a friend, and in part, also, the result to which they brought him. That this result was gloomy his friend knew; but not, as in the end it appeared, that it was despairing. Such, however, it was; and, accordingly, having satisfied himself that the chances of a happier destiny were for him slight or none, and having, by a last fruitless effort, ascertained that there was no hope whatever of mollifying his relatives, or of obtaining a year's delay of his sentence, he walked quietly up to the cloudy wildernesses within Blencathara; read his Æschylus (read, perhaps, those very scenes of the "Prome-

---

[1] St. Bees, on the Cumberland coast, where there is a theological college for the education of young men intended for orders in the Church of England. As this was not founded till 1816, De Quincey may refer to the Grammar School, which dates from the sixteenth century.—M.

theus" that pass amidst the wild valleys of the Caucasus, and below the awful summits, untrod by man, of the ancient Elborus); read him for the last time; for the last time fathomed the abyss-like subtleties of his favourite geometrician, the mighty Apollonius[1]; for the last time retraced some parts of the narrative, so simple in its natural grandeur, composed by that imperial captain, the most majestic man of ancient history—

"The foremost man of all this world"—

Julius the Dictator, the eldest of the Cæsars. These three authors—Æschylus, Apollonius, and Cæsar—he studied until the daylight waned and the stars began to appear. Then he made a little pile of the three volumes, that served him for a pillow; took a dose, such as he had heard would be sufficient, of laudanum; laid his head upon the monument which he himself seemed in fancy to have raised to the three mighty spirits; and, with his face upturned to the heavens and the stars, slipped quietly away into a sleep upon which no morning ever dawned. The laudanum—whether it were from the effect of the open air, or from some peculiarity of temperament—had not produced sickness in the first stage of its action, nor convulsions in the last. But, from the serenity of his countenance, and from the tranquil maintenance of his original supine position—for his head was still pillowed upon the three intellectual Titans, Greek and Roman, and his eyes were still directed towards the stars—it would appear that he had died placidly, and without a struggle. In this way the imprudent boy,—who, like Chatterton, would not wait for the change that a day might bring,—obtained the liberty he sought. I describe him as doing whatsoever he had described himself in his last conversations as wishing to do; for whatsoever in his last scene of life was not explained by the objects and the arrangement of the objects about him found a sufficient solution in the confidential explanations of his purposes which he had communicated, so far as he felt it safe, to his only friend.[2]

[1] Apollonius, a native of Perga in Pamphylia, and called "the Great Geometer," lived about B.C. 240.—M.

[2] This story has been made the subject of a separate poem, entitled

From this little special episode, where the danger was of a more exceptional kind, let us fall back on the more ordinary case of shepherds, whose duties, in searching after missing sheep, or after sheep surprised by sudden snow-drifts, are too likely, in all seasons of severity, to force them upon facing dangers which, in relation to their natural causes, must for ever remain the same. This uniformity it is, this monotony of the danger, which authorizes our surprise and our indignation that long ago the resources of art and human contrivance, in any one of many possible modes, should not have been applied to the relief of an evil so constantly recurrent. A danger that has no fixed root in our social system suggests its own natural excuse when it happens to be neglected. But this evil is one of frightful ruin when it *does* take effect, and of eternal menace when it does *not*. In some years it has gone near to the depopulation of a whole pastoral hamlet, as respects the most vigorous and hopeful part of its male population; and annually it causes, by its mere contemplation, the heartache to many a young wife and many an anxious mother. In reality, amongst all pastoral districts where the field of their labour lies in mountainous tracts, an allowance is as regularly made for the loss of human life, by mists or storms suddenly enveloping the hills and surprising the shepherds, as for the loss of sheep; some proportion out of each class—shepherds and sheep—is considered as a kind of tithe-offering to the stern Goddess of Calamity, and in the light of a ransom for those who escape. Grahame, the author of "The Sabbath,"

"The Student of St. Bees," by my friend Mr. James Payn of Cambridge. The volume is published by Macmillan, Cambridge, and contains thoughts of great beauty, too likely to escape the vapid and irreflective reader. [The volume so referred to by De Quincey was published in 1853 with the title "*Poems: by James Payn, Author of Stories from Boccaccio*"; and the particular poem mentioned is a piece of about a hundred lines in heroic couplets. It is a rather remarkable coincidence that in the *Life Drama* of Alexander Smith, which was published also in 1853, there is a passage, almost too daringly powerful, describing a suicide by night on a mountain-top, which one can suppose to have been suggested, just as Mr. Payn's poem was, by the present incident in De Quincey's Lake Reminiscences. There, however, it is not a scholar, but a poet, that is the victim of the suicidal melancholy.—M.]

says that (confining himself to Scotland) he has known winters in which a single parish lost as many as ten shepherds. And this mention of Grahame reminds me of a useful and feasible plan proposed by him for obviating the main pressure of such sudden perils amidst snow and solitude and night. I call it feasible with good reason; for Grahame, who doubtless had made the calculations, declares that, for so trifling a sum as a few hundred pounds, every square mile in the southern counties of Scotland (that is, I presume, throughout the Lowlands) might be fitted up with his apparatus. He prefaces his plan by one general remark, to which I believe that every mountaineer will assent, viz. that the vast majority of deaths in such cases is owing to the waste of animal power in trying to recover the right direction, and probably it *would* be recovered in a far greater number of instances were the advance persisted in according to any unity of plan. But, partly, the distraction of mind and irresolution under such circumstances cause the wanderer frequently to change his direction voluntarily, according to any new fancy that starts up to beguile him; and, partly, he changes it often insensibly and unconsciously, from the same cause which originally led him astray. Obviously, therefore, the primary object should be to compensate the loss of distinct vision,—which, for the present, is irreparable in that form,—by substituting an appeal to another sense. That error which has been caused by the obstruction of the eye may be corrected by the sounder information of the ear. Let crosses, such as are raised for other purposes in Catholic lands, be planted at intervals—suppose of one mile—in every direction. "Snow-storms," says Grahame, "are almost always accompanied with wind. "Suppose, then, a pole, fifteen feet high, well fixed in the "ground, with two cross spars placed near the bottom, to "denote the 'airts' (or points of the compass): a bell hung "at the top of this pole, with a piece of flat wood (attached "to it) projecting upwards, would ring with the slightest "breeze. As they would be purposely made to have different "tones, the shepherd would soon be able to distinguish one "from another. He could never be more than a mile from "one or other of them. On coming to the spot, he would at "once know the points of the compass, and, of course, the direction in which his home lay."[1] Another protecting circumstance would rise out of the simplicity of manners, which is pretty sure to prevail in a mountainous region, and the pious tenderness universally felt towards those situations of peril which are incident to all alike—men and women, parents and children, the strong and the weak. The crosses, I would answer for it, whenever they are erected, will be protected by a superstition, such as that which in Holland protects the stork. But it would be right to strengthen this feeling by instilling it as a principle of duty in the catechisms of mountainous regions; and perhaps, also, in order to invest this duty with a religious sanctity, at the approach of every winter there might be read from the altar a solemn commination, such as that which the English Church appoints for Ash-Wednesday — "Cursed is he that removeth his neighbour's landmark," etc.; to which might now be added, —" Cursed is he that causeth the steps of the wayfarer to go astray, and layeth snares for the wanderer on the hills: cursed is he that removeth the bell from the snow-cross." And every child might learn to fear a judgment of retribution upon its own steps in case of any such wicked action, by reading the tale of that Scottish sea-rover who, in order

"To plague the Abbot of Aberbrothock,"

removed the bell from the Inchcape Rock; which same rock, in after days, and for want of this very warning bell, inflicted miserable ruin upon himself, his ship, and his crew.[2] Once made sacred from violation, these crosses might afterwards be made subjects of suitable ornament; that is to say, they might be made as picturesque in form, and colour, and

---

[1] This, I think, is a quotation from Grahame's note to his poem *A Winter Sabbath Walk*; and in the original article of 1839 it was followed by a longish extract from that poem, and by these words with reference to Grahame's proposal—"A more useful suggestion "was never made. Many thousands of lives would be saved in each "century by the general adoption of Mr. Grahame's plan." The extract from Grahame's poem, and these words in his praise, were omitted in De Quincey's reprint of 1854.—M.

[2] Southey's well-known ballad of Sir Ralph the Rover and the Inchcape Rock.—M.

material, as the crosses of Alpine countries or the guide-posts of England often are. The associated circumstances of storm and solitude, of winter, of night, and wayfaring, would give dignity to almost any form which had become familiar to the eye as the one appropriated to this purpose; and the particular form of a cross or crucifix, besides its own beauty, would suggest to the mind a pensive allegoric memorial of that spiritual asylum offered by the same emblem to the poor erring roamer in our human pilgrimage, whose steps are beset with other snares, and whose heart is bewildered by another darkness and another storm,—by the darkness of guilt, or by the storm of affliction.[1]

[1] The original concluding paragraph of the paper in the Magazine article of 1839 had been about three times as long as that which De Quincey retained in 1854,—including, indeed, all that he then retained, but consisting for the rest of a fritter of remarks towards a practical modification of the poet Grahame's plan for preventing the deaths of travellers among hills or moors in snow-storms. De Quincey thought (1) that the storm-crosses proposed by Grahame might be useful even if, to save expense, they were placed at intervals of four miles instead of one, inasmuch as a traveller would then be always within two miles of one of them, and the wind would carry the sound of a bell that distance, (2) that the crosses might be made of cast-iron, (3) that each cross might be provided with a little box or cell, elevated about eight feet from the ground, accessible by a ladder, and capable of containing one person, (4) that it would not be amiss if, after the sanctity of the crosses had been sufficiently established to protect them from theft, a small supply of brandy and biscuits were lodged in each cell or box at the beginning of every winter, with a few rockets and matches for lighting them. "If iron were too costly," he adds, "it might be used only for the little cell; and the rest of "the structure might be composed with no expense at all, except the "labour (and that would generally be given by public contribution "from the neighbourhood), from the rude undressed stones which "are always found lying about in such situations, and which are so "sufficient for all purposes of strength that the field-walls, and by "far the greater number of the dwelling-houses, in Westmorland, "are built of such materials, and, until late years, without mortar." To this mention of the novelty of the use of mortar in Westmorland in such cases De Quincey could not resist subjoining a footnote, as follows:—"This recent change in the art of rustic masonry by the "adoption of mortar does not mark any advance in that art, but, on "the contrary, a decay of skill and care. Twenty years ago [1819], "when 'dry' walls were in general use except for a superior class of "houses, it was necessary to supply the want of mortar by a much "nicer adaptation of the stones to each other. But now this care is

"regarded as quite superfluous; for the largest gaps and cavities
"amongst the stones are filled up with mortar; meantime, the walls
"built in this way are not so impervious either to rain or wind as
"those built upon the old patent construction of the past generation."
—All this is interesting enough; but De Quincey, when he reprinted
the EARLY MEMORIALS OF GRASMERE in 1854, showed artistic tact in
sweeping it all away, and closing a paper of this kind poetically and
musically, rather than with a bristle of such mechanical minutiæ.
—M.

THE SPANISH MILITARY NUN[1]

1.—*An Extra Nuisance is introduced into Spain*

On a night in the year 1592 (but which night is a secret liable to 365 answers), a Spanish "*son of somebody*" (*i.e.* hidalgo), in the fortified town of St. Sebastian,[2] received the disagreeable intelligence from a nurse that his wife had just presented him with a daughter. No present that the poor misjudging lady could possibly have made him was so entirely useless towards any purpose of his. He had three daughters already; which happened to be more by $2+1$, according to *his* reckoning, than any reasonable allowance of daughters.

---

[1] This story appeared first in three instalments, each headed with the words "By Thomas De Quincey," in the numbers of *Tait's Edinburgh Magazine* for May, June, and July 1847. It appeared then, however, under the clumsier title of THE NAUTICO-MILITARY NUN OF SPAIN. The change of title was made in 1854, when De Quincey reprinted the paper in vol. III of the Collective Edition of his writings. There were alterations at the same time in the text of the story, and in some particulars of its form and arrangement. The most important of these was the division of the text, which had previously been printed in block, into a succession of short chapters, each topped with a smart descriptive summary of its purport, after the fashion of the Spanish novels of roguish adventure, and of some later English novels. This device is, of course, retained in the present reproduction. As the story professes to be a real one, derived from old Spanish records, something will have to be said respecting De Quincey's authorities and his immediate materials. The information, however, will be best given in an appended editorial note at the close.—M.

[2] *St. Sebastian*: a sea-coast town in the north of Spain, in that corner of the Bay of Biscay where Spain begins to be divided from France by the chain of the Pyrenees.—M.

A supernumerary son might have been stowed away; but supernumerary daughters were the very nuisance of Spain. He did, therefore, what in such cases every proud and lazy Spanish gentleman endeavoured to do. And surely I need not interrupt myself by any parenthesis to inform the base British reader, who makes it his glory to work hard, that the peculiar point of honour for the Spanish gentleman lay in precisely these two qualities of pride and laziness; for, if he were not proud, or had anything to do, what could you look for but ruin to the old Spanish aristocracy? some of whom boasted that no member of their house (unless illegitimate, and a mere *terræ filius*) had done a day's work since the Flood. In the ark they admitted that Noah kept them tightly to work; because, in fact, there was work to do that must be done by somebody. But, once anchored upon Ararat, they insisted upon it most indignantly that no ancestor of the Spanish *noblesse* had ever worked, except through his slaves. And with a view to new leases of idleness, through new generations of slaves, it was (as many people think) that Spain went so heartily into the enterprises of Cortez and Pizarro. A sedentary body of Dons, without needing to uncross their thrice-noble legs, would thus levy eternal tributes of gold and silver upon eternal mines, through eternal successions of nations that had been, and were to be, enslaved. Meantime, until these golden visions should be realised, aristocratic *daughters*, who constituted the hereditary torment of the true Castilian Don, were to be disposed of in the good old way, viz. by quartering them for life upon nunneries: a plan which entailed no sacrifice whatever upon any of the parties concerned, except, indeed, the little insignificant sacrifice of happiness and natural birthrights to the daughters. But this little inevitable wreck, when placed in the counter scale to the magnificent purchase of eternal idleness for an aristocracy so ancient, was surely entitled to little attention amongst philosophers. Daughters must perish by generations, and ought to be proud of perishing, in order that their papas, being hidalgos, might luxuriate in laziness. Accordingly, on this system, our hidalgo of St. Sebastian wrapped the new little daughter, odious to his paternal eyes, in a pocket-handkerchief, and then, wrapping up his own throat with a great deal more care, off he bolted to the neighbouring convent of St. Sebastian,—meaning by that term not merely a convent of that city, but also (amongst several convents) the one dedicated to that saint. It is well that in this quarrelsome world we quarrel furiously about tastes; since, agreeing too closely about the objects to be liked, we should agree too closely about the objects to be appropriated; which would breed much more fighting than is bred by disagreeing. That little human tadpole, which the old toad of a father would not suffer to stay ten minutes in his house, proved as welcome at the nunnery of St. Sebastian as she was odious at home. The lady superior of the convent was aunt, by the mother's side, to the new-born stranger. She therefore kissed and blessed the little lady. The poor nuns, who were never to have any babies of their own, and were languishing for some amusement, perfectly doated on this prospect of a wee pet. The superior thanked the hidalgo for his very splendid present. The nuns thanked him, each and all; until the old crocodile actually began to whimper sentimentally at what he now perceived to be excess of munificence in himself. Munificence, indeed, he remarked, was his foible, next after parental tenderness.

2.—*Wait a little, Hidalgo!*

What a luxury it is, sometimes, to a cynic that there go two words to a bargain. In the convent of St. Sebastian all was gratitude; gratitude (as aforesaid) to the hidalgo from all the convent for his present, until at last the hidalgo began to express gratitude to *them* for their gratitude to *him*. Then came a rolling fire of thanks to St. Sebastian: from the superior, for sending a future saint; from the nuns, for sending such a love of a plaything; and, finally, from papa, for sending such substantial board and well-bolted lodgings: "from which," said the malicious old fellow, "my pussy will never find her way out to a thorny and dangerous world." Won't she? I suspect, son of somebody, that the next time you see "pussy," which may happen to be also the last, will not be in a convent of any kind. At present, whilst this general rendering of thanks was going on, one person only took no part in them. That person was "pussy," whose little figure lay quietly stretched out in the arms of a smiling young nun, with eyes nearly shut, yet peering a little at the candles. Pussy said nothing. It's of no great use to say much when all the world is against you. But, if St. Sebastian had enabled her to speak out the whole truth, pussy *would* have said: "So, Mr. Hidalgo, you have been engaging lodgings for me, lodgings for life. Wait a little. We'll try that question when my claws are grown a little longer."

3.—*Symptoms of Mutiny*

Disappointment, therefore, was gathering ahead. But for the present there was nothing of the kind. That noble old crocodile, papa, was not in the least disappointed as regarded *his* expectation of having no anxiety to waste, and no money to pay, on account of his youngest daughter. He insisted on his right to forget her; and in a week *had* forgotten her, never to think of her again, but once. The lady superior, as regarded *her* demands, was equally content, and through a course of several years; for, as often as she asked pussy if she would be a saint, pussy replied that she would if saints were allowed plenty of sweetmeats. But least of all were the nuns disappointed. Everything that they had fancied possible in a human plaything fell short of what pussy realised in racketing, racing, and eternal plots against the peace of the elder nuns. No fox ever kept a hen-roost in such alarm as pussy kept the dormitory of the senior sisters; whilst the younger ladies were run off their legs by the eternal wiles, and had their gravity discomposed, even in chapel, by the eternal antics, of this privileged little kitten.

The kitten had long ago received a baptismal name,— which was Kitty, or Kate; and *that* in Spanish is Catalina. It was a good name, as it recalled her original name of "pussy." And, by the way, she had also an ancient and honourable surname—viz. *De Erauso*; which is to this day a name rooted in Biscay. Her father, the hidalgo, was a military officer in the Spanish service, and had little care whether his kitten should turn out a wolf or a lamb, having made over the fee-simple of his own interest in the little

Kate to St. Sebastian, "to have and to hold," so long as
Kate should keep her hold of this present life. Kate had
no apparent intention to let slip that hold; for she was
blooming as a rose-bush in June, tall and strong as a young
cedar. Yet, notwithstanding this robust health, which forbade one to think of separation from St. Sebastian by death,
and notwithstanding the strength of the convent walls, which
forbade one to think of any other separation, the time was
drawing near when St. Sebastian's lease in Kate must, in
legal phrase, "determine," and any *chateaux en Espagne* that
the saint might have built on the cloistral fidelity of his pet
Catalina must suddenly give way in one hour, like many
other vanities in our own days of Spanish growth, such as
Spanish constitutions and charters, Spanish financial reforms,
Spanish bonds, and other little varieties of Spanish ostentatious mendacity.

4.—*The Symptoms Thicken.*

After reaching her tenth year, Catalina became thoughtful
and not very docile. At times she was even headstrong and
turbulent, so that the gentle sisterhood of St. Sebastian, who
had no other pet or plaything in the world, began to weep
in secret, fearing that they might have been rearing by
mistake some future tigress; for, as to infancy, *that*, you
know, is playful and innocent even in the cubs of a tigress.
But *there* the ladies were going too far. Catalina was impetuous and aspiring, violent sometimes, headstrong and
haughty towards those who presumed upon her youth,
absolutely rebellious against all open harshness, but still
generous and most forgiving, disdainful of petty arts, and
emphatically a noble girl. She was gentle, if people would
let her be so. But woe to those who took liberties with *her!*
A female servant of the convent, in some authority, one day,
in passing up the aisle to matins, *wilfully* gave Kate a push;
and, in return, Kate, who never left her debts in arrear, gave
the servant for a keepsake such a look as that servant carried
with her in fearful remembrance to her grave. It seemed as
if Kate had tropic blood in her veins that continually called
her away to the tropics. It was all the fault of that "blue
rejoicing sky," of those purple Biscayan mountains, of that

glad tumultuous ocean, which she beheld daily from the nunnery gardens. Or, if only half of it was *their* fault, the other half lay in those golden tales, streaming upwards even into the sanctuaries of convents, like morning mists touched by earliest sunlight, of kingdoms overshadowing a new world which had been founded by her kinsmen with the simple aid of a horse and a lance. The reader is to remember that this is no romance, or at least no fiction, that he is reading; and it is proper to remind the reader of real romances in Ariosto or our own Spenser that such martial ladies as the *Marfisa* or *Bradamant* of the first, and *Britomart* of the other, were really not the improbabilities that modern society imagines. Many a stout man, as you will soon see, found that Kate, with a sabre in hand, and well mounted, was no romance at all, but far too serious a fact.

5.—*Good-night, St. Sebastian!*

The day is come—the evening is come—when our poor Kate, that had for fifteen years been so tenderly rocked in the arms of St. Sebastian and his daughters, and that henceforth shall hardly find a breathing space between eternal storms, must see her peaceful cell, must see the holy chapel, for the last time. It was at vespers, it was during the chanting of the vesper service, that she finally read the secret signal for her departure, which long she had been looking for. It happened that her aunt, the Lady Principal, had forgotten her breviary. As this was in a private scrutoire, the prudent lady did not choose to send a servant for it, but gave the key to her niece. The niece, on opening the scrutoire, saw, with that rapidity of eye-glance for the one thing needed in great emergencies which ever attended her through life, that *now* was the moment, *now* had the clock struck for an opportunity which, if neglected, might never return. There lay the total keys, in one massive *trousseau*, of that monastic fortress, impregnable even to armies from without. St. Sebastian! do you see what your pet is going to do? And do it she will, as sure as your name is St. Sebastian. Kate went back to her aunt with the breviary and the key, but taking good care to leave that awful door, on whose hinge revolved all her future life, unlocked. Delivering the two articles to the superior, she complained of headache—(ah, Kate! what did *you* know of headaches?)—upon which her aunt, kissing her forehead, dismissed her to bed. Now, then, through three-fourths of an hour Kate will have free elbow-room for unanchoring her boat, for unshipping her oars, and for pulling ahead right out of St. Sebastian's cove into the main ocean of life.

Catalina, the reader is to understand, does not belong to the class of persons in whom pre-eminently I profess an interest. But everywhere one loves energy and indomitable courage. And always what is best in its kind one admires, even where the kind may happen to be not specially attractive. Kate's advantages for her *rôle* in this life lay in four things: viz. in a well-built person and a particularly strong wrist; 2d, in a heart that nothing could appal; 3d, in a sagacious head, never drawn aside from the *hoc age* (from the instant question of the hour) by any weakness of imagination; 4th, in a tolerably thick skin,—not literally, for she was fair and blooming and eminently handsome, having such a skin, in fact, as became a young woman of family in northernmost Spain; but her sensibilities were obtuse as regarded *some* modes of delicacy, *some* modes of equity, *some* modes of the world's opinion, and *all* modes whatever of personal hardship. Lay a stress on that word *some*—for, as to delicacy, she never lost sight of that kind which peculiarly concerns her sex. Long afterwards she told the Pope himself, when confessing without disguise to the paternal old man her sad and infinite wanderings (and I feel convinced of her veracity), that in this respect—viz. all which concerned her sexual honour —even then she was as pure as a child. And, as to equity, it was only that she substituted the rude natural equity of camps for the specious and conventional equity of courts and towns. I must add, though at the cost of interrupting the story by two or three more sentences, that Catalina had also a fifth advantage, which sounds humbly, but is really of use in a world where even to fold and seal a letter adroitly is not the lowest of accomplishments. She was a *handy* girl. She could turn her hand to anything; of which I will give you two memorable instances. Was there ever a girl in this world but herself that cheated and snapped her fingers at that awful Inquisition which brooded over the convents of Spain? that did this without collusion from outside; trusting to nobody but to herself, and what beside? to one needle, two skeins of thread, and a bad pair of scissors! For that the scissors were bad, though Kate does not say so in her memoirs, I know by an *a priori* argument: viz. because *all* scissors were bad in the year 1607. Now, say all decent logicians, from a universal to a particular *valet consequentia*, the right of inference is good. *All* scissors were bad, *ergo some* scissors were bad. The second instance of her handiness will surprise you even more:—She once stood upon a scaffold, under sentence of death (but, understand, on the evidence of false witnesses). Jack Ketch—or, as the present generation calls him, "*Mr. Calcraft*," or "—— *Calcraft, Esq.*"—was absolutely tying the knot under her ear, and the shameful man of ropes fumbled so deplorably, that Kate (who by much nautical experience had learned from another sort of "Jack" how a knot *should* be tied in this world) lost all patience with the contemptible artist, told him she was ashamed of him, took the rope out of his hand, and tied the knot irreproachably herself. The crowd saluted her with a festal roll, long and loud, of *vivas*; and, this word *vira* being a word of good augury——But stop; let me not anticipate.

From this sketch of Catalina's character the reader is prepared to understand the decision of her present proceeding. She had no time to lose: the twilight, it is true, favoured her; but in any season twilight is as short-lived as a farthing rushlight; and she must get under hiding before pursuit commenced. Consequently she lost not one of her forty-five minutes in picking and choosing. No *shilly-shally* in Kate. She saw with the eyeball of an eagle what was indispensable. Some little money perhaps, in the first place, to pay the first toll-bar of life: so, out of four shillings in Aunty's purse, or what amounted to that English sum in various Spanish coins, she took one. You can't say *that* was exorbitant. Which of us wouldn't subscribe a shilling for poor Kate, to put into the first trouser-pockets that ever she will wear? I remember even yet, as a personal experience, that, when first arrayed, at four years old, in nankeen trousers, though still so far retaining hermaphrodite relations of dress as to wear a petticoat above my trousers, all my female friends (because they pitied me, as one that had suffered from years of ague) filled my pockets with half-crowns, of which I can render no account at this day. But what were my poor pretensions by the side of Kate's? Kate was a fine blooming girl of fifteen, with no touch of ague; and, before the next sun rises, Kate shall draw on her first trousers, made by her own hand; and, that she may do so, of all the valuables in aunty's repository she takes nothing beside, first (for I detest your ridiculous and most pedantic neologism of *firstly* [1])—first, the shilling, for which I have already given a receipt,—secondly, two skeins of suitable thread,—thirdly, one stout needle, and (as I told you before, if you would please to remember things) one bad pair of scissors. Now she was ready; ready to cast off St Sebastian's towing-rope; ready to cut and run for port anywhere; which port (according to a smart American adage) is to be looked for "at the back of beyond." The finishing touch of her preparations was to pick out the proper keys: even there she showed the same discretion. She did no gratuitous mischief. She did not take the wine-cellar key, which would have irritated the good father-confessor; she did not take the key of the closet which held the peppermint-water and other cordials, for *that* would have distressed the elderly nuns. *She* took those keys only that belonged to *her*, if ever keys did; for they were the keys that locked her out from her natural birthright of liberty. Very different views are taken by different parties of this particular act now meditated by Kate. The Court of Rome treats it as the immediate suggestion of Hell, and open to no forgiveness. Another Court, far loftier, ampler, and of larger authority—viz. the Court which holds its dreadful tribunal in the human heart and conscience—pronounces this act an inalienable privilege of man, and the mere reassertion of a birthright that can neither be bought nor sold.

[1] Characteristic of De Quincey, and worth remembering!—M.

6.—*Kate's First Bivouac and First March.*

Right or wrong, however, in Romish casuistry, Kate was resolved to let herself out; and *did*; and, for fear any man should creep in while vespers lasted, and steal the kitchen grate, she locked her old friends *in*. Then she sought a shelter. The air was moderately warm. She hurried into a chestnut wood; and upon withered leaves, which furnished to Kate her very first bivouac in a long succession of such experiences, she slept till earliest dawn. Spanish diet and youth leave the digestion undisordered, and the slumbers light. When the lark rose, up rose Catalina. No time to lose; for she was still in the dress of a nun, and therefore, by a law too flagrantly notorious, liable to the peremptory challenge and arrest of any man — the very meanest or poorest — in all Spain. With her *armed* finger (ay, by the way, I forgot the thimble; but Kate did *not*), she set to work upon her amply-embroidered petticoat. She turned it wrong side out; and, with the magic that only female hands possess, had she soon sketched and finished a dashing pair of Wellington trousers. All other changes were made according to the materials she possessed, and quite sufficiently to disguise the two main perils—her sex, and her monastic dedication. What was she to do next? Speaking of Wellington trousers anywhere in the north of Spain would remind *us*, but could hardly remind *her*, of Vittoria, where she dimly had heard of some maternal relative. To Vittoria, therefore, she bent her course [1]; and, like the Duke of Wellington, but arriving more than two centuries earlier, she gained a great victory at that place. She had made a two days' march, with no provisions but wild berries; she depended, for anything better, as light-heartedly as the duke, upon attacking sword in hand, storming her dear friend's intrenchments, and effecting a lodgment in his breakfast-room, should he happen to possess one. This amiable rela-

---

[1] "*Vittoria*":—A town in the same province of Spain as St. Sebastian, but about fifty miles inland. There Wellington gained one of his greatest Peninsular War victories over the French, on the 21st of June 1813.—M.

tive proved to be an elderly man, who had but one foible,—
or perhaps it was a virtue,—which had by continual
development overshadowed his whole nature: it was
pedantry. On that hint Catalina spoke: she knew by
heart, from the services of the convent, a good number of
Latin phrases. Latin!—Oh, but *that* was charming; and
in one so young! The grave Don owned the soft impeachment; relented at once, and clasped the hopeful young
gentleman in the Wellington trousers to his *uncular* and
rather angular breast. In this house the yarn of life was of
a mingled quality. The table was good, but that was
exactly what Kate cared least about. On the other hand,
the amusement was of the worst kind. It consisted chiefly
in conjugating Latin verbs, especially such as were obstinately irregular. To show him a withered frost-bitten verb,
that wanted its preterite, wanted its gerunds, wanted its
supines,—wanted, in fact, everything in this world, fruits or
blossoms, that make a verb desirable,—was to earn the Don's
gratitude for life. All day long he was, as you may say,
marching and counter-marching his favourite brigades of
verbs—verbs frequentative, verbs inceptive, verbs desidera-
tive—horse, foot, and artillery; changing front, advancing
from the rear, throwing out skirmishing parties; until Kate,
not given to faint, must have thought of such a resource,—as
once in her life she had thought so seasonably of a vesper
headache. This was really worse than St. Sebastian's. It
reminds one of a French gaiety in Thiebault; who describes
a rustic party, under equal despair, as employing themselves
in conjugating the verb *s'ennuyer*—*Je m'ennuie, tu t'ennuies, il
s'ennuit; nous nous ennuyons*, &c.; thence to the imperfect—
Je m'ennuyois, tu t'ennuyois, &c.; thence to the imperative—
Qu'il s'ennuye, &c.; and so on, through the whole dolorous
conjugation. Now, you know, when the time comes that
nous nous ennuyons, the best course is to part. Kate saw
that; and she walked off from the Don's (of whose amorous
passion for defective verbs one would have wished to know
the catastrophe), taking from his mantelpiece rather more
silver than she had levied on her aunt. But then, observe,
the Don also was a relative; and really he owed her a small
cheque on his banker for turning out on his field-days. A

man, if he *is* a kinsman, has no unlimited privilege of boring one; an uncle has a qualified right to bore his nephews, even when they happen to be nieces; but he has no right to bore either nephew or niece *gratis*.

7.—*Kate at Court, where she prescribes Phlebotomy, and is Promoted.*

From Vittoria, Kate was guided by a carrier to Valladolid.[1] Luckily, as it seemed at first,—but, in fact, it made little difference in the end,—here, at Valladolid, were assembled the King and his Court. Consequently, there was plenty of regiments, and plenty of regimental bands. Attracted by one of these, Catalina was quietly listening to the music, when some street ruffians, in derision of the gay colours and the particular form of her forest-made costume (rascals! what sort of trousers would *they* have made with no better scissors?), began to pelt her with stones. Ah, my friends of the genus *blackguard*, you little know who it is that you are selecting for experiments! This is the one creature of fifteen years old in all Spain, be the other male or female, whom nature, and temper, and provocation have qualified for taking the conceit out of you! This she very soon did, laying open with sharp stones more heads than either one or two, and letting out rather too little than too much of bad Valladolid blood. But mark the constant villainy of this world! Certain Alguazils[2]—very like some other Alguazils that I know of nearer home—having stood by quietly to see the friendless stranger insulted and assaulted, now felt it their duty to apprehend the poor nun for her most natural retaliation; and, had there been such a thing as a treadmill in Valladolid, Kate was booked for a place on it without further inquiry. Luckily, injustice does not *always* prosper. A gallant young cavalier, who had witnessed from his windows the whole affair, had seen the provocation, and admired Catalina's behaviour, equally patient

---

[1] *Valladolid*, in Old Castille, about 140 miles south-west from Vittoria.—M.

[2] *Alguazils*, police-officers: a Spanish word from the Arabic or Moorish *al* (the) and *wazir* (officer, *vizier*).—M.

at first and bold at last, hastened into the street, pursued the
officers, forced them to release their prisoner upon stating the
circumstances of the case, and instantly offered to Catalina a
situation amongst his retinue. He was a man of birth and
fortune; and the place offered, that of an honorary page, not
being at all degrading even to a "daughter of somebody," was
cheerfully accepted.

8.—*Too Good to Last!*

Here Catalina spent a happy quarter of a year. She was
now splendidly dressed in dark blue velvet, by a tailor that
did not work within the gloom of a chestnut forest. She
and the young cavalier, Don Francisco de Cardenas, were
mutually pleased, and had mutual confidence. All went
well, until one evening (but, luckily, not before the sun had
been set so long as to make all things indistinct) who should
march into the antechamber of the cavalier but that sublime
of crocodiles, *papa*, whom we lost sight of fifteen years ago,
and shall never see again after this night. He had his
crocodile tears all ready for use, in working order, like a
good industrious fire-engine. Whom will he speak to first
in this lordly mansion? It was absolutely to Catalina herself that he advanced; whom, for many reasons, he could
not be supposed to recognise—lapse of years, male attire,
twilight, were all against him. Still, she might have the
family countenance; and Kate fancied (but it must have
been a fancy) that he looked with a suspicious scrutiny into
her face, as he inquired for the young Don. To avert her
own face, to announce him to Don Francisco, to wish papa
on the shores of that ancient river, the Nile, furnished but
one moment's work to the active Catalina. She lingered,
however, as her place entitled her to do, at the door of the
audience-chamber. She guessed already, but in a moment
she *heard* from papa's lips, what was the nature of his
errand. His daughter Catherine, he informed the Don, had
eloped from the convent of St. Sebastian, a place rich in
delight, radiant with festal pleasure, overflowing with
luxury. Then he laid open the unparalleled ingratitude of
such a step. Oh, the unseen treasure that had been spent
upon that girl! Oh, the untold sums of money, the

unknown amounts of cash, that had been sunk in that
unhappy speculation! The nights of sleeplessness suffered
during her infancy! The fifteen years of solicitude thrown
away in schemes for her improvement! It would have
moved the heart of a stone. The *hidalgo* wept copiously
at his own pathos. And to such a height of grandeur
had he carried his Spanish sense of the sublime that
he disdained to mention—yes! positively not even in a
parenthesis would he condescend to notice—that pocket-
handkerchief which he had left at St. Sebastian's fifteen
years ago, by way of envelope for "pussy," and which, to
the best of pussy's knowledge, was the one sole memorandum
of papa ever heard of at St. Sebastian's. Pussy, however,
saw no use in revising and correcting the text of papa's
remembrances. She showed her usual prudence, and her
usual incomparable decision. It did not appear, as yet, that
she would be reclaimed (or was at all suspected for the fugitive) by her father, or by Don Cardenas. For it is an
instance of that singular fatality which pursued Catalina
through life that, to her own astonishment (as she now
collected from her father's conference), nobody had traced
her to Valladolid, nor had her father's visit any connexion
with any suspicious traveller in that direction. The case
was quite different. Strangely enough, her street row had
thrown her, by the purest of accidents, into the one sole
household in all Spain that had an official connexion with
St. Sebastian's That convent had been founded by the
young cavalier's family; and, according to the usage of
Spain, the young man (as present representative of his
house) was the responsible protector and official visitor of
the establishment. It was not to the Don as harbourer of
his daughter, but to the Don as hereditary patron of the
convent, that the hidalgo was appealing. This being so,
Kate might have staid safely some time longer. Yet, again,
that would but have multiplied the clues for tracing her;
and, finally, she would too probably have been discovered;
after which, with all his youthful generosity, the poor Don
could not have protected her. Too terrific was the vengeance that awaited an abettor of any fugitive nun; but, above
all, if such a crime were perpetrated by an official mandatory

of the Church. Yet, again, so far it was the more hazardous course to abscond that it almost revealed her to the young Don as the missing daughter. Still, if it really *had* that effect, nothing at present obliged him to pursue her, as might have been the case a few weeks later. Kate argued (I daresay) rightly, as she always did. Her prudence whispered eternally that safety there was none for her until she had laid the Atlantic between herself and St. Sebastian's. Life was to be for *her* a Bay of Biscay; and it was odds but she had first embarked upon this billowy life from the literal Bay of Biscay. Chance ordered otherwise. Or, as a Frenchman says, with eloquent ingenuity, in connexion with this very story, "Chance is but the *pseudonym* of God for those particular cases which he does not choose to subscribe openly with his own sign-manual." She crept upstairs to her bedroom. Simple are the travelling preparations of those that, possessing nothing, have no imperials to pack. She had Juvenal's qualification for carolling gaily through a forest full of robbers[1]; for she had nothing to lose but a change of linen, that rode easily enough under her left arm, leaving the right free for answering the questions of impertinent customers. As she crept downstairs, she heard the crocodile still weeping forth his sorrows to the pensive ear of twilight, and to the sympathetic Don Francisco. Ah! what a beautiful idea occurs to me at this point! Once, on the hustings at Liverpool, I saw a mob orator, whose brawling mouth, open to its widest expansion, suddenly some larking sailor, by the most dexterous of shots, plugged up with a paving-stone. Here, now, at Valladolid was another mouth that equally required plugging. What a pity, then, that some gay brother-page of Kate's had not been there to turn aside into the room armed with a roasted potato, and, taking a sportsman's aim, to have lodged it in the crocodile's abominable mouth! Yet, what an anachronism! There were no roasted potatoes in Spain at that date (1608); which

---

[1] An allusion to the line in Juvenal's Tenth Satire:—
"Cantabit vacuus coram latrone viator";
which may be translated:—
"The empty-pocketed tramp will sing in the face of a robber."—M.

can be apodeictically proved, because in Spain there were no potatoes at all, and very few in England. But anger drives a man to say anything.

9.—*How to choose Lodgings.*

Catalina had seen her last of friends and enemies in Valladolid. Short was her time there; but she had improved it so far as to make a few of both. There was an eye or two in Valladolid that would have glared with malice upon her, had she been seen by *all* eyes in that city as she tripped through the streets in the dusk; and eyes there were that would have softened into tears, had they seen the desolate condition of the child, or in vision had seen the struggles that were before her. But what's the use of wasting tears upon our Kate? Wait till to-morrow morning at sunrise, and see if she is particularly in need of pity. What, now, should a young lady do—I propose it as a subject for a prize essay—that finds herself in Valladolid at nightfall, having no letters of introduction, and not aware of any reason, great or small, for preferring this or that street in general, except so far as she knows of some reason for avoiding one street in particular? The great problem I have stated Kate investigated as she went along; and she solved it with the accuracy which she ever applied to *practical* exigencies. Her conclusion was—that the best door to knock at, in such a case, was the door where there was no need to knock at all, as being deliberately left open to all comers. For she argued that within such a door there would be nothing to steal, so that, at least, you could not be mistaken in the dark for a thief. Then, as to stealing from *her*, they might do that if they could.

Upon these principles, which hostile critics will in vain endeavour to undermine, she laid her hand upon what seemed a rude stable-door. Such it proved; and the stable was not absolutely empty: for there was a cart inside—a four-wheeled cart. True, there was so; but you couldn't take *that* away in your pocket; and there were also five loads of straw—but then of those a lady could take no more than her *reticule* would carry; which perhaps was allowed by the courtesy of

Spain. So Kate was right as to the difficulty of being challenged for a thief. Closing the door as gently as she had opened it, she dropped her person, handsomely dressed as she was, upon the nearest heap of straw. Some ten feet further were lying two muleteers, honest and happy enough, as compared with the lords of the bedchamber then in Valladolid; but still gross men, carnally deaf from eating garlic and onions and other horrible substances. Accordingly, they never heard her, nor were aware, until dawn, that such a blooming person existed. But she was aware of *them*, and of their conversation. In the intervals of their sleep, they talked much of an expedition to America, on the point of sailing under Don Ferdinand de Cordova. It was to sail from some Andalusian port. That was the thing for *her*. At daylight she woke, and jumped up, needing little more toilet than the birds that already were singing in the gardens, or than the two muleteers, who, — good, honest fellows, — saluted the handsome boy kindly, thinking no ill at his making free with *their* straw, though no leave had been asked.

With these philo-garlic men Kate took her departure. The morning was divine; and, leaving Valladolid with the transports that befitted such a golden dawn,—feeling also already, in the very obscurity of her exit, the pledge of her final escape,—she cared no longer for the crocodile, nor for St. Sebastian, nor (in the way of fear) for the protector of St. Sebastian, though of *him* she thought with some tenderness; so deep is the remembrance of kindness mixed with justice. Andalusia she reached rather slowly; many weeks the journey cost her; but, after all, what are weeks? She reached Seville many months before she was sixteen years old, and quite in time for the expedition.[1]

---

[1] Arrived at Seville in Andalusia after her long journey, Kate, the reader will understand, was now in the south of Spain, at the extreme opposite point of the map from her native St. Sebastian, having traversed the entire diagonal distance of more than 450 miles between the two places.—M.

10.—*An Ugly Dilemma, where Right and Wrong is reduced to a Question of Right or Left.*

Ugly indeed is that dilemma where shipwreck and the sea are on one side of you, and famine on the other, or, if a chance of escape is offered, apparently it depends upon taking the right road where there is no guide-post.

St. Lucar being the port of rendezvous for the Peruvian expedition, thither she went.[1] All comers were welcome on board the fleet; much more a fine young fellow like Kate. She was at once engaged as a mate; and *her* ship, in particular, after doubling Cape Horn without loss, made the coast of Peru. Paita was the port of her destination.[2] Very near to this port they were, when a storm threw them upon a coral reef. There was little hope of the ship from the first, for she was unmanageable, and was not expected to hold together for twenty-four hours. In this condition, with death before their faces, mark what Kate did; and please to remember it for her benefit, when she does any other little thing that angers you. The crew lowered the long-boat. Vainly the captain protested against this disloyal desertion of a king's ship, which might yet, perhaps, be run on shore, so as to save the stores. All the crew, to a man, deserted the captain. You may say *that* literally; for the single exception was *not* a man, being our bold-hearted Kate. She was the only sailor that refused to leave her captain, or the King of Spain's ship. The rest pulled away for the shore, and with fair hopes of reaching it. But one half-hour told another tale. Just about that time came a broad sheet of lightning, which, through the darkness of evening, revealed the boat in

[1] "*St Lucar*":—A seaport of Andalusia, at the mouth of the Guadalquivir, somewhat north of Cadiz.—M.

[2] The reader who would follow Kate's adventures geographically must not neglect these two short and hasty sentences. They carry her away from Spain and Europe altogether, across the Atlantic to South America,—nay, not only across the Atlantic to South America, but round Cape Horn, to the *west* or *Pacific* coast of South America, and to a point far north on that coast. Paita or Payta is a seaport of the Pacific in the extreme north of Peru, about five degrees below the Equator. All the long voyage of thousands of miles is suppressed.—M.

the very act of mounting like a horse upon an inner reef, instantly filling, and throwing out the crew, every man of whom disappeared amongst the breakers. The night which succeeded was gloomy for both the representatives of his Catholic Majesty. It cannot be denied by the underwriters at Lloyd's that the muleteer's stable at Valladolid was worth twenty such ships, though the stable was *not* insured against fire, and the ship *was* insured against the sea and the wind by some fellow that thought very little of his engagements. But what's the use of sitting down to cry? That was never any trick of Catalina's. By daybreak she was at work with an axe in her hand. I knew it, before ever I came to this place in her memoirs. I felt, as sure as if I had read it, that when day broke we should find Kate at work. Thimble or axe, trousers or raft, all one to *her*.

The captain, though true to his duty, faithful to his king, and on his king's account even hopeful, seems from the first to have desponded on his own. He gave no help towards the raft. Signs were speaking, however, pretty loudly that he must do something; for notice to quit was now served pretty liberally. Kate's raft was ready; and she encouraged the captain to think that it would give both of them something to hold by in swimming, if not even carry double. At this moment, when all was waiting for a start and the ship herself was waiting only for a final lurch to say *Good-bye* to the King of Spain, Kate went and did a thing which some erring people will misconstrue. She knew of a box laden with gold coins, reputed to be the King of Spain's, and meant for contingencies on the voyage out. This she smashed open with her axe, and took out a sum in ducats and pistoles equal to one hundred guineas English; which, having well secured in a pillow-case, she then lashed firmly to the raft. Now, this, you know, though not "*flotsam*," because it would not float, was certainly, by maritime law, "*jetsam*." It would be the idlest of scruples to fancy that the sea or a shark had a better right to it than a philosopher, or a splendid girl who showed herself capable of writing a very fair 8vo, to say nothing of her decapitating in battle, as you will find, more than one of the king's enemies, and recovering the king's banner. No sane moralist would hesitate to do the same

thing under the same circumstances, even on board an
English vessel, and though the First Lord of the Admiralty,
and the Secretary, that pokes his nose into everything
nautical, should be looking on. The raft was now thrown
into the sea. Kate jumped after it, and then entreated the
captain to follow her. He attempted it; but, wanting her
youthful agility, he struck his head against a spar, and sank
like lead, giving notice below that his ship was coming after
him as fast as she could make ready. Kate's luck was
better: she mounted the raft, and by the rising tide was
gradually washed ashore, but so exhausted as to have lost all
recollection. She lay for hours, until the warmth of the sun
revived her. On sitting up, she saw a desolate shore stretching both ways — nothing to eat, nothing to drink; but
fortunately the raft and the money had been thrown near
her, none of the lashings having given way: only what is
the use of a gold ducat, though worth nine shillings in
silver, or even of a hundred, amongst tangle and sea-gulls?
The money she distributed amongst her pockets, and soon
found strength to rise and march forward. But which *was*
forward? and which backward? She knew by the conversation of the sailors that Paita must be in the neighbourhood; and Paita, being a port, could not be in the inside of
Peru, but, of course, somewhere on its outside — and the
outside of a maritime land must be the shore; so that, if she
kept the shore, and went far enough, she could not fail of
hitting her foot against Paita at last, in the very darkest of
nights, provided only she could first find out which was *up*
and which was *down*: else she might walk her shoes off, and
find herself, after all, a thousand miles in the wrong. Here
was an awkward case, and all for want of a guide-post. Still,
when one thinks of Kate's prosperous horoscope,—that, after
so long a voyage, *she* only, out of the total crew, was thrown
on the American shore, with one hundred and five pounds in
her purse of clear gain on the voyage,—a conviction arises
that she *could* not guess wrongly. She might have tossed up,
having coins in her pocket, *heads or tails*! but this kind of
sortilege was then coming to be thought irreligious in
Christendom, as a Jewish and a heathen mode of questioning
the dark future. She simply guessed, therefore; and very

soon a thing happened which, though adding nothing to strengthen her guess as a true one, did much to sweeten it, if it should prove a false one. On turning a point of the shore, she came upon a barrel of biscuit washed ashore from the ship. Biscuit is one of the best things I know, even if not made by Mrs. Bobo[1]; but it is the soonest spoiled; and one would like to hear counsel on one puzzling point,—why it is that a touch of water utterly ruins it, taking its life, and leaving behind a *caput mortuum*. Upon this *caput*, in default of anything better, Kate breakfasted. And, breakfast being over, she rang the bell for the waiter to take away, and to—— *Stop! what nonsense!* There could be no bell; besides which, there could be no waiter. Well, then, without asking the waiter's aid, she that was always prudent packed up some of the Catholic king's biscuit, as she had previously packed up far too little of his gold. But in such cases a most delicate question occurs, pressing equally on dietetics and algebra. It is this: if you pack up too much, then, by this extra burden of salt provisions, you may retard for days your arrival at fresh provisions; on the other hand, if you pack up too little, you may famish, and never arrive at all. Catalina hit the *juste milieu*; and about twilight on the third day she found herself entering Paita, without having had to swim any *very* broad river in her walk.

[1] Who is Mrs. Bobo? The reader will say, "I know not Bobo." Possibly; but, for all *that*, Bobo is known to Senates. From the American Senate (Friday, March 10, 1854) Bobo received the amplest testimonials of merits that have not yet been matched. In the debate on William Nevins's claim for the extension of his patent for a machine that rolls and cuts crackers and biscuits, thus spoke Mr. Adams, a most distinguished senator, against Mr. Badger—"It is said this is a "discovery of the patentee for making the best biscuits. Now, if it "be so, he must have got his invention from Mrs. Bobo of Alabama; "for she certainly makes better biscuit than anybody in the world. I "can prove by my friend from Alabama (Mr. Clay), who sits beside "me, and by any man who ever staid at Mrs. Bobo's house, that she "makes better biscuit than anybody else in the world; and, if this "man has the best plan for making biscuit, he must have got it "from *her*." Henceforward I hope we know where to apply for biscuit.

11.—*From the Malice of the Sea to the Malice of Man and Woman*

The first thing, in such a case of distress, which a young lady does, even if she happens to be a young gentleman, is to beautify her dress. Kate always attended to *that*. The man she sent for was not properly a tailor, but one who employed tailors, he himself furnishing the materials. His name was Urquiza,—a fact of very little importance to us in 1854,[1] if it had stood only at the head and foot of Kate's little account. But, unhappily for Kate's *début* on this vast American stage, the case was otherwise. Mr. Urquiza had the misfortune (equally common in the Old World and the New) of being a knave, and also a showy, specious knave. Kate, who had prospered under sea allowances of biscuit and hardship, was now expanding in proportions. With very little vanity or consciousness on that head, she now displayed a really magnificent person; and, when dressed anew in the way that became a young officer in the Spanish service, she looked[2] the representative picture of a Spanish *caballador*. It is strange that such an appearance, and such a rank, should have suggested to Urquiza the presumptuous idea of wishing that Kate might become his clerk. He *did*, however, wish it; for Kate wrote a beautiful hand; and a stranger thing is that Kate accepted his proposal. This might arise from the difficulty of moving in those days to

---

[1] This date is substituted by De Quincey in the reprint in the Collective Edition of his works for the original "1847" in *Tait's Magazine*.—M.

[2] "*She looked*," etc. :—If ever the reader should visit Aix-la-Chapelle, he will probably feel interest enough in the poor, wild, impassioned girl to look out for a picture of her in that city, and the only one known *certainly* to be authentic. It is in the collection of Mr. Sempeller. For some time it was supposed that the best (if not the only) portrait of her lurked somewhere in Italy. Since the discovery of the picture at Aix-la-Chapelle that notion has been abandoned. But there is great reason to believe that both in Madrid and Rome many portraits of her must have been painted to meet the intense interest which arose in her history subsequently amongst all men of rank, military or ecclesiastical, whether in Italy or Spain. The date of these would range between sixteen and twenty-two years from the period which we have now reached (1608).

any distance in Peru. The ship which threw Kate ashore had been merely bringing stores to the station of Paita ; and no corps of the royal armies was readily to be reached, whilst something must be done at once for a livelihood. Urquiza had two mercantile establishments—one at Trujillo, to which he repaired in person, on Kate's agreeing to undertake the management of the other in Paita.[1] Like the sensible girl that we have always found her, she demanded specific instructions for her guidance in duties so new. Certainly she was in a fair way for seeing life. Telling her beads at St. Sebastian's, manœuvring irregular verbs at Vittoria, acting as gentleman-usher at Valladolid, serving his Spanish Majesty round Cape Horn, fighting with storms and sharks off the coast of Peru, and now commencing as book-keeper or *commis* to a draper at Paita—does she not justify the character that I myself gave her, just before dismissing her from St. Sebastian's, of being a "handy" girl? Mr. Urquiza's instructions were short, easy to be understood, but rather comic ; and yet (which is odd) they led to tragic results. There were two debtors of the shop (*many*, it is to be hoped, but two meriting his affectionate notice) with respect to whom he left the most opposite directions. The one was a very handsome lady ; and the rule as to *her* was that she was to have credit unlimited,—strictly unlimited. That seemed plain. The other customer, favoured by Mr. Urquiza's valedictory thoughts, was a young man, cousin to the handsome lady, and bearing the name of Reyes. This youth occupied in Mr. Urquiza's estimate the same hyperbolical rank as the handsome lady, but on the opposite side of the equation. The rule as to *him* was that he was to have *no* credit,—strictly none. In this case, also, Kate saw no difficulty ; and, when she came to know Mr. Reyes a little, she found the path of pleasure coinciding with the path of duty. Mr. Urquiza could not be more precise in laying down the rule than Kate was in enforcing it. But in the other case a scruple arose. *Unlimited* might be a word, not of Spanish law, but of Spanish rhetoric ; such as, "*Live a thousand years,*" which even annuity offices utter without a

---

[1] *Trujillo* or *Truxillo* is a coast-town of Peru, about 250 miles south from Paita.—M.

pang. Kate therefore wrote to Trujillo, expressing her honest fears, and desiring to have more definite instructions. These were positive. If the lady chose to send for the entire shop, her account was to be debited instantly with *that*. She had, however, as yet, not sent for the shop; but she began to manifest strong signs of sending for the shop*man*. Upon the blooming young Biscayan had her roving eye settled; and she was in the course of making up her mind to take Kate for a sweetheart. Poor Kate saw this with a heavy heart. And, at the same time that she had a prospect of a tender friend more than she wanted, she had become certain of an extra enemy that she wanted quite as little. What she had done to offend Mr. Reyes Kate could not guess, except as to the matter of the credit; but, then, in that she only followed her instructions. Still, Mr. Reyes was of opinion that there were two ways of executing orders. But the main offence was unintentional on Kate's part. Reyes (though as yet she did not know it) had himself been a candidate for the situation of clerk, and intended probably to keep the equation precisely as it was with respect to the allowance of credit,—only to change places with the handsome lady—keeping *her* on the negative side, himself on the affirmative: an arrangement, you know, that in the final result could have made no sort of pecuniary difference to Urquiza.

Thus stood matters when a party of vagrant comedians strolled into Paita. Kate, being a native Spaniard, ranked as one of the Paita aristocracy, and was expected to attend. She did so; and there also was the malignant Reyes. He came and seated himself purposely so as to shut out Kate from all view of the stage. She, who had nothing of the bully in her nature, and was a gentle creature when her wild Biscayan blood had not been kindled by insult, courteously requested him to move a little; upon which Reyes replied that it was not in his power to oblige the clerk as to that, but that he *could* oblige him by cutting his throat. The tiger that slept in Catalina wakened at once. She seized him, and would have executed vengeance on the spot, but that a party of young men interposed, for the present, to part them. The next day, when Kate (always ready to forget and forgive) was thinking no more of the row, Reyes passed: by spitting at the window, and other gestures insulting to Kate, again he roused her Spanish blood. Out she rushed, sword in hand; a duel began in the street; and very soon Kate's sword had passed into the heart of Reyes. Now that the mischief was done, the police were, as usual, all alive for the pleasure of avenging it. Kate found herself suddenly in a strong prison, and with small hopes of leaving it, except for execution.

12.—*From the Steps leading up to the Scaffold to the Steps leading down to Assassination*

The relatives of the dead man were potent in Paita, and clamorous for justice; so that the *corrégidor*, in a case where he saw a very poor chance of being corrupted by bribes, felt it his duty to be sublimely incorruptible. The reader knows, however, that amongst the connexions of the deceased bully was that handsome lady who differed as much from her cousin in her sentiments as to Kate as she did in the extent of her credit with Mr. Urquiza. To *her* Kate wrote a note; and, using one of the Spanish King's gold coins for bribing the jailer, got it safely delivered. That, perhaps, was unnecessary; for the lady had been already on the alert, and had summoned Urquiza from Trujillo. By some means not very luminously stated, and by paying proper fees in proper quarters, Kate was smuggled out of the prison at nightfall, and smuggled into a pretty house in the suburbs. Had she known exactly the footing she stood on as to the law, she would have been decided. As it was, she was uneasy, and jealous of mischief abroad; and, before supper, she understood it all. Urquiza briefly informed his clerk that it would be requisite for him (the clerk) to marry the handsome lady. But why? Because, said Urquiza, after talking for hours with the *corrégidor*, who was infamous for obstinacy, he had found it impossible to make him "hear reason" and release the prisoner until this compromise of marriage was suggested. But how could public justice be pacified for the clerk's unfortunate homicide of Reyes by a female cousin of the deceased man engaging to love, honour, and obey the clerk for life?

Kate could not see her way through this logic. "Nonsense, my friend," said Urquiza; "you don't comprehend. As it stands, the affair is a murder, and hanging the penalty. But, if you marry into the murdered man's house, then it becomes a little family murder—all quiet and comfortable amongst ourselves. What has the *corrégidor* to do with that? or the public either? Now, let me introduce the bride." Supper entered at that moment, and the bride immediately after. The thoughtfulness of Kate was narrowly observed, and even alluded to, but politely ascribed to the natural anxieties of a prisoner and the very imperfect state of his liberation even yet from prison *surveillance*. Kate had, indeed, never been in so trying a situation before. The anxieties of the farewell night at St. Sebastian were nothing to this; because, even if she had failed *then*, a failure might not have been always irreparable. It was but to watch and wait. But now, at this supper table, she was not more alive to the nature of the peril than she was to the fact that, if before the night closed she did not by some means escape from it, she never *would* escape with life. The deception as to her sex, though resting on no motive that pointed to these people, or at all concerned them, would be resented as if it had. The lady would regard the case as a mockery; and Urquiza would lose his opportunity of delivering himself from an imperious mistress. According to the usages of the times and country, Kate knew that within twelve hours she would be assassinated.

People of infirmer resolution would have lingered at the supper table, for the sake of putting off the evil moment of final crisis. Not so Kate. She had revolved the case on all its sides in a few minutes, and had formed her resolution. This done, she was as ready for the trial at one moment as another; and, when the lady suggested that the hardships of a prison must have made repose desirable, Kate assented, and instantly rose. A sort of procession formed, for the purpose of doing honour to the interesting guest, and escorting him in pomp to his bedroom. Kate viewed it much in the same light as that procession to which for some days she had been expecting an invitation from the *corrégidor*. Far ahead ran the servant-woman, as a sort of outrider; then came Urquiza, like a pacha of two tails, who granted two sorts of credit—viz. unlimited and none at all—bearing two wax-lights, one in each hand, and wanting only cymbals and kettle-drums to express emphatically the pathos of his Castilian strut; next came the bride, a little in advance of the clerk, but still turning obliquely towards him, and smiling graciously into his face; lastly, bringing up the rear, came the prisoner—our poor ensnared Kate—the nun, the page, the mate, the clerk, the homicide, the convict, and, for this night only, by particular desire, the bridegroom-elect.

It was Kate's fixed opinion that, if for a moment she entered any bedroom having obviously no outlet, her fate would be that of an ox once driven within the shambles. Outside, the bullock might make some defence with his horns; but, once in, with no space for turning, he is muffled and gagged. She carried her eye, therefore, like a hawk's, steady, though restless, for vigilant examination of every angle she turned. Before she entered any bedroom, she was resolved to reconnoitre it from the doorway, and, in case of necessity, show fight at once before entering, as the best chance in a crisis where all chances were bad. Everything ends; and at last the procession reached the bedroom-door, the outrider having filed off to the rear. One glance sufficed to satisfy Kate that windows there were none, and therefore no outlet for escape. Treachery appeared even in *that*; and Kate, though unfortunately without arms, was now fixed for resistance. Mr. Urquiza entered first, with a strut more than usually grandiose, and inexpressibly sublime—" Sound the trumpets! Beat the drums!" There were, as we know already, no windows; but a slight interruption to Mr. Urquiza's pompous tread showed that there were steps downwards into the room. Those, thought Kate, will suit me even better. She had watched the unlocking of the bedroom-door—she had lost nothing—she had marked that the key was left in the lock. At this moment, the beautiful lady, as one acquainted with the details of the house, turning with the air of a gracious monitress, held out her fair hand to guide Kate in careful descent of the steps. This had the air of taking out Kate to dance; and Kate, at that same moment, answering to it by the gesture of a modern waltzer, threw her arm behind the lady's waist, hurled her headlong down the steps right against Mr. Urquiza, draper and haberdasher, and then, with the speed of lightning, throwing the door *home* within its architrave, doubly locked the creditor and unlimited debtor into the rat-trap which they had prepared for herself.

The affrighted outrider fled with horror; she knew that the clerk had already committed one homicide; a second would cost him still less thought; and thus it happened that egress was left easy.

13.—*From Human Malice back again to the Malice of Winds and Waves*

But, when abroad, and free once more in the bright starry night, which way should Kate turn? The whole city would prove but one vast rap-trap for her, as bad as Mr. Urquiza's, if she was not off before morning. At a glance she comprehended that the sea was her only chance. To the port she fled. All was silent. Watchmen there were none; and she jumped into a boat. To use the oars was dangerous, for she had no means of muffling them. But she contrived to hoist a sail, pushed off with a boat-hook, and was soon stretching across the water for the mouth of the harbour, before a breeze light but favourable. Having cleared the difficulties of exit, she lay down, and unintentionally fell asleep. When she awoke, the sun had been up three or four hours; all was right otherwise; but, had she not served as a sailor, Kate would have trembled upon finding that, during her long sleep of perhaps seven or eight hours, she had lost sight of land; by what distance she could only guess; and in what direction was to some degree doubtful. All this, however, seemed a great advantage to the bold girl, throwing her thoughts back on the enemies she had left behind. The disadvantage was—having no breakfast, not even damaged biscuit; and some anxiety naturally arose as to ulterior prospects a little beyond the horizon of breakfast. But who's afraid? As sailors whistle for a wind, Catalina really had but to whistle for anything with energy, and it was sure to come. Like Cæsar to the pilot of Dyrrhachium, she might have said, for the comfort of her poor timorous boat (though a boat that in fact was destined soon to perish), "*Catalinam vehis, et fortunas ejus.*"[1] Meantime, being very doubtful as to the best course for sailing, and content if her course did but lie off shore, she "carried on," as sailors say, under easy sail,—going, in fact, just whither and just how the Pacific breezes suggested in the gentlest of whispers. *All right behind,* was Kate's opinion; and, what was better, very soon she might say, *all right ahead;* for, some hour or two before sunset, when dinner was for once becoming, even to Kate, the most interesting of subjects for meditation, suddenly a large ship began to swell upon the brilliant atmosphere. In those latitudes, and in those years, any ship was pretty sure to be Spanish: sixty years later, the odds were in favour of its being an English buccaneer; which would have given a new direction to Kate's energy. Kate continued to make signals with a handkerchief whiter than the crocodile's of Ann. Dom. 1592; else it would hardly have been noticed. Perhaps, after all, it would not, but that the ship's course carried her very nearly across Kate's. The stranger lay to for her. It was dark by the time Kate steered herself under the ship's quarter; and *then* was seen an instance of this girl's eternal wakefulness. Something was painted on the stern of her boat, she could not see *what*; but she judged that, whatever this might be, it would express some connexion with the port that she had just quitted. Now, it was her wish to break the chain of traces connecting her with such a scamp as Urquiza; since, else, through his commercial correspondence, he might disperse over Peru a portrait of herself by no means flattering. How should she accomplish this? It was dark; and she stood, as you may see an Etonian do at times, rocking her little boat from side to side, until it had taken in water as much as might be agreeable. Too much it proved for the boat's constitution, and the boat perished of dropsy—Kate declining to tap it. She got a ducking herself; but what cared she? Up the ship's side she went, as gaily as ever, in those years when she was called pussy, she had raced after the nuns of St. Sebastian; jumped

[1] "You carry Catalina, and her fortunes."—M.

upon deck, and told the first lieutenant, when he questioned her about her adventures, quite as much truth as any man, under the rank of admiral, had a right to expect.

14.—*Bright Gleams of Sunshine*

This ship was full of recruits for the Spanish army, and bound to Concepcion.[1] Even in that destiny was an iteration, or repeating memorial, of the significance that ran through Catalina's most casual adventures. She had enlisted amongst the soldiers; and, on reaching port, the very first person who came off from shore was a dashing young military officer, whom at once, by his name and rank (though she had never consciously seen him), she identified as her own brother. He was splendidly situated in the service, being the Governor-General's secretary, besides his rank as a cavalry officer; and, his errand on board being to inspect the recruits, naturally, on reading in the roll one of them described as a Biscayan, the ardent young man came up with high-bred courtesy to Catalina, took the young recruit's hand with kindness, feeling that to be a compatriot at so great a distance was to be a sort of relative, and asked with emotion after old boyish remembrances. There was a scriptural pathos in what followed, as if it were some scene of domestic reunion opening itself from patriarchal ages. The young officer was the eldest son of the house, and had left Spain when Catalina was only three years old. But, singularly enough, Catalina it was, the little wild cat that he yet remembered seeing at St. Sebastian's, upon whom his earliest inquiries settled. "Did the recruit know his family, the De Erausos?" Oh yes; everybody knew *them*. "Did the recruit know little Catalina?" Catalina smiled as she replied that she did; and gave such an animated description of the little fiery wretch as made the officer's eye flash with gratified tenderness, and with certainty that the recruit was no counterfeit Biscayan. Indeed, you know, if Kate couldn't give a good description of "pussy," *who* could? The issue of the interview was that the officer insisted on Kate's making a home

[1] "*Concepcion*":—On the coast of Chili, some 2400 miles south from Paita, on the shore of the Pacific.—M.

of his quarters. He did other services for his unknown sister. He placed her as a trooper in his own regiment, and favoured her in many a way that is open to one having authority. But the person, after all, that did most to serve our Kate, was Kate. War was then raging with Indians, both from Chili and Peru. Kate had always done her duty in action; but at length, in the decisive battle of Puren, there was an opening for doing something more. Havoc had been made of her own squadron; most of the officers were killed, and the standard was carried off. Kate gathered around her a small party—galloped after the Indian column that was carrying away the trophy—charged—saw all her own party killed—but, in spite of wounds on her face and shoulder, succeeded in bearing away the recovered standard. She rode up to the general and his staff; she dismounted; she rendered up her prize; and fainted away, much less from the blinding blood than from the tears of joy which dimmed her eyes as the general, waving his sword in admiration over her head, pronounced our Kate on the spot an *Alférez*,[1] or standard-bearer, with a commission from the King of Spain and the Indies. Bonny Kate! noble Kate! I would there were not two centuries laid between us, so that I might have the pleasure of kissing thy fair hand.

15.—*The Sunshine is Overcast*

Kate had the good sense to see the danger of revealing her sex, or her relationship, even to her own brother. The grasp of the Church never relaxed, never "prescribed," unless freely and by choice. The nun, if discovered, would have been taken out of the horse-barracks or the dragoon-saddle. She had the firmness, therefore, for many years, to resist the sisterly impulses that sometimes suggested such a confidence. For years, and those years the most important of her life—the years that developed her character—she lived undetected as a brilliant cavalry officer, under her brother's patronage. And the bitterest grief in poor Kate's whole life was the tragical (and, were it not fully attested,

---

[1] "*Alférez*":—This rank in the Spanish army is, or was, on a level with the modern *sous-lieutenant* of France.

one might say the ultra-scenical) event that dissolved their long connexion. Let me spend a word of apology on poor Kate's errors. We all commit many; both you and I, reader. No, stop; that's not civil. You, reader, I know, are a saint; I am *not*, though very near it. I *do* err at long intervals; and then I think with indulgence of the many circumstances that plead for this poor girl. The Spanish armies of that day inherited, from the days of Cortez and Pizarro, shining remembrances of martial prowess, and the very worst of ethics. To think little of bloodshed, to quarrel, to fight, to gamble, to plunder, belonged to the very atmosphere of a camp, to its indolence, to its ancient traditions. In your own defence, you were obliged to do such things. Besides all these grounds of evil, the Spanish army had just then an extra demoralisation from a war with savages— faithless and bloody. Do not think too much, reader, of killing a man—do not, I beseech you! That word "*kill*" is sprinkled over every page of Kate's own autobiography. It ought not to be read by the light of these days. Yet, how if a man that she killed were —— ? Hush! It was sad; but is better hurried over in a few words. Years after this period, a young officer, one day dining with Kate, entreated her to become his second in a duel. Such things were everyday affairs. However, Kate had reasons for declining the service, and did so. But the officer, as he was sullenly departing, said that, if he were killed (as he thought he *should* be), his death would lie at Kate's door. I do not take *his* view of the case, and am not moved by his rhetoric or his logic. Kate *was*, and relented. The duel was fixed for eleven at night, under the walls of a monastery. Unhappily, the night proved unusually dark, so that the two principals had to tie white handkerchiefs round their elbows, in order to descry each other. In the confusion they wounded each other mortally. Upon that, according to a usage not peculiar to Spaniards, but extending (as doubtless the reader knows) for a century longer to our own countrymen, the two seconds were obliged in honour to do something towards avenging their principals. Kate had her usual fatal luck. Her sword passed sheer through the body of her opponent: this unknown opponent, falling dead, had just breath left to cry out, "Ah, villain! you have killed me!" in a voice of horrific reproach; and the voice was the voice of her brother!

The monks of the monastery under whose silent shadows this murderous duel had taken place, roused by the clashing of swords and the angry shouts of combatants, issued out with torches, to find one only of the four officers surviving. Every convent and altar had the right of asylum for a short period. According to the custom, the monks carried Kate, insensible with anguish of mind, to the sanctuary of their chapel. There for some days they detained her; but then, having furnished her with a horse and some provisions, they turned her adrift. Which way should the unhappy fugitive turn? In blindness of heart, she turned towards the sea. It was the sea that had brought her to Peru; it was the sea that would perhaps carry her away. It was the sea that had first shown her this land and its golden hopes; it was the sea that ought to hide from her its fearful remembrances.[1] The sea it was that had twice spared her life in extremities; the sea it was that might now, if it chose, take back the bauble that it had spared in vain.

16.—*Kate's Ascent of the Andes*

Three days our poor heroine followed the coast.[2] Her horse was then almost unable to move; and on *his* account

[1] De Quincey seems to have forgotten that Kate was not now in Peru, but in Chili. Although the fightings with the Indians in which she had been engaged during the years that had elapsed since her arrival at the Chilian town of Concepcion may have carried her far enough north in Chili from that town, they could hardly have taken her back into Peru. So one fancies at least; for all has been left to fancy. The geography of the last few pages, telling the story of Kate's years of military service as a cavalry-officer under her brother, has been singularly vague. We have certainly been in the Spanish Indies all the while, but whether in Chili or Peru, or in both, we have not known, and have not inquired. The chronology is as vague as the geography; but Kate must have been ten or twelve years in South America by this time, and has to be imagined as about thirty years of age, more or less, at this point of her story.—M.

[2] It becomes necessary here to have some more definite conception of that matter of Kate's whereabouts at this time which has been mooted in the last note. Kate was about to commence her great feat of the ascent of the Andes; but the Andes are a mountain-chain, 4500

she turned inland to a thicket, for grass and shelter. As she drew near to it, a voice challenged, "*Who goes there?*"—Kate answered, "*Spain.*"—"*What people?*"—"*A friend.*" It was two soldiers, deserters, and almost starving. Kate shared her provisions with these men; and, on hearing their plan, which was to go over the Cordilleras,[1] she agreed to join the party. *Their* object was the wild one of seeking the river *Dorado*, whose waters rolled along golden sands, and whose pebbles were emeralds. *Hers* was to throw herself upon a line the least liable to pursuit, and the readiest for a new chapter of life, in which oblivion might be found for the past. After a few days of incessant climbing and fatigue, they found themselves in the regions of perpetual snow. Summer came even hither; but came as vainly to this kingdom of frost as to the grave of her brother. No fire but the fire of human blood in youthful veins could ever be kept burning in these aerial solitudes. Fuel was rarely to be found, and kindling a fire by interfriction of dry sticks was a secret almost exclusively Indian. However, our Kate can do everything; and she's the girl, if ever girl *did* such a thing, that I back at any odds for crossing the Cordilleras. I would bet you something now, reader, if I thought you would deposit your stakes by return of post (as they play at chess through the post-office), that Kate does the trick; that she gets down to the other side; that the soldiers do *not*; and that the horse, if preserved at all, is preserved in a way that will leave him very little to boast of.

The party had gathered wild berries and esculent roots at the foot of the mountains, and the horse was of very great use in carrying them. But this larder was soon emptied.

miles long, running parallel with the Pacific through the whole extent of the South American Continent from Panama to Patagonia. At what point in this vast range was Kate about to make the ascent? De Quincey is at his ease on the subject, and gives us no information. From evidence which will appear in the sequel, however, we have to assume that it was over the northern portion of the Chilian Andes that Kate's ascent was to be made. Accordingly, if any reader should think it worth his while to follow the poor girl's adventures on the map, he must imagine the piece of sea-shore along which she is now wandering, before her ascent begins, to be the northern coast of Chili.—M.

[1] "*Cordilleras*":—A general word for any mountain chain in Spanish America; applied here specifically to the Andes.—M.

There was nothing then to carry; so that the horse's value, as a beast of burden, fell cent per cent. In fact, very soon he could not carry himself, and it became easy to calculate when he would reach the bottom on the wrong side the Cordilleras. He took three steps back for one upwards. A council of war being held, the small army resolved to slaughter their horse. He, though a member of the expedition, had no vote; and, if he had, the votes would have stood three to one—majority, two against him. He was cut into quarters —a difficult fraction to distribute amongst a triad of claimants. No saltpetre or sugar could be had; but the frost was antiseptic. And the horse was preserved in as useful a sense as ever apricots were preserved, or strawberries; and *that* was the kind of preservation which one page ago I promised to the horse.

On a fire painfully devised out of broom and withered leaves a horse-steak was dressed; for drink, snow was allowed *à discretion*. This ought to have revived the party; and Kate, perhaps, it *did*. But the poor deserters were thinly clad, and they had not the boiling heart of Catalina. More and more they drooped. Kate did her best to cheer them. But the march was nearly at an end for *them*; and they were going, in one half-hour, to receive their last billet. Yet, before this consummation, they have a strange spectacle to see—such as few places could show but the upper chambers of the Cordilleras. They had reached a billowy scene of rocky masses, large and small, looking shockingly black on their perpendicular sides as they rose out of the vast snowy expanse. Upon the highest of these that was accessible Kate mounted to look around her, and she saw—oh, rapture at such an hour!—a man sitting on a shelf of rock, with a gun by his side. Joyously she shouted to her comrades, and ran down to communicate the good news. Here was a sportsman, watching, perhaps, for an eagle; and now they would have relief. One man's cheek kindled with the hectic of sudden joy, and he rose eagerly to march. The other was fast sinking under the fatal sleep that frost sends before herself as her merciful minister of death; but, hearing in his dream the tidings of relief, and assisted by his friends, he also staggeringly arose. It could not be three minutes' walk,

Kate thought, to the station of the sportsman. That thought supported them all. Under Kate's guidance, who had taken a sailor's glance at the bearings, they soon unthreaded the labyrinth of rocks so far as to bring the man within view. He had not left his resting-place; their steps on the soundless snow, naturally, he could not hear; and, as their road brought them upon him from the rear, still less could he see them. Kate hailed him; but so keenly was he absorbed in some speculation, or in the object of his watching, that he took no notice of them, not even moving his head. Coming close behind him, Kate touched his shoulder, and said, "My friend, are you sleeping?" Yes, he *was* sleeping—sleeping the sleep from which there is no awaking; and, the slight touch of Kate having disturbed the equilibrium of the corpse, down it rolled on the snow: the frozen body rang like a hollow iron cylinder; the face uppermost, and blue with mould, mouth open, teeth ghastly and bleaching in the frost, and a frightful grin upon the lips. This dreadful spectacle finished the struggles of the weaker man, who sank and died at once. The other made an effort with so much spirit that, in Kate's opinion, horror had acted upon him beneficially as a stimulant. But it was not really so. It was simply a spasm of morbid strength. A collapse succeeded; his blood began to freeze; he sat down in spite of Kate, and *he* also died without further struggle. Yes, gone are the poor suffering deserters; stretched out and bleaching upon the snow; and insulted discipline is avenged. Great kings have long arms; and sycophants are ever at hand for the errand of the potent. What had frost and snow to do with the quarrel? Yet *they* made themselves sycophantic servants to the King of Spain; and *they* it was that dogged his deserters up to the summit of the Cordilleras, more surely than any Spanish bloodhound, or any Spanish tirailleur's bullet.

17.—*Kate stands alone on the Summit of the Andes*

Now is our Kate standing alone on the summits of the Andes, and in solitude that is frightful, for she is alone with her own afflicted conscience. Twice before she had stood in solitude as deep upon the wild, wild waters of the Pacific;

but her conscience had been then untroubled. Now is there nobody left that can help; her horse is dead—the soldiers are dead. There is nobody that she can speak to, except God; and very soon you will find that she *does* speak to Him; for already on these vast aerial deserts He has been whispering to *her*. The condition of Kate in some respects resembled that of Coleridge's *Ancient Mariner*. But possibly, reader, you may be amongst the many careless readers that have never fully understood what that condition was. Suffer me to enlighten you; else you ruin the story of the mariner, and, by losing all its pathos, lose half its beauty.

There are three readers of the *Ancient Mariner*. The first is gross enough to fancy all the imagery of the mariner's visions delivered by the poet for actual facts of experience; which being impossible, the whole pulverises, for that reader, into a baseless fairy tale. The second reader is wiser than *that*; he knows that the imagery is the imagery of febrile delirium; really seen, but not seen as an external reality. The mariner had caught the pestilential fever which carried off all his mates; he only had survived. the delirium had vanished; but the visions that had haunted the delirium remained. "Yes," says the third reader, "they remained; naturally they did, being scorched by fever into his brain; but how did they happen to remain on his belief as gospel truths? The delirium had vanished; why had not the painted scenery of the delirium vanished except as visionary memorials of a sorrow that was cancelled? Why was it that craziness settled upon this mariner's brain, driving him, as if he were a Cain, or another Wandering Jew, to 'pass like night from land to land,' and, at certain intervals, wrenching him until he made rehearsal of his errors, even at the difficult cost of 'holding children from their play, and old men from the chimney corner'?"[1] That craziness, as the *third* reader deciphers, rose out of a deeper soil than any bodily affection. It had its root in penitential sorrow. Oh, bitter is the sorrow to a conscientious heart, when, too late, it discovers the depth of a love that has been trampled under foot! This mariner had slain the creature that, on all the earth, loved him best. In the dark-

[1] The beautiful words of Sir Philip Sidney, in his *Defense of Poesy*.

ness of his cruel superstition he had done it, to save his human brothers from a fancied inconvenience ; and yet, by that very act of cruelty, he had himself called destruction upon their heads. The Nemesis that followed punished *him* through *them*—him that wronged through those that wrongfully he sought to benefit. That spirit who watches over the sanctities of love is a strong angel—is a jealous angel ; and this angel it was

> "That loved the bird that loved the man
> That shot him with his bow."

He it was that followed the cruel archer into silent and slumbering seas .—

> "Nine fathom deep he had followed him,
> Through the realms of mist and snow."

This jealous angel it was that pursued the man into noonday darkness and the vision of dying oceans, into delirium, and finally (when recovered from disease) into an unsettled mind.

Not altogether unlike, though free from the criminal intention of the mariner, had been the offence of Kate ; not unlike, also, was the punishment that now is dogging her steps. She, like the mariner, had slain the one sole creature that loved her upon the whole wide earth ; she, like the mariner, for this offence, had been hunted into frost and snow—very soon will be hunted into delirium ; and from *that* (if she escapes with life) will be hunted into the trouble of a heart that cannot rest. There was the excuse of one darkness, physical darkness, for *her* ; there was the excuse of another darkness, the darkness of superstition, for the mariner. But, with all the excuses that earth, and the darkness of earth, can furnish, bitter it would be for any of us, reader, through every hour of life, waking or dreaming, to look back upon one fatal moment when we had pierced the heart that would have died for *us*. In this only the darkness had been merciful to Kate—that it had hidden for ever from her victim the hand that slew him. But now, in such utter solitude, her thoughts ran back to their earliest interview. She remembered with anguish how, on touching the shores of America, almost the first word that met her ear had been from *him*, the brother whom she had killed, about the "pussy" of times long past; how the gallant young man had hung upon her words, as in her native Basque she described her own mischievous little self, of twelve years back; how his colour went and came whilst his loving memory of the little sister was revived by her own descriptive traits, giving back, as in a mirror, the fawn-like grace, the squirrel-like restlessness, that once had kindled his own delighted laughter; how he would take no denial, but showed on the spot that simply to have touched—to have kissed—to have played with—the little wild thing that glorified by her innocence the gloom of St. Sebastian's cloisters, gave a *right* to his hospitality; how through *him* only she had found a welcome in camps; how through *him* she had found the avenue to honour and distinction. And yet this brother, so loving and generous, who, without knowing, had cherished and protected her, and all from pure holy love for herself as the innocent plaything of St. Sebastian's, *him* in a moment she had dismissed from life. She paused; she turned round, as if looking back for his grave; she saw the dreadful wildernesses of snow which already she had traversed. Silent they were at this season, even as in the panting heats of noon the Saharas of the torrid zone are oftentimes silent. Dreadful was the silence; it was the nearest thing to the silence of the grave. Graves were at the foot of the Andes,—*that* she knew too well; graves were at the summit of the Andes,—*that* she saw too well. And, as she gazed, a sudden thought flashed upon her, when her eyes settled upon the corpses of the poor deserters, —Could she, like *them*, have been all this while unconsciously executing judgment upon herself? Running from a wrath that was doubtful, into the very jaws of a wrath that was inexorable? Flying in panic—and behold! there was no man that pursued? For the first time in her life, Kate trembled. *Not* for the first time, Kate wept. Far less for the first time was it that Kate bent her knee—that Kate clasped her hands— that Kate prayed. But it *was* the first time that she prayed as *they* pray for whom no more hope is left but in prayer.

Here let me pause a moment, for the sake of making somebody angry. A Frenchman who sadly misjudges Kate, looking at her through a Parisian opera-glass, gives it as *his* opinion that, because Kate first *records* her prayer on this occasion, therefore now first of all she prayed.[1] *I* think not so. *I* love this Kate, bloodstained as she is; and I could not love a woman that never bent her knee in thankfulness or in supplication. However, we have all a right to our own little opinion; and it is not *you*, "*mon cher*," you Frenchman, that I am angry with, but somebody else that stands behind you. You, Frenchman, and your compatriots, I love oftentimes for your festal gaiety of heart; and I quarrel only with your levity, and that eternal worldliness that freezes too fiercely—that absolutely blisters with its frost, like the upper air of the Andes. *You* speak of Kate only as too readily you speak of all women; the instinct of a natural scepticism being to scoff at all hidden depths of truth. Else you are civil enough to Kate; and your "*homage*" (such as it may happen to be) is always at the service of a woman on the shortest notice. But behind *you* I see a worse fellow—a gloomy fanatic, a religious sycophant, that seeks to propitiate his circle by bitterness against the offences that are most unlike his own. And against him I must say one word for Kate to the too hasty reader. This villain opens his fire on our Kate under shelter of a lie. For there is a standing lie in the very constitution of civil society—a *necessity* of error, misleading us as to the proportions of crime. Mere necessity obliges man to create many acts into felonies, and to punish them as the heaviest offences, which his better sense teaches him secretly to regard as perhaps among the lightest. Those poor mutineers or deserters, for instance, were they necessarily without excuse? They might have been oppressively used; but, in critical times of war, no matter for the individual palliations, the mutineer *must* be shot: there is no help for it,—as, in extremities of general famine, we shoot the man (alas! we are *obliged* to shoot him) that is found robbing the common stores in order to feed his own perishing children, though the offence is hardly visible in the sight of God. Only blockheads adjust their scale of guilt to the scale of human punishments. Now, our wicked friend the fanatic, who calumniates Kate, abuses the advantage which, for such a purpose, he derives from

[1] Who this Frenchman was will appear from the Appended Editorial Note —M.

the exaggerated social estimate of all violence. Personal security being so main an object of social union, we are obliged to frown upon all modes of violence, as hostile to the central principle of that union. We are *obliged* to rate it according to the universal results towards which it tends, and scarcely at all according to the special condition of circumstances in which it may originate. Hence a horror arises for that class of offences, which is (philosophically speaking) exaggerated; and, by daily use, the ethics of a police-office translate themselves insensibly into the ethics even of religious people. But I tell that sycophantish fanatic —not this only, viz. that he abuses unfairly against Kate the advantage which he has from the *inevitably* distorted bias of society; but also I tell him this second little thing,— that, upon turning away the glass from that one obvious aspect of Kate's character, her too fiery disposition to vindicate all rights by violence, and viewing her in relation to *general* religious capacities, she was a thousand times more promisingly endowed than himself. It is impossible to be noble in many things without having many points of contact with true religion. If you deny *that*, you it is that calumniate religion. Kate *was* noble in many things. Her worst errors never took a shape of self-interest or deceit. She was brave, she was generous, she was forgiving, she bore no malice, she was full of truth—qualities that God loves either in man or woman. She hated sycophants and dissemblers. *I* hate them; and more than ever at this moment on her behalf. I wish she were but here, to give a punch on the head to that fellow who traduces her. And, coming round again to the occasion from which this short digression has started—viz. the question raised by the Frenchman, whether Kate were a person likely to *pray* under other circumstances than those of extreme danger—I offer it as *my* opinion that she was. Violent people are not always such from choice, but perhaps from situation. And, though the circumstances of Kate's position allowed her little means for realising her own wishes, it is certain that those wishes pointed continually to peace and an unworldly happiness, if *that* were possible. The stormy clouds that enveloped her in camps opened overhead at intervals, showing her a far-distant blue serene. She yearned, at many times, for the rest which is not in camps or armies; and it is certain that she ever combined with any plans or day-dreams of tranquillity, as their most essential ally, some aid derived from that dove-like religion which, at St. Sebastian's, from her infant days, she had been taught so profoundly to adore.

18.—*Kate begins to descend the Mighty Staircase*

Now, let us rise from this discussion of Kate against libellers, as Kate herself is rising from prayer, and consider, in conjunction with *her*, the character and promise of that dreadful ground which lies immediately before her. What is to be thought of it? I could wish we had a theodolite here, and a spirit-level, and other instruments, for settling some important questions. Yet, no: on consideration, if one *had* a wish allowed by that kind fairy without whose assistance it would be quite impossible to send even for the spirit-level, nobody would throw away the wish upon things so paltry. I would not put the fairy upon such an errand: I would order the good creature to bring no spirit-level, but a stiff glass of spirits for Kate; also, next after which, I would request a palanquin, and relays of fifty stout bearers —all drunk, in order that they might not feel the cold. The main interest at this moment, and the main difficulty— indeed, the "open question" of the case—was, to ascertain whether the ascent were yet accomplished or not, and when would the descent commence? or had it, perhaps, long commenced? The character of the ground, in those immediate successions that could be connected by the eye, decided nothing; for the undulations of the level had been so continual for miles as to perplex any eye, even an engineer's, in attempting to judge whether, upon the whole, the tendency were upwards or downwards. Possibly it was yet neither way. It is indeed probable that Kate had been for some time travelling along a series of terraces that traversed the whole breadth of the topmost area at that point of crossing the Cordilleras; and this area, perhaps, but not certainly, might compensate any casual tendencies downwards by corresponding reascents. Then came the question, how long would these terraces yet continue? and had the ascending parts *really* balanced the descending? Upon *that* seemed to rest the final chance for Kate. Because, unless she very soon reached a lower level and a warmer atmosphere, mere weariness would oblige her to lie down, under a fierceness of cold that would not suffer her to rise after once losing the warmth of motion; or, inversely, if she even continued in motion, continued extremity of cold would, of itself, speedily absorb the little surplus energy for moving which yet remained unexhausted by weariness: that is, in short, the excessive weariness would give a murderous advantage to the cold, or the excessive cold would give a corresponding advantage to the weariness.

At this stage of her progress, and whilst the agonising question seemed yet as indeterminate as ever, Kate's struggle with despair, which had been greatly soothed by the fervour of her prayer, revolved upon her in deadlier blackness. All turned, she saw, upon a race against time and the arrears of the road; and she, poor thing! how little qualified could *she* be, in such a condition, for a race of any kind—and against two such obstinate brutes as Time and Space! This hour of the progress, this noontide of Kate's struggle, must have been the very crisis of the whole. Despair was rapidly tending to ratify itself. Hope, in any degree, would be a cordial for sustaining her efforts. But to flounder along a dreadful chaos of snow-drifts, or snow-chasms, towards a point of rock which, being turned, should expose only another interminable succession of the same character— might *that* be endured by ebbing spirits, by stiffening limbs, by the ghastly darkness that was now beginning to gather upon the inner eye? And, if once despair became triumphant, all the little arrear of physical strength would collapse at once.

Oh! verdure of human fields, cottages of men and women (that now suddenly, in the eyes of Kate, seemed all brothers and sisters), cottages with children around them at play, that are so far below—oh! spring and summer, blossoms and flowers, to which, as to *his* symbols, God has given the gorgeous privilege of rehearsing for ever upon earth his most mysterious perfection—Life, and the resurrections of Life—

is it indeed true that poor Kate must never see you more
Mutteringly she put that question to herself. But strange
are the caprices of ebb and flow in the deep fountains of
human sensibilities. At this very moment, when the utter
incapacitation of despair was gathering fast at Kate's heart,
a sudden lightening, as it were, or flashing inspiration of
hope, shot far into her spirit, a reflux almost supernatural
from the earliest effects of her prayer. Dimmed and confused had been the accuracy of her sensations for hours; but
all at once a strong conviction came over her that more
and more was the sense of descent becoming steady and con-
tinuous. Turning round to measure backwards with her eye
the ground traversed through the last half-hour, she identified, by a remarkable point of rock, the spot near which the
three corpses were lying. The silence seemed deeper than
ever. Neither was there any phantom memorial of life for
the eye or for the ear, nor wing of bird, nor echo, nor green
leaf, nor creeping thing that moved or stirred, upon the
soundless waste. Oh, what a relief to this burden of silence
would be a human groan! Here seemed a motive for still
darker despair. And yet, at that very moment, a pulse of
joy began to thaw the ice at her heart. It struck her, as she
reviewed the ground from that point where the corpses lay,
that undoubtedly it had been for some time slowly descending. Her senses were much dulled by suffering; but this
thought it was, suggested by a sudden apprehension of a continued descending movement, which had caused her to turn
round. Sight had confirmed the suggestion first derived
from her own steps. The distance attained was now sufficient
to establish the tendency. Oh, yes, yes; to a certainty she
was descending—she *had* been descending for some time.
Frightful was the spasm of joy which whispered that the
worst was over. It was as when the shadow of midnight,
that murderers had relied on, is passing away from your beleaguered shelter, and dawn will soon be manifest. It was as
when a flood, that all day long has raved against the walls
of your house, ceases (you suddenly think) to rise; yes!
measured by a golden plummet, it *is* sinking beyond a
doubt, and the darlings of your household are saved. Kate
faced round in agitation to her proper direction. She saw,

what previously, in her stunning confusion, she had *not* seen, that hardly two stonethrows in advance lay a mass of rock, split as into a gateway. Through that opening it now became certain that the road was lying. Hurrying forward, she passed within these natural gates. Gates of paradise they were. Ah, what a vista did that gateway expose before her dazzled eye! what a revelation of heavenly promise! Full two miles long, stretched a long narrow glen, everywhere descending, and in many parts rapidly. All was now placed beyond a doubt. She *was* descending,—for hours, perhaps, *had* been descending insensibly,—the mighty staircase. Yes, Kate is leaving behind her the kingdom of frost and the victories of death. Two miles farther, there may be rest, if there is not shelter. And very soon, as the crest of her new-born happiness, she distinguished at the other end of that rocky vista a pavilion-shaped mass of dark green foliage—a belt of trees, such as we see in the lovely parks of England, but islanded by a screen of thick bushy undergrowth! Oh! verdure of dark olive foliage, offered suddenly to fainting eyes, as if by some winged patriarchal herald of wrath relenting—solitary Arab's tent, rising with saintly signals of peace in the dreadful desert—must Kate indeed die even yet, whilst she sees but cannot reach you? Outpost on the frontier of man's dominions, standing within life, but looking out upon everlasting death, wilt thou hold up the anguish of thy mocking invitation only to betray? Never, perhaps, in this world was the line so exquisitely grazed that parts salvation and ruin. As the dove to her dovecot from the swooping hawk—as the Christian pinnace to the shelter of Christian batteries from the bloody Mahometan corsair—so flew, so tried to fly, towards the anchoring thickets, that, alas! could not weigh their anchors, and make sail to meet her, the poor exhausted Kate from the vengeance of pursuing frost.

And she reached them; staggering, fainting, reeling, she entered beneath the canopy of umbrageous trees. But, as oftentimes the Hebrew fugitive to a city of refuge, flying for his life before the avenger of blood, was pressed so hotly that, on entering the archway of what seemed to *him* the heavenly city gate, as he kneeled in deep thankfulness to kiss its holy merciful shadow, he could not rise again, but sank instantly with infant weakness into sleep—sometimes to wake no more; so sank, so collapsed upon the ground, without power to choose her couch, and with little prospect of ever rising again to her feet, the martial nun. She lay as luck had ordered it, with her head screened by the undergrowth of bushes from any gales that might arise; she lay exactly as she sank, with her eyes up to heaven. and thus it was that the nun saw, before falling asleep, the two sights that upon earth are the fittest for the closing eyes of a nun, whether destined to open again or to close for ever. She saw the interlacing of boughs overhead forming a dome that seemed like the dome of a cathedral. She saw, through the fretwork of the foliage, another dome, far beyond the dome of an evening sky, the dome of some heavenly cathedral, not built with hands. She saw upon this upper dome the vesper lights, all alive with pathetic grandeur of colouring from a sunset that had just been rolling down like a chorus. She had not till now consciously observed the time of day; whether it were morning, or whether it were afternoon, in the confusion of her misery, she had not distinctly known. But now she whispered to herself, "*It is evening*"; and what lurked half unconsciously in these words might be, "The sun, that rejoices, has finished his daily toil; man, that labours, has finished *his*; I, that suffer, have finished mine." That might be what she thought; but what she *said* was "It is evening; and the hour is come when the *Angelus* is sounding through St. Sebastian." What made her think of St. Sebastian, so far away in the depth of space and time? Her brain was wandering, now that her feet were *not*; and, because her eyes had descended from the heavenly to the earthly dome, *that* made her think of earthly cathedrals, and of cathedral choirs, and of St. Sebastian's chapel, with its silvery bells that carried the echoing *Angelus* far into mountain recesses. Perhaps, as her wanderings increased, she thought herself back into childhood; became "pussy" once again; fancied that all since then was a frightful dream; that she was not upon the dreadful Andes, but still kneeling in the holy chapel at vespers; still innocent as then; loved as then she had been loved; and that all men were liars who said her hand was ever stained with blood. Little is mentioned of the delusions which possessed her; but that little gives a key to the impulse which her palpitating heart obeyed, and which her rambling brain for ever reproduced in multiplying mirrors. Restlessness kept her in waking dreams for a brief half-hour. But then fever and delirium would wait no longer; the killing exhaustion would no longer be refused; the fever, the delirium, and the exhaustion, swept in together with power like an army with banners; and the nun ceased through the gathering twilight any more to watch the cathedrals of earth, or the more solemn cathedrals that rose in the heavens above.

19.—*Kate's Bedroom is invaded by Horsemen*

All night long she slept in her verdurous St. Bernard's hospice without awaking; and whether she would *ever* awake seemed to depend upon accident. The slumber that towered above her brain was like that fluctuating silvery column which stands in scientific tubes, sinking, rising, deepening, lightening, contracting, expanding; or like the mist that sits, through sultry afternoons, upon the river of the American St. Peter, sometimes rarefying for minutes into sunny gauze, sometimes condensing for hours into palls of funeral darkness. You fancy that, after twelve hours of *any* sleep, she must have been refreshed; better, at least, than she was last night. Ah! but sleep is not always sent upon missions of refreshment. Sleep is sometimes the secret chamber in which death arranges his machinery, and stations his artillery. Sleep is sometimes that deep mysterious atmosphere in which the human spirit is slowly unsettling its wings for flight from earthly tenements. It is now eight o'clock in the morning; and, to all appearance, if Kate should receive no aid before noon, when next the sun is departing to his rest, then, alas! Kate will be departing to hers: when next the sun is holding out his golden Christian signal to man that the hour is come for letting his anger go down, Kate will be sleeping away for ever into the arms of brotherly forgiveness.

What is wanted just now for Kate, supposing Kate herself to be wanted by this world, is that this world would be kind enough to send her a little brandy before it is too late. The simple truth was, and a truth which I have known to take place in more ladies than Kate,—who died or did *not* die, accordingly as they had or had not an adviser like myself, capable of giving an opinion equal to Captain Bunsby's [1] on this point—viz. whether the jewelly star of life had descended too far down the arch towards setting for any chance of reascending by *spontaneous* effort. The fire was still burning in secret, but needed, perhaps, to be rekindled by potent artificial breath. It lingered, and *might* linger, but apparently would never culminate again without some stimulus from earthly vineyards.[2] Kate was ever lucky, though ever unfortunate; and the world, being of my opinion that Kate was worth saving, made up its mind about half-past eight o'clock in the morning to save her. Just at that time, when the night was over, and its sufferings were hidden—in one

---

[1] The sage Captain Bunsby in Dickens's *Dombey & Son*.—M.

[2] Though not exactly in the same circumstances as Kate, or sleeping, *à la belle étoile*, on a declivity of the Andes, I have known (or heard circumstantially reported) the cases of many ladies, besides Kate, who were in precisely the same critical danger of perishing for want of a little brandy. A dessert-spoonful or two would have saved them. Avaunt! you wicked "Temperance" medalist! repent as fast as ever you can, or, perhaps, the next time we hear of you, *anasarca* and *hydrothorax* will be running after you, to punish your shocking excesses in water. Seriously, the case is one of constant recurrence, and constantly ending fatally from *unseasonable* and pedantic rigour of temperance. Dr. Darwin, the famous author of *Zoonomia, The Botanic Garden*, &c., sacrificed his life to the very pedantry and superstition of temperance, by refusing a glass of brandy, in obedience to a system, at a moment when (according to the opinion of all around him) one single glass would have saved his life. The fact is that the medical profession composes the most generous and liberal body of men amongst us,—taken generally, by much the most enlightened; but, professionally, the most timid. Want of boldness in the administration of opium, &c., though they can be bold enough with mercury, is their besetting infirmity. And from this infirmity females suffer most. One instance I need hardly mention,—the fatal case of an august lady mourned by nations [the Princess Charlotte, who died in childbirth 6th Nov. 1817—M.]; with respect to whom it was, and is, the belief of multitudes to this hour (well able to judge) that she would have been saved by a glass of brandy; and her chief medical attendant, Sir R. C. [Sir Richard Croft—M.], who shot himself, came to think so too late—too late for *her*, and too late for himself. Amongst many cases of the same nature which personally I have been acquainted with, thirty years ago, a man illustrious for his intellectual

of those intermitting gleams that for a moment or two
lightened the clouds of her slumber—Kate's dull ear caught
a sound that for years had spoken a familiar language to
her. What was it? It was the sound, though muffled and
deadened, like the ear that heard it, of horsemen advancing.
Interpreted by the tumultuous dreams of Kate, was it the
cavalry of Spain, at whose head so often she had charged the
bloody Indian scalpers? Was it, according to the legend of
ancient days, cavalry that had been sown by her brother's
blood—cavalry that rose from the ground on an inquest of
retribution, and were racing up the Andes to seize her?
Her dreams, that had opened sullenly to the sound, waited
for no answer, but closed again into pompous darkness.
Happily, the horsemen had caught the glimpse of some bright
ornament, clasp or aiguillette, on Kate's dress. They were

---

accomplishments[1] mentioned to me that his own wife, during her first
or second confinement, was suddenly reported to him, by one of her
female attendants (who slipped away unobserved by the medical
people), as undoubtedly sinking fast. He hurried to her chamber, and
saw that it was so. On this, he suggested earnestly some stimulant
—laudanum or alcohol. The presiding medical authority, however,
was inexorable. "Oh, by no means," shaking his ambrosial wig;
"any stimulant at this crisis would be fatal." But no authority
could overrule the concurrent testimony of all symptoms, and of all
unprofessional opinions. By some pious falsehood, my friend smuggled
the doctor out of the room, and immediately smuggled a glass of
brandy into the poor lady's lips. She recovered as if under the
immediate afflatus of magic; so sudden was her recovery, and so complete. The doctor is now dead, and went to his grave under the
delusive persuasion that not any vile glass of brandy, but the stern
refusal of all brandy, was the thing that saved his collapsing patient.
The patient herself, who might naturally know something of the
matter, was of a different opinion. She sided with the factious body
around her bed (comprehending all beside the doctor), who felt sure
that death was rapidly approaching, *barring* that brandy. The same
result, in the same appalling crisis, I have known repeatedly produced
by twenty-five drops of laudanum. Many will say, "Oh, never
listen to a non-medical man like this writer. Consult in such a case
your medical adviser." You will, will you? Then let me tell you
that you are missing the very logic of all I have been saying for the
improvement of blockheads; which is—that you should consult any
man *but* a medical man, since no other man has any obstinate prejudice
of professional timidity.

---

[1] On second thoughts, I see no reason for scrupling to mention that this
man was Robert Southey.

hunters and foresters from below—servants in the household of a beneficent lady—and, in pursuit of some flying game, had wandered far beyond their ordinary limits. Struck by the sudden scintillation from Kate's dress played upon by the morning sun, they rode up to the thicket. Great was their surprise, great their pity, to see a young officer in uniform stretched within the bushes upon the ground, and apparently dying. Borderers from childhood on this dreadful frontier, sacred to winter and death, they understood the case at once. They dismounted, and, with the tenderness of women, raising the poor frozen cornet in their arms, washed her temples with brandy, whilst one, at intervals, suffered a few drops to trickle within her lips. As the restoration of a warm bed was now most likely to be the one thing needed, they lifted the helpless stranger upon a horse, walking on each side with supporting arms. Once again our Kate is in the saddle, once again a Spanish caballero. But Kate's bridle-hand is deadly cold. And her spurs, that she had never unfastened since leaving the monastic asylum, hung as idle as the flapping sail that fills unsteadily with the breeze upon a stranded ship.

This procession had many miles to go, and over difficult ground ; but at length it reached the forest-like park and the chateau of the wealthy proprietress. Kate was still half-frozen, and speechless, except at intervals. Heavens! can this corpse-like, languishing young woman be the Kate that once, in her radiant girlhood, rode with a handful of comrades into a column of two thousand enemies, that saw her comrades die, that persisted when all were dead, that tore from the heart of all resistance the banner of her native Spain ? Chance and change have "written strange defeatures in her face." Much is changed ; but some things are not changed, either in herself or in those about her : there is still kindness that overflows with pity ; there is still helplessness that asks for this pity without a voice : she is now received by a senora not less kind than that maternal aunt who, on the night of her birth, first welcomed her to a loving home ; and she, the heroine of Spain, is herself as helpless now as that little lady who, then at ten minutes of age, was kissed and blessed by all the household of St. Sebastian.[1]

[1] At this point De Quincey had reached the close of the *second*

20.—*A Second Lull in Kate's Stormy Life*

Let us suppose Kate placed in a warm bed. Let us suppose her in a few hours recovering steady consciousness; in a few days recovering some power of self-support; in a fortnight able to seek the gay saloon where the señora was sitting alone, and able to render thanks, with that deep sincerity which ever characterised our wild-hearted Kate, for the critical services received from that lady and her establishment.

This lady, a widow, was what the French call a *métisse*, the Spaniards a *mestizza*—that is, the daughter of a genuine Spaniard and an Indian mother. I will call her simply a *Creole*,[1] which will indicate her want of pure Spanish blood

---

part of the story as it originally appeared in *Tait's Edinburgh Magazine.* As the *first part* (May 1847) had closed with the intimation "*To be concluded in the next Number,*" he thought it necessary to apologise for the non-fulfilment of that promise and the protraction of the story into a *third part.* This he did in the following paragraph, inserted at this point in the magazine, but omitted, of course, in the reprint:—
"Last month, reader, I promised, or some one promised *for* me, that
"I should drive through to the end of the journey in the next stage.
"But, oh, dear reader! these Andes, in Jonathan's phrase, are a
"'severe' range of hills. It takes 'the kick' out of any horse, or,
"indeed, out of any cornet of horse, to climb up this cruel side of the
"range. Rest I really must, whilst Kate is resting. But next month
"I will carry you down the other side at such a flying gallop that you
"shall suspect me (though most unjustly) of a plot against your
"neck. Now, let me throw down the reins; and then, in our brother
"Jonathan's sweet sentimental expression, 'let's liquor.'"—There is some pathos now in this careless piece of slang, scribbled by De Quincey as a stop-gap for his magazine readers in 1847. "Rest I really must," "Let me throw down the reins," "Let's liquor,"—in these phrases, and with real fun in the last, one sees De Quincey yet, pen in hand more than forty years ago, in some fatigued moment in his Edinburgh abode.—M.

[1] "*Creole*":—At that time the infusion of negro or African blood was small. Consequently, none of the negro hideousness was diffused. After those intercomplexities had arisen between all complications and interweavings of descent from three original strands—European, American, African—the distinctions of social consideration founded on them bred names so many that a court calendar was necessary to keep you from blundering. As yet (*i.e.* in Kate's time) the varieties were few. Meantime, the word *Creole* has always been misapplied in our English colonies to a person (though of strictly European

sufficiently to explain her deference for those who had it. She was a kind, liberal woman; rich rather more than needed where there were no opera-boxes to rent; a widow about fifty years old in the wicked world's account, some forty-two in her own; and happy, above all, in the possession of a most lovely daughter, whom even the wicked world did not accuse of more than sixteen years. This daughter, Juana, was—— But stop—let her open the door of the saloon in which the senora and the cornet are conversing, and speak for herself. She did so, after an hour had passed; which length of time, to *her* that never had any business whatever in her innocent life, seemed sufficient to settle the business of the Old World and the New. Had Pietro Diaz (as Catalina now called herself) been really a Peter, and not a sham Peter, what a vision of loveliness would have rushed upon his sensibilities as the door opened. Do not expect me to describe her; for which, however, there are materials extant, sleeping in archives where they have slept for two hundred and twenty-eight years. It is enough that she is reported to have united the stately tread of Andalusian women with the innocent voluptuousness of Peruvian eyes. As to her complexion and figure, be it known that Juana's father was a gentleman from Grenada, having in his veins the grandest blood of all this earth—blood of Goths and Vandals, tainted (for which Heaven be thanked!) twice over with blood of Arabs—once through Moors, once through Jews [1];

blood) simply if *born* in the West Indies. In this English use, the word *Creole* expresses exactly the same difference as the Romans indicated by *Hispanus* and *Hispanicus*. The first meant a person of Spanish blood, a native of Spain; the second, a Roman born in Spain. So of *Germanus* and *Germanicus*, *Italus* and *Italicus*, *Anglus* and *Anglicus*, etc.: an important distinction, on which see Isaac Casaubon *apud Scriptores Hist. Augustan.*

[1] It is well known that the very reason why the Spanish beyond all nations became so gloomily jealous of a Jewish cross in the pedigree was because, until the vigilance of the Church rose into ferocity, in no nation was such a cross so common. The hatred of fear is ever the deepest. And men hated the Jewish taint, as once in Jerusalem they hated the leprosy, because, even whilst they raved against it, the secret proofs of it might be detected amongst their own kindred; even as in the Temple, whilst once a Hebrew king rose in mutiny against the priesthood (2 Chron. xxvi 16-20), suddenly the leprosy that dethroned him blazed out upon his forehead.

whilst from her grandmother Juana drew the deep subtle melancholy, and the beautiful contours of limb, which belonged to the Indian race—a race destined (ah, wherefore?) silently and slowly to fade away from the earth. No awkwardness was or could be in this antelope, when gliding with forest grace into the room; no town-bred shame; nothing but the unaffected pleasure of one who wishes to speak a fervent welcome, but knows not if she ought; the astonishment of a Miranda, bred in utter solitude, when first beholding a princely Ferdinand; and just so much reserve as to remind you that, if Catalina thought fit to dissemble her sex, she did *not*. And consider, reader, if you look back, and are a great arithmetician, that, whilst the senora had only fifty per cent of Spanish blood, Juana had seventy-five; so that her Indian melancholy, after all, was swallowed up for the present by her Visigothic, by her Vandal, by her Arab, by her Spanish, fire.

Catalina, seared as she was by the world, has left it evident in her memoirs that she was touched more than she wished to be by this innocent child. Juana formed a brief lull for Catalina in her too stormy existence. And, if for *her* in this life the sweet reality of a sister had been possible, here was the sister she would have chosen. On the other hand, what might Juana think of the cornet? To have been thrown upon the kind hospitalities of her native home, to have been rescued by her mother's servants from that fearful death which, lying but a few miles off, had filled her nursery with traditionary tragedies—*that* was sufficient to create an interest in the stranger. Such things it had been that wooed the heavenly Desdemona. But his bold martial demeanour, his yet youthful style of beauty, his frank manners, his animated conversation, that reported a hundred contests with suffering and peril, wakened for the first time her admiration. Men she had never seen before, except menial servants, or a casual priest. But here was a gentleman, young like herself, a splendid cavalier, that rode in the cavalry of Spain; that carried the banner of the only potentate whom Peruvians knew of—the King of the Spains and the Indies; that had doubled Cape Horn; that had crossed the Andes; that had suffered shipwreck; that had rocked upon fifty storms, and had wrestled for life through fifty battles.

The reader already guesses all that followed. The sisterly love which Catalina did really feel for this young mountaineer was inevitably misconstrued. Embarrassed, but not able, from sincere affection, or almost in bare propriety, to refuse such expressions of feeling as corresponded to the artless and involuntary kindnesses of the ingenuous Juana, one day the cornet was surprised by mamma in the act of encircling her daughter's waist with his martial arm, although waltzing was premature by at least two centuries in Peru.[1] She taxed him instantly with dishonourably abusing her confidence. The cornet made but a bad defence. He muttered something about "*fraternal affection*," about "esteem," and a great deal of metaphysical words that are destined to remain untranslated in their original Spanish. The good senora, though she could boast only of forty-two years' experience, or say forty-four, was not altogether to be "*had*" in that fashion: she was as learned as if she had been fifty, and she brought matters to a speedy crisis. "You are a Spaniard," she said, "a gentleman, therefore; *remember* that you are a gentleman. This very night, if your intentions are not serious, quit my house. Go to Tucuman; you shall command my horses and servants; but stay no longer to increase the sorrow that already you will have left behind you. My daughter loves you. That is sorrow enough, if you are trifling with us. But, if not, and you also love *her*, and can be happy in our solitary mode of life, stay with us—stay for ever. Marry Juana with my free consent. I ask not for wealth. Mine is sufficient for you both." The cornet protested that the honour was one never contemplated by *him*—that it was too great—that——. But, of course, reader, you know that "gammon" flourishes in Peru, amongst the silver mines, as well as in some more boreal lands that produce little better than copper and tin. "Tin," however, has its uses. The delighted senora overruled

---

[1] On the supposition that Catalina had crossed the Andes from some point in the north of Chili, she must now,—after having descended "the mighty staircase" on the other side, and found refuge in the house of the kind senora,—have been in the part of Spanish South America known as La Plata. But there have been many changes in the territorial divisions of South America since the beginning of the seventeenth century; and *Peru* or *Peruvia* was then a name for a much larger extent of Spanish South America than at present.—M.

all objections, great and small; and she confirmed Juana's
notion that the business of two worlds could be transacted
in an hour, by settling her daughter's future happiness in
exactly twenty minutes. The poor, weak Catalina, not acting now in any spirit of recklessness, grieving sincerely for
the gulf that was opening before her, and yet shrinking
effeminately from the momentary shock that would be
inflicted by a firm adherence to her duty, clinging to the
anodyne of a short delay, allowed herself to be installed as
the lover of Juana. Considerations of convenience, however,
postponed the marriage. It was requisite to make various
purchases; and for this it was requisite to visit Tucuman,
where also the marriage ceremony could be performed with
more circumstantial splendour. To Tucuman, therefore,
after some weeks' interval, the whole party repaired.[1] And
at Tucuman it was that the tragical events arose which,
whilst interrupting such a mockery for ever, left the poor
Juana still happily deceived, and never believing for a
moment that hers was a rejected or a deluded heart.

One reporter of Mr. De Ferrer's narrative forgets his usual
generosity when he says that the senora's gift of her daughter
to the Alférez was not quite so disinterested as it seemed to
be.[2] Certainly it was not so disinterested as European
ignorance might fancy it; but it was quite as much so as it
ought to have been in balancing the interests of a child.
Very true it is, that, being a genuine Spaniard, who was

---

[1] It is this mention of Tucuman that throws light at last on the
question, mooted in notes at pp. 191-2, as to the point at which
Catalina had crossed the Andes, and the part of Spanish America in
which she had found herself after that feat. Tucuman is the name of
one of the provinces of the present Republic of La Plata, in the interior
of South America; and the town Tucuman, which gives it the name,
and which has a present population of about 11,000, is between 250
and 300 miles east from the Andes frontier of North Chili. Therefore, unless Catalina had crossed the Andes from northern Chili, one
can hardly see how Tucuman could be the nearest town to that
residence of the Creole lady in which Catalina had been a guest after
having crossed them. But a large part of what is now La Plata was
then included in the viceroyalty of Peru.—M.

[2] This "reporter" is the same person as the Frenchman attacked
previously in pp 197-8. Who he was, and who Mr. De Ferrer was, is
explained in the Appended Editorial Note —M.

still a rare creature in so vast a world as Peru—being a Spartan amongst Helots—a Spanish Alférez would, in those days, and in that region, have been a natural noble. His alliance created honour for his wife and for his descendants. Something, therefore, the cornet would add to the family consideration. But, instead of selfishness, it argued just regard for her daughter's interest to build upon this, as some sort of equipoise to the wealth which her daughter would bring.

Spaniard, however, as she was, our Alférez, on reaching Tucuman, found no Spaniards to mix with, but, instead, twelve Portuguese.[1]

21.—*Kate once more in Storms.*

Catalina remembered the Spanish proverb, "Pump out of a Spaniard all his good qualities, and the remainder makes a pretty fair Portuguese"; but, as there was nobody else to gamble with, she entered freely into their society. Soon she suspected that there was foul play; for all modes of doctoring dice had been made familiar to *her* by the experience of camps. She watched; and, by the time she had lost her final coin, she was satisfied that she had been plundered. In her first anger, she would have been glad to switch the whole dozen across the eyes; but, as twelve to one were too great odds, she determined on limiting her vengeance to the immediate culprit. Him she followed into the street; and, coming near enough to distinguish his profile reflected on a wall, she continued to keep him in view from a short distance. The lighthearted young cavalier whistled, as he went, an old Portuguese ballad of romance, and in a quarter-of-an-hour came up to a house, the front-door of which he began to open with a pass-key. This operation was the signal for Catalina that the hour of vengeance had struck; and, stepping up hastily, she tapped the Portuguese on the shoulder, saying, "Senor, you are a robber!" The Portuguese turned coolly

---

[1] The interior parts of South America were then a meeting ground, and their native inhabitants a common prey, for the Spanish colonists of Peru, Chili, etc., in the west of South America, and for the Portuguese colonists of Brazil in the east of the same continent.—M.

round, and, seeing his gaming antagonist, replied, " Possibly, sir ; but I have no particular fancy for being told so," at the same time drawing his sword. Catalina had not designed to take any advantage , and the touching him on the shoulder, with the interchange of speeches, and the known character of Kate, sufficiently imply it. But it is too probable, in such cases, that the party whose intention had been regularly settled from the first will, and must, have an advantage unconsciously over a man so abruptly thrown on his defence. However this might be, they had not fought a minute before Catalina passed her sword through her opponent's body ; and, without a groan or a sigh, the Portuguese cavalier fell dead at his own door. Kate searched the street with her ears, and (as far as the indistinctness of night allowed) with her eyes. All was profoundly silent : and she was satisfied that no human figure was in motion. What should be done with the body ? A glance at the door of the house settled *that* : Fernando had himself opened it at the very moment when he received the summons to turn round. She dragged the corpse in, therefore, to the foot of the staircase, put the key by the dead man's side, and then, issuing softly into the street, drew the door close with as little noise as possible. Catalina again paused to listen and to watch, went home to the hospitable senora's house, retired to bed, fell asleep, and early the next morning was awakened by the corrégidor and four alguazils.

The lawlessness of all that followed strikingly exposes the frightful state of criminal justice at that time wherever Spanish law prevailed. No evidence appeared to connect Catalina in any way with the death of Fernando Acosta. The Portuguese gamblers, besides that perhaps they thought lightly of such an accident, might have reasons of their own for drawing off public attention from their pursuits in Tucuman. Not one of these men came forward openly ; else the circumstances at the gaming-table, and the departure of Catalina so closely on the heels of her opponent, would have suggested reasonable grounds for detaining her until some further light should be obtained. As it was, her imprisonment rested upon no colourable ground whatever, unless the magistrate had received some anonymous information,—

which, however, he never alleged. One comfort there was, meantime, in Spanish injustice: it did not loiter. Full gallop it went over the ground: one week often sufficed for informations—for trial—for execution; and the only bad consequence was that a second or a third week sometimes exposed the disagreeable fact that everything had been "premature"; a solemn sacrifice had been made to offended justice in which all was right except as to the victim; it was the wrong man; and *that* gave extra trouble; for then all was to do over again—another man to be executed, and, possibly, still to be caught.

Justice moved at her usual Spanish rate in the present case. Kate was obliged to rise instantly; not suffered to speak to anybody in the house, though, in going out, a door opened, and she saw the young Juana looking out with her saddest Indian expression. In one day the trial was finished. Catalina said (which was true) that she hardly knew Acosta, and that people of her rank were used to attack their enemies face to face, not by murderous surprises. The magistrates were impressed by Catalina's answers (yet answers to *what*, or to *whom*, in a case where there was no distinct charge, and no avowed accuser?) Things were beginning to look well when all was suddenly upset by two witnesses, whom the reader (who is a sort of accomplice after the fact, having been privately let into the truths of the case, and having concealed his knowledge) will know at once to be false witnesses, but whom the old Spanish buzwigs doated on as models of all that could be looked for in the best. Both were ill-looking fellows, as it was their duty to be. And the first deposed as follows.—That through *his* quarter of Tucuman the fact was notorious of Acosta's wife being the object of a criminal pursuit on the part of the Alférez (Catalina); that, doubtless, the injured husband had surprised the prisoner,—which, of course, had led to the murder, to the staircase, to the key, to everything, in short, that could be wished. No—stop! what am I saying?—to everything that ought to be abominated. Finally—for he had now settled the main question—that he had a friend who would take up the case where he himself, from short-sightedness, was obliged to lay it down. This friend—the

Pythias of this shortsighted Damon—started up in a frenzy of virtue at this summons, and, rushing to the front of the alguazils, said, "That, since his friend had proved sufficiently the fact of the Alférez having been lurking in the house, and having murdered a man, all that rested upon *him* to show was how that murderer got out of that house; which he could do satisfactorily; for there was a balcony running along the windows on the second floor, one of which windows he himself, lurking in a corner of the street, saw the Alférez throw up, and from the said balcony take a flying leap into the said street." Evidence like this was conclusive; no defence was listened to, nor indeed had the prisoner any to produce. The Alférez could deny neither the staircase nor the balcony; the street is there to this day, like the bricks in Jack Cade's chimney, testifying all that may be required; and, as to our friend who saw the leap, there he was— nobody could deny *him*. The prisoner might indeed have suggested that she never heard of Acosta's wife; nor had the existence of such a wife been proved, or even ripened into a suspicion. But the bench were satisfied; chopping logic in defence was henceforward impertinence; and sentence was pronounced—that, on the eighth day from the day of arrest, the Alférez should be executed in the public square.

It was not amongst the weaknesses of Catalina—who had so often inflicted death, and, by her own journal, thought so lightly of inflicting it (unless under cowardly advantages)— to shrink from facing death in her own person. Many incidents in her career show the coolness and even gaiety with which, in any case where death was apparently inevitable, she would have gone forward to meet it. But in this case she *had* a temptation for escaping it, which was certainly in her power. She had only to reveal the secret of her sex, and the ridiculous witnesses, beyond whose testimony there was nothing at all against her, must at once be covered with derision. Catalina had some liking for fun; and a main inducement to this course was that it would enable her to say to the judges, "Now, you see what old fools you've made of yourselves; every woman and child in Peru will soon be laughing at you." I must acknowledge my own weakness; this last temptation I could *not* have withstood; flesh is weak, and fun is strong. But Catalina *did*. On consideration, she fancied that, although the particular motive for murdering Acosta would be dismissed with laughter, still this might not clear her of the murder; which, on some *other* motive, she might be supposed to have committed. But, allowing that she were cleared altogether, what most of all she feared was that the publication of her sex would throw a reflex light upon many past transactions in her life: would instantly find its way to Spain; and would probably soon bring her within the tender attentions of the Inquisition. She kept firm, therefore, to the resolution of not saving her life by this discovery. And, so far as her fate lay in her own hands, she would to a certainty have perished—which to me seems a most fantastic caprice; it was to court a certain death and a present death, in order to evade a remote contingency of death. But even at this point how strange a case! A woman *falsely* accused (because accused by lying witnesses) of an act which she really *did* commit! And falsely accused of a true offence upon a motive that was impossible!

As the sun was setting upon the seventh day, when the hours were numbered for the prisoner, there filed into her cell four persons in religious habits. They came on the charitable mission of preparing the poor convict for death. Catalina, however, watching all things narrowly, remarked something earnest and significant in the eye of the leader, as of one who had some secret communication to make. She contrived, therefore, to clasp this man's hands, as if in the energy of internal struggles, and *he* contrived to slip into hers the very smallest of billets from poor Juana. It contained for indeed it *could* contain, only these three words—"Do not confess.—J." This one caution, so simple and so brief, proved a talisman. It did not refer to any confession of the crime; *that* would have been assuming what Juana was neither entitled nor disposed to assume; but it referred, in the technical sense of the Church, to the act of devotional confession. Catalina found a single moment for a glance at it; understood the whole; resolutely refused to confess, as a person unsettled in her religious opinions that needed spiritual instructions; and the four monks withdrew to make their report. The principal judge, upon hearing of the prisoner's impenitence, granted another day. At the end of *that*, no change having occurred either in the prisoner's mind or in the circumstances, he issued his warrant for the execution. Accordingly, as the sun went down, the sad procession formed within the prison. Into the great square of Tucuman it moved, where the scaffold had been built, and the whole city had assembled for the spectacle. Catalina steadily ascended the ladder of the scaffold; even then she resolved not to benefit by revealing her sex; even then it was that she expressed her scorn for the lubberly executioner's mode of tying a knot; did it herself in a "ship-shape," orthodox manner; received in return the enthusiastic plaudits of the crowd, and so far ran the risk of precipitating her fate; for the timid magistrates, fearing a rescue from the fiery clamours of the impetuous mob, angrily ordered the executioner to finish the scene. The clatter of a galloping horse, however, at this instant forced them to pause. The crowd opened a road for the agitated horseman, who was the bearer of an order from the President of La Plata to suspend the execution until two prisoners could be examined. The whole was the work of the senora and her daughter. The elder lady, having gathered informations against the witnesses, had pursued them to La Plata. There, by her influence with the governor, they were arrested, recognised as old malefactors, and in their terror had partly confessed their perjury. Catalina was removed to La Plata; solemnly acquitted; and, by the advice of the president, for the present the connexion with the senora's family was indefinitely postponed.[1]

22.—*Kate's Penultimate Adventure*

Now was the last-but-one adventure at hand that ever Catalina should see in the New World. Some fine sights

[1] The story thinks nothing of shifting Catalina some hundreds of miles in a mere sentence or two, and without any intimation of difficulty. The town once called *Plata* or *La Plata*, but now known as *Chuquisaca*, the capital of Bolivia, is about 600 miles due north of Tucuman. What is now Bolivia was then Upper Peru; and at Plata, even more than in Tucuman, Kate was among Peruvian Spaniards.—M.

she may yet see in Europe, but nothing after this (*which she has recorded*) in America. Europe, if it had ever heard of her name (as very shortly it *shall* hear),—Kings, Pope, Cardinals, if they were but aware of her existence (which in six months they *shall* be),—would thirst for an introduction to our Catalina. You hardly thought now, reader, that she was such a great person, or anybody's pet but yours and mine. Bless you, sir, she would scorn to look at *us*. I tell you, that Eminences, Excellencies, Highnesses—nay, even Royalties and Holinesses—are languishing to see her, or soon *will* be. But how can this come to pass, if she is to continue in her present obscurity? Certainly it cannot without some great *peripetteia*, or vertiginous whirl of fortune; which, therefore, you shall now behold taking place in one turn of her next adventure. *That* shall let in a light, *that* shall throw back a Claude Lorraine gleam over all the past, able to make kings, that would have cared not for her under Peruvian daylight, come to glorify her setting beams.

The senora—and, observe, whatever kindness she does to Catalina speaks secretly from two hearts, her own and Juana's —had, by the advice of Mr. President Mendonia, given sufficient money for Catalina's travelling expenses. So far well. But Mr. M. chose to add a little codicil to this bequest of the senora's, never suggested by her or by her daughter. "Pray," said this inquisitive president, who surely might have found business enough within his own neighbourhood— "pray, Senor Pietro Diaz, did you ever live at Concepcion? And were you ever acquainted there with Signor Miguel de Erauso? That man, sir, was my friend." What a pity that on this occasion Catalina could not venture to be candid! What a capital speech it would have made to say, "*Friend* were you? I think you could hardly be *that*, with seven hundred miles between you. But that man was *my* friend also; and, secondly, my brother. True it is I killed him. But, if you happen to know that this was by pure mistake in the dark, what an old rogue you must be to throw *that* in my teeth which is the affliction of my life!" Again, however, as so often in the same circumstances, Catalina thought that it would cause more ruin than it could heal to be candid; and, indeed if she were really *P. Diaz, Esq.*, how came she to be brother to the late Mr. Erauso? On consideration, also, if she could not tell *all*, merely to have professed a fraternal connexion which never was avowed by either whilst living together would not have brightened the reputation of Catalina. Still, from a kindness for poor Kate, I feel uncharitably towards the president for advising Senor Pietro "to travel for his health." What had *he* to do with people's health? However, Mr. Peter, as he had pocketed the senora's money, thought it right to pocket also the advice that accompanied its payment. That he might be in a condition to do so, he went off to buy a horse. On that errand, in all lands, for some reason only half explained, you must be in luck if you do not fall in, and eventually fall out, with a knave. But on this particular day Kate *was* in luck. For, beside money and advice, she obtained at a low rate a horse both beautiful and serviceable for a journey. To Paz it was, a city of prosperous name, that the cornet first moved.[1] But Paz did not fulfil the promise of its name. For it laid the grounds of a feud that drove our Kate out of America.

Her first adventure was a bagatelle, and fitter for a jest-book than for a serious history; yet it proved no jest either, since it led to the tragedy that followed. Riding into Paz, our gallant standard-bearer and her bonny black horse drew all eyes, *comme de raison*, upon their separate charms. This was inevitable amongst the indolent population of a Spanish town; and Kate was used to it. But, having recently had a little too much of the public attention, she felt nervous on remarking two soldiers eyeing the handsome horse and the handsome rider with an attention that seemed too earnest for mere *æsthetics*. However, Kate was not the kind of person to let anything dwell on her spirits, especially if it took the shape of impudence; and, whistling gaily, she was riding forward, when—who should cross her path but the Alcalde of Paz? Ah! alcalde, you see a person now that has a mission against you and all that you inherit; though a mission known to herself as little as to you. Good were it for you had you never crossed the path of this Biscayan Alférez.

---

[1] Another locomotive leap! Paz, or La Paz, the capital of the department of that name in the present Bolivia, is about 300 miles north-west from Plata or Chuquisaca.—M.

The alcalde looked so sternly that Kate asked if his worship had any commands. "Yes. These men," said the alcalde, "these two soldiers, say that this horse is stolen." To one who had so narrowly and so lately escaped the balcony witness and his friend, it was really no laughing matter to hear of new affidavits in preparation. Kate was nervous, but never disconcerted. In a moment she had twitched off a saddle-cloth on which she sat; and, throwing it over the horse's head, so as to cover up all between the ears and the mouth, she replied, "That she had bought and paid for the horse at La Plata. But now, your worship, if this horse has really been stolen from these men, they must know well of which eye it is blind; for it *can* be only in the right eye or the left." One of the soldiers cried out instantly that it was the left eye; but the other said, "No, no; you forget, it's the right." Kate maliciously called attention to this little schism. But the men said, "Ah, *that* was nothing—they were hurried; but now, on recollecting themselves, they were agreed that it was the left eye."—"Did they stand to that?"—"Oh yes, positive they were—left eye—left."

Upon which our Kate, twitching off the horse-cloth, said gaily to the magistrate, "Now, sir, please to observe that this horse has nothing the matter with either eye." And, in fact, it *was* so. Upon *that*, his worship ordered his alguazils to apprehend the two witnesses, who posted off to bread and water, with other reversionary advantages; whilst Kate rode in quest of the best dinner that Paz could furnish.

23.—*Preparation for Kate's Final Adventure in Peru*

This alcalde's acquaintance, however, was not destined to drop here. Something had appeared in the young caballero's bearing which made it painful to have addressed him with harshness, or for a moment to have entertained such a charge against such a person. He despatched his cousin, therefore, Don Antonio Calderon, to offer his apologies, and at the same time to request that the stranger, whose rank and quality he regretted not to have known, would do him the honour to come and dine with him This explanation, and the fact that Don Antonio had already proclaimed his own position as cousin to the magistrate, and nephew to the Bishop of Cuzco, obliged Catalina to say, after thanking the gentlemen for their obliging attentions, "I myself hold the rank of Alférez in the service of his Catholic Majesty. I am a native of Biscay, and I am now repairing to Cuzco on private business."[1]—"To Cuzco!" exclaimed Antonio; "and you from dear lovely Biscay! How very fortunate! My cousin is a Basque like you; and, like you, he starts for Cuzco to-morrow morning; so that, if it is agreeable to you, Senor Alférez, we will travel together." It was settled that they should. To travel—amongst "balcony witnesses," and anglers for "blind horses"—not merely with a just man, but with the very abstract idea and riding allegory of justice, was too delightful to the storm-wearied cornet; and he cheerfully accompanied Don Antonio to the house of the magistrate, called Don Pedro de Chavarria. Distinguished was his reception; the alcalde personally renewed his regrets for the ridiculous scene of the two scampish oculists, and presented Kate to his wife—a most splendid Andalusian beauty, to whom he had been married about a year.

This lady there is a reason for describing; and the French reporter of Catalina's memoirs dwells upon the theme. She united, he says, the sweetness of the German lady with the energy of the Arabian—a combination hard to judge of. "As to her feet," he adds, "I say nothing, for she had scarcely any at all. *Je ne parle point de ses pieds; elle n'en avait presque pas.*" "Poor lady!" says a compassionate rustic: "no feet! What a shocking thing that so fine a woman should have been so sadly mutilated!" Oh, my dear rustic, you're quite in the wrong box. The Frenchman means this as the very highest compliment. Beautiful, however, she must have been, and a Cinderella, I hope; but still not a Cinderellula, considering that she had the inimitable walk and step of Andalusian women, which cannot be accomplished without something of a proportionate basis to stand upon.

The reason which there is (as I have said) for describing

---

[1] Cuzco is about 300 miles north-west from La Paz. It was the capital of the native Peruvian Empire of the Incas, and is one of the most important cities, and the capital of one of the provinces, of the present and much-restricted Peru.—M.

this lady arises out of her relation to the tragic events which followed. She, by her criminal levity, was the cause of all. And I must here warn the moralising blunderer of two errors that he is likely to make: 1st, that he is invited to read some extract from a licentious amour, as if for its own interest; 2dly, or on account of Donna Catalina's memoirs, with a view to relieve their too martial character. I have the pleasure to assure him of his being so utterly in the darkness of error that any possible change he can make in his opinions, right or left, must be for the better: he cannot stir but he will mend,—which is a delightful thought for the moral and blundering mind. As to the first point, what little glimpse he obtains of a licentious amour is, as a court of justice will sometimes show him such a glimpse, simply to make intelligible the subsequent facts which depend upon it. Secondly, as to the conceit that Catalina wished to embellish her memoirs, understand that no such practice then existed—certainly not in Spanish literature. Her memoirs are electrifying by their facts; else, in the manner of telling these facts, they are systematically dry.

But let us resume. Don Antonio Calderon was a handsome, accomplished cavalier. And in the course of dinner Catalina was led to judge, from the behaviour to each other of this gentleman and the lady, the alcalde's beautiful wife, that they had an improper understanding. This also she inferred from the furtive language of their eyes. Her wonder was that the alcalde should be so blind; though upon that point she saw reason in a day or two to change her opinion. Some people see everything by affecting to see nothing. The whole affair, however, was nothing at all to *her*; and she would have dismissed it altogether from her thoughts, but for the dreadful events on the journey.

This went on but slowly, however steadily. Owing to the miserable roads, eight hours a-day of travelling was found quite enough for man and beast; the product of which eight hours was from ten to twelve leagues, taking the league at $2\frac{1}{4}$ miles. On the last day but one of the journey, the travelling party, which was precisely the original dinner party, reached a little town ten leagues short of Cuzco. The corrégidor of this place was a friend of the alcalde; and through *his* influence the party obtained better accommodations than those which they had usually commanded in a hovel calling itself a *venta*, or in a sheltered corner of a barn. The alcalde was to sleep at the corrégidor's house; the two young cavaliers, Calderon and our Kate, had sleeping-rooms at the public *locanda*; but for the lady was reserved a little pleasure-house in an enclosed garden. This was a mere toy of a house; but, the season being summer, and the house surrounded with tropical flowers, the lady preferred it (in spite of its loneliness) to the damp mansion of the official grandee, who, in her humble opinion, was quite as fusty as his mansion, and his mansion not much less so than himself.

After dining gaily together at the *locanda*, and possibly taking a "rise" out of his worship the corrégidor, as a repeating echo of Don Quixote (then growing popular in Spanish America), the young man Don Antonio, who was no young officer, and the young officer Catalina, who was no young man, lounged down together to the little pavilion in the flower-garden, with the purpose of paying their respects to the presiding belle. They were graciously received, and had the honour of meeting there his mustiness the alcalde, and his fustiness the corrégidor; whose conversation ought surely to have been edifying, since it was anything but brilliant. How they got on under the weight of two such muffs has been a mystery for two centuries. But they *did* to a certainty, for the party did not break up till eleven. *Tea and turn out* you could not call it; for there was the *turn-out* in rigour, but not the *tea*. One thing, however, Catalina by mere accident had an opportunity of observing, and observed with pain. The two official gentlemen, on taking leave, had gone down the steps into the garden. Catalina, having forgot her hat, went back into the little vestibule to look for it. There stood the lady and Don Antonio, exchanging a few final words (they *were* final) and a few final signs. Amongst the last Kate observed distinctly this, and distinctly she understood it. First of all, by raising her forefinger, the lady drew Calderon's attention to the act which followed as one of significant pantomime; which done, she snuffed out one of the candles. The young man answered it by a look of intelligence; and then all three passed down the steps together. The lady was disposed to take the cool air, and accompanied them to the garden-gate; but, in passing down the walk, Catalina noticed a second ill-omened sign that all was not right. Two glaring eyes she distinguished amongst the shrubs for a moment, and a rustling immediately after. "What's that?" said the lady; and Don Antonio answered, carelessly, "A bird flying out of the bushes." But birds do not amuse themselves by staying up to midnight; and birds do not wear rapiers.

Catalina, as usual, had read everything. Not a wrinkle or a rustle was lost upon *her*. And therefore, when she reached the *locanda*, knowing to an iota all that was coming, she did not retire to bed, but paced before the house. She had not long to wait: in fifteen minutes the door opened softly, and out stepped Calderon. Kate walked forward, and faced him immediately; telling him laughingly that it was not good for his health to go abroad on this night. The young man showed some impatience; upon which, very seriously, Kate acquainted him with her suspicions, and with the certainty that the alcalde was not so blind as he had seemed. Calderon thanked her for the information; would be upon his guard; but, to prevent further expostulation, he wheeled round instantly into the darkness. Catalina was too well convinced, however, of the mischief on foot to leave him thus. She followed rapidly, and passed silently into the garden, almost at the same time with Calderon. Both took their stations behind trees,—Calderon watching nothing but the burning candles, Catalina watching circumstances to direct her movements. The candles burned brightly in the little pavilion. Presently one was extinguished. Upon this, Calderon pressed forward to the steps, hastily ascended them, and passed into the vestibule. Catalina followed on his traces. What succeeded was all one scene of continued, dreadful dumb show; different passions of panic, or deadly struggle, or hellish malice, absolutely suffocated all articulate utterances.

In the first moments a gurgling sound was heard, as of a wild beast attempting vainly to yell over some creature that it was strangling. Next came a tumbling out at the door of one black mass, which heaved and parted at intervals into two figures, which closed, which parted again, which at last fell down the steps together. Then appeared a figure in white. It was the unhappy Andalusian; and she, seeing the outline of Catalina's person, ran up to her, unable to utter one syllable. Pitying the agony of her horror, Catalina took her within her own cloak, and carried her out at the garden gate. Calderon had by this time died; and the maniacal alcalde had risen up to pursue his wife. But Kate, foreseeing what he would do, had stepped silently within the shadow of the garden wall. Looking down the road to the town, and seeing nobody moving, the maniac, for some purpose, went back to the house. This moment Kate used to recover the *locanda*, with the lady still panting in horror. What was to be done? To think of concealment in this little place was out of the question. The alcalde was a man of local power, and it was certain that he would kill his wife on the spot. Kate's generosity would not allow her to have any collusion with this murderous purpose. At Cuzco, the principal convent was ruled by a near relative of the Andalusian; and there she would find shelter. Kate therefore saddled her horse rapidly, placed the lady behind, and rode off in the darkness.

24.—*A Steeplechase*

About five miles out of the town their road was crossed by a torrent, over which they could not hit the bridge. "Forward!" cried the lady, "Oh, heavens! forward!"; and, Kate repeating the word to the horse, the docile creature leaped down into the water. They were all sinking at first; but, having its head free, the horse swam clear of all obstacles through midnight darkness, and scrambled out on the opposite bank. The two riders were dripping from the shoulders downward. But, seeing a light twinkling from a cottage window, Kate rode up, obtaining a little refreshment, and the benefit of a fire, from a poor labouring man. From this man she also bought a warm mantle for the lady; who besides her torrent bath, was dressed in a light evening robe, so that but for the horseman's cloak of Kate she would have perished. But there was no time to lose. They had already lost two hours from the consequences of their cold bath.

Cuzco was still eighteen miles distant; and the alcalde's shrewdness would at once divine this to be his wife's mark. They remounted: very soon the silent night echoed the hoofs of a pursuing rider; and now commenced the most frantic race, in which each party rode as if the whole game of life were staked upon the issue. The pace was killing; and Kate has delivered it as her opinion, in the memoirs which she wrote, that the alcalde was the better mounted. This may be doubted. And certainly Kate had ridden too many years in the Spanish cavalry to have any fear of his worship's horsemanship; but it was a prodigious disadvantage that *her* horse had to carry double, while the horse ridden by her opponent was one of those belonging to the murdered Don Antonio, and known to Kate as a powerful animal. At length they had come within three miles of Cuzco. The road after this descended the whole way to the city, and in some places rapidly, so as to require a cool rider. Suddenly a deep trench appeared, traversing the whole extent of a broad heath. It was useless to evade it. To have hesitated was to be lost. Kate saw the necessity of clearing it; but she doubted much whether her poor exhausted horse, after twenty-one miles of work so severe, had strength for the effort. However, the race was nearly finished; a score of dreadful miles had been accomplished; and Kate's maxim, which never yet had failed, both figuratively for life, and literally for the saddle, was—to ride at everything that showed a front of resistance. She did so now. Having come upon the trench rather too suddenly, she wheeled round for the advantage of coming down upon it with more impetus, rode resolutely at it, cleared it, and gained the opposite bank. The hind feet of her horse were sinking back from the rottenness of the ground; but the strong supporting bridle-hand of Kate carried him forward; and in ten minutes more they would be in Cuzco. This being seen by the vengeful alcalde, who had built great hopes on the trench, he unslung his carbine, pulled up, and fired after the bonny black horse and its two bonny riders. But this vicious manœuvre would have lost his worship any bet that he might have had depending on this admirable steeplechase. For the bullets, says Kate in her memoirs, whistled round the poor clinging lady *en croupe*—luckily none struck *her*; but one wounded the horse. And that settled the odds. Kate now planted herself well in her stirrups to enter Cuzco, almost dangerously a winner; for the horse was so maddened by the wound, and the road so steep, that he went like blazes; and it really became difficult for Kate to guide him with any precision through narrow episcopal[1] paths. Henceforwards the wounded horse required unintermitting attention; and yet, in the mere luxury of strife, it was impossible for Kate to avoid turning a little in her saddle to see the alcalde's performance on this tight-rope of the trench. His worship's horsemanship being, perhaps, rather rusty, and he not perfectly acquainted with his horse, it would have been agreeable for *him* to compromise the case by riding round, or dismounting. But all *that* was impossible. The job must be done. And I am happy to report, for the reader's satisfaction, the sequel—so far as Kate could attend the performance. Gathering himself up for mischief, the alcalde took a mighty sweep, as if ploughing out the line of some vast encampment, or tracing the *pomœrium* for some future Rome; then, like thunder and lightning, with arms flying aloft in the air, down he came upon the trembling trench. But the horse refused the leap; to take the leap was impossible; absolutely to refuse it, the horse felt, was immoral; and therefore, as the only compromise that *his* unlearned brain could suggest, he threw his worship right over his ears, lodging him safely in a sand-heap, that rose with clouds of dust and screams of birds into the morning air. Kate had now no time to send back her compliments in a musical halloo. The alcalde missed breaking his neck on this occasion very narrowly; but his neck was of no use to him in twenty minutes more, as the reader will find. Kate rode right onwards; and, coming in with a lady behind her, horse bloody, and pace such as no hounds could have lived with, she ought to have made a great sensation in Cuzco. But, unhappily, the people of Cuzco, the spectators that *should* have been, were fast asleep in bed.[2]

[1] "*Episcopal*":—The roads around Cuzco were made, and maintained, under the patronage and control of the bishop.
[2] As the ride from Paz to Cuzco has been described with exceptional

The steeplechase into Cuzco had been a fine headlong thing, considering the torrent, the trench, the wounded horse, the lovely Andalusian lady, with her agonising fears, mounted behind Kate, together with the meek dove-like dawn; but the finale crowded together the quickest succession of changes that out of a melodrama ever *can* have been witnessed. Kate reached the convent in safety; carried into the cloisters, and delivered like a parcel, the fair Andalusian. But to rouse the servants and obtain admission to the convent caused a long delay; and, on returning to the street through the broad gateway of the convent, whom should she face but the alcalde! How he had escaped the trench who can tell? He had no time to write memoirs; his horse was too illiterate. But he *had* escaped; temper not at all improved by that adventure, and now raised to a hell of malignity by seeing that he had lost his prey. The

spirit and minuteness, so that our attention has been bespoken more strongly for Cuzco than for any other of the towns in the circuit of Kate's South American wanderings since she left Paita (except perhaps Concepcion and Tucuman), the following account of Cuzco from the description of Peru given in Heylyn's *Cosmography* may not be unwelcome:—" Cusco, in the latitude of 13 degrees and 30 minutes,
" about 130 leagues to the east of Lima, and situate in a rugged and
" uneven soil, begirt with mountains, but on both sides of a pleasant
" and commodious river. Once the Seat-Royal of the Ingas or
" Peruvian Kings; who, the more to beautifie this city, commanded
" every one of the nobility to build here a palace for their continual
" abode. Still of most credit in this country, both for beauty and
" bigness and the multitudes of inhabitants; here being thought to
" dwell 3000 Spaniards and 10,000 of the natives, besides women and
" children. The Palace of the King, advanced on a lofty mountain,
" was held to be a work of so great magnificence, built of such huge
" and massive stones, that the Spaniards thought it to have been the
" work rather of devils than of men. Now miserably defaced, most
" of the stones being tumbled down to build private houses in the
" city: some of the churches raised also by the ruins of it; and
" amongst them perhaps both the Bishop's Palace and Cathedral,
" whose annual rents are estimated at 20,000 ducats. Yet did not
" this vast building yield more lustre to the City of Cusco than a
" spacious Market-place, the centre in which those highways did
" meet together which the Ingas had caused to be made cross the king-
" dom, both for length and breadth, with most incredible charge and
" pains, for the use of their subjects."—This description of Cuzco by Heylyn in the middle of the seventeenth century may serve for Cuzco as Kate came into it and saw it some twenty-five years earlier.—M.

morning light showed him how to use his sword, and whom he had before him; and he attacked Kate with fury. Both were exhausted; and Kate, besides that she had no personal quarrel with the alcalde, having now accomplished her sole object in saving the lady, would have been glad of a truce. She could with difficulty wield her sword; and the alcalde had so far the advantage that he wounded Kate severely. That roused her ancient Biscayan blood; and she turned on him now with deadly determination. At that moment in rode two servants of the alcalde, who took part with their master. These odds strengthened Kate's resolution, but weakened her chances. Just then, however, rode in, and ranged himself on Kate's side, the servant of the murdered Don Calderon. In an instant Kate had pushed her sword through the alcalde; who died upon the spot. In an instant the servant of Calderon had fled. In an instant the alguazils had come up. They and the servants of the alcalde pressed furiously on Kate, who was again fighting for her life with persons not even known to her by sight. Against such odds, she was rapidly losing ground; when, in an instant, on the opposite side of the street, the great gates of the Episcopal Palace rolled open. Thither it was that Calderon's servant had fled. The bishop and his attendants hurried across. "Senor Caballero," said the bishop, "in the name of the Virgin, I enjoin you to surrender your sword."—"My lord," said Kate, "I dare not do it with so many enemies about me."—"But I," replied the bishop, "become answerable to the law for your safe keeping." Upon which, with filial reverence, all parties dropped their swords. Kate being severely wounded, the bishop led her into his palace. In another instant came the catastrophe: Kate's discovery could no longer be delayed; the blood flowed too rapidly; and the wound was in her bosom. She requested a private interview with the bishop: all was known in a moment; surgeons and attendants were summoned hastily; and Kate had fainted. The good bishop pitied her, and had her attended in his palace; then removed to a convent; then to a second convent at Lima; and, after many months had passed, his report of the whole extraordinary case in all its details to the supreme government at Madrid drew from the king,

Philip IV, and from the papal legate, an order that the nun should be transferred to Spain.[1]

25.—*St. Sebastian is finally Checkmated*

Yes, at length the warrior lady, the blooming cornet—this nun that is so martial, this dragoon that is so lovely—must visit again the home of her childhood, which now for seventeen years she has not seen.[2] All Spain, Portugal, Italy, rang with her adventures. Spain, from north to south, was frantic with desire to behold her fiery child, whose girlish romance, whose patriotic heroism, electrified the national imagination. The King of Spain must kiss his *faithful* daughter, that would not suffer his banner to see dishonour. The Pope must kiss his *wandering* daughter, that henceforwards will be a lamb travelling back into the Christian fold. Potentates so great as these, when *they* speak words of love, do not speak in vain. All was forgiven,—the sacrilege, the bloodshed, the flight, and the scorn of St. Sebastian's (consequently of St. Peter's) keys; the pardons were made out, were signed, were sealed; and the chanceries of earth were satisfied.

Ah! what a day of sorrow and of joy was *that* one day,

---

[1] Lima, the capital of Peru, is on the Pacific coast, about 300 miles north-west from Cuzco, and about 600 miles south from the Peruvian town of Paita where Kate's South American adventures had begun sixteen years before. The geography of her transatlantic wanderings during those sixteen years may therefore be now reviewed thus:—(1) By sea from Paita in Peru to Concepcion in Chili, a distance of 2400 miles. (2) In Chili and Peru, or backwards and forwards between them, in military service in the Spanish armies, for an indefinite number of years. (3) Across the Andes, presumably somewhere from the north of Chili, and so to her residence with the Creole Senora somewhere at the eastern foot of the Andes, in what is now La Plata, but was then part of Peru. (4) At Tucuman in that part of Peru; thence to La Plata or Chuquisaca; thence to La Paz; thence to Cuzco, where her sex was discovered and her game was at an end; and so finally to Lima, where she was nearer her original starting-point of Paita than she had been yet in all her long previous circuit from it, and whence she was to be shipped back to Spain.—M.

[2] These seventeen years had brought her, if the data are correct, from 1608, when she landed in South America at Paita, a girl of seventeen, to 1624, when she embarked on her return voyage to Spain from Lima, at the age of thirty-three.—M.

in the first week of November 1624, when the returning Kate drew near to the shore of Andalusia; when, descending into the ship's barge, she was rowed to the piers of Cadiz by bargemen in the royal liveries; when she saw every ship, street, house, convent, church, crowded, as if on some mighty day of judgment, with human faces, with men, with women, with children, all bending the lights of their flashing eyes upon herself! Forty myriads of people had gathered in Cadiz alone. All Andalusia had turned out to receive her.[1] Ah! what joy for *her*, if she had not looked back to the Andes, to their dreadful summits, and their more dreadful feet. Ah! what sorrow, if she had not been forced by music, and endless banners, and the triumphant jubilations of her countrymen, to turn away from the Andes, and to fix her thoughts for the moment upon that glad tumultuous shore which she approached.

Upon this shore stood, ready to receive her, in front of all this mighty crowd, the Prime Minister of Spain, that same Condé Olivarez[2] who but one year before had been so haughty and so defying to our haughty and defying Duke of Buckingham. But a year ago the Prince of Wales had been in Spain, seeking a Spanish bride, and he also was welcomed with triumph and great joy[3]; but not with the hundredth part of that enthusiasm which now met the returning nun.

---

[1] The precise day of this reception of Catalina at Cadiz on her return from the New World is given as 1st November 1624 in other documents.—M.

[2] Olivarez was Prime Minister in Spain from 1621 to 1643.—M.

[3] It was in February 1622-3 that James I. of England despatched his heir-apparent, Prince Charles, afterwards Charles I., to Spain, under the escort of the splendid royal favourite, George Villiers, then Marquis of Buckingham, on the famous business of the Spanish Match, —*i.e.* for the conclusion of the long-pending negotiations for a marriage between the Prince and the Spanish Infanta, daughter of the late Philip III of Spain, and sister of Philip IV. The Prince and Buckingham remained at the Spanish Court some months,—the Prince eager for the match, but Buckingham's attitude in the matter becoming that of obstruction and of open quarrel with the Spanish officials. In September 1623 the two were back in England, reporting that they had been duped; and, greatly to the delight of the English people, the Spanish Match business and all friendly relations with Roman Catholic Spain were at an end. Buckingham had been raised to the dignity of Duke during his absence.—M.

And Olivarez, that had spoken so roughly to the English duke, to *her* "was sweet as summer."[1] Through endless crowds of welcoming compatriots he conducted her to the king. The king folded her in his arms, and could never be satisfied with listening to her. He sent for her continually to his presence; he delighted in her conversation, so new, so natural, so spirited, he settled a pension upon her (at the time of unprecedented amount); and by *his* desire, because the year 1625 was a year of jubilee,[2] she departed in a few months from Madrid to Rome. She went through Barcelona, —there and everywhere welcomed as the lady whom the king delighted to honour. She travelled to Rome, and all doors flew open to receive her. She was presented to his Holiness, with letters from his Most Catholic Majesty. But letters there needed none. The Pope admired her as much as all before had done. He caused her to recite all her adventures; and what he loved most in her account was the sincere and sorrowing spirit in which she described herself as neither better nor worse than she had been. Neither proud was Kate, nor sycophantishly and falsely humble. Urban VIII it was then that filled the chair of St. Peter.[3] He did not neglect to raise his daughter's thoughts from earthly things: he pointed her eyes to the clouds that were floating in mighty volumes above the dome of St. Peter's Cathedral; he told her what the cathedral had told her amongst the gorgeous clouds of the Andes and the solemn vesper lights— how sweet a thing, how divine a thing, it was for Christ's sake to forgive all injuries, and how he trusted that no more she would think of bloodshed, but that, if again she should suffer wrongs, she would resign all vindictive retaliation for them into the hands of God, the final Avenger. I

---

[1] Griffith in Shakspere, when vindicating, in that immortal scene with Queen Catharine, Cardinal Wolsey.

[2] "*A year of jubilee*":—This is an institution of the Roman Catholic Church, dating from 1300, when, by a bull of Pope Boniface VIII, a plenary indulgence was granted to all pilgrims who visited Rome in that year, and complied with certain other conditions. It was then intended that the festival should be repeated every hundredth year; but the interval was afterwards abridged to fifty years, and latterly, with changed conditions, to twenty-five years. The jubilee of 1625 was the seventh on the twenty-five years' system.—M.

[3] Urban VIII was Pope from 1623 to 1644.—M.

must also find time to mention, although the press and the compositors are in a fury at my delays, that the Pope, in his farewell audience to his dear daughter, whom he was to see no more, gave her a general licence to wear henceforth in all countries—even *in partibus Infidelium*—a cavalry officer's dress, boots, spurs, sabre; in fact, anything that she and the Horse Guards might agree upon. Consequently, reader, say not one word, nor suffer any tailor to say one word, or the ninth part of a word, against those Wellington trousers made in the chestnut forest; for, understanding that the papal indulgence as to this point runs backwards as well as forwards, it sanctions equally those trousers in the forgotten rear and all possible trousers yet to come.

From Rome, Kate returned to Spain. She even went to St. Sebastian's—to the city; but—whether it was that her heart failed her or not—never to the convent. She roamed up and down; everywhere she was welcome—everywhere an honoured guest; but everywhere restless. The poor and humble never ceased from their admiration of her; and amongst the rich and aristocratic of Spain, with the king at their head, Kate found especial love from two classes of men. The cardinals and bishops all doated upon her, as their daughter that was returning. The military men all doated upon her, as their sister that was retiring.

26.—*Farewell to the Daughter of St. Sebastian!*

Now, at this moment, it has become necessary for me to close; but I allow to the reader one question before laying down my pen. Come now, reader, be quick; "look sharp," and ask what you *have* to ask; for in one minute and a-half I am going to write in capitals the word FINIS; after which, you know, I am not at liberty to add a syllable. It would be shameful to do so; since that word *Finis* enters into a secret covenant with the reader that he shall be molested no more with words, small or great. Twenty to one, I guess what your question will be. You desire to ask me, What became of Kate? What was her end?

Ah, reader! but, if I answer that question, you will say I have *not* answered it. If I tell you that secret, you will say that the secret is still hidden. Yet, because I have promised, and because you will be angry if I do not, let me do my best.

After ten years of restlessness in Spain, with thoughts always turning back to the dreadful Andes, Kate heard of an expedition on the point of sailing to Spanish America.[1] All soldiers knew *her*, so that she had information of everything which stirred in camps. Men of the highest military rank were going out with the expedition; but Kate was a sister everywhere privileged; she was as much cherished and as sacred, in the eyes of every brigade or *tertia*, as their own regimental colours; and every member of the staff, from the highest to the lowest, rejoiced to hear that she would join their mess on board ship. This ship, with others, sailed; whither finally bound, I really forget. But, on reaching America, all the expedition touched at *Vera Cruz*.[2] Thither a great crowd of the military went on shore. The leading officers made a separate party for the same purpose. Their intention was to have a gay, happy dinner, after their long confinement to a ship, at the chief hotel; and happy in perfection the dinner could not be unless Kate would consent to join it. She, that was ever kind to brother soldiers, agreed to do so. She descended into the boat along with them, and in twenty minutes the boat touched the shore. All the bevy of gay laughing officers, junior and senior, like so many schoolboys let loose from school, jumped on shore, and walked hastily, as their time was limited, up to the hotel. Arriving there, all turned round in eagerness, saying, "Where is our dear Kate?" Ah, yes, my dear Kate, at that solemn moment, where, indeed, were *you*? She had,

---

[1] This brings us to the year 1635, when Kate, after her ten years or so of attempted rest and quasi-respectability in Spain or elsewhere in Europe, had attained the forty-third year of her age.—M.

[2] If De Quincey had not been here huddling up the conclusion of his story for *Tait's Magazine* on pressure from the printers, he would certainly have explained that Vera Cruz is not on that western or Pacific shore of South America with which Kate had already been familiar by her previous adventures, nor in any part of South America at all, but is on the East or Atlantic side of Spanish North America, —being, in fact, the chief port of Mexico, and situated far within the Gulf of Mexico, about 190 miles from the inland city of Mexico itself. —M.

beyond all doubt, taken her seat in the boat: that was certain, though nobody, in the general confusion, was certain of having seen her actually step ashore. The sea was searched for her—the forests were ransacked. But the sea did not give up its dead, if *there* indeed she lay; and the forests made no answer to the sorrowing hearts which sought her amongst *them*. Have I never formed a conjecture of my own upon the mysterious fate which thus suddenly enveloped her, and hid her in darkness for ever? Yes, I have. But it is a conjecture too dim and unsteady to be worth repeating. Her brother soldiers, that should naturally have had more materials for guessing than myself, were all lost in sorrowing perplexity, and could never arrive even at a plausible conjecture.[1]

That happened two hundred and twenty-one years ago! And here is the brief upshot of all:—This nun sailed from Spain to Peru, and she found no rest for the sole of her foot. This nun sailed back from Peru to Spain, and she found no rest for the agitations of her heart. This nun sailed again from Spain to America, and she found—the rest which all of us find. But where it was could never be made known to the father of Spanish camps, that sat in Madrid, nor to Kate's spiritual father, that sat in Rome. Known it is to the great Father of All, that once whispered to Kate on the Andes; but else it has been a secret for more than two centuries; and to man it remains a secret for ever and ever!

[1] See Appended Editorial Note.—M.

AUTHOR'S POSTSCRIPT IN 1854

THERE are some narratives which, though pure fictions from first to last, counterfeit so vividly the air of grave realities that, if deliberately offered for such, they would for a time impose upon everybody. In the opposite scale there are other narratives, which, whilst rigorously true, move amongst characters and scenes so remote from our ordinary experience, and through a state of society so favourable to an adventurous cast of incidents, that they would everywhere pass for romances, if severed from the documents which attest their fidelity to facts. In the former class stand the admirable novels of Defoe, and, on a lower range within the same category, the inimitable *Vicar of Wakefield*; upon which last novel, without at all designing it, I once became the author of the following instructive experiment:—I had given a copy of this little novel to a beautiful girl of seventeen, the daughter of a 'statesman in Westmorland, not designing any deception (nor so much as any concealment) with respect to the fictitious character of the incidents and of the actors in that famous tale. Mere accident it was that had intercepted those explanations as to the extent of fiction in these points which in this case it would have been so natural to make. Indeed, considering the exquisite verisimilitude of the work, meeting with such absolute inexperience in the reader, it was almost a duty to have made them. This duty, however, something had caused me to forget; and, when next I saw the young mountaineer, I forgot that I *had* forgotten it. Consequently, at first I was perplexed by the unfaltering gravity with which my fair young friend spoke of Dr. Primrose, of Sophia and her sister, of Squire Thornhill, etc., as real and probably living personages, who could sue and be sued. It appeared that this artless young rustic, who had never heard of novels and romances as a bare possibility amongst all the shameless devices of London swindlers, had read with religious fidelity every word of this tale, so thoroughly life-like, surrendering her perfect faith and loving sympathy to the different persons in the tale and the natural distresses in which they are involved, without suspecting for a moment that, by so much as a breathing of exaggeration or of embellishment, the pure gospel truth of the narrative could have been sullied. She listened in a kind of breathless stupor to my frank explanation that not part only, but the whole, of this natural tale was a pure invention. Scorn and indignation flashed from her eyes. She regarded herself as one who had been hoaxed and swindled; begged me to take back the book; and never again, to the end of her life, could endure to look into the book, or to be reminded of that criminal imposture which Dr. Oliver Goldsmith had practised upon her youthful credulity.

In that case, a book altogether fabulous, and not meaning to offer itself for anything else, had been read as genuine history. Here, on the other hand, the adventures of the Spanish Nun, which, in every detail of time and place have since been sifted and authenticated, stood a good chance at one period of being classed as the most lawless of romances. It is, indeed, undeniable—and this arises as a natural result from the bold adventurous character of the heroine, and from the unsettled state of society at that period in Spanish America—that a reader the most credulous would at times be startled with doubts upon what seems so unvarying a tenor of danger and lawless violence. But, on the other hand, it is also undeniable that a reader the most obstinately sceptical would be equally startled in the very opposite direction, on remarking that the incidents are far from being such as a romance-writer would have been likely to invent; since, if striking, tragic, and even appalling, they are at times repulsive. And it seems evident that, once putting himself to the cost of a wholesale fiction, the writer would have used his privilege more freely for his own advantage, whereas the author of these memoirs clearly writes under the coercion and restraint of a notorious reality, that would not suffer him to ignore or to modify the leading facts. Then, as to the objection that few people or none have an experience presenting such uniformity of perilous adventure, a little closer attention shows that the experience in this case is *not* uniform; and so far otherwise that a period of several years in Kate's South American life is confessedly suppressed, and on no other ground whatever than that this long parenthesis is *not* adventurous, not essentially differing from the monotonous character of ordinary Spanish life.

Suppose the case, therefore, that Kate's Memoirs had been thrown upon the world with no vouchers for their authenticity beyond such internal presumptions as would have occurred to thoughtful readers when reviewing the entire succession of incidents, I am of opinion that the person best qualified by legal experience to judge of evidence would finally have pronounced a favourable award; since it is easy to understand that in a world so vast as the Peru, the Mexico, the Chili, of Spaniards during the first quarter of the seventeenth century, and under the slender modification of Indian manners as yet effected by the Papal Christianisation of these countries, and in the neighbourhood of a river-system so awful, of a mountain-system so unheard-of in Europe, there would probably, by blind, unconscious sympathy, grow up a tendency to lawless and gigantesque ideals of adventurous life, under which, united with the duelling code of Europe, many things would become trivial and commonplace experiences that to us home-bred English ("*qui musas colimus severiores*") seem monstrous and revolting.

Left, therefore, to itself, *my* belief is that the story of the Military Nun would have prevailed finally against the demurs of the sceptics. However, in the meantime, all such demurs were suddenly and *officially* silenced for ever. Soon after the publication of Kate's Memoirs, in what you may call an early stage of her *literary* career, though two centuries after her *personal* career had closed, a regular controversy arose upon the degree of credit due to these extraordinary confessions (such they may be called) of the poor conscience-haunted nun. Whether these in Kate's original MS. were entitled "Autobiographic Sketches," or "Selections Grave and Gay, from the Military Experiences of a Nun," or possibly "The Confessions of a Biscayan Fire-Eater," is more than I know. No matter: confessions they were; and confessions that, when at length published, were absolutely mobbed and hustled by a gang of misbelieving (*i.e. miscreant*) critics. And this fact is most remarkable, that the person who originally headed the incredulous party—viz. Senor De Ferrer, a learned Castilian—was the very same who finally authenticated, by *documentary* evidence, the extraordinary narrative in those parts which had most of all invited scepticism. The progress of the dispute threw the decision at length upon the archives of the Spanish Marine. Those for the southern ports of Spain had been transferred, I believe, from Cadiz and St. Lucar to Seville: chiefly, perhaps, through the confusions incident to the two French invasions of Spain in our own day (1st, that under Napoleon, 2dly, that under the Duc d'Angoulême). Amongst these archives,—subsequently amongst those of Cuzco in South America,—3dly amongst the records of some royal courts in Madrid,—4thly by collateral proof from the Papal Chancery,—5thly from Barcelona—have been drawn together ample attestations of all the incidents recorded by Kate. The elopement from St Sebastian's, the doubling of Cape Horn, the shipwreck on the coast of Peru, the rescue of the royal banner from the Indians of Chili, the fatal duel in the dark, the astonishing passage of the Andes, the tragical scenes at Tucuman and Cuzco, the return to Spain in obedience to a royal and a papal summons, the visit to Rome and the interview with the Pope; finally, the return to South America, and the mysterious disappearance at Vera Cruz, upon which no light was ever thrown,—all these capital heads of the narrative have been established beyond the reach of scepticism; and, in consequence, the story was soon after adopted as historically established, and was reported at length by journals of the highest credit in Spain and Germany, and by a Parisian journal so cautious and so distinguished for its ability as the *Revue des Deux Mondes*. I must not leave the impression upon my readers that this complex body of documentary evidences has been searched and appraised by myself. Frankly, I acknowledge that, on the sole occasion when any opportunity offered itself for such a labour, I shrank from it as too fatiguing, and also as superfluous; since, if the proofs had satisfied the compatriots of Catalina, who came to the investigation with hostile feelings of partisanship, and not dissembling their incredulity,—armed also (and in Mr. De Ferrer's case conspicuously armed) with the appropriate learning for giving effect to this incredulity,—it could not become a stranger to suppose himself qualified for disturbing a judgment that had been so deliberately delivered. Such a tribunal of native Spaniards being satisfied, there was no further opening for demur. The ratification of poor Kate's Memoirs is now therefore to be understood as absolute and without reserve.[1]

This being stated—viz. such an attestation from competent authorities to the truth of Kate's narrative, as may save all readers from my fair Westmorland friend's disaster—it remains to give such an answer as without further research *can* be given to a question pretty sure of arising in all reflective readers' thoughts—viz. Does there anywhere survive a portrait of Kate? I answer—and it would be both mortifying and perplexing if I could *not*—*Yes*. One such portrait there is confessedly; and seven years ago this was to be found at Aix-la-Chapelle, in the collection of Herr Sempeller. The name of the artist I am not able to report; neither can I say whether Herr Sempeller's collection still remains intact, and remains at Aix-la-Chapelle.

But, inevitably, to most readers who review the circumstances of a case so extraordinary it will occur that beyond a doubt *many* portraits of the adventurous nun must have been executed. To have affronted the wrath of the Inquisition, and to have survived such an audacity, would of itself be enough to found a title for the martial nun to a national interest. It is true that Kate had not taken the veil; she had stopped short of the deadliest crime known to the Inquisition; but still her transgressions were such as to require a special indulgence; and this indulgence was granted by a

---

[1] See Appended Editorial Note.—M.

Pope to the intercession of a King—the greatest then reigning. It was a favour that could not have been asked by any greater man in this world, nor granted by any less. Had no other distinction settled upon Kate, this would have been enough to fix the gaze of her own nation. But her whole life constituted Kate's supreme distinction. There can be no doubt, therefore, that from the year 1624 (*i.e.* the last year of our James I.) she became the object of an admiration in her own country that was almost idolatrous. And this admiration was not of a kind that rested upon any partisan-schism amongst her countrymen. So long as it was kept alive by her bodily presence amongst them, it was an admiration equally aristocratic and popular, shared alike by the rich and the poor, by the lofty and the humble. Great, therefore, would be the demand for her portrait. There is a tradition that Velasquez, who had in 1623 executed a portrait of Charles I. (then Prince of Wales), was amongst those who in the three or four following years ministered to this demand.[1] It is believed also that, in travelling from Genoa and Florence to Rome, she sat to various artists, in order to meet the interest about herself already rising amongst the cardinals and other dignitaries of the Romish Church. It is probable, therefore, that numerous pictures of Kate are yet lurking both in Spain and Italy, but not known as such. For, as the public consideration granted to her had grown out of merits and qualities purely personal, and were kept alive by no local or family memorials rooted in the land, or surviving herself, it was inevitable that, as soon as she herself died, all identification of her portraits would perish; and the portraits would thenceforwards be confounded with the similar memorials, past all numbering, which every year accumulates as the wrecks from household remembrances of generations that are passing or passed, that are fading or faded, that are dying or buried. It is well, therefore, amongst so many

---

[1] Velasquez, b. 1599, d. 1660. His great celebrity may be said to date from 1623, when, on his second visit to Madrid at the age of twenty-four, he painted portraits of Philip IV, Olivarez, and other Spanish magnates, besides that of the English Prince Charles mentioned in the text,—which last, unfortunately, has been lost.—M.

irrecoverable ruins, that in the portrait at Aix-la-Chapelle we still possess one undoubted representation (and therefore in some degree a means for identifying *other* representations) of a female so memorably adorned by nature; gifted with capacities so unparalleled both of doing and suffering; who lived a life so stormy, and perished by a fate so unsearchably mysterious.

APPENDED EDITORIAL NOTE

[The following is substantially a repetition of a Note which I appended to a reprint of the story of the Spanish Military Nun contained in a Selection of De Quincey's Essays published in two volumes in 1888 by Messrs. Black.—M]

De Quincey was often secretive when there was little need for being so; and he would have saved himself trouble if, instead of mystifying his readers with the elaborate explanations in his Postscript, he had simply informed them that his story of the Spanish Military Nun was a cooked, and spiced, and De Quinceyfied (which means electrified and glorified) translation from the French.

Such, at all events, is the fact. In the *Revue des Deux Mondes* of 15th February 1847, or two months and a half before the publication of the first instalment of De Quincey's story in *Tait's Edinburgh Magazine*, there appeared, under the title "Catalina de Erauso," an article of forty-nine pages, signed "Alexis de Valon," and containing the same tissue of adventures which De Quincey thought it worth his while to turn into English. The writer of that article announced, near the beginning of it, that he took his facts from autobiographic Memoirs in the old Castilian tongue left by the heroine herself, and bearing the title *Historia de la Monja Alferez Donna Catalina de Erauso, escrita por ella misma* ("History of the Nun-Lieutenant Donna Catalina de Erauso, written by herself"); and the last section of the article was devoted to a farther account of what the author called "the history of this history" ("*l'histoire de cette histoire*").

According to this account, a certain M. de Ferrer, at one time a Spanish political refugee in France, having, in his readings in Spanish records, come upon some glowing mention of the exploits of the Nun of St. Sebastian, and feeling the more interested because he was himself a native of the province to which the Nun belonged, remembered that he had heard of her original manuscript memoirs as one of the preserved curiosities in the Royal Library of Seville, and of a copy of them as existing among the archives of the Office of Marine at Madrid. Having made inquiries and obtained a copy for his own use, he was sceptical at first as to the authenticity of the memoirs,—the copyist having written *Araujo* for *Erauso*, and M. de Ferrer not recognising

Araujo as ever having been the name of any family in his province. When the error was rectified, however, all became plain. On writing to St. Sebastian, M. de Ferrer obtained, we are told, the most definite testimony, from parish registers, the convent registers, etc., as to the existence of a Catalina de Erauso in that town at the time alleged, and as to the accuracy of the particulars in the earlier part of her reputed Autobiography. Research among the Government records at Seville, especially those relating to the Spanish American Colonies in the seventeenth century, having proved the substantial accuracy of all the rest, and traces having been found of a portrait of the Nun as having once existed in Rome, and an actual portrait of her having been discovered at Aix-la-Chapelle, M. de Ferrer no longer hesitated. "He published, for himself and his friends, the manuscript of "Catalina. This was just before the Revolution of July [1830], and "it was an ill-chosen time. The political excitement whirled away "the unfortunate book, which disappeared as mysteriously as the "heroine whose history it related. It can hardly have been seen by "more than a few rare amateurs, and it has passed now into the state "of a bibliographical curiosity." M. Alexis de Valon, the writer in the *Revue des Deux Mondes* for February 1847, we are to assume, had a copy then before him, and founded his article upon it.

Of the Memoirs themselves M. Alexis de Valon gives no very favourable opinion. "The original memoirs of Catalina," he writes, "are, it is my duty to say, clumsily written. They are less a narra-"tive than matter for a narrative; they are a dry and short summary, "without animation and without life. One feels that the hand which "held the pen had been hardened by holding a sword; and I find in "the very inexperience of the narrator the best guarantee of her "veracity. If a fiction, these memoirs would have been wholly "different; a writer of fiction would have done better or otherwise. "The style of Catalina is rude, coarse, often obscure, and sometimes "of an untranslateable frankness, verging on impudence. On the "whole, the narrative, though Spanish, is far from being orthodox. "If a scrupulous reader should find it even deplorable from the point "of view of morality, I should be noway surprised: plenty of rogues "have been hanged who were infinitely more respectable characters, I "fancy, than the Nun-Lieutenant. Her faults, however, great as "they may have been, do not inspire disgust. Hers is a savage, self-"abandoned nature, which has a conscience neither for good nor for "evil. Bred up to the age of fifteen by ignorant *religieuses*, aban-"doned from that time to all the hazards of a wandering life, all the "instincts of a vulgar nature, Catalina could learn no other morality "than that of the highways, camps, and life on board ship. She "evidently did not know what she did; she herself tells, without "malice, without bragging, without even thinking of excusing herself, "of actions of hers such as now-a-days would come before an assize-"court. She robs with candour, worthy woman, and she kills with "*naïveté*. For her a man's death is a very small thing."—So much for the criticism of the memoirs themselves and their author by the writer in the *Revue des Deux Mondes*. His criticism on their editor, M. de Ferrer, is good-natured on the whole, but rather sarcastic in parts. M. de Ferrer's painstaking research is praised; but he is quizzed for his over-enthusiasm for his subject, and for having written about a person who, at the best, was but a man-woman adventuress of the seventeenth century, entitled to the same kind of interest as that which attached to the famous Chevalier d'Eon of the eighteenth, as if there had been the makings in her of a Saint Theresa, an Aspasia, or a Madame de Stael.—One passage quoted from M. de Ferrer, purporting to be a description of Catalina's personal appearance in her more advanced life by a contemporary Spanish historian, may be worth re-quotation here:—"She is of large size for a woman," reports this authority, "without, however, having the stature of a fine man. "She has no throat or bust to speak of. Her figure is neither good "nor bad. Her eyes are black, brilliant, and well-opened; and her "features have been changed more by the fatigues she has undergone "than by age. She has black hair, short like that of a man, and "pomaded in the fashion. She is dressed like a Spaniard. Her "gait is elegant and light, and she carries a sword well. She has a "martial air. Her hands alone have a something feminine about "them, and this more in their *pose* than in their shape. Finally, her "upper lip is covered with a slight brown down, which, without "being actually a moustache, yet gives a certain virile aspect to her "physiognomy."

All this is from the last section of the article by M. Alexis de Valon in the *Revue des Deux Mondes*, the whole of the preceding forty-five pages of the article having consisted of a pretty skilful and vivid narrative of the adventures of Donna Catalina, as the writer had been able to conceive them from the rude autobiographical original, with the aid of M. de Ferrer's editorial elucidations. How far he adhered to the original, and how far he dressed it up into a romance suitable for modern French tastes, no one can tell who has not seen M. de Ferrer's own book.

De Quincey, I am pretty sure, had never seen that book. There is not, so far as I know, a copy of it in Edinburgh now; and there can hardly have been a copy of it in Edinburgh in De Quincey's time. His chief authority, I believe, when he wrote his paper for *Tait's Magazine*, was the previous paper by M. Alexis de Valon in the *Revue des Deux Mondes*. But it is fair to give his own account of the matter.

In an introductory paragraph prefixed to the first instalment of the story in *Tait* for May 1847, and vouching for its authenticity, he wrote:—" No memoir exists, or personal biography, that is so trebly "authenticated by proofs and attestations, direct and collateral. "From the archives of the Royal Marine at Seville, from the auto- "biography of the heroine, from contemporary chroniclers, and from "several official sources scattered in and out of Spain, some of them "ecclesiastical, the amplest proofs have been drawn, and may yet be "greatly extended, of the extraordinary events here recorded. M.

"de Ferrer, a Spaniard of much research, and originally incredulous as
"to the facts, published about seventeen years ago a selection from
"the leading documents, accompanied by his *palinode* as to their
"accuracy. His materials have been since used for the basis of more
"than one narrative, not inaccurate, in French, German, and Spanish
"journals of high authority. It is seldom that the French writers err
"by prolixity. They have done so in this case. The present narra-
"tive, which contains no one sentence derived from any foreign one,
"has the great advantage of close compression; my own pages, after
"equating the size, being as 1 to 3 of the shortest continental form."
One remarks here, in the first place, that De Quincey's own complete paper in *Tait's Magazine* is decidedly longer than its predecessor in the *Revue des Deux Mondes*, and, in the second place, not without some surprise, that, while mentioning vaguely other continental versions of the story of Donna Catalina, in German, Spanish, and French, he has avoided mentioning that one in particular!—In the reprint of 1854 he does mention it. In that reprint the introductory paragraph of 1847 just quoted was cancelled, and what had to be told of "the history of the history" was relegated, as we have seen, to a more formal *Postscript*, restating in detail the case for the authenticity of Kate's memoirs. There had been a controversy on the subject after their first publication, he there says; but, the researches of De Ferrer and others having been conclusive, the narrative had at last been adopted as "historically established," and had been "reported at length by journals of "the highest credit in Spain and Germany, and by a Parisian journal "so cautious and so distinguished for its ability as the *Revue des Deux* "*Mondes.*" Better late than never, though still, I think, not up to the proper mark! What follows is more significant. "I must not "leave the impression upon my readers," he says, "that this complex "body of documentary evidence has been searched and appraised by "myself. Frankly I acknowledge that, on the sole occasion when "any opportunity offered itself for such a labour, I shrank from it as "too fatiguing." This seems to be De Quincey's way of saying that, to as late as 1854, he had never had an opportunity of examining the original of Kate's memoirs in M. de Ferrer's book, and had therefore reprinted his story of her adventures much as it stood in his magazine papers of 1847.

My own final impression of the whole matter is that De Quincey, having read the article in the *Revue des Deux Mondes* in February or March 1847, said to himself, "This is a capital subject; I will do it over again," and that there and then he *proceeded* to do it over again, with little or nothing else than the article in the *Revue des Deux Mondes* for his material. Incident for incident, situation for situation, at all events, the story in the two papers is one and the same. Necessarily also the phraseology of the one corresponds to that of the other to a great extent throughout, though here De Quincey's craft in language enabled him to make good his assertion that *his* narrative contained "no one sentence derived from any foreign one." He had the art of De Quinceyfying whatever he borrowed; and his SPANISH MILITARY

NUN is, in reality, I repeat, a De Quinceyfied translation from the French. But much is involved in the word "De Quinceyfied." Not only are there passages in which we see him throwing ironical sideglances at the French original he is using, and refusing its version, or any French version, of the facts and circumstances; not only are there digressions, in which De Quincey leaves the track of the original altogether, to amuse himself and his readers for some moments with some crank or whimsy before returning to it, but the key of playful wit in which he has set the whole narrative of the Nun's life and adventures from its very start in the first few sentences, and the humour with which some of the situations and the sketches of some of the characters are suffused, are entirely De Quincey's. Above all, the Catalina of his story emerges as a much higher being than the Catalina of the French original; and, if ever that wild Spanish eccentric, that masculine nun-adventuress from Biscay, with her black eyes and black hair, the tinge of brown down on her upper lip, and the sword by her side, shall take permanent hold of the imagination of those who read books, it will be because her portrait, after having been attempted by rougher hands, was repainted more sympathetically by this greater artist.

At the same time, M. Alexis de Valon deserves the credit of having, in his fashion, told his story well. We have to go to him, in fact, for the exact chronology of Kate's life:—Born in 1592, she escaped from the nunnery of St. Sebastian on the 18th of March 1607, when she was in her fifteenth year. It was in the following year that, after her intermediate adventures in other Spanish towns, she embarked for Spanish America. Her various adventures there extended over a period of sixteen or seventeen years; and, when she returned to Spain in November 1624 as the famous detected woman-soldier, she was thirty-two years of age. The decree for the pension bestowed upon her by the Spanish King, Philip IV, and said to be still extant at Seville, was signed in August 1625. It was during the subsequent ten years of her vague residence in Spain and visits to Italy that several likenesses of her were taken, and those observations of her personal appearance and habits were made which M. de Ferrer gathered up. She was forty-three years of age when, in the year 1635, she took that fatal voyage back to America which ended in her mysterious disappearance on a stormy night at the landing-place of Vera Cruz on the Mexican coast, when all the other passengers got safely ashore and were surprised that she was not among them. De Quincey had formed a conjecture of his own, he says, on the subject of this mysterious disappearance; but, as he does not give it, we may quote that of her French biographer. "No need to say," M. Alexis de Valon writes, "that this mysterious "disappearance occasioned the most contradictory suppositions. Had "Catalina, passionate for a return to a life of wandering, fled again "into the wilds? How then should no farther traces of her have "been discovered? Or, in the dark of that stormy night, was she "drowned in disembarking, no one observing the accident? This "opinion seems the most reasonable, and yet her body was not found "in the harbour. A shark, no doubt, had swallowed Catalina:

"many persons more respectable than she have had no other sepulture."

The reader will understand now who that Frenchman was whom De Quincey, without naming him, takes to task several times in the course of his story, and once so severely, for insufficient appreciation of the character of the Spanish Military Nun. He was M. Alexis de Valon, the author of that article in the *Revue des Deux Mondes* for 15th February 1847 of the matter of which De Quincey's story in *Tait's Edinburgh Magazine* for May, June, and July of the same year was a De Quinceyfied reproduction. One can go back now with increased interest to that paragraph (pp. 197-200) where De Quincey, commenting on one passage of his French original, takes occasion to declare polemically, once for all, the fundamental difference of his own mood throughout the narrative from that of his unnamed French authority. "Left alone, the wanderer knelt down, took to weeping, and prayed "to God with fervour, doubtless for the first time in her life": so M. Alexis de Valon had written, in his description of Kate in her terrible solitude on the heights of the Andes after the deaths of her two companions. For the last phrase De Quincey is down upon him in an instant. He is "a Frenchman, who sadly misjudges Kate, looking at her through a Parisian opera-glass"; and, as for himself, not only does he believe that Kate had prayed many times before without mentioning the fact, but he will champion Kate in many other matters against all Frenchmen and all gainsayers whatever! It is here that he breaks out, "*I* love this Kate, bloodstained as she is," and that he proceeds to an ethical dissertation in her behalf, winding up with the assertion that "Kate *was* noble in many things," possessing "qualities that God loves either in man or woman," and with the wish that she were still alive "to give a punch on the head to that fellow who traduces her." This difference in De Quincey's conception of his heroine from that of the French critic of her Memoirs is maintained to the very end, but is perhaps nowhere more conspicuous than in the contrast between the two accounts of the unexplained disappearance of the heroine at last in the harbour of Vera Cruz. "Fell overboard, and probably eaten by a shark!" is substantially, as we have seen, our last glimpse of Kate in the French account of her life. De Quincey refuses a close so precise and so prosaic. He will not tell even his own hypothesis on the subject, but rises into the mysterious unknown, and leaves us there. The reader may choose between the two moods, and the two versions of Kate's story which they respectively inspire; and all is subject, of course, to any re-inquiry that may yet be moved into the historical authenticity of Kate's professed Autobiography.—M.

SORTILEGE AND ASTROLOGY [1]

SUDDENLY, about the middle of February, I received a request for some contribution of my own proper writing to a meditated ALBUM of a new Literary Institution, called the Athenæum, in a great western city. What was to be done? The 13th of the month had already dawned before the request reached me; "return of post" was the sharp limitation notified within which my communication must revolve; whilst the request itself was dated February 10th: so that already three "returns of post" had finished their brief career on earth. I am not one of those people who, in respect of bread, insist on the discretionary allowance (*pain à discrétion*) of Paris *restaurants*; but, in respect to time, I do. Positively, for all efforts of thought I must have time *à discrétion*. And thus it happened that there was no resource available but one; which was this:—In my study I have a bath, large enough to swim in, provided the swimmer, not being an ambitious man, is content with going ahead to the extent of three inches at the utmost. This bath, having been superseded (as regards its original purpose) by a better, has yielded a secondary service to me as a

---

[1] Appeared originally in a printed little collection of pieces, in prose and verse, got up as a contribution to a Ladies' Bazaar held on the 22d and 23d of March 1848 in aid of the Library of the Glasgow Athenæum. The volume, which is now scarce, bears the title *Glasgow Athenæum Album*, 1848. De Quincey's paper bears his name, and is placed first. Among the other contributors were Robert Chambers, James Hedderwick, George Gilfillan, Samuel Brown, and Mrs. Crowe. De Quincey's paper was reprinted by himself in 1858 in vol. ix. of his Collected Writings.—M.

reservoir for my MSS. Filled to the brim it is by papers of all sorts and sizes. Every paper written *by* me, *to* me, *for* me, *of* or *concerning* me, and, finally, *against* me, is to be found, after an impossible search, in this capacious repertory. Those papers, by the way, that come under the last (or hostile) subdivision are chiefly composed by shoemakers and tailors—an affectionate class of men, who stick by one to the last like pitch-plasters. One admires this fidelity; but it shows itself too often in waspishness, and all the little nervous irritabilities of attachment too jealous. They are wretched if they do not continually hear what one is "about," what one is "up to," and which way one is going to travel. Me, because I am a political economist, they plague for my private opinions on the currency, especially on that part of it which consists in bills at two years after date; and they always want an answer by return of post.

Now, from this reservoir I resolved to draw some paper for the use of the Athenæum. It was my fixed determination that this Institution should receive full justice, so far as human precautions could secure it. Four dips into the bath I decreed that the Athenæum should have; whereas an individual man, however hyperbolically illustrious, could have had but one. On the other hand, the Athenæum must really content itself with what fortune might send, and not murmur at me as if I had been playing with loaded dice. To cut off all pretence for such allegations, I requested the presence of three young ladies, haters of everything unfair, as female lawyers to watch the proceedings on behalf of the Athenæum, to see that the dipping went on correctly, and also to advise the court in case of any difficulties arising. At six P.M. all was reported right for starting in my study. The bath had been brilliantly illuminated from above, so that no tricks *could* be played in that quarter; and the young man who was to execute the dips had finished dressing in a new potato-sack, with holes cut through the bottom for his legs. Now, as the sack was tied with distressing tightness about his throat, leaving only a loophole for his right arm to play freely, it is clear that, however sincerely fraudulent in his intentions, and in possible collusion with myself, he could not assist me by secreting any papers about his person, or by any other knavery that we might wish to perpetrate. The young ladies having taken their seats in stations admirably chosen for overlooking any irregular movements, the proceedings opened. The inaugural step was made in a neat speech from myself, complaining that I was the object of unjust suspicions, and endeavouring to re-establish my character for absolute purity of intentions; but, I regret to say, ineffectually. I declared, with some warmth, that in the bath, but whereabouts I could not guess, there lay a particular paper which I valued as equal to the half of my possessions. "But for all that," I went on, "if our honourable friend in the potato sack should chance to haul up this very paper, I am resolved to stand by the event: yes, in that case, to the half of my kingdom I will express my interest in the Institution. Should even *that* prize be drawn, out of this house it shall pack off to the Athenæum, this very night." Upon this, the leader of the attorneys, whom, out of honour to Shakspere,[1] I may as well call Portia, chilled my enthusiasm disagreeably by saying— "There was no occasion for any extra zeal on *my* part in such an event, since, as to packing out of this house to the Athenæum, she and her learned sisters would take good care that it *did* ;"—in fact, *I* was to have no merit whatever I did. Upon this, by way of driving away the melancholy caused by the obstinate prejudices of the attorneys, I called for a glass of wine; and, turning to the west, I drank the health of the Athenæum, under the allegoric idea of a young lady about to come of age and enter upon the enjoyment of her estates. "Here's to your prosperity, my dear lass," I said; "you're very young; but that's a fault which, according to the old Greek adage, is mending every day; and I'm sure you'll always continue as amiable as you are now towards strangers in distress for books and journals. Never grow churlish, my dear, as some of your sex are" (saying which, I looked savagely at Portia). And then I made the signal to the young man for getting to work — Portia's eyes, as I noticed privately, brightening like a hawk's. "*Prepare to dip!*" I called aloud; and soon after—"*Dip!*" At the "*prepare*," Potato-sack went on his right knee (his face being

[1] *Merchant of Venice.*

at right angles to the bath); at the "Dip!" he plunged his right arm into the billowy ocean of papers. For one minute he worked amongst them as if he had been pulling an oar; and then, at the peremptory order "*Haul up!*" he raised aloft in air, like Brutus refulgent from the stroke of Cæsar, his booty. It was handed, of course, to the attorneys; who showed a little female curiosity at first, for it was a letter with the seal as yet unbroken, and might prove to be some old love-letter of my writing, recently sent back to me by the Dead-Letter Office. It still looked fresh and blooming. So, if there was no prize for the Athenæum, there might still be an interesting secret for the benefit of the attorneys. What it was, and what each successive haul netted, I will register under corresponding numbers.

No. 1.—This was a dinner invitation for the 15th of February, which I had neglected to open. It was, as bill-brokers say, "coming to maturity," but luckily not *past due* (in which case you have but a poor remedy); for it had still two days to run before it could be presented for payment. A debate arose with the attorneys—Whether this might not do for the *Album*, in default of any better haul? I argued for the affirmative—that, although a dinner invitation cannot in reason be looked to for very showy writing, its motto being *Esse quam videri* (which is good Latin for *To eat*[1] *rather than make believe to eat*, as at Barmecide banquets), yet, put the case that I should send this invitation to the Athenæum, accompanied with a power-of-attorney to eat the dinner in my stead, might not *that* solid bonus as an enclosure weigh down the levity of the letter considered as a contribution to the *Album*, and take off the edge of the Athenæum's displeasure? Portia argued *contra*—that such a thing was impossible; because the Athenæum had 2000 mouths, and would, therefore, require 2000 dinners;—an argument which I admitted to be showy, but, legally speaking, hardly tenable:

---

[1] *Esse*, to eat:—The reader who may chance to be no great scholar as regards Latin will yet perhaps be aware of this meaning attached of old to the verb *Esse*, from a Latin enigma current amongst schoolboys, viz. *Pes est caput*; which at first sight seems to say that *the foot is the head*, but in the true version means—*Pes* (in its secondary sense the same as *Pediculus*, an insect not to be named) *est*, eats, *caput*, the head.

because the Athenæum had power to appoint a plenipotentiary—some man of immense calibre—to eat the dinner as representative of the collective 2000. What there was to laugh at I don't see; but, at this hot skirmish between me and Portia, Potato-sack began to laugh so immoderately that I was obliged to pull him up by giving the word rather imperiously—"*Prepare to dip!*" Before he could obey, I was myself pulled up by Portia, with a triumph in her eye that alarmed me. She and her sister-attorneys had been examining the dinner invitation — "And," said Portia maliciously to me, "it's quite correct; as you observe there are two days good to the dinner hour on the 15th. Only, by misfortune, the letter is in the wrong year; it is four years old!" Oh! fancy the horror of this; since, besides the mortification from Portia's victory, I had perhaps narrowly escaped an indictment from the plenipotentiary for sending him what might *now* be considered a swindle. I hurried to cover my confusion by issuing the two orders "*Prepare to dip!*" and "*Dip!*" almost in the same breath. No. 1, after all the waste of legal learning upon it, had suddenly burst like a soap-bubble; and the greater stress of expectation, therefore, had now settled on No. 2. With considerable trepidation of voice, I gave the final order—"*Haul up!*"

No. 2.— It is disagreeable to mention that this haul brought up "a dun." Disgust was written upon every countenance; and I fear that suspicion began to thicken upon myself, as having possibly (from my personal experience in these waters) indicated to our young friend where to dredge for duns with most chance of success. But I protest fervently my innocence. It is true that I had myself long remarked that part of the channel to be dangerously infested with duns. In searching for literary or philosophic papers, it would often happen for an hour together that I brought up little else than variegated specimens of the dun. And one vast bank there was which I called the Goodwin Sands, because nothing within the memory of man was ever known to be hauled up from it except eternal varieties of the dun— some grey with antiquity, some of a neutral tint, some green and lively. With grief it was that I had seen our dipper shoaling his water towards that dangerous neighbourhood.

But what could I do? If I had warned him off, Portia would have been sure to fancy that there was some great oyster-bed or pearl-fishery in that region; and all I should have effected by my honesty would have been a general conviction of my treachery. Exactly below that very spot where he had dipped lay, as stationary as if he had been anchored, a huge and ferocious dun of great antiquity. Age had not at all softened the atrocious expression of his countenance, but rather aided it by endowing him with a tawny hue. The size of this monster was enormous, nearly two square feet; and I fancied at times that, in spite of his extreme old age, he had not done growing. I knew him but too well; because, whenever I happened to search in that region of the bath, let me be seeking what I would, and let me miss what I might, always I was sure to haul up *him* whom I never wanted to see again. Sometimes I even found him basking on the very summit of the papers; and I conceived an idea, which may be a mere fancy, that he came up for air in particular states of the atmosphere. At present he was *not* basking on the surface: better for the Athenæum if he *had*; for then the young man would have been cautious. Not being above, *he* was certainly below, and underneath the very centre of the dipper's plunge. Unable to control my feelings, I cried out — "Bear away to the right!" But Portia protested with energy against this intermeddling of mine, as perfidy too obvious. "Well," I said, "have it your own way: "you'll see what will happen."

No. 3.—This, it is needless to say, turned out the horrid old shark, as I had long christened him. I knew his vast proportions, and his bilious aspect, the moment that the hauling-up commenced, which in *his* case occupied some time. Portia was the more angry because she had thrown away her right to *express* any anger by neutralizing my judicious interference. She grew even more angry because I, though sorry for the Athenæum, really could not help laughing when I saw the truculent old wretch expanding his huge dimensions — all umbered by time and ill-temper — under the eyes of the wondering young ladies; so mighty was the contrast between this sallow behemoth and a rose-coloured little billet of their own. By the way, No. 2 had been a specimen of the dulcet dun, breathing only zephyrs of request and persuasion; but this No. 3 was a specimen of the polar opposite—the dun horrific and Gorgonian— blowing great guns of menace. As ideal specimens in their several classes, might they not have a value for the *museum* of the Athenæum, if it *has* one, or even for the *Album*? This was *my* suggestion, but overruled, like everything else that I proposed,—and on the ground that a great city had too vast a conservatory of duns, native and indigenous, to need any exotic specimens. This settled, we hurried to the next dip; which, being by contract the last, made us all nervous.

No. 4.—This, alas! turned out a lecture addressed to myself by an ultra-moral friend,—a lecture on procrastination, and not badly written. I feared that something of the sort was coming; for, at the moment of dipping, I called out to the dipper—"Starboard your helm! you're going smack upon the Goodwins: in thirty seconds you'll founder." Upon this, in an agony of fright, the dipper forged off, but evidently quite unaware that vast spurs stretched off from the Goodwins—shoals and sand-banks—where it was mere destruction to sail without a special knowledge of the soundings. He had run upon an ethical sand-bank. "Yet, after all, since this is to be the last dip," said Portia, "if the lecture is well written, might it not be acceptable to the Athenæum?" "Possibly," I replied; "but it is too personal. I could not allow myself to be advertised in a book as a procrastinator on principle, unless the Athenæum would add a postscript under its official seal expressing entire disbelief of the accusation; which I have private reasons for thinking that the Athenæum may decline to do."

"Well, then," said Portia, "as you wilfully rob the Athenæum of No. 4, which by contract is the undoubted property of that body, then you are bound to give us a fifth dip; particularly as you have been so treacherous all along." In the tone of an injured man I cried out, "My friend Potato-sack! will you quietly listen to this charge upon me? If it is a crime in me to know, and in you *not* to know, where the Goodwins lie, why, then, let you and me sheer off to the other side of the room, and let Portia try if *she* can do better. I allow her motion. I grant a fifth dip: and the more because it is an old saying—that there is luck in odd numbers: *numero deus impare gaudet*; only I must request of Portia to be the dipper on this final occasion." All the three attorneys blushed a rosy red on this unexpected summons. It was one thing to criticise, but quite another thing to undertake the performance: and the fair attorneys trembled for their professional reputation. Secretly, however, I whispered to Potato-sack, "You'll see now, such is female art and readiness that, whatever sort of monster they haul up, they'll proclaim it a great prize, and contrive to extract some use from it that may place *us* in the wrong."

No. 5.—Thrilling, therefore, were the doubts, fears, expectations of us all, when Portia "prepared to dip," and secondly "dipped." She shifted her hand, and "ploitered" amongst the papers for full five minutes. I winked at this in consideration of past misfortunes; but, strictly speaking, she had no right to "ploiter" for more than one minute. She contended that she knew, by intuition, the sort of paper upon which "duns" were written; and, whatever else might come up, she was resolved it should not be a dun. "Don't be too sure," I said; and, at last, when she seemed to have settled her choice, I called out the usual word of command, "*Haul up!*"

"What is it?" we said; "what's the prize?" one and all rushing up to Portia. Oh Gemini! my sympathizing reader;—it was a sheet of blank paper!

Did we laugh, or did we cry? I, for my part, was afraid to do either. I really felt for Portia, and, at the same time, for the Athenæum. But, bless you, reader! there was no call for pity to Portia. With the utmost coolness she said, so ready were *her* wits for facing any issue, "Oh! this is *carte blanche* for receiving your latest thoughts. This is the paper on which you are to write an essay for the Athenæum; and thus we are providentially enabled to assure our client the Athenæum of something expressly manufactured for the occasion, and not an old wreck from the Goodwins. Fortune loves the Athenæum; and her four blanks at starting were only meant to tease that Institution, and to enhance the value of her final favour." "Ah, indeed!" I said in an under tone: "*meant to tease!* there are other ladies who understand that little science beside Fortune!" However, there is no disobeying the commands of Portia; so I sat down to write a paper on ASTROLOGY. But, before beginning, I looked at Potato-sack, whispering only, "You see; I told you what would happen."

ASTROLOGY

As my contribution to their *Album*, I will beg the Athenæum to accept a single thought on this much-injured subject. Astrology I greatly respect; but it is singular that my respect for the science arose out of my contempt for its professors,—not exactly as a direct logical consequence, but as a casual suggestion from that contempt. I believe in Astrology, but not in astrologers; as to *them* I am an incorrigible infidel. First, let me state the occasion upon which my astrological thought arose; and then, secondly, the thought itself.

When about seventeen years old, I was wandering as a pedestrian tourist in North Wales. For some little time, the centre of my ramblings (upon which I still revolved from all my excursions, whether elliptical, circular, or zigzag) was Llangollen in Denbighshire, or else Rhuabon, not more than a few miles distant. One morning I was told by a young married woman, at whose cottage I had received some kind hospitalities, that an astrologer lived in the neighbourhood. "What might be his name?" Very good English it was that my young hostess had hitherto spoken; and yet, in this instance, she chose to answer me in Welsh. *Mochinahante* was her brief reply. I daresay that my spelling of the word will not stand Welsh criticism; but what can you expect from a man's first attempt at Welsh orthography? which at that time was, and (I believe) still is, a very rare accomplishment in the six counties of North Wales. But what did *Mochinahante* mean? For a man might as well be anonymous, or call himself X Y Z, as offer one his visiting card indorsed with a name so frightful to look at—so torturing to utter—so impossible to spell—as *Mochinahante*. And that it had a translatable meaning—that it was not a proper name but an appellative, in fact some playful *sobriquet*,—I felt certain, from observing the young woman to smile whilst she uttered it. My next question drew from her that this Pagan-looking monster of a name meant *Pig-in-the-dingle*. But really, now, between the original monster and this English interpretation there was very little to choose; in fact the interpretation, as often happens, strikes one as the harder to understand of the two. "To be sure it does," says a lady sitting at my elbow, and tormented by a passion so totally unfeminine as curiosity; "to be sure—very much harder; for *Mochina—what-do-you-call-it*? might, you know, mean something or other, for anything that you or I could say to the contrary; but, as to *Pig-in-the-dingle* — what dreadful nonsense! what an impossible description of an astrologer! A man that—let me see—does something or other about the stars: how can *he* be described as a pig? pig in *any* sense, you know; pig in *any* place? But *Pig-in-a-dingle*; why, if he's a pig at all, he must be *Pig-on-a-steeple*, or *Pig-on-the-top-of-a-hill*, that he may rise above the mists and vapours. Now, I insist, my dear creature, on your explaining all this riddle on the spot. *You* know it; you came to the end of the mystery; but none of *us* that are sitting here can guess at the meaning; we shall all be ill if you keep us waiting—I've a headache beginning already; so say the thing at once, and put us out of torment."

What's to be done? I *must* explain the thing to the Athenæum; and, if I stop to premise an oral explanation for the lady's separate use, there will be no time to save the village post; which waits for no man, and is deaf even to female outcries. By way of compromise, therefore, I request of the lady that she will follow my pen with her radiant eyes; by which means she will obtain the earliest intelligence, and the speediest relief to her headache. I, on my part, will not loiter, but will make my answer as near to a telegraphic answer, in point of speed, as a rigid metallic pen will allow.

I divide this answer into two heads: the first concerning "*in the dingle*"; the second concerning "*pig*." My philosophic researches, and a visit to the astrologer, ascertained a profound reason for describing him as *in-the-dingle*; viz.

because he *was* in a dingle. He was the sole occupant of a little cove amongst the hills—the sole householder; and so absolutely such that, if ever any treason should be hatched in the dingle, clear it was to my mind that *Mochinahante* would be found at the bottom of it; if ever war should be levied in this dingle, *Mochinahante* must be the sole belligerent; and, if a forced contribution were ever imposed upon this dingle, *Mochinahante* (poor man!) must pay it all out of his own pocket. The lady interrupts me at this point to say—" Well, I understand all *that*; that's all very clear. But what I want to know about is—*Pig*. Come to *Pig*. Why *Pig*? How *Pig*? In what sense *Pig*? You can't have any profound reason, you know, for *that*."

Yes, I have: a *very* profound reason; and satisfactory to the most sceptical of philosophers, viz. that he *was* a Pig. I was presented by my fair hostess to the great interpreter of the stars in person; for I was anxious to make the acquaintance of an astrologer, and especially of one who, whilst owning to so rare a profession, owned also to the soft impeachment of so very significant a name. Having myself enjoyed so favourable an opportunity for investigating the reasonableness of that name, *Mochinahante*, as applied to the Denbighshire astrologer, I venture to pronounce it unimpeachable. About his dress there was a forlornness, and an ancient tarnish or *ærugo*, which went far to justify the name; and upon his face there sat that lugubrious rust (or what medallists technically call *patina*) which bears so costly a value when it is found on the *coined* face of a Syro-Macedonian prince long since compounded with dust, but, alas! bears no value at all if found upon the flesh-and-blood face of a living philosopher. Speaking humanly, one would have insinuated that the star-gazer wanted much washing and scouring; but, astrologically speaking, perhaps he would have been spoiled by earthly waters for his celestial vigils.

Mochinahante was civil enough,—a pig, if by accident dirty, is not therefore rude; and, after seating me in his chair of state, he prepared for his learned labours by cross-examination as to the day and hour of my birth. The *day* I knew to a certainty; and even about the *hour* I could tell quite as much as ought in reason to be expected from one who certainly had not been studying a chronometer when that event occurred. These points settled, the astrologer withdrew into an adjoining room, for the purpose (as he assured me) of scientifically constructing my horoscope; but, unless the drawing of corks is a part of that process, I should myself incline to think that the great man, instead of minding my interests amongst the stars and investigating my horoscope, had been seeking consolation for himself in bottled porter. Within half-an-hour he returned; looking more lugubrious than ever—more grim—more grimy (if *grime* yields any such adjective)—a little more rusty—rather more *patinous*, if numismatists will lend me that word—and a great deal more in want of scouring. He had a paper of diagrams in his hand, which was supposed to contain some short-hand memoranda upon my horoscope; but, from its smokiness, a malicious visitor might have argued a possibility that it had served for more customers than myself. Under his arm he carried a folio book, which (he said) was a manuscript of unspeakable antiquity. This he was jealous of my seeing; and, before he would open it, as if I and the book had been two prisoners at the bar suspected of meditating some collusive mischief (such as tying a cracker to the judge's wig), he separated us as widely from each other as the dimensions of the room allowed. These solemnities finished, we were all ready—I, and the folio volume, and Pig-in-the-dingle—for our several parts in the play.

Mochinahante began. He opened the pleadings in a deprecatory tone, protesting, almost with tears, that, if anything should turn out amiss in the forthcoming revelations, it was much against his will—that *he* was powerless, and could not justly be held responsible for any part of the disagreeable message which it might be his unhappiness to deliver. I hastened to assure him that I was incapable of such injustice; that I should hold the stars responsible for the whole; by nature, that I was very forgiving; that any little malice which I might harbour for a year or so should all be reserved for the use of the particular constellations concerned in the plot against myself; and, lastly, that I was now quite ready to stand the worst of their thunders. Pig was pleased with this reasonableness—he saw that he had to deal with a philosopher—and, in a more cheerful tone, he now explained that my "case" was mystically contained in the diagrams: these smoke-dried documents submitted, as it were, a series of questions to the book; which book it was —a book of unspeakable antiquity—that gave the inflexible answers, like the gloomy oracle that it was. But I was not to be angry with the book, any more than with himself, since ——! "Of course not," I replied, interrupting him; "the book did but utter the sounds which were predetermined by the white and black keys struck in the smoky diagrams; and I could no more be angry with the book for speaking what it conscientiously believed to be the truth than with a decanter of port wine, or a bottle of porter, for declining to yield more than one or two wine-glasses of the precious liquor at the moment when I was looking for a dozen, under a transient forgetfulness, incident to the greatest minds, that I myself, ten minutes before, had nearly drunk up the whole." This comparison, though to a critic wide awake it might have seemed slightly personal, met with the entire approbation of *Pig-in-the-dingle*. A better frame of mind for receiving disastrous news, he evidently conceived, could not exist or be fancied by the mind of man than existed at that moment in myself. *He* was in a state of intense pathos from the bottled porter. *I* was in a state of intense excitement (pathos combined with horror) at the prospect of a dreadful lecture on my future life, now ready to be thundered into my ears from that huge folio of unspeakable antiquity, prompted by those wretched smoke-dried diagrams. I believe we were in magnetical rapport! Think of *that*, reader! Pig and I in magnetical rapport! Both making passes at each other! What in the world would have become of us if suddenly we should have taken to somnambulizing? Pig would have abandoned his dingle to me; and I should have dismissed Pig to that life of wandering which must have betrayed the unscoured and patinous condition of the astrologer to the astonished eyes of Cambria:—

"Stout Glo'ster stood aghast [or *might* have stood] in speechless trance.
 To arms! cried Mortimer [or at least *might* have cried], and couch'd his quivering lance"

But Pig was a greater man than he seemed. He yielded neither to magnetism nor to bottled porter; but commenced reading from the black book in the most awful tone of voice, and, generally speaking, most correctly. Certainly he made one dreadful mistake; he started from the very middle of a sentence, instead of the beginning; but then *that* had a truly lyrical effect, and also it was excused by the bottled porter. The words of the prophetic denunciation, from which he started, were these—"also *he* [that was myself, you understand] shall have red hair." "*There* goes a bounce," I said in an under tone; "the stars, it seems, can tell falsehoods as well as other people." "Also," for Pig went on without stopping, "he shall have seven-and-twenty children." Too horror-struck I was by this news to utter one word of protest against it. "Also," Pig yelled out at the top of his voice, "he shall desert them." Anger restored my voice, and I cried out, "That's not only a lie in the stars, but a libel; and, if an action lay against a constellation, I should recover damages." Vain it would be to trouble the reader with all the monstrous prophecies that Pig read against me. He read with a steady Pythian fury. Dreadful was his voice; dreadful were the starry charges against myself—things that I *was* to do—things that I *must* do; dreadful was the wrath with which secretly I denounced all participation in the acts which these wicked stars laid to my charge. But this infirmity of good-nature besets me,—that, if a man shows trust and absolute faith in any agent or agency whatever, heart there is not in me to resist him, or to expose his folly. Pig trusted—O how profoundly!—in his black book of unspeakable antiquity. It would have killed him on the spot to prove that the black book was a hoax, and that he himself was another. Consequently, I submitted in silence to pass for the monster that Pig, under the coercion of the stars, had pronounced me, rather than part in anger from the solitary man, who, after all, was not to blame, acting only in a ministerial capacity, and reading only what the stars obliged him to read. I rose without saying one word, advanced to the table, and paid my fees; for it is a disagreeable fact to record, that astrologers grant no credit, nor even discount upon prompt payment. I shook hands with *Mochinahante*;

we exchanged kind farewells: he smiling benignly upon me, in total forgetfulness that he had just dismissed me to a life of storms and crimes; I, in return, as the very best benediction that I could think of, saying secretly, "O Pig, may the heavens rain their choicest soap-suds upon thee!"

Emerging into the open air, I told my fair hostess of the red hair which the purblind astrologer had obtained for me from the stars, and which, with *their* permission, I would make over to *Mochinahante* for a reversionary wig in his days of approaching baldness. But I said not one word upon that too bountiful allowance of children with which *Moch.* had endowed me. I retreated by nervous anticipation from that inextinguishable laughter which, I was too certain, would follow upon *her* part; and yet, when we reached the outlet of the dingle, and turned round to take a parting look of the astrological dwelling, I myself was overtaken by fits of laughter; for suddenly I figured in vision my own future return to this mountain recess with the young legion of twenty-seven children. "*I* desert them, the darlings!" I exclaimed; "far from it! Backed by this filial army, I shall feel myself equal to the task of taking vengeance on the stars for the affronts they have put upon me through Pig, their servant. It will be like the return of the Heracleidæ to the Peloponnesus. The sacred legion will storm the 'dingle,' whilst *I* storm Pig; the rising generation will take military possession of '-*inahante*,' whilst I deal with '*Moch*' (which I presume to be the part in the long word belonging to *Pig*)." My hostess laughed in sympathy with *my* laughter; but I was cautious of letting her have a look into my vision of the sacred legion. For the female mind is naturally but too prone to laughter. We quitted the dingle for ever; and so ended my first visit, being also my last, to an astrologer.

This, reader, was the true general occasion of my one thought upon astrology; and, before I mention that thought, I may add that the immediate impulse drawing my mind in any such direction was this:—On walking to the table where the astrologer sat, in order to pay my fees, naturally I came nearer to the folio book than astrological prudence would generally have allowed. But Pig's attention was diverted for the moment to the silver coins laid before him: these he reviewed with the care reasonable in one so poor, and in a state of the coinage so neglected as in 1802 it was. By that moment of avarice in Pig I profited so far as to look over the astrologer's person, sitting and bending forward full upon the book. This was spread open; and at a glance I saw that it was no MS., but a printed book, in black-letter types. The month of August stood as a rubric at the head of the broad margin; and below it stood some days of that month in orderly succession. "So, then, Pig," said I in my thoughts, "it seems that any person whatever, born on my particular day and hour of August, is to have the same exact fate as myself. But a king and a beggar may chance thus far to agree. And be you assured, Pig, that all the infinite variety of cases lying between these two *termini* differ from each other in fortunes and incidents of life as much, though not so notoriously, as king and beggar."

Hence arose a confirmation of my contempt for astrology. It seemed as if *necessarily* false—false by an *a priori* principle, viz. that the possible differences in human fortunes, which are infinite, cannot be measured by the possible differences in the particular moments of birth, which are too strikingly finite. It strengthened me in this way of thinking that subsequently I found the very same objection in Macrobius. Macrobius may have stolen the idea; but certainly not from me—*as* certainly I did not steal it from him; so that here is a concurrence of two people independently, *one* of them a great philosopher, in the very same annihilating objection.

Now comes my one thought. Both of us were wrong, Macrobius and myself. Even the great philosopher is obliged to confess it. The objection, truly valued, is—to astrologers, not to astrology. No two events ever *did* coincide in point of time. Every event has, and must have, a certain duration; this you may call its *breadth*; and the true *locus* of the event in time is the central point of that breadth, which never was or will be the same for any two separate events, though grossly held to be contemporaneous. It is the mere imperfection of our human means for chasing the infinite subdivisibilities of time which causes us to regard two events as even by possibility concurring in their central moments. This imperfection is crushing to the pretensions of astrologers; but astrology laughs at it in the heavens; and astrology, armed with celestial chronometers, is true!

Suffer me to illustrate the case a little:—It is rare that a metaphysical difficulty can be made as clear as a pike-staff. This can. Suppose two events to occur in the same quarter of a minute—that is, in the same fifteen seconds; then, if they started precisely together, and ended precisely together, they would not only have the same breadth, but this breadth would accurately coincide in all its parts or fluxions; consequently, the central moment, viz. the eighth, would coincide rigorously with the centre of each event. But suppose that one of the two events,—A, for instance,—commenced a single second before B, the other: then, because we are still supposing them to have the same breadth or extension, A will have ended in the second before B ends, and consequently, the centres will be different, for the eighth second of A will be the seventh of B. The disks of the two events will overlap: A will overlap B at the beginning; B will overlap A at the end. Now, go on to assume that, in a particular case, this overlapping does not take place, but that the two events *eclipse* each other, lying as truly surface to surface as two sovereigns in a tight *rouleau* of sovereigns, or one dessert-spoon nestling in the bosom of another; in that case, the eighth or central second will be the centre for both. But even here a question will arise as to the degree of rigour in the coincidence; for divide the eighth second into a thousand parts of sub-moments, and perhaps the centre of A will be found to hit the 450th sub-moment, whilst that of B may hit the 600th. Or suppose, again, even this trial surmounted: the two harmonious creatures, A and B, running neck and neck together, have both hit simultaneously the true centre of the thousand sub-moments which lies half-way between the 500th and the 501st. All is right so far—" all right behind"; but go on, if you please; subdivide this last centre, which we will call X, into a thousand lesser fractions. Take, in fact, a railway express-train of decimal fractions, and give chase to A and B; my word for it that you will come up with them in some stage or other of the journey, and arrest them in the very act of separating their centres—which is a dreadful crime in the eye of astrology; for it is utterly impossible that the initial moment, or *sub*-moment, or *sub-sub*-moment of A and B should absolutely coincide. Such a thing as a perfect start was never heard of at Doncaster. Now, this severe accuracy is not wanted on earth. Archimedes, it is well known, never saw a perfect circle, nor even, with his leave, a decent circle; for, doubtless, the reader knows the following fact,—viz. that, if you take the most perfect Vandyking ever cut out of paper or silk, by the most delicate of female fingers, with the most exquisite of Salisbury scissors, upon viewing it through a microscope you will find the edges frightfully ragged; but, if you apply the same microscope to a case of God's Vandyking on the corolla of a flower, you will find it as truly cut and as smooth as a moonbeam. We on earth, I repeat, need no such rigorous truth. For instance, you and I, my reader, want little perhaps with circles, except now and then to bore one with an auger in a ship's bottom, when we wish to sink her, and to cheat the underwriters; or, by way of variety, to cut one with a centre-bit through shop-shutters, in order to rob a jeweller;—so *we* don't care much whether the circumference is ragged or not. But that won't do for a constellation! The stars *n'entendent pas la raillerie* on the subject of geometry. The pendulum of the starry heavens oscillates truly; and, if the Greenwich time of the *Empyreum* can't be repeated upon earth without an error, a horoscope is as much a chimera as the perpetual motion, or as an agreeable income-tax. In fact, in casting a nativity, to swerve from the true centre by the trillionth of a centillionth is as fatal as to leave room for a coach-and-six to turn between your pistol shot and the bull's eye. If you haven't done the trick, no matter how near you've come to it. And to overlook this is as absurd as was the answer of that Lieutenant M. who, being asked whether he had any connexion with another officer of the same name, replied—"O yes! a very close one." "But in what way?" "Why, you see, I'm in the 50th regiment of foot, and he's in the 49th": walking, in fact, just behind him! Yet, for all this, horoscopes may be calculated very truly by the stars amongst themselves; and my conviction is—that they are.

They are perhaps even printed hieroglyphically, and published as regularly as a nautical almanac. Only, they cannot be republished upon earth by any mode of piracy yet discovered amongst sublunary booksellers. Astrology, in fact, is a very profound, or, at least, a very lofty science; but astrologers are humbugs.

I have finished, and I am vain of my work; for I have accomplished three considerable things: I have floored Macrobius; I have cured a lady of her headache; and, lastly, which is best of all, I have expressed my sincere interest in the prosperity of a new-born Athenæum.

But our village post (a boy, in fact, who rides a pony) is mounting; and the chances are that this letter of mine will be too late,—a fact which, amongst all the dangers besetting me in this life, the wretched Pig forgot to warn me of.

THE ENGLISH MAIL-COACH[1]

Section I—The Glory of Motion

SOME twenty or more years before I matriculated at Oxford, Mr. Palmer, at that time M.P. for Bath, had accomplished two things, very hard to do on our little planet, the Earth, however cheap they may be held by eccentric people in comets: he had invented mail-coaches, and he had married the daughter of a duke.[2] He was, therefore, just twice as

---

[1] In October 1849 there appeared in *Blackwood's Magazine* an article entitled "*The English Mail-Coach, or the Glory of Motion.*" There was no intimation that it was to be continued, but in December 1849 there followed in the same magazine an article in two sections, headed by a paragraph explaining that it was by the author of the previous article in the October number, and was to be taken in connexion with that article. One of the sections of this second article was entitled "*The Vision of Sudden Death*," and the other "*Dream-Fugue on the above theme of Sudden Death.*" When De Quincey revised the papers in 1854 for republication in volume iv of the Collective Edition of his writings, he brought the whole under the one general title of "*The English Mail-Coach,*" dividing the text, as at present, into three sections or chapters, the first with the sub-title *The Glory of Motion*, the second with the sub-title *The Vision of Sudden Death*, and the third with the sub-title *Dream-Fugue, founded on the preceding theme of Sudden Death*. Great care was bestowed on the revision. Passages that had appeared in the magazine articles were omitted; new sentences were inserted; and the language was retouched throughout. —M.

[2] Mr. John Palmer, a native of Bath, and from about 1768 the energetic proprietor of the Theatre Royal in that city, had been led, by the wretched state in those days of the means of intercommunication between Bath and London, and his own consequent difficulties in arranging for a punctual succession of good actors at his theatre, to turn his attention to the improvement of the whole system of Post-

great a man as Galileo, who did certainly invent (or, which is the same thing,[1] discover) the satellites of Jupiter, those very next things extant to mail-coaches in the two capital pretensions of speed and keeping time, but, on the other hand, who did *not* marry the daughter of a duke.

These mail-coaches, as organised by Mr. Palmer, are entitled to a circumstantial notice from myself, having had so large a share in developing the anarchies of my subsequent dreams: an agency which they accomplished, 1st, through velocity at that time unprecedented—for they first revealed the glory of motion; 2dly, through grand effects for the eye between lamp-light and the darkness upon solitary roads; 3dly, through animal beauty and power so often displayed in the class of horses selected for this mail service; 4thly, Office conveyance, and of locomotive machinery generally, in the British Islands. The result was a scheme for superseding, on the great roads at least, the then existing system of sluggish and irregular stage-coaches, the property of private persons and companies, by a new system of government coaches, in connexion with the Post-Office, carrying the mails, and also a regulated number of passengers, with clock-work precision, at a rate of comparative speed, which he hoped should ultimately be not less than ten miles an hour. The opposition to the scheme was, of course, enormous; coach-proprietors, innkeepers, the Post-Office officials themselves, were all against Mr. Palmer; he was voted a crazy enthusiast and a public bore. Pitt, however, when the scheme was submitted to him, recognised its feasibility; on the 8th of August 1784 the first mail-coach on Mr. Palmer's plan started from London at 8 o'clock in the morning and reached Bristol at 11 o'clock at night; and from that day the success of the new system was assured.—Mr. Palmer himself, having been appointed Surveyor and Comptroller-General of the Post-Office, took rank as an eminent and wealthy public man, M.P. for Bath and what not, and lived till 1818. De Quincey makes it one of his distinctions that he "had married the daughter of a duke"; and in a footnote to that paragraph he gives the lady's name as "Lady Madeline Gordon." From an old Debrett, however, I learn that Lady Madelina Gordon, second daughter of Alexander, fourth Duke of Gordon, was first married, on the 3d of April 1789, to Sir Robert Sinclair, Bart., and next, on the 25th of November 1805, to *Charles Palmer, of Lockley Park, Berks, Esq*. If Debrett is right, her second husband was not the John Palmer of Mail-Coach celebrity, and De Quincey is wrong.—M.

[1] "*The same thing*":—Thus, in the calendar of the Church Festivals, the discovery of the true cross (by Helen, the mother of Constantine) is recorded (and, one might think, with the express consciousness of sarcasm) as the *Invention* of the Cross.

through the conscious presence of a central intellect, that, in the midst of vast distances[1]—of storms, of darkness, of danger—overruled all obstacles into one steady co-operation to a national result. For my own feeling, this post-office service spoke as by some mighty orchestra, where a thousand instruments, all disregarding each other, and so far in danger of discord, yet all obedient as slaves to the supreme *baton* of some great leader, terminate in a perfection of harmony like that of heart, brain, and lungs in a healthy animal organisation. But, finally, that particular element in this whole combination which most impressed myself, and through which it is that to this hour Mr. Palmer's mail-coach system tyrannises over my dreams by terror and terrific beauty, lay in the awful *political* mission which at that time it fulfilled. The mail-coach it was that distributed over the face of the land, like the opening of apocalyptic vials, the heart-shaking news of Trafalgar, of Salamanca, of Vittoria, of Waterloo.[2] These were the harvests that, in the grandeur of their reaping, redeemed the tears and blood in which they had been sown. Neither was the meanest peasant so much below the grandeur and the sorrow of the times as to confound battles such as these, which were gradually moulding the destinies of Christendom, with the vulgar conflicts of ordinary warfare, so often no more than gladiatorial trials of national prowess. The victories of England in this stupendous contest rose of themselves as natural *Te Deums* to heaven; and it was felt by the thoughtful that such victories, at such a crisis of general prostration, were not more beneficial to ourselves than finally to France, our enemy, and to the nations of all western or central Europe, through whose pusillanimity it was that the French domination had prospered.

The mail-coach, as the national organ for publishing these mighty events, thus diffusively influential, became itself a spiritualised and glorified object to an impassioned heart;

---

[1] "*Vast distances*":—One case was familiar to mail-coach travellers where two mails in opposite directions, north and south, starting at the same minute from points six hundred miles apart, met almost constantly at a particular bridge which bisected the total distance.

[2] Battle of Trafalgar, Nelson's last victory, 21st October 1805; Battle of Salamanca, 22d July 1812; Battle of Vittoria, 21st June 1813; Battle of Waterloo, 18th June 1815.—M.

and naturally, in the Oxford of that day, *all* hearts were impassioned, as being all (or nearly all) in *early* manhood. In most universities there is one single college; in Oxford there were five-and-twenty, all of which were peopled by young men, the *élite* of their own generation; not boys, but men: none under eighteen. In some of these many colleges the custom permitted the student to keep what are called "short terms"; that is, the four terms of Michaelmas, Lent, Easter, and Act, were kept by a residence, in the aggregate, of ninety-one days, or thirteen weeks. Under this interrupted residence, it was possible that a student might have a reason for going down to his home four times in the year. This made eight journeys to and fro. But, as these homes lay dispersed through all the shires of the island, and most of us disdained all coaches except his majesty's mail, no city out of London could pretend to so extensive a connexion with Mr. Palmer's establishment as Oxford. Three mails, at the least, I remember as passing every day through Oxford, and benefiting by my personal patronage—viz. the Worcester, the Gloucester, and the Holyhead mail. Naturally, therefore, it became a point of some interest with us, whose journeys revolved every six weeks on an average, to look a little into the executive details of the system. With some of these Mr. Palmer had no concern; they rested upon bye-laws enacted by posting-houses for their own benefit, and upon other bye-laws, equally stern, enacted by the inside passengers for the illustration of their own haughty exclusiveness. These last were of a nature to rouse our scorn; from which the transition was not very long to systematic mutiny. Up to this time, say 1804, or 1805 (the year of Trafalgar), it had been the fixed assumption of the four inside people (as an old tradition of all public carriages derived from the reign of Charles II) that they, the illustrious quaternion, constituted a porcelain variety of the human race, whose dignity would have been compromised by exchanging one word of civility with the three miserable delf-ware outsides. Even to have kicked an outsider might have been held to attain the foot concerned in that operation, so that, perhaps, it would have required an act of Parliament to restore its purity of blood. What words, then, could express the horror, and the sense of treason, in that case, which *had* happened, where all three outsides (the trinity of Pariahs[1]) made a vain attempt to sit down at the same breakfast-table or dinner-table with the consecrated four? I myself witnessed such an attempt; and on that occasion a benevolent old gentleman endeavoured to soothe his three holy associates, by suggesting that, if the outsides were indicted for this criminal attempt at the next assizes, the court would regard it as a case of lunacy or *delirium tremens* rather than of treason. England owes much of her grandeur to the depth of the aristocratic element in her social composition, when pulling against her strong democracy. I am not the man to laugh at it. But sometimes, undoubtedly, it expressed itself in comic shapes. The course taken with the infatuated outsiders, in the particular attempt which I have noticed, was that the waiter, beckoning them away from the privileged *salle-à-manger*, sang out, "This way, my good men," and then enticed these good men away to the kitchen. But that plan had not always answered. Sometimes, though rarely, cases occurred where the intruders, being stronger than usual, or more vicious than usual, resolutely refused to budge, and so far carried their point as to have a separate table arranged for themselves in a corner of the general room. Yet, if an Indian screen could be found ample enough to plant them out from the very eyes of the high table, or *dais*, it then became possible to assume as a fiction of law that the three delf fellows, after all, were not present. They could be ignored by the porcelain men, under the maxim that objects not appearing and objects not existing are governed by the same logical construction.[2]

Such being, at that time, the usage of mail-coaches, what was to be done by us of young Oxford? We, the most aristocratic of people, who were addicted to the practice of looking down superciliously even upon the insides themselves as often very questionable characters—were we, by voluntarily

---

[1] This word *Pariah* for "social outcast" (from the name of the lowest of the Hindoo ranks) was a favourite word in De Quincey's vocabulary, for which he often found very serious use.—M.

[2] *De non apparentibus*, etc. [*De non apparentibus et non existentibus eadem est lex*].

going outside, to court indignities? If our dress and bearing sheltered us generally from the suspicion of being "raff" (the name at that period for "snobs"[1]), we really *were* such constructively by the place we assumed. If we did not submit to the deep shadow of eclipse, we entered at least the skirts of its penumbra. And the analogy of theatres was valid against us,—where no man can complain of the annoyances incident to the pit or gallery, having his instant remedy in paying the higher price of the boxes. But the soundness of this analogy we disputed. In the case of the theatre, it cannot be pretended that the inferior situations have any separate attractions, unless the pit may be supposed to have an advantage for the purposes of the critic or the dramatic reporter. But the critic or reporter is a rarity. For most people, the sole benefit is in the price. Now, on the contrary, the outside of the mail had its own incommunicable advantages. These we could not forgo. The higher price we would willingly have paid, but not the price connected with the condition of riding inside; which condition we pronounced insufferable. The air, the freedom of prospect, the proximity to the horses, the elevation of seat: these were what we required; but, above all, the certain anticipation of purchasing occasional opportunities of driving.

Such was the difficulty which pressed us; and under the coercion of this difficulty we instituted a searching inquiry into the true quality and valuation of the different apartments about the mail. We conducted this inquiry on metaphysical principles; and it was ascertained satisfactorily that the roof of the coach, which by some weak men had been called the attics, and by some the garrets, was in reality the drawing-room; in which drawing-room the box was the chief ottoman or sofa; whilst it appeared that the *inside*, which had been traditionally regarded as the only room tenantable by gentlemen, was, in fact, the coal-cellar in disguise.

Great wits jump. The very same idea had not long

---

[1] "*Snobs*," and its antithesis, "*nobs*," arose among the internal factions of shoemakers perhaps ten years later. Possibly enough, the terms may have existed much earlier; but they were then first made known, picturesquely and effectively, by a trial at some assizes which happened to fix the public attention.

before struck the celestial intellect of China. Amongst the presents carried out by our first embassy to that country was a state-coach. It had been specially selected as a personal gift by George III; but the exact mode of using it was an intense mystery to Pekin. The ambassador, indeed (Lord Macartney), had made some imperfect explanations upon this point; but, as His Excellency communicated these in a diplomatic whisper at the very moment of his departure, the celestial intellect was very feebly illuminated, and it became necessary to call a cabinet council on the grand state question, "Where was the Emperor to sit?" The hammer-cloth happened to be unusually gorgeous; and, partly on that consideration, but partly also because the box offered the most elevated seat, was nearest to the moon, and undeniably went foremost, it was resolved by acclamation that the box was the imperial throne, and, for the scoundrel who drove,—he might sit where he could find a perch. The horses, therefore, being harnessed, solemnly his imperial majesty ascended his new English throne under a flourish of trumpets, having the first lord of the treasury on his right hand, and the chief jester on his left. Pekin gloried in the spectacle; and in the whole flowery people, constructively present by representation, there was but one discontented person, and *that* was the coachman. This mutinous individual audaciously shouted, "Where am *I* to sit?" But the privy council, incensed by his disloyalty, unanimously opened the door, and kicked him into the inside. He had all the inside places to himself; but such is the rapacity of ambition that he was still dissatisfied. "I say," he cried out in an extempore petition addressed to the Emperor through the window— "I say, how am I to catch hold of the reins?"—"Anyhow," was the imperial answer; "don't trouble *me*, man, in my glory. How catch the reins? Why, through the windows, through the keyholes—*anyhow*." Finally this contumacious coachman lengthened the check-strings into a sort of juryreins communicating with the horses; with these he drove as steadily as Pekin had any right to expect. The Emperor returned after the briefest of circuits; he descended in great pomp from his throne, with the severest resolution never to remount it. A public thanksgiving was ordered for his majesty's happy escape from the disease of broken neck; and the state-coach was dedicated thenceforward as a votive offering to the god Fo Fo — whom the learned more accurately called Fi Fi.[1]

A revolution of this same Chinese character did young Oxford of that era effect in the constitution of mail-coach society. It was a perfect French Revolution; and we had good reason to say, ça ira.[2] In fact, it soon became *too* popular. The "public"—a well-known character, particularly disagreeable, though slightly respectable, and notorious for affecting the chief seats in synagogues—had at first loudly opposed this revolution; but, when the opposition showed itself to be ineffectual, our disagreeable friend went into it with headlong zeal. At first it was a sort of race between us; and, as the public is usually from thirty to fifty years old, naturally we of young Oxford, that averaged about twenty, had the advantage. Then the public took to bribing, giving fees to horse-keepers, &c., who hired out their persons as warming-pans on the box-seat. *That*, you know, was shocking to all moral sensibilities. Come to bribery, said we, and there is an end to all morality,—Aristotle's, Zeno's, Cicero's, or anybody's. And, besides, of what use was it? For *we* bribed also. And, as our bribes, to those of the public, were as five shillings to sixpence, here again young Oxford had the advantage. But the contest was ruinous to the principles of the stables connected with the mails. This whole corporation was constantly bribed, rebribed, and often sur-rebribed; a mail-coach yard was like the hustings in a contested election; and a horse-keeper, ostler, or helper, was held by the philosophical at that time to be the most corrupt character in the nation

There was an impression upon the public mind, natural enough from the continually augmenting velocity of the mail, but quite erroneous, that an outside seat on this class of carriages was a post of danger. On the contrary, I main-

[1] This paragraph is a caricature of a story told in Staunton's Account of the Earl of Macartney's Embassy to China in 1792.—M.
[2] Ça ira ("This will do," "This is the go"), a proverb of the French Revolutionists when they were hanging the aristocrats in the streets, &c., and the burden of one of the popular revolutionary songs —"Ça ira, ça ira, ça ira"—M.

tained that, if a man had become nervous from some gipsy prediction in his childhood, allocating to a particular moon now approaching some unknown danger, and he should inquire earnestly, "Whither can I fly for shelter? Is a prison the safest retreat? or a lunatic hospital? or the British Museum?" I should have replied, "Oh no; I'll tell you what to do. Take lodgings for the next forty days on the box of his majesty's mail. Nobody can touch you there. If it is by bills at ninety days after date that you are made unhappy—if noters and protesters are the sort of wretches whose astrological shadows darken the house of life —then note you what I vehemently protest: viz. that, no matter though the sheriff and under-sheriff in every county should be running after you with his *posse*, touch a hair of your head he cannot whilst you keep house and have your legal domicile on the box of the mail. It is felony to stop the mail; even the sheriff cannot do that. And an *extra* touch of the whip to the leaders (no great matter if it grazes the sheriff) at any time guarantees your safety." In fact, a bedroom in a quiet house seems a safe enough retreat; yet it is liable to its own notorious nuisances—to robbers by night, to rats, to fire. But the mail laughs at these terrors. To robbers, the answer is packed up and ready for delivery in the barrel of the guard's blunderbuss. Rats again! there *are* none about mail-coaches, any more than snakes in Von Troil's Iceland[1]; except, indeed, now and then a parliamentary rat, who always hides his shame in what I have shown to be the "coal-cellar." And, as to fire, I never knew but one in a mail-coach; which was in the Exeter mail, and caused by an obstinate sailor bound to Devonport. Jack, making light of the law and the lawgiver that had set their faces against his offence, insisted on taking up a forbidden seat[2] in the rear of the roof, from which he could exchange

---

[1] "*Von Troil's Iceland*":—The allusion is to a well-known chapter in Von Troil's work, entitled, "Concerning the Snakes of Iceland." The entire chapter consists of these six words—"*There are no snakes in Iceland.*"

[2] "*Forbidden seat*".—The very sternest code of rules was enforced upon the mails by the Post-office. Throughout England, only three outsides were allowed, of whom one was to sit on the box, and the other two immediately behind the box; none, under any pretext, to

his own yarns with those of the guard. No greater offence was then known to mail-coaches; it was treason, it was *læsa majestas*, it was by tendency arson; and the ashes of Jack's pipe, falling amongst the straw of the hinder boot, containing the mail-bags, raised a flame which (aided by the wind of our motion) threatened a revolution in the republic of letters. Yet even this left the sanctity of the box unviolated. In dignified repose, the coachman and myself sat on, resting with benign composure upon our knowledge that the fire would have to burn its way through four inside passengers before it could reach ourselves. I remarked to the coachman, with a quotation from Virgil's *Æneid* really too hackneyed—

"Jam proximus ardet Ucalegon."

But, recollecting that the Virgilian part of the coachman's education might have been neglected, I interpreted so far as to say that perhaps at that moment the flames were catching hold of our worthy brother and inside passenger, Ucalegon. The coachman made no answer,—which is my own way when a stranger addresses me either in Syriac or in Coptic; but by his faint sceptical smile he seemed to insinuate that he knew better,—for that Ucalegon, as it happened, was not in the way-bill, and therefore could not have been booked.

No dignity is perfect which does not at some point ally itself with the mysterious. The connexion of the mail with

come near the guard; an indispensable caution; since else, under the guise of a passenger, a robber might by any one of a thousand advantages—which sometimes are created, but always are favoured, by the animation of frank social intercourse—have disarmed the guard. Beyond the Scottish border, the regulation was so far relaxed as to allow of *four* outsides, but not relaxed at all as to the mode of placing them. One, as before, was seated on the box, and the other three on the front of the roof, with a determinate and ample separation from the little insulated chair of the guard. This relaxation was conceded by way of compensating to Scotland her disadvantages in point of population. England, by the superior density of her population, might always count upon a large fund of profits in the fractional trips of chance passengers riding for short distances of two or three stages. In Scotland this chance counted for much less. And therefore, to make good the deficiency, Scotland was allowed a compensatory profit upon one *extra* passenger.

the state and the executive government—a connexion obvious, but yet not strictly defined—gave to the whole mail establishment an official grandeur which did us service on the roads, and invested us with seasonable terrors. Not the less impressive were those terrors because their legal limits were imperfectly ascertained. Look at those turnpike gates: with what deferential hurry, with what an obedient start, they fly open at our approach! Look at that long line of carts and carters ahead, audaciously usurping the very crest of the road. Ah! traitors, they do not hear us as yet; but, as soon as the dreadful blast of our horn reaches them with proclamation of our approach, see with what frenzy of trepidation they fly to their horses' heads, and deprecate our wrath by the precipitation of their crane-neck quarterings. Treason they feel to be their crime; each individual carter feels himself under the ban of confiscation and attainder; his blood is attainted through six generations; and nothing is wanting but the headsman and his axe, the block and the sawdust, to close up the vista of his horrors. What! shall it be within benefit of clergy to delay the king's message on the high road?—to interrupt the great respirations, ebb and flood, *systole* and *diastole*, of the national intercourse?—to endanger the safety of tidings running day and night between all nations and languages? Or can it be fancied, amongst the weakest of men, that the bodies of the criminals will be given up to their widows for Christian burial? Now, the doubts which were raised as to our powers did more to wrap them in terror, by wrapping them in uncertainty, than could have been effected by the sharpest definitions of the law from the Quarter Sessions. We, on our parts (we, the collective mail, I mean), did our utmost to exalt the idea of our privileges by the insolence with which we wielded them. Whether this insolence rested upon law that gave it a sanction, or upon conscious power that haughtily dispensed with that sanction, equally it spoke from a potential station; and the agent, in each particular insolence of the moment, was viewed reverentially, as one having authority.

Sometimes after breakfast his majesty's mail would become frisky; and, in its difficult wheelings amongst the intricacies of early markets, it would upset an apple-cart, a cart loaded with eggs, &c. Huge was the affliction and dismay, awful was the smash. I, as far as possible, endeavoured in such a case to represent the conscience and moral sensibilities of the mail; and, when wildernesses of eggs were lying poached under our horses' hoofs, then would I stretch forth my hands in sorrow, saying (in words too celebrated at that time, from the false echoes[1] of Marengo), "Ah! wherefore have we not time to weep over you?"—which was evidently impossible, since, in fact, we had not time to laugh over them. Tied to post-office allowance in some cases of fifty minutes for eleven miles, could the royal mail pretend to undertake the offices of sympathy and condolence? Could it be expected to provide tears for the accidents of the road? If even it seemed to trample on humanity, it did so, I felt, in discharge of its own more peremptory duties.

Upholding the morality of the mail, *a fortiori* I upheld its rights; as a matter of duty, I stretched to the uttermost its privilege of imperial precedency, and astonished weak minds by the feudal powers which I hinted to be lurking constructively in the charters of this proud establishment. Once I remember being on the box of the Holyhead mail, between Shrewsbury and Oswestry, when a tawdry thing from Birmingham, some "Tallyho" or "Highflyer," all flaunting with green and gold, came up alongside of us. What a contrast to our royal simplicity of form and colour in this plebeian wretch! The single ornament on our dark ground of chocolate colour was the mighty shield of the imperial arms, but emblazoned in proportions as modest as a signet-ring bears to a seal of office. Even this was displayed only on a single panel, whispering, rather than proclaiming, our relations to the mighty state; whilst the beast from Birmingham, our green-and-gold friend from false, fleeting, perjured Brummagem, had as much writing and painting on its sprawling flanks as would have puzzled a decipherer from

---

[1] "*False echoes*":—Yes, false! for the words ascribed to Napoleon, as breathed to the memory of Desaix, never were uttered at all. They stand in the same category of theatrical fictions as the cry of the foundering line-of-battle ship *Vengeur*, as the vaunt of General Cambronne at Waterloo, "*La Garde meurt, mais ne se rend pas*," or as the repartees of Talleyrand.

the tombs of Luxor. For some time this Birmingham machine ran along by our side—a piece of familiarity that already of itself seemed to me sufficiently jacobinical. But all at once a movement of the horses announced a desperate intention of leaving us behind. "Do you see *that*?" I said to the coachman.—"I see," was his short answer. He was wide awake,—yet he waited longer than seemed prudent; for the horses of our audacious opponent had a disagreeable air of freshness and power. But his motive was loyal; his wish was that the Birmingham conceit should be full-blown before he froze it. When *that* seemed right, he unloosed, or, to speak by a stronger word, he *sprang*, his known resources: he slipped our royal horses like cheetahs, or hunting-leopards, after the affrighted game. How they could retain such a reserve of fiery power after the work they had accomplished seemed hard to explain. But on our side, besides the physical superiority, was a tower of moral strength, namely the king's name, "which they upon the adverse faction wanted." Passing them without an effort, as it seemed, we threw them into the rear with so lengthening an interval between us as proved in itself the bitterest mockery of their presumption; whilst our guard blew back a shattering blast of triumph that was really too painfully full of derision.

I mention this little incident for its connexion with what followed. A Welsh rustic, sitting behind me, asked if I had not felt my heart burn within me during the progress of the race? I said, with philosophic calmness, *No*; because we were not racing with a mail, so that no glory could be gained. In fact, it was sufficiently mortifying that such a Birmingham thing should dare to challenge us. The Welshman replied that he didn't see *that*, for that a cat might look at a king, and a Brummagem coach might lawfully race the Holyhead mail. "*Race* us, if you like," I replied, "though even *that* has an air of sedition; but not *beat* us. This would have been treason; and for its own sake I am glad that the 'Tallyho' was disappointed." So dissatisfied did the Welshman seem with this opinion that at last I was obliged to tell him a very fine story from one of our elder dramatists: viz. that once, in some far oriental kingdom, when the sultan of all the land, with his princes, ladies, and chief omrahs, were flying their falcons, a hawk suddenly flew at a majestic eagle, and, in defiance of the eagle's natural advantages, in contempt also of the eagle's traditional royalty, and before the whole assembled field of astonished spectators from Agra and Lahore, killed the eagle on the spot. Amazement seized the sultan at the unequal contest, and burning admiration for its unparalleled result. He commanded that the hawk should be brought before him; he caressed the bird with enthusiasm; and he ordered that, for the commemoration of his matchless courage, a diadem of gold and rubies should be solemnly placed on the hawk's head, but then that, immediately after this solemn coronation, the bird should be led off to execution, as the most valiant indeed of traitors, but not the less a traitor, as having dared to rise rebelliously against his liege lord and anointed sovereign, the eagle. "Now," said I to the Welshman, "to you and me, as men of refined sensibilities, how painful it would have been that this poor Brummagem brute, the 'Tallyho,' in the impossible case of a victory over us, should have been crowned with Birmingham tinsel, with paste diamonds and Roman pearls, and then led off to instant execution." The Welshman doubted if that could be warranted by law. And, when I hinted at the 6th of Edward Longshanks, chap. 18, for regulating the precedency of coaches, as being probably the statute relied on for the capital punishment of such offences, he replied drily that, if the attempt to pass a mail really were treasonable, it was a pity that the "Tallyho" appeared to have so imperfect an acquaintance with law.

The modern modes of travelling cannot compare with the old mail-coach system in grandeur and power. They boast of more velocity,—not, however, as a consciousness, but as a fact of our lifeless knowledge, resting upon *alien* evidence: as, for instance, because somebody *says* that we have gone fifty miles in the hour, though we are far from feeling it as a personal experience; or upon the evidence of a result, as that actually we find ourselves in York four hours after leaving London. Apart from such an assertion, or such a result, I myself am little aware of the pace. But, seated on the old mail-coach, we needed no evidence out of ourselves to indicate the velocity. On this system the word was not *magna loquimur*, as upon railways, but *vivimus*. Yes, "magna *vivimus*"; we do not make verbal ostentation of our grandeurs, we realise our grandeurs in act, and in the very experience of life. The vital experience of the glad animal sensibilities made doubts impossible on the question of our speed; we heard our speed, we saw it, we felt it as a thrilling; and this speed was not the product of blind insensate agencies, that had no sympathy to give, but was incarnated in the fiery eyeballs of the noblest amongst brutes, in his dilated nostril, spasmodic muscles, and thunder-beating hoofs. The sensibility of the horse, uttering itself in the maniac light of his eye, might be the last vibration of such a movement; the glory of Salamanca might be the first. But the intervening links that connected them, that spread the earthquake of battle into the eyeball of the horse, were the heart of man and its electric thrillings—kindling in the rapture of the fiery strife, and then propagating its own tumults by contagious shouts and gestures to the heart of his servant the horse. But now, on the new system of travelling, iron tubes and boilers have disconnected man's heart from the ministers of his locomotion. Nile nor Trafalgar has power to raise an extra bubble in a steam-kettle. The galvanic cycle is broken up for ever; man's imperial nature no longer sends itself forward through the electric sensibility of the horse; the inter-agencies are gone in the mode of communication between the horse and his master out of which grew so many aspects of sublimity under accidents of mists that hid, or sudden blazes that revealed, of mobs that agitated, or midnight solitudes that awed. Tidings fitted to convulse all nations must henceforwards travel by culinary process; and the trumpet that once announced from afar the laurelled mail, heart-shaking when heard screaming on the wind and proclaiming itself through the darkness to every village or solitary house on its route, has now given way for ever to the pot-wallopings of the boiler. Thus have perished multiform openings for public expressions of interest, scenical yet natural, in great national tidings,—for revelations of faces and groups that could not offer themselves amongst the fluctuating mobs of a railway station. The gatherings of gazers about a laurelled mail had one centre, and acknowledged one sole interest. But the crowds attending at a railway station have as little unity as running water, and own as many centres as there are separate carriages in the train.

How else, for example, than as a constant watcher for the dawn, and for the London mail that in summer months entered about daybreak amongst the lawny thickets of Marlborough forest, couldst thou, sweet Fanny of the Bath road, have become the glorified inmate of my dreams? Yet Fanny, as the loveliest young woman for face and person that perhaps in my whole life I have beheld, merited the station which even now, from a distance of forty years, she holds in my dreams; yes, though by links of natural association she brings along with her a troop of dreadful creatures, fabulous and not fabulous, that are more abominable to the heart than Fanny and the dawn are delightful.

Miss Fanny of the Bath road, strictly speaking, lived at a mile's distance from that road, but came so continually to meet the mail that I on my frequent transits rarely missed her, and naturally connected her image with the great thoroughfare where only I had ever seen her. Why she came so punctually I do not exactly know; but I believe with some burden of commissions, to be executed in Bath, which had gathered to her own residence as a central rendezvous for converging them. The mail-coachman who drove the Bath mail and wore the royal livery[1] happened to be Fanny's grandfather. A good man he was, that loved his beautiful granddaughter, and, loving her wisely, was vigilant over her deportment in any case where young Oxford might happen to be concerned. Did my vanity then suggest that I myself, individually, could fall within

---

[1] "*Wore the royal livery*":—The general impression was that the royal livery belonged of right to the mail-coachmen as their professional dress. But that was an error. To the guard it *did* belong, I believe, and was obviously essential as an official warrant, and as a means of instant identification for his person, in the discharge of his important public duties. But the coachman, and especially if his place in the series did not connect him immediately with London and the General Post-Office, obtained the scarlet coat only as an honorary distinction after long (or, if not long, trying and special) service.

the line of his terrors? Certainly not, as regarded any physical pretensions that I could plead; for Fanny (as a chance passenger from her own neighbourhood once told me) counted in her train a hundred and ninety-nine professed admirers, if not open aspirants to her favour; and probably not one of the whole brigade but excelled myself in personal advantages. Ulysses even, with the unfair advantage of his accursed bow, could hardly have undertaken that amount of suitors. So the danger might have seemed slight —only that woman is universally aristocratic; it is amongst her nobilities of heart that she *is* so. Now, the aristocratic distinctions in my favour might easily with Miss Fanny have compensated my physical deficiencies. Did I then make love to Fanny? Why, yes; about as much love as one *could* make whilst the mail was changing horses—a process which, ten years later, did not occupy above eighty seconds; but *then*,—viz. about Waterloo—it occupied five times eighty. Now, four hundred seconds offer a field quite ample enough for whispering into a young woman's ear a great deal of truth, and (by way of parenthesis) some trifle of falsehood. Grandpapa did right, therefore, to watch me. And yet, as happens too often to the grandpapas of earth in a contest with the admirers of granddaughters, how vainly would he have watched me had I meditated any evil whispers to Fanny! She, it is my belief, would have protected herself against any man's evil suggestions. But he, as the result showed, could not have intercepted the opportunities for such suggestions. Yet, why not? Was he not active? Was he not blooming? Blooming he was as Fanny herself.

"Say, all our praises why should lords——"

Stop, that's not the line.

"Say, all our roses why should girls engross?"

The coachman showed rosy blossoms on his face deeper even than his granddaughter's—*his* being drawn from the ale-cask, Fanny's from the fountains of the dawn. But, in spite of his blooming face, some infirmities he had; and one particularly in which he too much resembled a crocodile. This lay in a monstrous inaptitude for turning round. The crocodile,

I presume, owes that inaptitude to the absurd *length* of his back; but in our grandpapa it arose rather from the absurd *breadth* of his back, combined, possibly, with some growing stiffness in his legs. Now, upon this crocodile infirmity of his I planted a human advantage for tendering my homage to Miss Fanny. In defiance of all his honourable vigilance, no sooner had he presented to us his mighty Jovian back (what a field for displaying to mankind his royal scarlet!), whilst inspecting professionally the buckles, the straps, and the silvery turrets[1] of his harness, than I raised Miss Fanny's hand to my lips, and, by the mixed tenderness and respectfulness of my manner, caused her easily to understand how happy it would make me to rank upon her list as No. 10 or 12: in which case a few casualties amongst her lovers (and, observe, they *hanged* liberally in those days) might have promoted me speedily to the top of the tree; as, on the other hand, with how much loyalty of submission I acquiesced by anticipation in her award, supposing that she should plant me in the very rearward of her favour, as No. 199 + 1. Most truly I loved this beautiful and ingenuous girl; and, had it not been for the Bath mail, timing all courtships by post-office allowance, heaven only knows what might have come of it. People talk of being over head and ears in love; now, the mail was the cause that I sank only over ears in love,—which, you know, still left a trifle of brain to overlook the whole conduct of the affair.

Ah, reader! when I look back upon those days, it seems to me that all things change—all things perish. "Perish the roses and the palms of kings": perish even the crowns and trophies of Waterloo: thunder and lightning are not the thunder and lightning which I remember. Roses are de-

---

[1] "*Turrets*"·—As one who loves and venerates Chaucer for his unrivalled merits of tenderness, of picturesque characterisation, and of narrative skill, I noticed with great pleasure that the word *torrettes* is used by him to designate the little devices through which the reins are made to pass ["torettz fyled rounde" occurs in line 1294 of the *Knightes Tale*; where, however, the reference is not to horse-trappings.—M.] This same word, in the same exact sense, I heard uniformly used by many scores of illustrious mail-coachmen to whose confidential friendship I had the honour of being admitted in my younger days.

generating. The Fannies of our island—though this I say with reluctance—are not visibly improving; and the Bath Road is notoriously superannuated. Crocodiles, you will say, are stationary. Mr. Waterton tells me that the crocodile does *not* change,—that a cayman, in fact, or an alligator, is just as good for riding upon as he was in the time of the Pharaohs. *That* may be; but the reason is that the crocodile does not live fast—he is a slow coach. I believe it is generally understood among naturalists that the crocodile is a blockhead. It is my own impression that the Pharaohs were also blockheads. Now, as the Pharaohs and the crocodile domineered over Egyptian society, this accounts for a singular mistake that prevailed through innumerable generations on the Nile. The crocodile made the ridiculous blunder of supposing man to be meant chiefly for his own eating. Man, taking a different view of the subject, naturally met that mistake by another: he viewed the crocodile as a thing sometimes to worship, but always to run away from. And this continued till Mr. Waterton[1] changed the relations between the animals. The mode of escaping from the reptile he showed to be not by running away, but by leaping on its back booted and spurred. The two animals had misunderstood each other. The use of the crocodile has now been cleared up—viz. to be ridden; and the final cause of man is that he may improve the health of the crocodile by riding him a-foxhunting before breakfast. And it is pretty certain that any crocodile who has been regularly hunted through the season, and is master of the weight he carries, will take a six-barred gate now as well as ever he would have done in the infancy of the pyramids.

[1] "*Mr. Waterton*."—Had the reader lived through the last generation, he would not need to be told that, some thirty or thirty-five years back, Mr. Waterton, a distinguished country gentleman of ancient family in Northumberland [Charles Waterton, naturalist, born 1782, died 1865—M.], publicly mounted and rode in top-boots a savage old crocodile, that was restive and very impertinent, but all to no purpose. The crocodile jibbed and tried to kick, but vainly. He was no more able to throw the squire than Sinbad was to throw the old scoundrel who used his back without paying for it, until he discovered a mode (slightly immoral, perhaps, though some think not) of murdering the old fraudulent jockey, and so circuitously of unhorsing him.

If, therefore, the crocodile does *not* change, all things else undeniably *do*: even the shadow of the pyramids grows less. And often the restoration in vision of Fanny and the Bath road makes me too pathetically sensible of that truth. Out of the darkness, if I happen to call back the image of Fanny, up rises suddenly from a gulf of forty years a rose in June; or, if I think for an instant of the rose in June, up rises the heavenly face of Fanny. One after the other, like the antiphonies in the choral service, rise Fanny and the rose in June, then back again the rose in June and Fanny. Then come both together, as in a chorus—roses and Fannies, Fannies and roses, without end, thick as blossoms in paradise. Then comes a venerable crocodile, in a royal livery of scarlet and gold, with sixteen capes; and the crocodile is driving four-in-hand from the box of the Bath mail. And suddenly we upon the mail are pulled up by a mighty dial, sculptured with the hours, that mingle with the heavens and the heavenly host. Then all at once we are arrived at Marlborough forest, amongst the lovely households[1] of the roe-deer; the deer and their fawns retire into the dewy thickets; the thickets are rich with roses; once again the roses call up the sweet countenance of Fanny; and she, being the granddaughter of a crocodile, awakens a dreadful host of semi-legendary animals—griffins, dragons, basilisks, sphinxes— till at length the whole vision of fighting images crowds into one towering armorial shield, a vast emblazonry of human charities and human loveliness that have perished, but quartered heraldically with unutterable and demoniac natures, whilst over all rises, as a surmounting crest, one fair female hand, with the forefinger pointing, in sweet, sorrowful admonition, upwards to heaven, where is sculptured the eternal writing which proclaims the frailty of earth and her children.[2]

[1] "*Households*":—Roe-deer do not congregate in herds like the fallow or the red deer, but by separate families, parents and children; which feature of approximation to the sanctity of human hearths, added to their comparatively miniature and graceful proportions, conciliates to them an interest of peculiar tenderness, supposing even that this beautiful creature is less characteristically impressed with the grandeurs of savage and forest life.

[2] This paragraph is but about one-fifth of the length of the corre-

GOING DOWN WITH VICTORY

But the grandest chapter of our experience within the whole mail-coach service was on those occasions when we went down from London with the news of victory. A

sponding paragraph as it appeared originally in *Blackwood*, De Quincey's taste having led him, on revision in 1854, to cancel the other four-fifths as forced or irrelevant. The condensation was judicious for its particular purpose; but, as the original paragraph is too characteristic to be sacrificed altogether, we reproduce it here entire in detached form:—"Perhaps, therefore, the crocodile does *not* change, but all
"things else *do*; even the shadow of the Pyramids grows less. And
"often the restoration in vision of Fanny and the Bath road makes
"me too pathetically sensible of that truth Out of the darkness, if
"I happen to call up the image of Fanny from thirty-five years back,
"arises suddenly a rose in June; or, if I think for an instant of a
"rose in June, up rises the heavenly face of Fanny. One after the
"other, like the antiphonies in a choral service, rises Fanny and the
"rose in June, then back again the rose in June and Fanny Then
"come both together, as in a chorus; roses and Fannies, Fannies and
"roses, without end—thick as blossoms in paradise. Then comes a
"venerable crocodile, in a royal livery of scarlet and gold, or in a
"coat with sixteen capes; and the crocodile is driving four-in-hand
"from the box of the Bath mail. And suddenly we upon the mail
"are pulled up by a mighty dial, sculptured with the hours, and with
"the dreadful legend of Too Late. Then all at once we are arrived
"in Marlborough forest, amongst the lovely households of the roe-
"deer: these retire into the dewy thickets; the thickets are rich
"with roses; the roses call up (as ever) the sweet countenance of
"Fanny, who, being the granddaughter of a crocodile, awakens a dread-
"ful host of wild semi-legendary animals—griffins, dragons, basilisks,
"sphinxes—till at length the whole vision of fighting images crowds
"into one towering armorial shield, a vast emblazonry of human
"charities and human loveliness that have perished, but quartered
"heraldically with unutterable horrors of monstrous and demoniac
"natures; whilst over all rises, as a surmounting crest, one fair
"female hand, with the fore-finger pointing, in sweet, sorrowful
"admonition, upwards to heaven, and having power (which, without
"experience, I never could have believed) to awaken the pathos that
"kills, in the very bosom of the horrors that madden, the grief that
"gnaws at the heart, together with the monstrous creations of dark-
"ness that shock the belief, and make dizzy the reason, of man. This
"is the peculiarity that I wish the reader to notice, as having first
"been made known to me for a possibility by this early vision of
"Fanny on the Bath road. The peculiarity consisted in the conflu-
"ence of two different keys, though apparently repelling each other,
"into the music and governing principles of the same dream; horror,
"such as possesses the maniac, and yet, by momentary transitions,

period of about ten years stretched from Trafalgar to Waterloo; the second and third years of which period (1806 and 1807) were comparatively sterile; but the other nine (from 1805 to 1815 inclusively) furnished a long succession of victories, the least of which, in such a contest of Titans, had

"grief, such as may be supposed to possess the dying mother when
"leaving her infant children to the mercies of the cruel. Usually,
"and perhaps always, in an unshaken nervous system, these two
"modes of misery exclude each other—here first they met in horrid
"reconciliation. There was always a separate peculiarity in the
"quality of the horror. This was afterwards developed into far more
"revolting complexities of misery and incomprehensible darkness;
"and perhaps I am wrong in ascribing any value as a *causative*
"agency to this particular case on the Bath road—possibly it fur-
"nished merely an *occasion* that accidentally introduced a mode of
"horrors certain, at any rate, to have grown up, with or without the
"Bath road, from more advanced stages of the nervous derangement.
"Yet, as the cubs of tigers or leopards, when domesticated, have been
"observed to suffer a sudden development of their latent ferocity
"under too eager an appeal to their playfulness—the gaieties of sport
"in *them* being too closely connected with the fiery brightness of their
"murderous instincts—so I have remarked that the caprices, the gay
"arabesques, and the lively floral luxuriations of dreams, betray a
"shocking tendency to pass into finer maniacal splendours. That
"gaiety, for instance (for such at first it was), in the dreaming
"faculty, by which one principal point of resemblance to a crocodile
"in the mail-coachman was soon made to clothe him with the form
"of a crocodile, and yet was blended with accessory circumstances
"derived from his *human* functions, passed rapidly into a further
"development, no longer gay or playful, but terrific, the most terrific
"that besieges dreams—viz. the horrid inoculation upon each other
"of incompatible natures. This horror has always been secretly felt
"by man; it was felt even under pagan forms of religion, which
"offered a very feeble, and also a very limited, gamut for giving
"expression to the human capacities of sublimity or of horror. We
"read it in the fearful composition of the sphinx. The dragon,
"again, is the snake inoculated upon the scorpion. The basilisk
"unites the mysterious malice of the evil eye, unintentional on the
"part of the unhappy agent, with the intentional venom of some
"other malignant natures. But these horrid complexities of evil
"agency are but *objectively* horrid; they inflict the horror suitable to
"their compound nature; but there is no insinuation that they *feel*
"that horror. Heraldry is so full of these fantastic creatures that, in
"some zoologies, we find a separate chapter or a supplement dedi-
"cated to what is denominated heraldic zoology. And why not?
"For these hideous creatures, however visionary, have a real tradi-
"tionary ground in medieval belief—sincere and partly reasonable,
"though adulterating with mendacity, blundering, credulity, and

an inappreciable value of position: partly for its absolute interference with the plans of our enemy, but still more from its keeping alive through central Europe the sense of a deep-seated vulnerability in France. Even to tease the coasts of our enemy, to mortify them by continual blockades, to insult them by capturing if it were but a baubling schooner under the eyes of their arrogant armies, repeated from time to time a sullen proclamation of power lodged in one quarter to which the hopes of Christendom turned in secret. How much more loudly must this proclamation have spoken in the audacity [1] of having bearded the *élite* of their troops, and

" intense superstition. But the dream-horror which I speak of is far
" more frightful. The dreamer finds housed within himself—occupy-
" ing, as it were, some separate chamber in his brain—holding, per-
" haps, from that station a secret and detestable commerce with his
" own heart—some horrid alien nature. What if it were his own
" nature repeated,—still, if the duality were distinctly perceptible,
" even that—even this mere numerical double of his own conscious-
" ness—might be a curse too mighty to be sustained. But how if
" the alien nature contradicts his own, fights with it, perplexes and
" confounds it? How, again, if not one alien nature, but two, but
" three, but four, but five, are introduced within what once he
" thought the inviolable sanctuary of himself? These, however, are
" horrors from the kingdom of anarchy and darkness, which, by their
" very intensity, challenge the sanctity of concealment, and gloomily
" retire from exposition Yet it was necessary to mention them,
" because the first introduction to such appearances (whether causal
" or merely casual) lay in the heraldic monsters, which monsters were
" themselves introduced (though playfully) by the transfigured coach-
" man of the Bath mail."—M.

[1] "*Audacity*":—Such the French accounted it; and it has struck me that Soult would not have been so popular in London, at the period of her present Majesty's coronation [28th June 1838], or in Manchester, on occasion of his visit to that town [July 1838], if they had been aware of the insolence with which he spoke of us in notes written at intervals from the field of Waterloo. As though it had been mere felony in our army to look a French one in the face, he said in more notes than one, dated from two to four P.M. on the field of Waterloo, "Here are the English—we have them; they are caught *en flagrant delit*." Yet no man should have known us better; no man had drunk deeper from the cup of humiliation than Soult had in 1809, when ejected by us with headlong violence from Oporto, and pursued through a long line of wrecks to the frontier of Spain; and subsequently at Albuera, in the bloodiest of recorded battles [16th May 1811], to say nothing of Toulouse [10th April 1814], he should have learned our pretensions.

having beaten them in pitched battles! Five years of life it was worth paying down for the privilege of an outside place on a mail-coach, when carrying down the first tidings of any such event. And it is to be noted that, from our insular situation, and the multitude of our frigates disposable for the rapid transmission of intelligence, rarely did any unauthorised rumour steal away a prelibation from the first aroma of the regular despatches. The government news was generally the earliest news.

From eight P.M. to fifteen or twenty minutes later imagine the mails assembled on parade in Lombard Street; where, at that time,[1] and not in St. Martin's-le-Grand, was seated the General Post-office.[2] In what exact strength we mustered I do not remember; but, from the length of each separate *attelage*, we filled the street, though a long one, and though we were drawn up in double file. On *any* night the spectacle was beautiful. The absolute perfection of all the appointments about the carriages and the harness, their strength, their brilliant cleanliness; their beautiful simplicity —but, more than all, the royal magnificence of the horses— were what might first have fixed the attention. Every carriage on every morning in the year was taken down to an official inspector for examination: wheels, axles, linchpins, pole, glasses, lamps, were all critically probed and tested. Every part of every carriage had been cleaned, every horse had been groomed, with as much rigour as if they belonged to a private gentleman; and that part of the spectacle offered itself always. But the night before us is a night of victory; and, behold! to the ordinary display what a heart-shaking addition!—horses, men, carriages, all are dressed in laurels and flowers, oak-leaves and ribbons. The guards, as being officially his Majesty's servants, and of the coachmen such as are within the privilege of the post-office, wear the royal liveries of course; and, as it is summer (for all the *land* victories were naturally won in summer), they wear, on this fine evening, these liveries exposed to view, without any covering of upper coats. Such a costume, and the elaborate

---

[1] "*At that time*":—I speak of the era previous to Waterloo.

[2] The present General Post-office in St. Martin's-le-Grand was opened 23d Sept. 1829.—M.

arrangement of the laurels in their hats, dilate their hearts, by giving to them openly a personal connexion with the great news in which already they have the general interest of patriotism. That great national sentiment surmounts and quells all sense of ordinary distinctions. Those passengers who happen to be gentlemen are now hardly to be distinguished as such except by dress; for the usual reserve of their manner in speaking to the attendants has on this night melted away. One heart, one pride, one glory, connects every man by the transcendent bond of his national blood. The spectators, who are numerous beyond precedent, express their sympathy with these fervent feelings by continual hurrahs. Every moment are shouted aloud by the post-office servants, and summoned to draw up, the great ancestral names of cities known to history through a thousand years— Lincoln, Winchester, Portsmouth, Gloucester, Oxford, Bristol, Manchester, York, Newcastle, Edinburgh, Glasgow, Perth, Stirling, Aberdeen—expressing the grandeur of the empire by the antiquity of its towns, and the grandeur of the mail establishment by the diffusive radiation of its separate missions. Every moment you hear the thunder of lids locked down upon the mail-bags. That sound to each individual mail is the signal for drawing off; which process is the finest part of the entire spectacle. Then come the horses into play. Horses! can these be horses that bound off with the action and gestures of leopards? What stir!— what sea-like ferment!—what a thundering of wheels!— what a trampling of hoofs!—what a sounding of trumpets! —what farewell cheers—what redoubling peals of brotherly congratulation, connecting the name of the particular mail— "Liverpool for ever!"—with the name of the particular victory—" Badajoz for ever!" or "Salamanca for ever!" The half-slumbering consciousness that all night long, and all the next day—perhaps for even a longer period—many of these mails, like fire racing along a train of gunpowder, will be kindling at every instant new successions of burning joy, has an obscure effect of multiplying the victory itself, by multiplying to the imagination into infinity the stages of its progressive diffusion. A fiery arrow seems to be let loose, which from that moment is destined to travel, without intermission, westwards for three hundred[1] miles—northwards for six hundred; and the sympathy of our Lombard Street friends at parting is exalted a hundredfold by a sort of visionary sympathy with the yet slumbering sympathies which in so vast a succession we are going to awake.

Liberated from the embarrassments of the city, and issuing into the broad uncrowded avenues of the northern suburbs, we soon begin to enter upon our natural pace of ten miles an hour. In the broad light of the summer evening, the sun, perhaps, only just at the point of setting, we are seen from every storey of every house. Heads of every age crowd to the windows; young and old understand the language of

[1] "*Three hundred*":—Of necessity, this scale of measurement, to an American, if he happens to be a thoughtless man, must sound ludicrous. Accordingly, I remember a case in which an American writer indulges himself in the luxury of a little fibbing, by ascribing to an Englishman a pompous account of the Thames, constructed entirely upon American ideas of grandeur, and concluding in something like these terms:—"And, sir, arriving at London, this mighty father of rivers attains a breadth of at least two furlongs, having, in its winding course, traversed the astonishing distance of one hundred and seventy miles." And this the candid American thinks it fair to contrast with the scale of the Mississippi. Now, it is hardly worth while to answer a pure fiction gravely; else one might say that no Englishman out of Bedlam ever thought of looking in an island for the rivers of a continent, nor, consequently, could have thought of looking for the peculiar grandeur of the Thames in the length of its course, or in the extent of soil which it drains. Yet, if he *had* been so absurd, the American might have recollected that a river, not to be compared with the Thames even as to volume of water—viz. the Tiber—has contrived to make itself heard of in this world for twenty-five centuries to an extent not reached as yet by any river, however corpulent, of his own land. The glory of the Thames is measured by the destiny of the population to which it ministers, by the commerce which it supports, by the grandeur of the empire in which, though far from the largest, it is the most influential stream. Upon some such scale, and not by a transfer of Columbian standards, is the course of our English mails to be valued. The American may fancy the effect of his own valuations to our English ears by supposing the case of a Siberian glorifying his country in these terms:—"These wretches, sir, in France and England, cannot march half a mile in any direction without finding a house where food can be had and lodging; whereas such is the noble desolation of our magnificent country that in many a direction for a thousand miles I will engage that a dog shall not find shelter from a snow-storm, nor a wren find an apology for breakfast."

our victorious symbols; and rolling volleys of sympathising cheers run along us, behind us, and before us. The beggar, rearing himself against the wall, forgets his lameness—real or assumed — thinks not of his whining trade, but stands erect, with bold exulting smiles, as we pass him. The victory has healed him, and says, Be thou whole! Women and children, from garrets alike and cellars, through infinite London, look down or look up with loving eyes upon our gay ribbons and our martial laurels; sometimes kiss their hands; sometimes hang out, as signals of affection, pocket-handkerchiefs, aprons, dusters, anything that, by catching the summer breezes, will express an aerial jubilation. On the London side of Barnet, to which we draw near within a few minutes after nine, observe that private carriage which is approaching us. The weather being so warm, the glasses are all down; and one may read, as on the stage of a theatre, everything that goes on within. It contains three ladies— one likely to be "mamma," and two of seventeen or eighteen, who are probably her daughters. What lovely animation, what beautiful unpremeditated pantomime, explaining to us every syllable that passes, in these ingenuous girls! By the sudden start and raising of the hands on first discovering our laurelled equipage, by the sudden movement and appeal to the elder lady from both of them, and by the heightened colour on their animated countenances, we can almost hear them saying, "See, see! Look at their laurels! Oh, mamma! there has been a great battle in Spain; and it has been a great victory." In a moment we are on the point of passing them. We passengers—I on the box, and the two on the roof behind me—raise our hats to the ladies; the coachman makes his professional salute with the whip; the guard even, though punctilious on the matter of his dignity as an officer under the crown, touches his hat. The ladies move to us, in return, with a winning graciousness of gesture; all smile on each side in a way that nobody could misunderstand, and that nothing short of a grand national sympathy could so instantaneously prompt. Will these ladies say that we are nothing to *them*? Oh no; they will not say *that*. They cannot deny—they do not deny—that for this night they are our sisters; gentle or simple, scholar or illiterate servant, for twelve hours to come, we on the outside have the honour to be their brothers. Those poor women, again, who stop to gaze upon us with delight at the entrance of Barnet, and seem, by their air of weariness, to be returning from labour—do you mean to say that they are washerwomen and charwomen? Oh, my poor friend, you are quite mistaken. I assure you they stand in a far higher rank; for this one night they feel themselves by birthright to be daughters of England, and answer to no humbler title.

Every joy, however, even rapturous joy—such is the sad law of earth—may carry with it grief, or fear of grief, to some. Three miles beyond Barnet, we see approaching us another private carriage, nearly repeating the circumstances of the former case. Here, also, the glasses are all down; here, also, is an elderly lady seated; but the two daughters are missing; for the single young person sitting by the lady's side seems to be an attendant—so I judge from her dress, and her air of respectful reserve. The lady is in mourning; and her countenance expresses sorrow. At first she does not look up; so that I believe she is not aware of our approach, until she hears the measured beating of our horses' hoofs. Then she raises her eyes to settle them painfully on our triumphal equipage. Our decorations explain the case to her at once; but she beholds them with apparent anxiety, or even with terror. Some time before this, I, finding it difficult to hit a flying mark when embarrassed by the coachman's person and reins intervening, had given to the guard a *Courier* evening paper, containing the gazette, for the next carriage that might pass. Accordingly he tossed it in, so folded that the huge capitals expressing some such legend as GLORIOUS VICTORY might catch the eye at once. To see the paper, however, at all, interpreted as it was by our ensigns of triumph, explained everything; and, if the guard were right in thinking the lady to have received it with a gesture of horror, it could not be doubtful that she had suffered some deep personal affliction in connexion with this Spanish war.

Here, now, was the case of one who, having formerly suffered, might, erroneously perhaps, be distressing herself with anticipations of another similar suffering. That same night, and hardly three hours later, occurred the reverse case. A poor woman, who too probably would find herself, in a day or two, to have suffered the heaviest of afflictions by the battle, blindly allowed herself to express an exultation so unmeasured in the news and its details as gave to her the appearance which amongst Celtic Highlanders is called *fey*.[1] This was at some little town where we changed horses an hour or two after midnight. Some fair or wake had kept the people up out of their beds, and had occasioned a partial illumination of the stalls and booths, presenting an unusual but very impressive effect. We saw many lights moving about as we drew near; and perhaps the most striking scene on the whole route was our reception at this place. The flashing of torches and the beautiful radiance of blue lights (technically, Bengal lights) upon the heads of our horses; the fine effect of such a showery and ghostly illumination falling upon our flowers and glittering laurels[2]; whilst all around ourselves, that formed a centre of light, the darkness gathered on the rear and flanks in massy blackness: these optical splendours, together with the prodigious enthusiasm of the people, composed a picture at once scenical and affecting, theatrical and holy. As we staid for three or four minutes, I alighted; and immediately from a dismantled stall in the street, where no doubt she had been presiding through the earlier part of the night, advanced eagerly a middle-aged woman. The sight of my newspaper it was that had drawn her attention upon myself. The victory which we were carrying down to the provinces on *this* occasion was the imperfect one of Talavera—imperfect for its results, such was the virtual treachery of the Spanish general, Cuesta, but not imperfect in its ever-memorable

---

[1] *Fey*, fated, doomed to die: not a Celtic word, but an Anglo-Saxon word preserved in Lowland Scotch. "You are surely *fey*" would be said in Scotland to a person observed to be in extravagantly high spirits, or in any mood surprisingly beyond the bounds of his ordinary temperament,—the notion being that the excitement is supernatural, and a presage of his approaching death or of some other calamity about to befall him.—M.

[2] "*Glittering laurels*":—I must observe that the colour of *green* suffers almost a spiritual change and exaltation under the effect of Bengal lights.

heroism.[1] I told her the main outline of the battle. The agitation of her enthusiasm had been so conspicuous when listening, and when first applying for information, that I could not but ask her if she had not some relative in the Peninsular army. Oh yes; her only son was there. In what regiment? He was a trooper in the 23d Dragoons. My heart sank within me as she made that answer. This sublime regiment, which an Englishman should never mention without raising his hat to their memory, had made the most memorable and effective charge recorded in military annals. They leaped their horses—*over* a trench where they could; *into* it, and with the result of death or mutilation, when they could *not*. What proportion cleared the trench is nowhere stated. Those who *did* closed up and went down upon the enemy with such divinity of fervour (I use the word *divinity* by design: the inspiration of God must have prompted this movement to those whom even then He was calling to His presence) that two results followed. As regarded the enemy, this 23d Dragoons, not, I believe, originally three hundred and fifty strong, paralysed a French column six thousand strong, then ascended the hill, and fixed the gaze of the whole French army. As regarded themselves, the 23d were supposed at first to have been barely not annihilated; but eventually, I believe, about one in four survived. And this, then, was the regiment—a regiment already for some hours glorified and hallowed to the ear of all London, as lying stretched, by a large majority, upon one bloody aceldama — in which the young trooper served whose mother was now talking in a spirit of such joyous enthusiasm. Did I tell her the truth? Had I the heart to break up her dreams? No. To-morrow, said I to myself—to-morrow, or the next day, will publish the worst. For one night more wherefore should she not sleep in peace? After to-morrow the chances are too many that peace will forsake her pillow. This brief respite, then, let her owe to *my* gift and *my* forbearance. But, if I told her not of the bloody price that had been paid, not therefore was I silent

---

[1] Battle of Talavera, in Spain, but close to the Portuguese frontier, fought by Wellington (then Sir Arthur Wellesley) 27th and 28th July 1809.—M.

on the contributions from her son's regiment to that day's service and glory. I showed her not the funeral banners under which the noble regiment was sleeping. I lifted not the overshadowing laurels from the bloody trench in which horse and rider lay mangled together. But I told her how these dear children of England, officers and privates, had leaped their horses over all obstacles as gaily as hunters to the morning's chase. I told her how they rode their horses into the mists of death,—saying to myself, but not saying to *her*, "and laid down their young lives for thee, O mother England! as willingly — poured out their noble blood as cheerfully—as ever, after a long day's sport, when infants, they had rested their wearied heads upon their mother's knees, or had sunk to sleep in her arms." Strange it is, yet true, that she seemed to have no fears for her son's safety, even after this knowledge that the 23d Dragoons had been memorably engaged; but so much was she enraptured by the knowledge that *his* regiment, and therefore that *he*, had rendered conspicuous service in the dreadful conflict — a service which had actually made them, within the last twelve hours, the foremost topic of conversation in London —so absolutely was fear swallowed up in joy—that, in the mere simplicity of her fervent nature, the poor woman threw her arms round my neck, as she thought of her son, and gave to *me* the kiss which secretly was meant for *him*.

SECTION II—THE VISION OF SUDDEN DEATH [1]

What is to be taken as the predominant opinion of man, reflective and philosophic, upon SUDDEN DEATH? It is remarkable that, in different conditions of society, sudden death has been variously regarded as the consummation of an earthly career most fervently to be desired, or, again, as that consummation which is with most horror to be deprecated. Cæsar the Dictator, at his last dinner-party (*cœna*), on the

---

[1] In *Blackwood* for December 1849 there was prefixed to this Paper a paragraph within brackets, explaining its connexion with the preceding Section, which had appeared in October, and also its connexion with the subsequent "Dream-Fugue." See *ante*, p 270, footnote.—M.

very evening before his assassination, when the minutes of his earthly career were numbered, being asked what death, in *his* judgment, might be pronounced the most eligible, replied "That which should be most sudden." On the other hand, the divine Litany of our English Church, when breathing forth supplications, as if in some representative character, for the whole human race prostrate before God, places such a death in the very van of horrors: " From lightning and tempest; from plague, pestilence, and famine; from battle and murder, and from SUDDEN DEATH—*Good Lord, deliver us.*" Sudden death is here made to crown the climax in a grand ascent of calamities; it is ranked among the last of curses; and yet by the noblest of Romans it was ranked as the first of blessings. In that difference most readers will see little more than the essential difference between Christianity and Paganism. But this, on consideration, I doubt. The Christian Church may be right in its estimate of sudden death; and it is a natural feeling, though after all it may also be an infirm one, to wish for a quiet dismissal from life, as that which *seems* most reconcilable with meditation, with penitential retrospects, and with the humilities of farewell prayer. There does not, however, occur to me any direct scriptural warrant for this earnest petition of the English Litany, unless under a special construction of the word "sudden." It seems a petition indulged rather and conceded to human infirmity than exacted from human piety. It is not so much a doctrine built upon the eternities of the Christian system as a plausible opinion built upon special varieties of physical temperament. Let that, however, be as it may, two remarks suggest themselves as prudent restraints upon a doctrine which else *may* wander, and *has* wandered, into an uncharitable superstition. The first is this: that many people are likely to exaggerate the horror of a sudden death from the disposition to lay a false stress upon words or acts simply because by an accident they have become *final* words or acts. If a man dies, for instance, by some sudden death when he happens to be intoxicated, such a death is falsely regarded with peculiar horror; as though the intoxication were suddenly exalted into a blasphemy. But *that* is unphilosophic. The man was, or he was not, *habitu-*

ally a drunkard. If not, if his intoxication were a solitary accident, there can be no reason for allowing special emphasis to this act simply because through misfortune it became his final act. Nor, on the other hand, if it were no accident, but one of his *habitual* transgressions, will it be the more habitual or the more a transgression because some sudden calamity, surprising him, has caused this habitual transgression to be also a final one. Could the man have had any reason even dimly to foresee his own sudden death, there would have been a new feature in his act of intemperance—a feature of presumption and irreverence, as in one that, having known himself drawing near to the presence of God, should have suited his demeanour to an expectation so awful. But this is no part of the case supposed. And the only new element in the man's act is not any element of special immorality, but simply of special misfortune.

The other remark has reference to the meaning of the word *sudden*. Very possibly Cæsar and the Christian Church do not differ in the way supposed,—that is, do not differ by any difference of doctrine as between Pagan and Christian views of the moral temper appropriate to death; but perhaps they are contemplating different cases. Both contemplate a violent death, a $Βιαθανατος$—death that is $βιαιος$, or, in other words, death that is brought about, not by internal and spontaneous change, but by active force having its origin from without.[1] In this meaning the two authorities agree. Thus far they are in harmony. But the difference is that the Roman by the word "sudden" means *unlingering*, whereas the Christian Litany by "sudden death" means a death *without warning*, consequently without any available summons to religious preparation. The poor mutineer who kneels down to gather into his heart the bullets from twelve firelocks of his pitying comrades dies by a most sudden death in Cæsar's sense; one shock, one mighty spasm, one (possibly *not* one) groan, and all is over. But, in the sense of the Litany, the mutineer's death is far from sudden: his offence originally, his imprisonment, his trial, the interval between his sentence and its execution, having

---

[1] *Biaios*, Greek for "forcible" or "violent": hence *Biathanatos*, violent death.—M.

all furnished him with separate warnings of his fate—having all summoned him to meet it with solemn preparation.

Here at once, in this sharp verbal distinction, we comprehend the faithful earnestness with which a holy Christian Church pleads on behalf of her poor departing children that God would vouchsafe to them the last great privilege and distinction possible on a death-bed, viz. the opportunity of untroubled preparation for facing this mighty trial. Sudden death, as a mere variety in the modes of dying where death in some shape is inevitable, proposes a question of choice which, equally in the Roman and the Christian sense, will be variously answered according to each man's variety of temperament. Meantime, one aspect of sudden death there is, one modification, upon which no doubt can arise, that of all martyrdoms it is the most agitating—viz. where it surprises a man under circumstances which offer (or which seem to offer) some hurrying, flying, inappreciably minute chance of evading it. Sudden as the danger which it affronts must be any effort by which such an evasion can be accomplished. Even *that*, even the sickening necessity for hurrying in extremity where all hurry seems destined to be vain,—even that anguish is liable to a hideous exasperation in one particular case: viz. where the appeal is made not exclusively to the instinct of self-preservation, but to the conscience, on behalf of some other life besides your own, accidentally thrown upon *your* protection. To fail, to collapse in a service merely your own, might seem comparatively venial; though, in fact, it is far from venial. But to fail in a case where Providence has suddenly thrown into your hands the final interests of another,—a fellow-creature shuddering between the gates of life and death: this, to a man of apprehensive conscience, would mingle the misery of an atrocious criminality with the misery of a bloody calamity. You are called upon, by the case supposed, possibly to die, but to die at the very moment when, by any even partial failure or effeminate collapse of your energies, you will be self-denounced as a murderer. You had but the twinkling of an eye for your effort, and that effort might have been unavailing; but to have risen to the level of such an effort would have rescued you, though not from dying, yet from dying as a traitor to your final and farewell duty.

The situation here contemplated exposes a dreadful ulcer, lurking far down in the depths of human nature. It is not that men generally are summoned to face such awful trials. But potentially, and in shadowy outline, such a trial is moving subterraneously in perhaps all men's natures. Upon the secret mirror of our dreams such a trial is darkly projected, perhaps, to every one of us. That dream, so familiar to childhood, of meeting a lion, and, through languishing prostration in hope and the energies of hope, that constant sequel of lying down before the lion, publishes the secret frailty of human nature—reveals its deep-seated falsehood to itself—records its abysmal treachery. Perhaps not one of us escapes that dream; perhaps, as by some sorrowful doom of man, that dream repeats for every one of us, through every generation, the original temptation in Eden. Every one of us, in this dream, has a bait offered to the infirm places of his own individual will; once again a snare is presented for tempting him into captivity to a luxury of ruin; once again, as in aboriginal Paradise, the man falls by his own choice; again, by infinite iteration, the ancient earth groans to Heaven, through her secret caves, over the weakness of her child. "Nature, from her seat, sighing through all her works," again "gives signs of woe that all is lost"; and again the counter-sigh is repeated to the sorrowing heavens for the endless rebellion against God. It is not without probability that in the world of dreams every one of us ratifies for himself the original transgression. In dreams, perhaps under some secret conflict of the midnight sleeper, lighted up to the consciousness at the time, but darkened to the memory as soon as all is finished, each several child of our mysterious race completes for himself the treason of the aboriginal fall.

The incident, so memorable in itself by its features of horror, and so scenical by its grouping for the eye, which furnished the text for this reverie upon *Sudden Death*, occurred to myself in the dead of night, as a solitary spectator, when seated on the box of the Manchester and Glasgow mail, in the second or third summer after Waterloo. I find it necessary to relate the circumstances, because they are such as could not have occurred unless under a singular combination of accidents. In those days, the oblique and lateral communications with many rural post-offices were so arranged, either through necessity or through defect of system, as to make it requisite for the main north-western mail (*i.e.* the *down* mail) on reaching Manchester to halt for a number of hours; how many, I do not remember; six or seven, I think; but the result was that, in the ordinary course, the mail recommenced its journey northwards about midnight. Wearied with the long detention at a gloomy hotel, I walked out about eleven o'clock at night for the sake of fresh air; meaning to fall in with the mail and resume my seat at the post-office. The night, however, being yet dark, as the moon had scarcely risen, and the streets being at that hour empty, so as to offer no opportunities for asking the road, I lost my way, and did not reach the post-office until it was considerably past midnight; but, to my great relief (as it was important for me to be in Westmorland by the morning), I saw in the huge saucer eyes of the mail, blazing through the gloom, an evidence that my chance was not yet lost. Past the time it was; but, by some rare accident, the mail was not even yet ready to start. I ascended to my seat on the box, where my cloak was still lying as it had lain at the Bridgewater Arms. I had left it there in imitation of a nautical discoverer, who leaves a bit of bunting on the shore of his discovery, by way of warning off the ground the whole human race, and notifying to the Christian and the heathen worlds, with his best compliments, that he has hoisted his pocket-handkerchief once and for ever upon that virgin soil: thenceforward claiming the *jus dominii* to the top of the atmosphere above it, and also the right of driving shafts to the centre of the earth below it; so that all people found after this warning either aloft in upper chambers of the atmosphere, or groping in subterraneous shafts, or squatting audaciously on the surface of the soil, will be treated as trespassers—kicked, that is to say, or decapitated, as circumstances may suggest, by their very faithful servant, the owner of the said pocket-handkerchief. In the present case, it is probable that my cloak might not have been respected, and the *jus gentium* might have been cruelly violated in my person—for, in the dark, people commit deeds of darkness, gas being a great ally of morality; but it so happened that on this night there was no other outside passenger; and thus the crime, which else was but too probable, missed fire for want of a criminal.

Having mounted the box, I took a small quantity of laudanum, having already travelled two hundred and fifty miles—viz. from a point seventy miles beyond London. In the taking of laudanum there was nothing extraordinary. But by accident it drew upon me the special attention of my assessor on the box, the coachman. And in *that* also there was nothing extraordinary. But by accident, and with great delight, it drew my own attention to the fact that this coachman was a monster in point of bulk, and that he had but one eye. In fact, he had been foretold by Virgil as

"Monstrum horrendum, informe, ingens, cui lumen ademptum."

He answered to the conditions in every one of the items:— 1, a monster he was; 2, dreadful; 3, shapeless; 4, huge; 5, who had lost an eye. But why should *that* delight me? Had he been one of the Calendars in the *Arabian Nights*, and had paid down his eye as the price of his criminal curiosity, what right had *I* to exult in his misfortune? I did *not* exult; I delighted in no man's punishment, though it were even merited. But these personal distinctions (Nos. 1, 2, 3, 4, 5) identified in an instant an old friend of mine whom I had known in the south for some years as the most masterly of mail-coachmen. He was the man in all Europe that could (if *any* could) have driven six-in-hand full gallop over *Al Sirat*—that dreadful bridge of Mahomet, with no side battlements, and of *extra* room not enough for a razor's edge—leading right across the bottomless gulf. Under this eminent man, whom in Greek I cognominated Cyclops-*Diphrélates* (Cyclops the Charioteer), I, and others known to me, studied the diphrelatic art. Excuse, reader, a word too elegant to be pedantic[1] As a pupil, though I paid extra

---

[1] For the last two sentences the original in *Blackwood* had these four:—" I used to call him *Cyclops Mastigophorus*, Cyclops the Whip-

fees, it is to be lamented that I did not stand high in his esteem. It showed his dogged honesty (though, observe, not his discernment) that he could not see my merits. Let us excuse his absurdity in this particular by remembering his want of an eye. Doubtless *that* made him blind to my merits. In the art of conversation, however, he admitted that I had the whip-hand of him. On this present occasion great joy was at our meeting. But what was Cyclops doing here? Had the medical men recommended northern air, or how? I collected, from such explanations as he volunteered, that he had an interest at stake in some suit-at-law now pending at Lancaster; so that probably he had got himself transferred to this station for the purpose of connecting with his professional pursuits an instant readiness for the calls of his lawsuit.

Meantime, what are we stopping for? Surely we have now waited long enough. Oh, this procrastinating mail, and this procrastinating post-office! Can't they take a lesson upon that subject from *me*? Some people have called *me* procrastinating. Yet you are witness, reader, that I was here kept waiting for the post-office. Will the post-office lay its hand on its heart, in its moments of sobriety, and assert that ever it waited for me? What are they about? The guard tells me that there is a large extra accumulation of foreign mails this night, owing to irregularities caused by war, by wind, by weather, in the packet service, which as yet does not benefit at all by steam. For an *extra* hour, it seems, the post-office has been engaged in threshing out the pure wheaten correspondence of Glasgow, and winnowing it from the chaff of all baser intermediate towns. But at last all is finished. Sound your horn, guard! Manchester, good-bye!; we've lost an hour by your criminal conduct at

bearer, until I observed that his skill made whips useless, except to fetch off an impertinent fly from a leader's head; upon which I changed his Grecian name to Cyclops *Diphrēlates* (Cyclops the Charioteer). I, and others known to me, studied under him the diphrelatic art. Excuse, reader, a word too elegant to be pedantic. And also take this remark from me as a *gage d'amitié*—that no word ever was or *can* be pedantic which, by supporting a distinction, supports the accuracy of logic, or which fills up a chasm for the understanding."—M.

the post-office: which, however, though I do not mean to part with a serviceable ground of complaint, and one which really *is* such for the horses, to me secretly is an advantage, since it compels us to look sharply for this lost hour amongst the next eight or nine, and to recover it (if we can) at the rate of one mile extra per hour. Off we are at last, and at eleven miles an hour; and for the moment I detect no changes in the energy or in the skill of Cyclops.

From Manchester to Kendal, which virtually (though not in law) is the capital of Westmorland, there were at this time seven stages of eleven miles each. The first five of these, counting from Manchester, terminate in Lancaster; which is therefore fifty-five miles north of Manchester, and the same distance exactly from Liverpool. The first three stages terminate in Preston (called, by way of distinction from other towns of that name, *Proud* Preston); at which place it is that the separate roads from Liverpool and from Manchester to the north become confluent.[1] Within these first three stages lay the foundation, the progress, and termination of our night's adventure. During the first stage, I found out that Cyclops was mortal: he was liable to the shocking affection of sleep—a thing which previously I had never suspected. If a man indulges in the vicious habit of sleeping, all the skill in aurigation of Apollo himself, with the horses of Aurora to execute his notions, avails him nothing. "Oh, Cyclops!" I exclaimed, "thou art mortal. My friend, thou snorest." Through the first eleven miles, however, this infirmity—which I grieve to say that he shared with the whole Pagan Pantheon—betrayed itself only by brief snatches. On waking up, he made an apology for himself which, instead of mending matters, laid open a gloomy vista of coming disasters. The summer assizes, he reminded me, were now going on at Lancaster: in consequence of which for three nights and three days he had not lain down in a bed. During

---

[1] "*Confluent*":—Suppose a capital Y (the Pythagorean letter): Lancaster is at the foot of this letter; Liverpool at the top of the *right* branch; Manchester at the top of the *left*; Proud Preston at the centre, where the two branches unite. It is thirty-three miles along either of the two branches; it is twenty-two miles along the stem—viz. from Preston in the middle to Lancaster at the root. There's a lesson in geography for the reader!

the day he was waiting for his own summons as a witness on the trial in which he was interested, or else, lest he should be missing at the critical moment, was drinking with the other witnesses under the pastoral surveillance of the attorneys. During the night, or that part of it which at sea would form the middle watch, he was driving. This explanation certainly accounted for his drowsiness, but in a way which made it much more alarming; since now, after several days' resistance to this infirmity, at length he was steadily giving way. Throughout the second stage he grew more and more drowsy. In the second mile of the third stage he surrendered himself finally and without a struggle to his perilous temptation. All his past resistance had but deepened the weight of this final oppression. Seven atmospheres of sleep rested upon him; and, to consummate the case, our worthy guard, after singing "Love amongst the Roses" for perhaps thirty times, without invitation and without applause, had in revenge moodily resigned himself to slumber—not so deep, doubtless, as the coachman's, but deep enough for mischief. And thus at last, about ten miles from Preston, it came about that I found myself left in charge of his Majesty's London and Glasgow mail, then running at the least twelve miles an hour.

What made this negligence less criminal than else it must have been thought was the condition of the roads at night during the assizes. At that time, all the law business of populous Liverpool, and also of populous Manchester, with its vast cincture of populous rural districts, was called up by ancient usage to the tribunal of Lilliputian Lancaster. To break up this old traditional usage required, 1, a conflict with powerful established interests, 2, a large system of new arrangements, and 3, a new parliamentary statute. But as yet this change was merely in contemplation. As things were at present, twice in the year[1] so vast a body of business rolled northwards from the southern quarter of the county that for a fortnight at least it occupied the severe exertions of two judges in its despatch. The consequence of this was

[1] "*Twice in the year*":—There were at that time only two assizes even in the most populous counties—viz. the Lent Assizes and the Summer Assizes.

that every horse available for such a service, along the whole line of road, was exhausted in carrying down the multitudes of people who were parties to the different suits. By sunset, therefore, it usually happened that, through utter exhaustion amongst men and horses, the road sank into profound silence. Except the exhaustion in the vast adjacent county of York from a contested election, no such silence succeeding to no such fiery uproar was ever witnessed in England.

On this occasion the usual silence and solitude prevailed along the road. Not a hoof nor a wheel was to be heard. And, to strengthen this false luxurious confidence in the noiseless roads, it happened also that the night was one of peculiar solemnity and peace. For my own part, though slightly alive to the possibilities of peril, I had so far yielded to the influence of the mighty calm as to sink into a profound reverie. The month was August; in the middle of which lay my own birthday—a festival to every thoughtful man suggesting solemn and often sigh-born [1] thoughts. The county was my own native county—upon which, in its southern section, more than upon any equal area known to man past or present, had descended the original curse of labour in its heaviest form, not mastering the bodies only of men, as of slaves, or criminals in mines, but working through the fiery will. Upon no equal space of earth was, or ever had been, the same energy of human power put forth daily. At this particular season also of the assizes, that dreadful hurricane of flight and pursuit, as it might have seemed to a stranger, which swept to and from Lancaster all day long, hunting the county up and down, and regularly subsiding back into silence about sunset, could not fail (when united with this permanent distinction of Lancashire as the very metropolis and citadel of labour) to point the thoughts pathetically upon that counter-vision of rest, of saintly repose from strife and sorrow, towards which, as to their secret haven, the profounder aspirations of man's heart are in solitude continually travelling. Obliquely upon our left we were nearing the sea; which also must, under the present

---

[1] "*Sigh-born*":—I owe the suggestion of this word to an obscure remembrance of a beautiful phrase in "Giraldus Cambrensis"—viz. *suspiriosæ cogitationes*.

circumstances, be repeating the general state of halcyon repose. The sea, the atmosphere, the light, bore each an orchestral part in this universal lull. Moonlight and the first timid tremblings of the dawn were by this time blending; and the blendings were brought into a still more exquisite state of unity by a slight silvery mist, motionless and dreamy, that covered the woods and fields, but with a veil of equable transparency. Except the feet of our own horses,—which, running on a sandy margin of the road, made but little disturbance,—there was no sound abroad. In the clouds and on the earth prevailed the same majestic peace; and, in spite of all that the villain of a schoolmaster has done for the ruin of our sublimer thoughts, which are the thoughts of our infancy, we still believe in no such nonsense as a limited atmosphere. Whatever we may swear with our false feigning lips, in our faithful hearts we still believe, and must for ever believe, in fields of air traversing the total gulf between earth and the central heavens. Still, in the confidence of children that tread without fear *every* chamber in their father's house, and to whom no door is closed, we, in that Sabbatic vision which sometimes is revealed for an hour upon nights like this, ascend with easy steps from the sorrow-stricken fields of earth upwards to the sandals of God.

Suddenly, from thoughts like these I was awakened to a sullen sound, as of some motion on the distant road. It stole upon the air for a moment; I listened in awe; but then it died away. Once roused, however, I could not but observe with alarm the quickened motion of our horses. Ten years' experience had made my eye learned in the valuing of motion; and I saw that we were now running thirteen miles an hour. I pretend to no presence of mind. On the contrary, my fear is that I am miserably and shamefully deficient in that quality as regards action. The palsy of doubt and distraction hangs like some guilty weight of dark unfathomed remembrances upon my energies when the signal is flying for *action*. But, on the other hand, this accursed gift I have, as regards *thought*, that in the first step towards the possibility of a misfortune I see its total evolution; in the radix of the series I see too certainly and too instantly its entire expansion; in the first syllable of the dreadful sentence I read already the last. It was not that I feared for ourselves. *Us* our bulk and impetus charmed against peril in any collision. And I had ridden through too many hundreds of perils that were frightful to approach, that were matter of laughter to look back upon, the first face of which was horror, the parting face a jest—for any anxiety to rest upon *our* interests. The mail was not built, I felt assured, nor bespoke, that could betray *me* who trusted to its protection. But any carriage that we could meet would be frail and light in comparison of ourselves. And I remarked this ominous accident of our situation,—we were on the wrong side of the road. But then, it may be said, the other party, if other there was, might also be on the wrong side; and two wrongs might make a right. *That* was not likely. The same motive which had drawn *us* to the right-hand side of the road—viz. the luxury of the soft beaten sand as contrasted with the paved centre—would prove attractive to others. The two adverse carriages would therefore, to a certainty, be travelling on the same side; and from this side, as not being ours in law, the crossing over to the other would, of course, be looked for from *us*.[1] Our lamps, still lighted, would give the impression of vigilance on our part And every creature that met us would rely upon *us* for quartering.[2] All this, and if the separate links of the anticipation had been a thousand times more, I saw, not discursively, or by effort, or by succession, but by one flash of horrid simultaneous intuition.

Under this steady though rapid anticipation of the evil which *might* be gathering ahead, ah! what a sullen mystery of fear, what a sigh of woe, was that which stole upon the air, as again the far-off sound of a wheel was heard! A whisper it was—a whisper from, perhaps, four miles off—

---

[1] It is true that, according to the law of the case as established by legal precedents, all carriages were required to give way before royal equipages, and therefore before the mail as one of them. But this only increased the danger, as being a regulation very imperfectly made known, very unequally enforced, and therefore often embarrassing the movements on both sides.

[2] "*Quartering*":—This is the technical word, and, I presume, derived from the French *cartayer*, to evade a rut or any obstacle

secretly announcing a ruin that, being foreseen, was not the less inevitable; that, being known, was not therefore healed. What could be done—who was it that could do it—to check the storm-flight of these maniacal horses? Could I not seize the reins from the grasp of the slumbering coachman? You, reader, think that it would have been in *your* power to do so. And I quarrel not with your estimate of yourself. But, from the way in which the coachman's hand was viced between his upper and lower thigh, this was impossible. Easy was it? See, then, that bronze equestrian statue. The cruel rider has kept the bit in his horse's mouth for two centuries. Unbridle him for a minute, if you please, and wash his mouth with water. Easy was it? Unhorse me, then, that imperial rider; knock me those marble feet from those marble stirrups of Charlemagne.

The sounds ahead strengthened, and were now too clearly the sounds of wheels. Who and what could it be? Was it industry in a taxed cart? Was it youthful gaiety in a gig? Was it sorrow that loitered, or joy that raced? For as yet the snatches of sound were too intermitting, from distance, to decipher the character of the motion. Whoever were the travellers, something must be done to warn them. Upon the other party rests the active responsibility, but upon *us*—and, woe is me! that *us* was reduced to my frail opium-shattered self—rests the responsibility of warning. Yet, how should this be accomplished? Might I not sound the guard's horn? Already, on the first thought, I was making my way over the roof to the guard's seat. But this, from the accident which I have mentioned, of the foreign mails being piled upon the roof, was a difficult and even dangerous attempt to one cramped by nearly three hundred miles of outside travelling. And, fortunately, before I had lost much time in the attempt, our frantic horses swept round an angle of the road which opened upon us that final stage where the collision must be accomplished and the catastrophe sealed. All was apparently finished. The court was sitting; the case was heard; the judge had finished; and only the verdict was yet in arrear.

Before us lay an avenue straight as an arrow, six hundred yards, perhaps, in length; and the umbrageous trees, which rose in a regular line from either side, meeting high overhead, gave to it the character of a cathedral aisle. These trees lent a deeper solemnity to the early light; but there was still light enough to perceive, at the further end of this Gothic aisle, a frail reedy gig, in which were seated a young man, and by his side a young lady. Ah, young sir! what are you about? If it is requisite that you should whisper your communications to this young lady—though really I see nobody, at an hour and on a road so solitary, likely to overhear you—is it therefore requisite that you should carry your lips forward to hers? The little carriage is creeping on at one mile an hour; and the parties within it, being thus tenderly engaged, are naturally bending down their heads. Between them and eternity, to all human calculation, there is but a minute and a-half. Oh heavens! what is it that I shall do? Speaking or acting, what help can I offer? Strange it is, and to a mere auditor of the tale might seem laughable, that I should need a suggestion from the *Iliad* to prompt the sole resource that remained. Yet so it was. Suddenly I remembered the shout of Achilles, and its effect. But could I pretend to shout like the son of Peleus, aided by Pallas? No: but then I needed not the shout that should alarm all Asia militant; such a shout would suffice as might carry terror into the hearts of two thoughtless young people and one gig-horse. I shouted—and the young man heard me not. A second time I shouted—and now he heard me, for now he raised his head.

Here, then, all had been done that, by me, *could* be done; more on *my* part was not possible. Mine had been the first step; the second was for the young man; the third was for God. If, said I, this stranger is a brave man, and if indeed he loves the young girl at his side—or, loving her not, if he feels the obligation, pressing upon every man worthy to be called a man, of doing his utmost for a woman confided to his protection—he will at least make some effort to save her. If *that* fails, he will not perish the more, or by a death more cruel, for having made it; and he will die as a brave man should, with his face to the danger, and with his arm about the woman that he sought in vain to save. But, if he makes no effort,—shrinking without a struggle from his duty,—he himself will not the less certainly perish for this baseness of poltroonery. He will die no less: and why not? Wherefore should we grieve that there is one craven less in the world? No; *let* him perish, without a pitying thought of ours wasted upon him; and, in that case, all our grief will be reserved for the fate of the helpless girl who now, upon the least shadow of failure in *him*, must by the fiercest of translations—must without time for a prayer—must within seventy seconds—stand before the judgment-seat of God.

But craven he was not: sudden had been the call upon him, and sudden was his answer to the call. He saw, he heard, he comprehended, the ruin that was coming down: already its gloomy shadow darkened above him; and already he was measuring his strength to deal with it. Ah! what a vulgar thing does courage seem when we see nations buying it and selling it for a shilling a-day: ah! what a sublime thing does courage seem when some fearful summons on the great deeps of life carries a man, as if running before a hurricane, up to the giddy crest of some tumultuous crisis from which he two courses, and a voice says to him audibly, "One way lies hope; take the other, and mourn for ever!" How grand a triumph if, even then, amidst the raving of all around him, and the frenzy of the danger, the man is able to confront his situation—is able to retire for a moment into solitude with God, and to seek his counsel from *Him!*

For seven seconds, it might be, of his seventy, the stranger settled his countenance stedfastly upon us, as if to search and value every element in the conflict before him. For five seconds more of his seventy he sat immovably, like one that mused on some great purpose. For five more, perhaps, he sat with eyes upraised, like one that prayed in sorrow, under some extremity of doubt, for light that should guide him to the better choice. Then suddenly he rose; stood upright; and, by a powerful strain upon the reins, raising his horse's fore-feet from the ground, he slewed him round on the pivot of his hind-legs, so as to plant the little equipage in a position nearly at right angles to ours. Thus far his condition was not improved; except as a first step had been taken towards the possibility of a second. If no more were done, nothing was done; for the little carriage still occupied the very centre of our path, though in an altered direction. Yet even now it may not be too late: fifteen of the seventy seconds may still be unexhausted; and one almighty bound may avail to clear the ground. Hurry, then, hurry! for the flying moments—*they* hurry. Oh, hurry, hurry, my brave young man! for the cruel hoofs of our horses—*they* also hurry! Fast are the flying moments, faster are the hoofs of our horses. But fear not for *him*, if human energy can suffice; faithful was he that drove to his terrific duty; faithful was the horse to *his* command. One blow, one impulse given with voice and hand, by the stranger, one rush from the horse, one bound as if in the act of rising to a fence, landed the docile creature's fore-feet upon the crown or arching centre of the road. The larger half of the little equipage had then cleared our over-towering shadow: *that* was evident even to my own agitated sight. But it mattered little that one wreck should float off in safety if upon the wreck that perished were embarked the human freightage. The rear part of the carriage—was *that* certainly beyond the line of absolute ruin? What power could answer the question? Glance of eye, thought of man, wing of angel, which of these had speed enough to sweep between the question and the answer, and divide the one from the other? Light does not tread upon the steps of light more indivisibly than did our all-conquering arrival upon the escaping efforts of the gig. *That* must the young man have felt too plainly. His back was now turned to us; not by sight could he any longer communicate with the peril; but, by the dreadful rattle of our harness, too truly had his ear been instructed that all was finished as regarded any effort of *his*. Already in resignation he had rested from his struggle; and perhaps in his heart he was whispering, "Father, which art in heaven, do Thou finish above what I on earth have attempted." Faster than ever mill-race we ran past them in our inexorable flight.[1]

---

[1] Among the many modifications of the original wording made by De Quincey in revising these paragraphs for the reprint in his Collected Works may be noted, as particularly characteristic, his substitution of this form of the present sentence for the original form; which was, "We ran past them faster than ever mill-race in our inexorable flight." His sensitiveness to fit sound, at such a moment of wild rapidity, suggested the inversion.—M.

Oh, raving of hurricanes that must have sounded in their young ears at the moment of our transit! Even in that moment the thunder of collision spoke aloud. Either with the swingle-bar, or with the haunch of our near leader, we had struck the off-wheel of the little gig; which stood rather obliquely, and not quite so far advanced as to be accurately parallel with the near-wheel. The blow, from the fury of our passage, resounded terrifically. I rose in horror, to gaze upon the ruins we might have caused. From my elevated station I looked down, and looked back upon the scene; which in a moment told its own tale, and wrote all its records on my heart for ever.

Here was the map of the passion that now had finished.[1] The horse was planted immovably, with his fore-feet upon the paved crest of the central road. He of the whole party might be supposed untouched by the passion of death. The little cany carriage—partly, perhaps, from the violent torsion of the wheels in its recent movement, partly from the thundering blow we had given to it—as if it sympathised with human horror, was all alive with tremblings and shiverings. The young man trembled not, nor shivered. He sat like a rock. But *his* was the steadiness of agitation frozen into rest by horror. As yet he dared not to look round; for he knew that, if anything remained to do, by him it could no longer be done. And as yet he knew not for certain if their safety were accomplished. But the lady——

But the lady——! Oh, heavens! will that spectacle ever depart from my dreams, as she rose and sank upon her seat, sank and rose, threw up her arms wildly to heaven, clutched at some visionary object in the air, fainting, praying, raving, despairing? Figure to yourself, reader, the elements of the case; suffer me to recall before your mind the circumstances of that unparalleled situation. From the silence and deep peace of this saintly summer night—from the pathetic blending of this sweet moonlight, dawnlight, dreamlight—from the manly tenderness of this flattering, whispering, mur-

---

[1] This sentence, "Here was the map," etc., is an insertion in the reprint; and one observes how artistically it causes the due pause between the horror as still in rush of transaction and the backward look at the wreck when the crash was past.—M.

muring love—suddenly as from the woods and fields—suddenly as from the chambers of the air opening in revelation—suddenly as from the ground yawning at her feet, leaped upon her, with the flashing of cataracts, Death the crowned phantom, with all the equipage of his terrors, and the tiger roar of his voice.

The moments were numbered; the strife was finished; the vision was closed. In the twinkling of an eye, our flying horses had carried us to the termination of the umbrageous aisle; at the right angles we wheeled into our former direction; the turn of the road carried the scene out of my eyes in an instant, and swept it into my dreams for ever.

Section III.—Dream-Fugue:

FOUNDED ON THE PRECEDING THEME OF SUDDEN DEATH

> " Whence the sound
> Of instruments, that made melodious chime,
> Was heard, of harp and organ ; and who moved
> Their stops and chords was seen ; his volant touch
> Instinct through all proportions, low and high,
> Fled and pursued transverse the resonant fugue."
> *Par. Lost,* Bk. XI.

Tumultuosissimamente

Passion of sudden death! that once in youth I read and interpreted by the shadows of thy averted signs![1]—rapture of panic taking the shape (which amongst tombs in churches I have seen) of woman bursting her sepulchral bonds—of woman's Ionic form bending forward from the ruins of her grave with arching foot, with eyes upraised, with clasped adoring hands—waiting, watching, trembling, praying for the trumpet's call to rise from dust for ever! Ah, vision too fearful of shuddering humanity on the brink of almighty abysses!—vision that didst start back, that didst reel away,

---

[1] "*Averted signs*":—I read the course and changes of the lady's agony in the succession of her involuntary gestures; but it must be remembered that I read all this from the rear, never once catching the lady's full face, and even her profile imperfectly.

like a shrivelling scroll from before the wrath of fire racing on the wings of the wind! Epilepsy so brief of horror, wherefore is it that thou canst not die? Passing so suddenly into darkness, wherefore is it that still thou sheddest thy sad funeral blights upon the gorgeous mosaics of dreams? Fragment of music too passionate, heard once, and heard no more, what aileth thee, that thy deep rolling chords come up at intervals through all the worlds of sleep, and after forty years have lost no element of horror?

I

Lo, it is summer—almighty summer! The everlasting gates of life and summer are thrown open wide; and on the ocean, tranquil and verdant as a savannah, the unknown lady from the dreadful vision and I myself are floating—she upon a fairy pinnace, and I upon an English three-decker. Both of us are wooing gales of festal happiness within the domain of our common country, within that ancient watery park, within the pathless chase of ocean, where England takes her pleasure as a huntress through winter and summer, from the rising to the setting sun. Ah, what a wilderness of floral beauty was hidden, or was suddenly revealed, upon the tropic islands through which the pinnace moved! And upon her deck what a bevy of human flowers: young women how lovely, young men how noble, that were dancing together, and slowly drifting towards *us* amidst music and incense, amidst blossoms from forests and gorgeous corymbi[1] from vintages, amidst natural carolling, and the echoes of sweet girlish laughter. Slowly the pinnace nears us, gaily she hails us, and silently she disappears beneath the shadow of our mighty bows. But then, as at some signal from heaven, the music, and the carols, and the sweet echoing of girlish laughter—all are hushed. What evil has smitten the pinnace, meeting or overtaking her? Did ruin to our friends couch within our own dreadful shadow? Was our shadow the shadow of death? I looked over the bow for an answer, and, behold! the pinnace was dismantled; the revel and the revellers were found no more; the glory of the vintage was

[1] *Corymbus*, a cluster of fruit or flowers. —M.

dust; and the forests with their beauty were left without a witness upon the seas. "But where," and I turned to our crew—"where are the lovely women that danced beneath the awning of flowers and clustering corymbi? Whither have fled the noble young men that danced with *them*?" Answer there was none. But suddenly the man at the mast-head, whose countenance darkened with alarm, cried out, "Sail on the weather beam! Down she comes upon us · in seventy seconds she also will founder."

II

I looked to the weather side, and the summer had departed. The sea was rocking, and shaken with gathering wrath. Upon its surface sat mighty mists, which grouped themselves into arches and long cathedral aisles. Down one of these, with the fiery pace of a quarrel from a cross-bow,[1] ran a frigate right athwart our course. "Are they mad?" some voice exclaimed from our deck. "Do they woo their ruin?" But in a moment, as she was close upon us, some impulse of a heady current or local vortex gave a wheeling bias to her course, and off she forged without a shock. As she ran past us, high aloft amongst the shrouds stood the lady of the pinnace. The deeps opened ahead in malice to receive her, towering surges of foam ran after her, the billows were fierce to catch her. But far away she was borne into desert spaces of the sea: whilst still by sight I followed her, as she ran before the howling gale, chased by angry sea-birds and by maddening billows; still I saw her, as at the moment when she ran past us, standing amongst the shrouds, with her white draperies streaming before the wind. There she stood, with hair dishevelled, one hand clutched amongst the tackling—rising, sinking, fluttering, trembling, praying; there for leagues I saw her as she stood, raising at intervals one hand to heaven, amidst the fiery crests of the pursuing waves and the

---

[1] *Quarrel*, a cross-bow bolt, an arrow with a four-square head; connected with *quadratus*, made square. Richardson's Dictionary gives this example from Robert Brunne—
"A quarrelle lete he flie,
And smote him in the schank."—M.

raving of the storm; until at last, upon a sound from afar of malicious laughter and mockery, all was hidden for ever in driving showers; and afterwards, but when I know not, nor how,

III

Sweet funeral bells from some incalculable distance, wailing over the dead that die before the dawn, awakened me as I slept in a boat moored to some familiar shore. The morning twilight even then was breaking; and, by the dusky revelations which it spread, I saw a girl, adorned with a garland of white roses about her head for some great festival, running along the solitary strand in extremity of haste. Her running was the running of panic; and often she looked back as to some dreadful enemy in the rear. But, when I leaped ashore, and followed on her steps to warn her of a peril in front, alas! from me she fled as from another peril, and vainly I shouted to her of quicksands that lay ahead. Faster and faster she ran; round a promontory of rocks she wheeled out of sight; in an instant I also wheeled round it, but only to see the treacherous sands gathering above her head. Already her person was buried; only the fair young head and the diadem of white roses around it were still visible to the pitying heavens; and, last of all, was visible one white marble arm. I saw by the early twilight this fair young head, as it was sinking down to darkness—saw this marble arm, as it rose above her head and her treacherous grave, tossing, faltering, rising, clutching, as at some false deceiving hand stretched out from the clouds —saw this marble arm uttering her dying hope, and then uttering her dying despair. The head, the diadem, the arm —these all had sunk; at last over these also the cruel quicksand had closed; and no memorial of the fair young girl remained on earth, except my own solitary tears, and the funeral bells from the desert seas, that, rising again more softly, sang a requiem over the grave of the buried child, and over her blighted dawn.

I sat, and wept in secret the tears that men have ever given to the memory of those that died before the dawn, and by the treachery of earth, our mother. But suddenly

the tears and funeral bells were hushed by a shout as of
many nations, and by a roar as from some great king's
artillery, advancing rapidly along the valleys, and heard afar
by echoes from the mountains. "Hush!" I said, as I bent
my ear earthwards to listen—"hush!—this either is the
very anarchy of strife, or else"—and then I listened more
profoundly, and whispered as I raised my head—" or else,
oh heavens! it is *victory* that is final, victory that swallows
up all strife."

IV

Immediately, in trance, I was carried over land and sea
to some distant kingdom, and placed upon a triumphal car,
amongst companions crowned with laurel. The darkness of
gathering midnight, brooding over all the land, hid from us
the mighty crowds that were weaving restlessly about ourselves as a centre: we heard them, but saw them not.
Tidings had arrived, within an hour, of a grandeur that
measured itself against centuries; too full of pathos they
were, too full of joy, to utter themselves by other language
than by tears, by restless anthems, and *Te Deums* reverber-
ated from the choirs and orchestras of earth. These tidings
we that sat upon the laurelled car had it for our privilege
to publish amongst all nations. And already, by signs
audible through the darkness, by snortings and tramplings,
our angry horses, that knew no fear of fleshly weariness,
upbraided us with delay. Wherefore *was* it that we delayed?
We waited for a secret word, that should bear witness to the
hope of nations as now accomplished for ever. At midnight
the secret word arrived; which word was—*Waterloo and
Recovered Christendom!* The dreadful word shone by its own
light; before us it went; high above our leaders' heads it
rode, and spread a golden light over the paths which we
traversed. Every city, at the presence of the secret word,
threw open its gates. The rivers were conscious as we
crossed. All the forests, as we ran along their margins,
shivered in homage to the secret word. And the darkness
comprehended it.

Two hours after midnight we approached a mighty
Minster. Its gates, which rose to the clouds, were closed.

But, when the dreadful word that rode before us reached them with its golden light, silently they moved back upon their hinges; and at a flying gallop our equipage entered the grand aisle of the cathedral. Headlong was our pace; and at every altar, in the little chapels and oratories to the right hand and left of our course, the lamps, dying or sickening, kindled anew in sympathy with the secret word that was flying past. Forty leagues we might have run in the cathedral, and as yet no strength of morning light had reached us, when before us we saw the aerial galleries of organ and choir. Every pinnacle of the fretwork, every station of advantage amongst the traceries, was crested by white-robed choristers that sang deliverance; that wept no more tears, as once their fathers had wept, but at intervals that sang together to the generations, saying,

"Chant the deliverer's praise in every tongue,"

and receiving answers from afar,

"Such as once in heaven and earth were sung."

And of their chanting was no end; of our headlong pace was neither pause nor slackening.

Thus as we ran like torrents—thus as we swept with bridal rapture over the Campo Santo[1] of the cathedral graves—suddenly we became aware of a vast necropolis rising upon the far-off horizon—a city of sepulchres, built within the saintly cathedral for the warrior dead that rested from their feuds on earth. Of purple granite was the necropolis; yet, in the first minute, it lay like a purple stain

[1] "*Campo Santo*":—It is probable that most of my readers will be acquainted with the history of the Campo Santo (or cemetery) at Pisa, composed of earth brought from Jerusalem from a bed of sanctity, as the highest prize which the noble piety of crusaders could ask or imagine. To readers who are unacquainted with England, or who (being English) are yet unacquainted with the cathedral cities of England, it may be right to mention that the graves within-side the cathedrals often form a flat pavement over which carriages and horses *might* run; and perhaps a boyish remembrance of one particular cathedral, across which I had seen passengers walk and burdens carried, as about two centuries back they were through the middle of St. Paul's in London, may have assisted my dream.

upon the horizon, so mighty was the distance. In the second minute it trembled through many changes, growing into terraces and towers of wondrous altitude, so mighty was the pace. In the third minute already, with our dreadful gallop, we were entering its suburbs. Vast sarcophagi rose on every side, having towers and turrets that, upon the limits of the central aisle, strode forward with haughty intrusion, that ran back with mighty shadows into answering recesses. Every sarcophagus showed many bas-reliefs—bas-reliefs of battles and of battle-fields; battles from forgotten ages, battles from yesterday; battle-fields that, long since, nature had healed and reconciled to herself with the sweet oblivion of flowers; battle-fields that were yet angry and crimson with carnage. Where the terraces ran, there did *we* run; where the towers curved, there did *we* curve. With the flight of swallows our horses swept round every angle. Like rivers in flood wheeling round headlands, like hurricanes that ride into the secrets of forests, faster than ever light unwove the mazes of darkness, our flying equipage carried earthly passions, kindled warrior instincts, amongst the dust that lay around us—dust oftentimes of our noble fathers that had slept in God from Créci to Trafalgar. And now had we reached the last sarcophagus, now were we abreast of the last bas-relief, already had we recovered the arrow-like flight of the illimitable central aisle, when coming up this aisle to meet us we beheld afar off a female child, that rode in a carriage as frail as flowers. The mists which went before her hid the fawns that drew her, but could not hide the shells and tropic flowers with which she played—but could not hide the lovely smiles by which she uttered her trust in the mighty cathedral, and in the cherubim that looked down upon her from the mighty shafts of its pillars. Face to face she was meeting us; face to face she rode, as if danger there were none. "Oh, baby!" I exclaimed, "shalt thou be the ransom for Waterloo? Must we, that carry tidings of great joy to every people, be messengers of ruin to thee!" In horror I rose at the thought; but then also, in horror at the thought, rose one that was sculptured on a bas-relief—a Dying Trumpeter. Solemnly from the field of battle he rose to his feet; and, unslinging his stony trumpet, carried it, in his dying anguish, to his stony lips—sounding once, and yet once again; proclamation that, in *thy* ears, oh baby! spoke from the battlements of death. Immediately deep shadows fell between us, and aboriginal silence. The choir had ceased to sing. The hoofs of our horses, the dreadful rattle of our harness, the groaning of our wheels, alarmed the graves no more. By horror the bas-relief had been unlocked unto life. By horror we, that were so full of life, we men and our horses, with their fiery fore-legs rising in mid air to their everlasting gallop, were frozen to a bas-relief. Then a third time the trumpet sounded; the seals were taken off all pulses; life, and the frenzy of life, tore into their channels again; again the choir burst forth in sunny grandeur, as from the muffling of storms and darkness; again the thunderings of our horses carried temptation into the graves. One cry burst from our lips, as the clouds, drawing off from the aisle, showed it empty before us.— "Whither has the infant fled?—is the young child caught up to God?" Lo! afar off, in a vast recess, rose three mighty windows to the clouds; and on a level with their summits, at height insuperable to man, rose an altar of purest alabaster. On its eastern face was trembling a crimson glory. A glory was it from the reddening dawn that now streamed *through* the windows? Was it from the crimson robes of the martyrs painted *on* the windows? Was it from the bloody bas-reliefs of earth? There, suddenly, within that crimson radiance, rose the apparition of a woman's head, and then of a woman's figure. The child it was—grown up to woman's height. Clinging to the horns of the altar, voiceless she stood—sinking, rising, raving, despairing; and behind the volume of incense that, night and day, streamed upwards from the altar, dimly was seen the fiery font, and the shadow of that dreadful being who should have baptized her with the baptism of death. But by her side was kneeling her better angel, that hid his face with wings; that wept and pleaded for *her*; that prayed when *she* could *not*; that fought with Heaven by tears for *her* deliverance; which also, as he raised his immortal countenance from his wings, I saw, by the glory in his eye, that from Heaven he had won at last.

V

Then was completed the passion of the mighty fugue. The golden tubes of the organ, which as yet had but muttered at intervals—gleaming amongst clouds and surges of incense—threw up, as from fountains unfathomable, columns of heart-shattering music. Choir and anti-choir were filling fast with unknown voices. Thou also, Dying Trumpeter, with thy love that was victorious, and thy anguish that was finishing, didst enter the tumult; trumpet and echo—farewell love, and farewell anguish—rang through the dreadful *sanctus*. Oh, darkness of the grave! that from the crimson altar and from the fiery font wert visited and searched by the effulgence in the angel's eye—were these indeed thy children? Pomps of life, that, from the burials of centuries, rose again to the voice of perfect joy, did ye indeed mingle with the festivals of Death? Lo! as I looked back for seventy leagues through the mighty cathedral, I saw the quick and the dead that sang together to God, together that sang to the generations of man. All the hosts of jubilation, like armies that ride in pursuit, moved with one step. Us, that, with laurelled heads, were passing from the cathedral, they overtook, and, as with a garment, they wrapped us round with thunders greater than our own. As brothers we moved together; to the dawn that advanced, to the stars that fled; rendering thanks to God in the highest—that, having hid His face through one generation behind thick clouds of War, once again was ascending, from the Campo Santo of Waterloo was ascending, in the visions of Peace; rendering thanks for thee, young girl! whom having overshadowed with His ineffable passion of death, suddenly did God relent, suffered thy angel to turn aside His arm, and even in thee, sister unknown! shown to me for a moment only to be hidden for ever, found an occasion to glorify His goodness. A thousand times, amongst the phantoms of sleep, have I seen thee entering the gates of the golden dawn, with the secret word riding before thee, with the armies of the grave behind thee,—seen thee sinking, rising, raving, despairing; a thousand times in the worlds of sleep have seen thee followed by God's angel through storms, through desert seas, through the darkness of quicksands, through dreams and the dreadful revelations that are in dreams; only that at the last, with one sling of His victorious arm, He might snatch thee back from ruin, and might emblazon in thy deliverance the endless resurrections of His love!

AUTHOR'S POSTSCRIPT[1]

"THE ENGLISH MAIL-COACH."—This little paper, according to my original intention, formed part of the "Suspiria de Profundis"; from which, for a momentary purpose, I did not scruple to detach it, and to publish it apart, as sufficiently intelligible even when dislocated from its place in a larger whole. To my surprise, however, one or two critics, not carelessly in conversation, but deliberately in print, professed their inability to apprehend the meaning of the whole, or to follow the links of the connexion between its several parts. I am myself as little able to understand where the difficulty lies, or to detect any lurking obscurity, as these critics found themselves to unravel my logic. Possibly I may not be an indifferent and neutral judge in such a case. I will therefore sketch a brief abstract of the little paper according to my original design, and then leave the reader to judge how far this design is kept in sight through the actual execution.

Thirty-seven years ago, or rather more, accident made me, in the dead of night, and of a night memorably solemn, the solitary witness of an appalling scene, which threatened instant death in a shape the most terrific to two young people whom I had no means of assisting, except in so far as I was able to give them a most hurried warning of their danger; but even *that* not until they stood within the very shadow of

[1] What is now printed properly as a "Postscript" was printed by De Quincey himself as a portion of the Preface which he prefixed in 1854 to the volume of his Collected Writings containing *The English Mail-Coach.*—M.

the catastrophe, being divided from the most frightful of deaths by scarcely more, if more at all, than seventy seconds.

Such was the scene, such in its outline, from which the whole of this paper radiates as a natural expansion. This scene is circumstantially narrated in Section the Second, entitled "The Vision of Sudden Death."

But a movement of horror, and of spontaneous recoil from this dreadful scene, naturally carried the whole of that scene, raised and idealised, into my dreams, and very soon into a rolling succession of dreams. The actual scene, as looked down upon from the box of the mail, was transformed into a dream, as tumultuous and changing as a musical fugue. This troubled dream is circumstantially reported in Section the Third, entitled "Dream-Fugue on the theme of Sudden Death." What I had beheld from my seat upon the mail,— the scenical strife of action and passion, of anguish and fear, as I had there witnessed them moving in ghostly silence,— this duel between life and death narrowing itself to a point of such exquisite evanescence as the collision neared: all these elements of the scene blended, under the law of association, with the previous and permanent features of distinction investing the mail itself; which features at that time lay— 1st, in velocity unprecedented, 2dly, in the power and beauty of the horses, 3dly, in the official connexion with the government of a great nation, and, 4thly, in the function, almost a consecrated function, of publishing and diffusing through the land the great political events, and especially the great battles, during a conflict of unparalleled grandeur. These honorary distinctions are all described circumstantially in the First or introductory Section (" The Glory of Motion "). The three first were distinctions maintained at all times; but the fourth and grandest belonged exclusively to the war with Napoleon; and this it was which most naturally introduced Waterloo into the dream. Waterloo, I understand, was the particular feature of the "Dream-Fugue" which my censors were least able to account for. Yet surely Waterloo, which, in common with every other great battle, it had been our special privilege to publish over all the land, most naturally entered the dream under the licence of our privilege. If not —if there be anything amiss—let the Dream be responsible.

The Dream is a law to itself; and as well quarrel with a rainbow for showing, or for *not* showing, a secondary arch So far as I know, every element in the shifting movements of the Dream derived itself either primarily from the incidents of the actual scene, or from secondary features associated with the mail. For example, the cathedral aisle derived itself from the mimic combination of features which grouped themselves together at the point of approaching collision—viz. an arrow-like section of the road, six hundred yards long, under the solemn lights described, with lofty trees meeting overhead in arches. The guard's horn, again—a humble instrument in itself—was yet glorified as the organ of publication for so many great national events. And the incident of the Dying Trumpeter, who rises from a marble bas-relief, and carries a marble trumpet to his marble lips for the purpose of warning the female infant, was doubtless secretly suggested by my own imperfect effort to seize the guard's horn, and to blow a warning blast. But the Dream knows best; and the Dream. I say again, is the responsible party.

SUSPIRIA DE PROFUNDIS

BEING A SEQUEL TO

"THE CONFESSIONS OF AN ENGLISH OPIUM-EATER"

[De Quincey began in 1845 a special series of contributions to *Blackwood's Magazine* under the title of SUSPIRIA DE PROFUNDIS: BEING A SEQUEL TO THE CONFESSIONS OF AN ENGLISH OPIUM-EATER. It seems clear that he intended this series to be a collection of fragments or papers, some perhaps already beside him in manuscript, but others still to be written, all in that species of prose-phantasy, and some more particularly in that vein of dream-phantasy, of which his CONFESSIONS OF AN OPIUM-EATER had been, as he believed, the first example set in English Literature. Hence the propriety of announcing the new series as a projected sequel to those celebrated earlier papers. For some reason or other, however, whether because De Quincey himself became languid, or because a long continuity of papers under the melancholy title of "Sighs from the Depths" did not suit the editorial arrangements of *Blackwood*, the series broke down after it had run through four numbers of the Magazine. In the number for March 1845 there had appeared, by way of opening, an "*Introductory Notice*" on the subject of Dreaming in general, but especially of Opium-Dreaming, followed by an autobiographic paper entitled "*The Affliction of Childhood*" and a few separate and untitled paragraphs of lyrical prose; in the number for April there were a few more pages of autobiographical and lyrical matter, undistinguished by any sub-titles, but offered together as a continuation of "Part I" of the SUSPIRIA; in the number for June the said "Part I" was announced as "concluded,"—the conclusion consisting of four independent short papers, sub-titled respectively "*The Palimpsest*," "*Levana and Our Ladies of Sorrow*," "*The Apparition of the Brocken*," and "*Savannah-la-Mar*"; and in the number for July appeared the first instalment of a "Part II," printed continuously as such, without subdivision or subtitling. There the series stopped; the rest of Part II, and the whole of Parts III and IV (for it had been announced that there were to be four

Parts in all) remaining hopelessly due.——There is proof, however, that De Quincey still secretly persevered in his notion of making SUSPIRIA DE PROFUNDIS the collective name for a miscellany of such papers or shreds as might prove his unabated vigour in his later years in his old craft of prose-phantasy. His sketch called *The Daughter of Lebanon* purports to have been one of a number of little things he was privately penning for appearance at some time or other in this projected collection, and we have his own word for the fact that *The English Mail-Coach* itself was originally meant to be part of the same. ——In the case of this last paper there was an afterthought; for, when it got into *Blackwood* in 1849 (see *ante*, p. 270), it appeared there independently, and without the least intimation of any connexion between it and the interrupted and unfinished SUSPIRIA papers of 1845. This, in itself, was a considerable subtraction from the stock that was in reserve for the special SUSPIRIA series; and, before De Quincey's death, there was to be, also by his own act, a still further diminution of the quantity of his writings that could in future claim the striking name. For, when he was engaged, from 1853 onwards, in bringing out the Collective Edinburgh Edition of his writings, he pillaged at his pleasure, for the purposes of that edition, whatever of his own, printed or in manuscript, he could conveniently lay his hands on, the SUSPIRIA gatherings included. The result, as regarded *these*, was rather perplexing. Thus, not only was *The Daughter of Lebanon* attached to the enlarged edition of the CONFESSIONS OF AN ENGLISH OPIUM-EATER which formed volume v. of the collective issue (see *ante*, Vol. III, p. 222 and p. 450), and not only was there no replacing of *The English Mail-Coach* in its originally intended relationship; but so much of the original SUSPIRIA in *Blackwood* of 1845 was utilised, in recast shape, in new connexions,—*The Affliction of Childhood* and *The Apparition of the Brocken*, for example, being worked into the Volume of "Autobiographic Sketches" (see *ante*, Vol. I, pp. 28-54)—that nothing tangible remained of what had once been "Part I" and the fragment of "Part II" in *Blackwood*, except *The Introductory Notice, The Palimpsest, Levana and Our Ladies of Sorrow, Savannah-la-Mar*, and a few stray paragraphs besides. De Quincey had been revising and retouching these too; but what he would have done with them if he had lived to extend his Collective Edition, and to introduce into it a SUSPIRIA DE PROFUNDIS series in finally arranged form, one can hardly guess. As it was, though there was frequent mention of the SUSPIRIA DE PROFUNDIS in the course of the fourteen volumes of his Collective Edition issued between 1853 and 1860, not a single paper appeared under that express title in the whole range of the volumes.——The defect was remedied in 1871 in the second of the two supplementary volumes of Messrs. Black's augmented edition of De Quincey's Collected Writings. Among the additions in that volume to the matter of the previous edition were forty-nine pages bearing the general title of SUSPIRIA DE PROFUNDIS: BEING A SEQUEL TO THE CONFESSIONS OF AN ENGLISH OPIUM-EATER, and consisting of six separate short papers, sub-titled as follows:—(1)

Dreaming, (2) *The Palimpsest of the Human Brain*, (3) *Levana and Our Ladies of Sorrow*, (4) *Savannah-la-Mar*, (5) *Vision of Life*, (6) *Memorial Suspiria*. With respect to the volume generally it was announced in the Preface that most of the papers contained in it had been acquired from De Quincey's "original publishers, Messrs. James Hogg & Son," and that, with the exception of those that were reprinted from the *London Magazine*, all had had "the benefit of the Author's revision and correction"; and in a special further note prefixed to the six SUSPIRIA papers themselves there was the repeated intimation that they were "printed with the Author's latest corrections."——One can see now how it had happened. The *Blackwood Suspiria* of 1845, both Part I and the fragments of Part II, having been pillaged for the purposes of the Collective Edition of the writings, and so much of their matter having been worked into the *Autobiographic Sketches* in vol. 1 of that edition, and into the enlarged *Confessions of an Opium-Eater* in vol. v, it was only the residue that De Quincey could regard as available for future use in any publication that could then be offered as the SUSPIRIA proper. This residue, accordingly, he had conserved and corrected, retaining the original *Blackwood* sub-titles for three of the six short articles into which it broke itself, and fitting suitable sub-titles to the other three.——How great an improvement had been thus effected will be seen by any one who will take the trouble of comparing the original *Blackwood Suspiria* (of which the *Suspiria* as given in the American Collective Edition of De Quincey is a mere reprint) with the *Suspiria* of the conserved and corrected residue. The original *Blackwood Suspiria*, when read now, annoy one as a kind of clotted confusion, in which duplicates of portions of the *Autobiographic Sketches* and the enlarged *Confessions* interrupt and disturb the succession of the pieces of phantasy that constitute the *Suspiria* properly and essentially; whereas in De Quincey's reduction of that heterogeneous original these pieces are rescued into impressive independence and stand on their own merits.——At all events it is the six papers printed in Messrs. Black's supplementary volume of 1871, and there vouched for as having been left by De Quincey ready for use in case there should be a posthumous publication of his SUSPIRIA DE PROFUNDIS,—it is these that we have to reproduce here. For reasons which will appear presently, and which will seem sufficient to all, the order of their arrangement is slightly changed.—M.]

DREAMING [1]

IN 1821, as a contribution to a periodical work,—in 1822, as a separate volume,—appeared the "Confessions of an

[1] This is De Quincey's revised form of what appeared in *Blackwood* for March 1845 as the "Introductory Notice" to Part I of the original SUSPIRIA (see *ante*, p. 331). Though the title is changed, it still serves as an "introduction," inasmuch as it avowedly connects the SUSPIRIA DE PROFUNDIS with the CONFESSIONS OF AN ENGLISH OPIUM-EATER, and explains the nature of the connexion.—M.

English Opium-Eater."[1] The object of that work was to reveal something of the grandeur which belongs *potentially* to human dreams. Whatever may be the number of those in whom this faculty of dreaming splendidly can be supposed to lurk, there are not, perhaps, very many in whom it is developed. He whose talk is of oxen will probably dream of oxen; and the condition of human life which yokes so vast a majority to a daily experience incompatible with much elevation of thought oftentimes neutralises the tone of grandeur in the reproductive faculty of dreaming, even for those whose minds are populous with solemn imagery. Habitually to dream magnificently, a man must have a constitutional determination to reverie. This in the first place; and even this, where it exists strongly, is too much liable to disturbance from the gathering agitation of our present English life. Already, what by the procession through fifty years of mighty revolutions amongst the kingdoms of the earth, what by the continual development of vast physical agencies,—steam in all its applications, light getting under harness as a slave for man, powers from heaven descending upon education and accelerations of the press, powers from hell (as it might seem, but these also celestial) coming round upon artillery and the forces of destruction,—the eye of the calmest observer is troubled; the brain is haunted as if by some jealousy of ghostly beings moving amongst us; and it becomes too evident that, unless this colossal pace of advance can be retarded (a thing not to be expected), or, which is happily more probable, can be met by counter-forces of corresponding magnitude,—forces in the direction of religion or profound philosophy that shall radiate centrifugally against this storm of life so perilously centripetal towards the vortex of the merely human,—left to itself, the natural tendency of so chaotic a tumult must be to evil; for some minds to lunacy,

---

[1] As has been explained *ante*, Vol. III, pp. 5-7, the "Confessions" appeared originally in the *London Magazine* for September and October 1821, and the reprint of them in book-form by the proprietors of the magazine was in 1822. It is to this original form of the famous book that De Quincey refers in the above sentence, written in 1845. His revised and enlarged edition, swelling the "Confessions" to nearly three times their original bulk, and therefore completely superseding the original edition, did not appear till 1855.—M.

for others a reagency of fleshly torpor. How much this fierce condition of eternal hurry upon an arena too exclusively human in its interests is likely to defeat the grandeur which is latent in all men, may be seen in the ordinary effect from living too constantly in varied company. The word *dissipation*, in one of its uses, expresses that effect; the action of thought and feeling is consciously dissipated and squandered. To reconcentrate them into meditative habits, a necessity is felt by all observing persons for sometimes retiring from crowds. No man ever will unfold the capacities of his own intellect who does not at least checker his life with solitude. How much solitude, so much power. Or, if not true in that rigour of expression, to this formula undoubtedly it is that the wise rule of life must approximate.

Among the powers in man which suffer by this too intense life of the *social* instincts, none suffers more than the power of dreaming. Let no man think this a trifle. The machinery for dreaming planted in the human brain was not planted for nothing. That faculty, in alliance with the mystery of darkness, is the one great tube through which man communicates with the shadowy. And the dreaming organ, in connexion with the heart, the eye, and the ear, composes the magnificent apparatus which forces the infinite into the chambers of a human brain, and throws dark reflections from eternities below all life upon the mirrors of that mysterious *camera obscura*—the sleeping mind.

But, if this faculty suffers from the decay of solitude, which is becoming a visionary idea in England, on the other hand it is certain that some merely physical agencies can and do assist the faculty of dreaming almost preternaturally. Amongst these is intense exercise,—to some extent at least, for some persons; but beyond all others is opium: which indeed seems to possess a *specific* power in that direction; not merely for exalting the colours of dream-scenery, but for deepening its shadows, and, above all, for strengthening the sense of its fearful *realities*.

The *Opium Confessions* were written with some slight secondary purpose of exposing this specific power of opium upon the faculty of dreaming, but much more with the purpose of displaying the faculty itself; and the outline of the work travelled in this course:—Supposing a reader acquainted with the true object of the *Confessions* as here stated,—namely, the revelation of dreaming,—to have put this question :

"But how came you to dream more splendidly than others ?"

The answer would have been—

"Because (*præmissis præmittendis*) I took excessive quantities of opium."

Secondly, suppose him to say, "But how came you to take opium in this excess ?"

The answer to *that* would be, "Because some early events in my life had left a weakness in one organ which required (or seemed to require) that stimulant."

Then, because the opium dreams could not always have been understood without a knowledge of these events, it became necessary to relate them. Now, these two questions and answers exhibit the *law* of the work,—that is, the principle which determined its form,—but precisely in the inverse or regressive order. The work itself opened with the narration of my early adventures. These, in the natural order of succession, led to the opium as a resource for healing their consequences ; and the opium as naturally led to the dreams. But, in the synthetic order of presenting the facts, what stood last in the succession of development stood first in the order of my purposes.

At the close of this little work, the reader was instructed to believe, and *truly* instructed, that I had mastered the tyranny of opium. The fact is that *twice* I mastered it, and by efforts even more prodigious in the second of these cases than in the first. But one error I committed in both. I did not connect with the abstinence from opium, so trying to the fortitude under *any* circumstances, that enormity of exercise which (as I have since learned) is the one sole resource for making it endurable. I overlooked, in those days, the one *sine quâ non* for making the triumph permanent. Twice I sank, twice I rose again. A third time I sank ; partly from the cause mentioned (the oversight as to exercise), partly from other causes, on which it avails not now to trouble the reader. I could moralise, if I chose ; and perhaps *he* will moralise, whether I choose it or not.

But, in the meantime, neither of us is acquainted properly with the circumstances of the case : I, from natural bias of judgment, not altogether acquainted ; and he (with his permission) not at all.

During this third prostration before the dark idol, and after some years, new and monstrous phenomena began slowly to arise. For a time, these were neglected as accidents, or palliated by such remedies as I knew of. But, when I could no longer conceal from myself that these dreadful symptoms were moving forward for ever, by a pace steadily, solemnly, and equably increasing, I endeavoured, with some feeling of panic, for a third time to retrace my steps. But I had not reversed my motions for many weeks before I became profoundly aware that this was impossible Or, in the imagery of my dreams, which translated everything into their own language, I saw, through vast avenues of gloom, those towering gates of ingress which hitherto had always seemed to stand open now at last barred against my retreat, and hung with funeral crape.

As applicable to this tremendous situation (the situation of one escaping by some refluent current from the maelstrom roaring for him in the distance, who finds suddenly that this current is but an eddy wheeling round upon the same maelstrom), I have since remembered a striking incident in a modern novel.

A lady-abbess of a convent, herself suspected of Protestant leanings, and in that way already disarmed of all effectual power, finds one of her own nuns (whom she knows to be innocent) accused of an offence leading to the most terrific of punishments. The nun will be immured alive if she is found guilty, and there is no chance that she will not,—for the evidence against her is strong, unless something were made known that cannot be made known, and the judges are hostile. All follows in the order of the reader's fears. The witnesses depose ; the evidence is without effectual contradiction ; the conviction is declared ; the judgment is delivered ; nothing remains but to see execution done. At this crisis, the abbess, alarmed too late for effectual interposition, considers with herself that, according to the regular forms, there will be one single night open, during which the prisoner cannot be withdrawn from her own separate jurisdiction. This one night, therefore, she will use, at any hazard to herself, for the salvation of her friend. At midnight, when all is hushed in the convent, the lady traverses the passages which lead to the cells of prisoners. She bears a master-key under her professional habit. As this will open every door in every corridor, already, by anticipation, she feels the luxury of holding her emancipated friend within her arms. Suddenly she has reached the door; she descries a dusky object; she raises her lamp; and, ranged within the recess of the entrance, she beholds the funeral banner of the holy office, and the black robes of its inexorable officials.

I apprehend that, in a situation such as this, supposing it a real one, the lady-abbess would not start, would not show any marks externally of consternation or horror. The case was beyond *that*. The sentiment which attends the sudden revelation that *all is lost* silently is gathered up into the heart; it is too deep for gestures or for words; and no part of it passes to the outside. Were the ruin conditional, or were it in any point doubtful, it would be natural to utter ejaculations, and to seek sympathy. But, where the ruin is understood to be absolute, where sympathy cannot be consolation, and counsel cannot be hope, this is otherwise. The voice perishes; the gestures are frozen; and the spirit of man flies back upon its own centre. I, at least, upon seeing those awful gates closed and hung with draperies of woe, as for a death already past, spoke not, nor started, nor groaned. One profound sigh ascended from my heart, and I was silent for days.[1]

. . . .

In the *Opium Confessions* I touched a little upon the extraordinary power connected with opium (after long use) of amplifying the dimensions of time. Space, also, it amplifies by degrees that are sometimes terrific. But time it is upon which the exalting and multiplying power of opium chiefly spends its operation. Time becomes infinitely elastic, stretching out to such immeasurable and vanishing termini that it seems ridiculous to compute the sense of it, on waking,

---

[1] To this point the paper is substantially the same as the "Introductory Notice" in *Blackwood* for March 1845. See *ante*, p. 331.—M.

by expressions commensurate to human life. As in starry fields one computes by diameters of the Earth's orbit, or of Jupiter's, so, in valuing the *virtual* time lived during some dreams, the measurement by generations is ridiculous—by millennia is ridiculous; by æons, I should say, if æons were more determinate, would be also ridiculous.

Here pause, reader! Imagine yourself seated in some cloud-scaling swing, oscillating under the impulse of lunatic hands; for the strength of lunacy may belong to human dreams, the fearful caprice of lunacy, and the malice of lunacy, whilst the *victim* of those dreams may be all the more certainly removed from lunacy; even as a bridge gathers cohesion and strength from the increasing resistance into which it is forced by increasing pressure. Seated in such a swing, fast as you reach the lowest point of depression, may you rely on racing up to a starry altitude of corresponding ascent. Ups and downs you will see, heights and depths, in our fiery course together, such as will sometimes tempt you to look shyly and suspiciously at me, your guide, and the ruler of the oscillations. Here, at the point where I have called a halt, the reader has reached the lowest depths in my nursery afflictions. From that point according to the principles of *art* which govern the movement of these Confessions, I had meant to launch him upwards through the whole arch of ascending visions which seemed requisite to balance the sweep downwards, so recently described in his course. But accidents of the press have made it impossible to accomplish this purpose. There is reason to regret that the advantages of position which were essential to the full effect of passages planned for the equipoise and mutual resistance have thus been lost. Meantime, upon the principle of the mariner who rigs a *jury*-mast in default of his regular spars, I find my resource in a sort of "jury" peroration, not sufficient in the way of a balance by its *proportions*, but sufficient to indicate the *quality* of the balance which I had contemplated. He who has *really* read the preceding parts of these present Confessions will be aware that a stricter scrutiny of the past, such as was natural after the whole economy of the dreaming faculty had been convulsed beyond all precedents on record, led me to the conviction that not one agency, but two agencies had co-operated to the tremendous result. The nursery experience had been the ally and the natural coefficient of the opium. For that reason it was that the nursery experience has been narrated. Logically it bears the very same relation to the convulsions of the dreaming faculty as the opium. The idealising tendency existed in the dream-theatre of my childhood; but the preternatural strength of its action and colouring was first developed after the confluence of the *two* causes. The reader must suppose me at Oxford; twelve years and a half are gone by; I am in the glory of youthful happiness: but I have now first tampered with opium; and now first the agitations of my childhood reopened in strength; now first they swept in upon the brain with power and the grandeur of recovered life under the separate and the concurring inspirations of opium.[1]

The Palimpsest of the Human Brain.[2]

You know perhaps, masculine reader, better than I can tell you, what is a *Palimpsest*. Possibly you have one in your own library. But yet, for the sake of others who may *not* know, or may have forgotten, suffer me to explain it here, lest any female reader who honours these papers with

---

[1] The two closing paragraphs are the somewhat abrupt substitution left by De Quincey for five closing paragraphs of the paper as it stood originally in *Blackwood* for March 1845. Those five closing paragraphs were intended to prepare the reader for what immediately followed in the same number of the magazine, in the shape of that section of "Part I" of the SUSPIRIA which bore the title *The Affliction of Childhood*; and De Quincey's feeling seems to have been that there was no need to retain the paragraphs after *The Affliction of Childhood* had been removed from among the SUSPIRIA, for partial incorporation with his AUTOBIOGRAPHIC SKETCHES. But I have doubts whether De Quincey did really mean to close his present paper with the two paragraphs that now appear in such ragged shape to do duty for the omitted original conclusion of the "Introductory Notice" in *Blackwood*. The two paragraphs, I find, are clippings from the superseded "Affliction of Childhood"; and it seems more natural to suppose that they had been preserved inadvertently than that De Quincey thought they could be moved back suitably to where they now are. The paper seems to end more fitly without them.—M.

[2] Printed originally, but with the title of "The Palimpsest" merely, in *Blackwood* for June 1845. See *ante*, p. 331.—M.

her notice should tax me with explaining it once too seldom; which would be worse to bear than a simultaneous complaint from twelve proud men that I had explained it three times too often. You, therefore, fair reader, understand that for *your* accommodation exclusively I explain the meaning of this word. It is Greek; and our sex enjoys the office and privilege of standing counsel to yours in all questions of Greek. We are, under favour, perpetual and hereditary dragomans to you. So that if, by accident, you know the meaning of a Greek word, yet by courtesy to us, your counsel learned in that matter, you will always seem *not* to know it.

A palimpsest, then, is a membrane or roll cleansed of its manuscript by reiterated successions.

What was the reason that the Greeks and the Romans had not the advantage of printed books? The answer will be, from ninety-nine persons in a hundred,—Because the mystery of printing was not then discovered. But this is altogether a mistake. The secret of printing must have been discovered many thousands of times before it was used, or *could* be used. The inventive powers of man are divine; and also his stupidity is divine, as Cowper so playfully illustrates in the slow development of the *sofa* through successive generations of immortal dulness. It took centuries of blockheads to raise a joint stool into a chair; and it required something like a miracle of genius, in the estimate of elder generations, to reveal the possibility of lengthening a chair into a *chaise-longue*, or a sofa. Yes, these were inventions that cost mighty throes of intellectual power. But still, as respects printing, and admirable as is the stupidity of man, it was really not quite equal to the task of evading an object which stared him in the face with so broad a gaze. It did not require an Athenian intellect to read the main secret of printing in many scores of processes which the ordinary uses of life were *daily* repeating. To say nothing of analogous artifices amongst various mechanic artizans, all that is essential in printing must have been known to every nation that struck coins and medals. Not, therefore, any want of a printing art,—that is, of an art for multiplying impressions,—but the want of a cheap material for *receiving* such impressions, was the obstacle to an intro-

duction of printed books even as early as Pisistratus. The
ancients *did* apply printing to records of silver and gold; to
marble, and many other substances cheaper than gold or
silver, they did *not*, since each monument required a *separate*
effort of inscription. Simply this defect it was of a cheap
material for receiving impresses which froze in its very
fountains the early resources of printing.

Some twenty years ago this view of the case was luminously
expounded by Dr. Whately, and with the merit, I believe, of
having first suggested it. Since then, this theory has received
indirect confirmation. Now, out of that original scarcity
affecting all materials proper for durable books, which continued up to times comparatively modern, grew the opening
for palimpsests. Naturally, when once a roll of parchment
or of vellum had done its office, by propagating through a
series of generations what once had possessed an interest for
them, but which, under changes of opinion or of taste, had
faded to their feelings or had become obsolete for their under-
takings, the whole *membrana* or vellum skin, the twofold product of human skill and costly material, and the costly freight
of thought which it carried, drooped in value concurrently—
supposing that each were inalienably associated to the other.
Once it had been the impress of a human mind which
stamped its value upon the vellum; the vellum, though
costly, had contributed but a secondary element of value to
the total result. At length, however, this relation between
the vehicle and its freight has gradually been undermined.
The vellum, from having been the setting of the jewel, has
risen at length to be the jewel itself; and the burden of
thought, from having given the chief value to the vellum,
has now become the chief obstacle to its value; nay, has
totally extinguished its value, unless it can be dissociated
from the connexion. Yet, if this unlinking *can* be effected,
then, fast as the inscription upon the membrane is sinking
into rubbish, the membrane itself is reviving in its separate
importance; and, from bearing a ministerial value, the
vellum has come at last to absorb the whole value.

Hence the importance for our ancestors that the separation *should* be effected. Hence it arose in the Middle Ages as
a considerable object for chemistry to discharge the writing

from the roll, and thus to make it available for a new succession of thoughts. The soil, if cleansed from what once had been hot-house plants, but now were held to be weeds, would be ready to receive a fresh and more appropriate crop. In that object the monkish chemists succeeded; but after a fashion which seems almost incredible,—incredible not as regards the extent of their success, but as regards the delicacy of restraints under which it moved,—so equally adjusted was their success to the immediate interests of that period, and to the reversionary objects of our own. They did the thing, but not so radically as to prevent us, their posterity, from *undoing* it. They expelled the writing sufficiently to leave a field for the new manuscript, and yet not sufficiently to make the traces of the elder manuscript irrecoverable for us. Could magic, could Hermes Trismegistus, have done more? What would you think, fair reader, of a problem such as this:—to write a book which should be sense for your own generation, nonsense for the next; should revive into sense for the next after that, but again become nonsense for the fourth; and so on by alternate successions sinking into night or blazing into day, like the Sicilian river Arethusa and the English river Mole,[1] or like the undulating motions of a flattened stone which children cause to skim the breast of a river, now diving below the water, now grazing its surface, sinking heavily into darkness, rising buoyantly into light, through a long vista of alternations? Such a problem, you say, is impossible. But really it is a problem not harder apparently than to bid a generation kill, so that a subsequent generation may call back into life; bury, so that posterity may command to rise again. Yet *that* was what the rude chemistry of past ages effected when coming into combination with the reaction from the more refined chemistry of our own. Had *they* been better chemists, had *we* been worse, the mixed result,—namely, that, dying

---

[1] The famous Sicilian fountain of Arethusa is said to be still visible, though in shrunken dimensions, in the ancient quarter of Syracuse called Ortygia. The English Mole is in Surrey, and has, or had, the trick of disappearing in summer, for a part of its course, into a subterranean channel: whence Milton's line in his poem *At a Vacation Exercise*:—

"Or sullen Mole, that runneth underneath."—M.

for *them*, the flower should revive for *us*,—could not have been effected. They did the thing proposed to them: they did it effectually, for they founded upon it all that was wanted: and yet ineffectually, since we unravelled their work,—effacing all above which they had superscribed, restoring all below which they had effaced.

Here, for instance, is a parchment which contained some Grecian tragedy,—the Agamemnon of Æschylus, or the Phœnissæ of Euripides. This had possessed a value almost inappreciable in the eyes of accomplished scholars, continually growing rarer through generations. But four centuries are gone by since the destruction of the Western Empire. Christianity, with towering grandeurs of another class, has founded a different empire; and some bigoted, yet perhaps holy monk has washed away (as he persuades himself) the heathen's tragedy, replacing it with a monastic legend; which legend is disfigured with fables in its incidents, and yet in a higher sense is true, because interwoven with Christian morals, and with the sublimest of Christian revelations. Three, four, five, centuries more find man still devout as ever; but the language has become obsolete; and even for Christian devotion a new era has arisen, throwing it into the channel of crusading zeal or of chivalrous enthusiasm. The *membrana* is wanted now for a knightly romance—for "My Cid" or Cœur de Lion, for Sir Tristrem or Lybæus Disconus. In this way, by means of the imperfect chemistry known to the mediæval period, the same roll has served as a conservatory for three separate generations of flowers and fruits, all perfectly different, and yet all specially adapted to the wants of the successive possessors. The Greek tragedy, the monkish legend, the knightly romance, each has ruled its own period. One harvest after another has been gathered into the garners of man through ages far apart. And the same hydraulic machinery has distributed, through the same marble fountains, water, milk, or wine, according to the habits and training of the generations that came to quench their thirst.

Such were the achievements of rude monastic chemistry. But the more elaborate chemistry of our own days has reversed all these motions of our simple ancestors, with results in every stage that to *them* would have realised the most fantastic amongst the promises of thaumaturgy. Insolent vaunt of Paracelsus, that he would restore the original rose or violet out of the ashes settling from its combustion—*that* is now rivalled in this modern achievement. The traces of each successive handwriting, regularly effaced, as had been imagined, have, in the inverse order, been regularly called back : the footsteps of the game pursued, wolf or stag, in each several chase, have been unlinked, and hunted back through all their doubles; and, as the chorus of the Athenian stage unwove through the antistrophe every step that had been mystically woven through the strophe, so, by our modern conjurations of science, secrets of ages remote from each other have been exorcised [1] from the accumulated shadows of centuries. Chemistry, a witch as potent as the Erictho of Lucan (*Pharsalia*, lib. vi or vii),[2] has extorted by her torments, from the dust and ashes of forgotten centuries, the secrets of a life extinct for the general eye, but still glowing in the embers. Even the fable of the Phœnix, that secular bird who propagated his solitary existence, and his solitary births, along the line of centuries, through eternal relays of funeral mists,[3] is but a type of what we have done

---

[1] Some readers may be apt to suppose, from all English experience, that the word *exorcise* means properly banishment to the shades. Not so. Citation *from* the shades, or sometimes the torturing coercion of mystic adjurations, is more truly the primary sense.

[2] The passage in Lucan referred to is in Book VI of his *Pharsalia*, lines 507 *et seq.* ; where the name, however, is spelt "Erichtho."—M.

[3] The fable respecting the Phœnix was that it was a marvellous Arabian bird, the sole bird of the sort alive, which went every 500 years to Egypt, to die there, and leave its own burnt ashes as relics out of which might spring its sole successor, the next Phœnix. De Quincey had in his mind Milton's passage near the close of his *Samson Agonistes* :—

> "So Virtue, given for lost,
> Depressed and overthrown, as seemed,
> Like that self-begotten bird
> In the Arabian woods embost,
> That no second knows nor third,
> And lay erewhile a holocaust,
> From out her ashy womb now teemed,
> Revives, reflourishes, then vigorous most
> When most unactive deemed ;
> And, though her body die, her fame survives,
> A secular bird, ages of lives."—M.

with Palimpsests. We have backed upon each phœnix in the long *regressus*, and forced him to expose his ancestral phœnix, sleeping in the ashes below his own ashes. Our good old forefathers would have been aghast at our sorceries; and, if they speculated on the propriety of burning Dr. Faustus, *us* they would have burned by acclamation. Trial there would have been none; and they could not otherwise have satisfied their horror of the brazen profligacy marking our modern magic than by ploughing up the houses of all who had been parties to it, and sowing the ground with salt.

Fancy not, reader, that this tumult of images, illustrative or allusive, moves under any impulse or purpose of mirth. It is but the coruscation of a restless understanding, often made ten times more so by irritation of the nerves, such as you will first learn to comprehend (its *how* and its *why*) some stage or two ahead. The image, the memorial, the record, which for me is derived from a palimpsest as to one great fact in our human being, and which immediately I will show you, is but too repellent of laughter; or, even if laughter *had* been possible, it would have been such laughter as oftentimes is thrown off from the fields of ocean,[1]—laughter that hides, or that seems to evade, mustering tumult; foam-bells that weave garlands of phosphoric radiance for one moment round the eddies of gleaming abysses; mimicries of earth-born flowers that for the eye raise phantoms of gaiety, as oftentimes for the ear they raise the echoes of fugitive laughter, mixing with the ravings and choir-voices of an angry sea.

What else than a natural and mighty palimpsest is the human brain? Such a palimpsest is my brain; such a palimpsest, oh reader! is yours. Everlasting layers of ideas, images, feelings, have fallen upon your brain softly as light. Each succession has seemed to bury all that went before. And yet, in reality, not one has been extinguished. And, if

[1] Many readers will recall, though, at the moment of writing, my own thoughts did *not* recall, the well-known passage in the *Prometheus*—

———ποντίων τε κυμάτων
Ανηριθμον γελασμα.

"O multitudinous laughter of the ocean billows!" It is not clear whether Æschylus contemplated the laughter as addressing the ear or the eye.

in the vellum palimpsest, lying amongst the other *diplomata* of human archives or libraries, there is anything fantastic or which moves to laughter, as oftentimes there is in the grotesque collisions of those successive themes, having no natural connexion, which by pure accident have consecutively occupied the roll, yet, in our own heaven-created palimpsest, the deep memorial palimpsest of the brain, there are not and cannot be such incoherencies. The fleeting accidents of a man's life, and its external shows, may indeed be irrelate and incongruous; but the organising principles which fuse into harmony, and gather about fixed predetermined centres, whatever heterogeneous elements life may have accumulated from without, will not permit the grandeur of human unity greatly to be violated, or its ultimate repose to be troubled, in the retrospect from dying moments, or from other great convulsions.

Such a convulsion is the struggle of gradual suffocation, as in drowning, and in the original Opium Confessions I mentioned a case of that nature communicated to me by a lady from her own childish experience. The lady was then still living, though of unusually great age; and I may mention that amongst her faults never was numbered any levity of principle, or carelessness of the most scrupulous veracity, but, on the contrary, such faults as arise from austerity, too harsh, perhaps, and gloomy, indulgent neither to others nor herself. And, at the time of relating this incident, when already very old, she had become religious to asceticism.[1] According to my present belief, she had completed her ninth year when, playing by the side of a solitary brook, she fell into one of its deepest pools. Eventually, but after what lapse of time nobody ever knew, she was saved from death by a farmer, who, riding in some distant lane, had seen her rise to the surface; but not until she had descended within the abyss of death and looked into its secrets, as far, perhaps, as ever human eye *can* have looked that had permission to return. At a certain stage of this descent, a blow seemed to strike her; phosphoric radiance sprang forth from her eyeballs; and immediately a mighty theatre expanded within

---

[1] The description partly suits the known character of De Quincey's own mother; and perhaps it is she that is meant.—M.

her brain. In a moment, in the twinkling of an eye, every act, every design of her past life, lived again, arraying themselves not as a succession, but as parts of a coexistence. Such a light fell upon the whole path of her life backwards into the shades of infancy as the light, perhaps, which wrapt the destined Apostle on his road to Damascus. Yet that light blinded for a season; but hers poured celestial vision upon the brain, so that her consciousness became omnipresent at one moment to every feature in the infinite review.

This anecdote was treated sceptically at the time by some critics. But, besides that it has since been confirmed by other experience essentially the same, reported by other parties in the same circumstances, who had never heard of each other, the true point for astonishment is not the *simultaneity* of arrangement under which the past events of life, though in fact successive, had formed their dread line of revelation. This was but a secondary phenomenon; the deeper lay in the resurrection itself, and the possibility of resurrection for what had so long slept in the dust. A pall, deep as oblivion, had been thrown by life over every trace of these experiences; and yet suddenly, at a silent command, at the signal of a blazing rocket sent up from the brain, the pall draws up, and the whole depths of the theatre are exposed. Here was the greater mystery. Now, this mystery is liable to no doubt; for it is repeated, and ten thousand times repeated, by opium, for those who are its martyrs.

Yes, reader, countless are the mysterious handwritings of grief or joy which have inscribed themselves successively upon the palimpsest of your brain; and, like the annual leaves of aboriginal forests, or the undissolving snows on the Himalaya, or light falling upon light, the endless strata have covered up each other in forgetfulness. But by the hour of death, but by fever, but by the searchings of opium, all these can revive in strength. They are not dead, but sleeping. In the illustration imagined by myself from the case of some individual palimpsest, the Grecian tragedy had seemed to be displaced, but was *not* displaced, by the monkish legend; and the monkish legend had seemed to be displaced, but was *not* displaced, by the knightly romance. In some potent convulsion of the system, all wheels back into its earliest elementary stage. The bewildering romance, light tarnished with darkness, the semi-fabulous legend, truth celestial mixed with human falsehoods, these fade even of themselves as life advances. The romance has perished that the young man adored; the legend has gone that deluded the boy; but the deep, deep tragedies of infancy, as when the child's hands were unlinked for ever from his mother's neck, or his lips for ever from his sister's kisses, these remain lurking below all, and these lurk to the last. Alchemy there is none of passion or disease that can scorch away these immortal impresses; and the dream which closed the preceding section,[1] together with the succeeding dreams of this (which may be viewed as in the nature of choruses winding up the overture contained in Part I [2]), are but illustrations of this truth, such as every man probably will meet experimentally who passes through similar convulsions of dreaming or delirium from any similar or equal disturbance in his nature.[3]

[1] These words, as used in *Blackwood* for June 1845, referred to a dream of his sister's funeral with an account of which the preceding section of the SUSPIRIA, in the April number of the magazine, had closed; and, as the whole of that section, this dream included, is now removed from the context of the SUSPIRIA, having been converted into a chapter of the AUTOBIOGRAPHIC SKETCHES (see *ante*, Vol. I. pp 32-50) the words are now irrelevant. They are retained, however, in order that *The Palimpsest* may end as De Quincey ended it, and that his final footnote may be saved.—M.

[2] The reader will remember that the papers published in *Blackwood*, in March, April, and June 1845, with the title of SUSPIRIA DE PROFUNDIS, formed together only what was offered as Part I of the projected series.—M.

[3] This, it may be said, requires a corresponding duration of experience; but, as an argument for this mysterious power lurking in our nature, I may remind the reader of one phenomenon open to the notice of everybody,—namely, the tendency of very aged persons to throw back and concentrate the light of their memory upon scenes of early childhood, as to which they recall many traces that had faded even to *themselves* in middle life, whilst they often forget altogether the whole intermediate stages of their experience. This shows that naturally, and without violent agencies, the human brain is by tendency a palimpsest.

Vision of Life [1]

Upon me, as upon others scattered thinly by tens and twenties over every thousand years, fell too powerfully and too early the vision of life. The horror of life mixed itself already in earliest youth with the heavenly sweetness of life; that grief which one in a hundred has sensibility enough to gather from the sad retrospect of life in its closing stage for *me* shed its dews as a prelibation upon the fountains of life whilst yet sparkling to the morning sun. I saw from afar and from before what I was to see from behind. Is this the description of an early youth passed in the shades of gloom? No; but of a youth passed in the divinest happiness. And, if the reader has (which so few have) the passion without which there is no reading of the legend and superscription upon man's brow, if he is not (as most are) deafer than the grave to every *deep* note that sighs upwards from the Delphic caves of human life, he will know that the rapture of life (or anything which by approach can merit that name) does not arise, unless as perfect music arises, music of Mozart or Beethoven, by the confluence of the mighty and terrific discords with the subtile concords. Not by contrast, or as reciprocal foils, do these elements act,—which is the feeble conception of many,—but by union. They are the sexual forces in music: "male and female created he them"; and these mighty antagonists do not put forth their hostilities by repulsion, but by deepest attraction.

As "in to-day already walks to-morrow," so in the past experience of a youthful life may be seen dimly the future. The collisions with alien interests or hostile views of a child, boy, or very young man, so insulated as each of these is sure to be,—those aspects of opposition which such a person *can* occupy,—are limited by the exceedingly few and trivial lines of connexion along which he is able to radiate any essential influence whatever upon the fortunes or happiness of others. Circumstances may magnify his importance for the moment; but, after all, any cable which he carries out upon other

---

[1] A conserved portion of "Part II" of the Suspiria as published in *Blackwood* for July 1845. See *ante*, p. 331.—M.

vessels is easily slipped upon a feud arising. Far otherwise is the state of relations connecting an adult or responsible man with the circles around him as life advances. The network of these relations is a thousand times more intricate, the jarring of these intricate relations a thousand times more frequent, and the vibrations a thousand times harsher which these jarrings diffuse. This truth is felt beforehand, misgivingly and in troubled vision, by a young man who stands upon the threshold of manhood. One earliest instinct of fear and horror would darken his spirit if it could be revealed to itself and self-questioned at the moment of birth: a second instinct of the same nature would again pollute that tremulous mirror if the moment were as punctually marked as physical birth is marked which dismisses him finally upon the tides of absolute self-control. A dark ocean would seem the total expanse of life from the first; but far darker and more appalling would seem that inferior and second chamber of the ocean which called him away for ever from the direct accountability of others. Dreadful would be the morning which should say, "Be thou a human child incarnate"; but more dreadful the morning which should say, "Bear thou henceforth the sceptre of thy self-dominion through life, and the passion of life!" Yes, dreadful would be both; but without a basis of the dreadful there is no perfect rapture. It is in part through the sorrow of life, growing out of dark events, that this basis of awe and solemn darkness slowly accumulates. *That* I have illustrated. But, as life expands, it is more through the *strife* which besets us, strife from conflicting opinions, positions, passions, interests, that the funereal ground settles and deposits itself which sends upward the dark lustrous brilliancy through the jewel of life, else revealing a pale and superficial glitter. Either the human being must suffer and struggle, as the price of a more searching vision, or his gaze must be shallow and without intellectual revelation.

Memorial Suspiria [1]

Heavens! when I look back to the sufferings which I have

[1] Another conserved portion of the *Blackwood* Part II of the Suspiria. See *ante*, p. 331.—M.

witnessed or heard of, I say, if life could throw open its long suites of chambers to our eyes from some station *beforehand*,—if from some secret stand we could look *by anticipation* along its vast corridors, and aside into the recesses opening upon them from either hand halls of tragedy or chambers of retribution,—simply in that small wing and no more of the great caravanserai which we ourselves shall haunt,—simply in that narrow tract of time, and no more, where we ourselves shall range, and confining our gaze to those and no others for whom personally we shall be interested,—What a recoil we should suffer of horror in our estimate of life! What if those sudden catastrophes, or those inexpiable afflictions, which *have* already descended upon the people within my own knowledge, and almost below my own eyes, all of them now gone past, and some long past, had been thrown open before me as a secret exhibition when first I and they stood within the vestibule of morning hopes,— when the calamities themselves had hardly begun to gather in their elements of possibility, and when some of the parties to them were as yet no more than infants! The past viewed not *as* the past, but by a spectator who steps back ten years deeper into the rear in order that he may regard it as a future,—the calamity of 1840 contemplated from the station of 1830,—the doom that rang the knell of happiness viewed from a point of time when as yet it was neither feared nor would even have been intelligible,—the name that killed in 1843 which in 1835 would have struck no vibration upon the heart,—the portrait that on the day of her Majesty's coronation would have been admired by you with a pure disinterested admiration, but which, if seen to-day, would draw forth an involuntary groan : cases such as these are strangely moving for all who add deep thoughtfulness to deep sensibility. As the hastiest of improvisations, accept, fair reader (for such reader it is that will chiefly feel such an invocation of the past), three or four illustrations from my own experience :—

Who is this distinguished-looking young woman, with her eyes drooping, and the shadow of a dreadful shock yet fresh upon every feature ? Who is the elderly lady, with her eyes flashing fire ? Who is the downcast child of sixteen ? What is that torn paper lying at their feet? Who is the writer? Whom does the paper concern? Ah! if she, if the central figure in the group—twenty-two at the moment when she is revealed to us—could, on her happy birthday at sweet seventeen, have seen the image of herself five years onwards just as *we* see it now, would she have prayed for life as for an absolute blessing? or would she not have prayed to be taken from the evil to come—to be taken away one evening, at least, before this day's sun arose? It is true, she still wears a look of gentle pride, and a relic of that noble smile which belongs to *her* that suffers an injury which many times over she would have died sooner than inflict. Womanly pride refuses itself before witnesses to the total prostration of the blow; but, for all *that*, you may see that she longs to be left alone, and that her tears will flow without restraint when she is so. This room is her pretty boudoir, in which, till to-night—poor thing!—she has been glad and happy. There stands her miniature conservatory, and there expands her miniature library; as we circumnavigators of literature are apt (you know) to regard all female libraries in the light of miniatures. None of these will ever rekindle a smile on *her* face; and there, beyond, is her music, which only of all that she possesses will now become dearer to her than ever; but, not, as once, to feed a self-mocked pensiveness, or to cheat a half-visionary sadness. She will be sad, indeed. But she is one of those that will suffer in silence. Nobody will ever detect *her* failing in any point of duty, or querulously seeking the support in others which she can find for herself in this solitary room. Droop she will not in the sight of men; and, for all beyond, nobody has any concern with *that*, except God. You shall hear what becomes of her before we take our departure; but now let me tell you what has happened.

In the main outline I am sure you guess already, without aid of mine; for we leaden-eyed men, in such cases, see nothing by comparison with you our quick-witted sisters. That haughty-looking lady, with the Roman cast of features, who must once have been strikingly handsome,—an Agrippina even yet in a favourable presentation,—is the younger lady's aunt. She, it is rumoured, once sustained, in her younger days, some injury of that same cruel nature which has this day assailed her niece, and ever since she has worn an air of disdain, not altogether unsupported by real dignity, towards men. This aunt it was that tore the letter which lies upon the floor. It deserved to be torn; and yet she that had the best right to do so would *not* have torn it. That letter was an elaborate attempt on the part of an accomplished young man to release himself from sacred engagements. What need was there to argue the case of *such* engagements? Could it have been requisite with pure female dignity to plead anything, or do more than *look* an indisposition to fulfil them? The aunt is now moving towards the door,—which I am glad to see; and she is followed by that pale, timid girl of sixteen, a cousin, who feels the case profoundly, but is too young and shy to offer an intellectual sympathy.

One only person in this world there is who *could* to-night have been a supporting friend to our young sufferer; and *that* is her dear, loving twin-sister, that for eighteen years read and wrote, thought and sang, slept and breathed, with the dividing-door open for ever between their bed-rooms, and never once a separation between their hearts. But she is in a far distant land. Who else is there at her call? Except God, nobody. Her aunt had somewhat sternly admonished her, though still with a relenting in her eye as she glanced aside at the expression in her niece's face, that she must "call pride to her assistance." Ay, true; but pride, though a strong ally in public, is apt in private to turn as treacherous as the worst of those against whom she is invoked. How could it be dreamed, by a person of sense, that a brilliant young man, of merits various and eminent in spite of his baseness, to whom for nearly two years this young woman had given her whole confiding love, might be dismissed from a heart like hers on the earliest summons of pride, simply because she herself had been dismissed from *his*, or seemed to have been dismissed, on a summons of mercenary calculation? Look! now that she is relieved from the weight of an unconfidential presence, she has sat for two hours with her head buried in her hands. At last she rises to look for something. A thought has struck her; and, taking a little golden key which hangs by a chain within her bosom, she searches for something locked up amongst her few jewels. What is it? It is a Bible exquisitely illuminated, with a letter attached by some pretty silken artifice to the blank leaves at the end. This letter is a beautiful record, wisely and pathetically composed, of maternal anxiety still burning strong in death, and yearning, when all objects beside were fast fading from *her* eyes, after one parting act of communion with the twin darlings of her heart. Both were thirteen years old, within a week or two, as on the night before her death they sat weeping by the bedside of their mother, and hanging on her lips, now for farewell whispers and now for farewell kisses. They both knew that, as her strength had permitted during the latter month of her life, she had thrown the last anguish of love in her beseeching heart into a letter of counsel to themselves. Through this, of which each sister had a copy, she trusted long to converse with her orphans. And the last promise which she had entreated on this evening from both was that in either of two contingencies they would review her counsels, and the passages to which she pointed their attention in the Scriptures: namely, first, in the event of any calamity that, for one sister or for both, should overspread their paths with total darkness; and, secondly, in the event of life flowing in too profound a stream of prosperity, so as to threaten them with an alienation of interest from all spiritual objects. She had not concealed that, of these two extreme cases, she would prefer for her own children the first. And now had that case arrived, indeed, which she in spirit had desired to meet. Nine years ago, just as the silvery voice of a dial in the dying lady's bed-room was striking nine, upon a summer evening, had the last visual ray streamed from her seeking eyes upon her orphan twins; after which, throughout the night, she had slept away into heaven. Now again had come a summer evening memorable for unhappiness; now again the daughter thought of those dying lights of love which streamed at sunset from the closing eyes of her mother; again, and just as she went back in thought to this image, the same silvery voice of the dial sounded nine o'clock. Again she remembered her mother's dying request; again her own tear-hallowed promises; and, with her heart in her mother's grave, she now rose to fulfil it. Here, then, when this solemn recurrence to a testamentary counsel has ceased to be a mere office of duty towards the departed, having taken the shape of a consolation for herself, let us pause.

Now, fair companion in this exploring voyage of inquest into hidden scenes or forgotten scenes of human life, perhaps it might be instructive to direct our glasses upon the false, perfidious lover. It might. But do not let us do so. We might like him better, or pity him more, than either of us would desire. His name and memory have long since dropped out of everybody's thoughts. Of prosperity, and (what is more important) of internal peace, he is reputed to have had no gleam from the moment when he betrayed his faith, and in one day threw away the jewel of good conscience, and "a pearl richer than all his tribe." But, however that may be, it is certain that, finally, he became a wreck; and of any *hopeless* wreck it is painful to talk,—much more so when through him others also became wrecks.

Shall we, then, after an interval of nearly two years has passed over the young lady in the boudoir, look in again upon *her*? You hesitate, fair friend; and I myself hesitate. For, in fact, she also has become a wreck; and it would grieve us both to see her altered. At the end of twenty-one months she retains hardly a vestige of resemblance to the fine young woman we saw on that unhappy evening with her aunt and cousin. On consideration, therefore, let us do this:—We will direct our glasses to her room at a point of time about six weeks further on. Suppose this time gone; suppose her now dressed for her grave, and placed in her coffin. The advantage of that is that, though no change can restore the ravages of the past, yet (as often is found to happen with young persons) the expression has revived from her girlish years. The child-like aspect has revolved, and settled back upon her features. The wasting away of the flesh is less apparent in the face; and one might imagine that in this sweet marble countenance was seen the very same upon which, eleven years ago, her mother's darkening eyes had lingered to the last, until clouds had swallowed up the vision of her beloved *twins*. Yet, if that were in part a fancy, this, at least, is no fancy,—that not only much of a child-like truth and simplicity has reinstated itself in the temple of her now reposing features, but also tranquillity and perfect peace, such as are appropriate to eternity, but which from the *living* countenance had taken their flight for ever on that memorable evening when we looked in upon the impassioned group,—upon the towering and denouncing aunt, the sympathising but silent cousin, the poor, blighted niece, and the wicked letter lying in fragments at their feet.

Cloud, that hast revealed to us this young creature and her blighted hopes, close up again! And now, a few years later,—not more than four or five,—give back to us the latest arrears of the changes which thou concealest within thy draperies. Once more, "open sesame!" and show us a third generation.

Behold a lawn islanded with thickets! How perfect is the verdure; how rich the blossoming shrubberies that screen with verdurous walls from the possibility of intrusion, whilst by their own wandering line of distribution they shape, and umbrageously embay, what one might call lawny saloons and vestibules, sylvan galleries and closets! Some of these recesses, which unlink themselves as fluently as snakes, and unexpectedly as the shyest nooks, watery cells, and crypts, amongst the shores of a forest-lake, being formed by the mere caprices and ramblings of the luxuriant shrubs, are so small and so quiet that one might fancy them meant for *boudoirs*. Here is one that in a less fickle climate would make the loveliest of studies for a writer of breathings from some solitary heart, or of *suspiria* from some impassioned memory! And, opening from one angle of this embowered study, issues a little narrow corridor, that, after almost wheeling back upon itself in its playful mazes, finally widens into a little circular chamber; out of which there is no exit (except back again by the entrance), small or great; so that, adjacent to his study, the writer would command how sweet a bed-room, permitting him to lie the summer through, gazing all night long at the burning host of heaven. How silent *that* would be at the noon of summer nights,—how grave-like in its quiet! And yet need there be asked a stillness or a silence more profound than is felt at this present noon of day? One reason for such peculiar repose, over and above the tranquil character of the day, and the distance of the place from the high-roads, is the outer zone of woods which almost on every quarter invests the shrubberies, swathing them (as one may express it), belting them and overlooking them, from a varying distance of two and three furlongs, so as oftentimes to keep the winds at a distance. But, however caused and supported, the silence of these fanciful lawns and lawny chambers is oftentimes oppressive in the depths of summer to people unfamiliar with solitudes either mountainous or sylvan; and many would be apt to suppose that the villa to which these pretty shrubberies form the chief dependencies must be untenanted. But that is not the case. The house is inhabited, and by its own legal mistress, the proprietress of the whole domain; and not at all a silent mistress, but as noisy as most little ladies of five years old; for that is her age. Now, and just as we are speaking, you may hear her little joyous clamour, as she issues from the house. This way she comes, bounding like a fawn; and soon she rushes into the little recess which I pointed out as a proper study for any man who should be weaving the deep harmonies of memorial *suspiria*. But I fancy that she will soon dispossess it of that character, for her *suspiria* are not many at this stage of her life. Now she comes dancing into sight; and you see that, if she keeps the promise of her infancy, she will be an interesting creature to the eye in after-life. In other respects, also, she is an engaging child,—loving, natural, and wild as any one of her neighbours for some miles round, —namely, leverets, squirrels, and ring-doves. But what will surprise you most is that, although a child of pure English blood, she speaks very little English, but more Bengalee than perhaps you will find it convenient to construe. That is her ayah, who comes up from behind at a pace so different from her youthful mistress's. But, if their paces are different, in other things they agree most cordially; and dearly they love each other. In reality, the child has passed her whole life in the arms of this ayah. She remembers nothing elder than *her*; eldest of things is the ayah in her eyes; and, if the ayah should insist on her worshipping herself as the goddess Railroadina or Steamboatina, that made England, and the sea, and Bengal, it is certain that the little thing would do so, asking no question but this,—whether kissing would do for worshipping.

Every evening at nine o'clock, as the ayah sits by the little creature lying awake in bed, the silvery tongue of a dial tolls the hour. Reader, you know who she is. She is the grand-daughter of her that faded away about sunset in gazing at her twin orphans. Her name is Grace. And she is the niece of that elder and once happy Grace who spent so much of her happiness in this very room, but whom, in her utter desolation, we saw in the boudoir, with the torn letter at her feet. She is the daughter of that other sister, wife to a military officer who died abroad. Little Grace never saw her grandmamma, nor her lovely aunt that was her namesake, nor consciously her mamma. She was born six months after the death of the elder Grace; and her mother saw her only through the mists of mortal suffering, which carried her off three weeks after the birth of her daughter.

This view was taken several years ago; and since then the younger Grace, in her turn, is under a cloud of affliction. But she is still under eighteen; and of her there may be hopes. Seeing such things in so short a space of years,—for the grandmother died at thirty-two,—we say,—"Death we can face; but, knowing as some of us do what is human life, which of us is it that without shuddering could (if consciously we were summoned) face the hour of birth?"

SAVANNAH-LA-MAR [1]

God smote Savannah-la-mar, and in one night, by earthquake, removed her, with all her towers standing and population sleeping, from the steadfast foundations of the shore to the coral floors of ocean. And God said,—"Pompeii did I bury and conceal from men through seventeen centuries: this city I will bury, but not conceal. She shall be a monument to men of my mysterious anger, set in azure light through generations to come; for I will enshrine her in a

[1] Originally in *Blackwood* for June 1845. See *ante*, p. 331.—M.

crystal dome of my tropic seas." This city, therefore, like a mighty galleon with all her apparel mounted, streamers flying, and tackling perfect, seems floating along the noiseless depths of ocean; and oftentimes in glassy calms, through the translucid atmosphere of water that now stretches like an air-woven awning above the silent encampment, mariners from every clime look down into her courts and terraces, count her gates, and number the spires of her churches. She is one ample cemetery, and *has* been for many a year; but, in the mighty calms that brood for weeks over tropic latitudes, she fascinates the eye with a *Fata-Morgana* revelation, as of human life still subsisting in submarine asylums sacred from the storms that torment our upper air.

Thither, lured by the loveliness of cerulean depths, by the peace of human dwellings privileged from molestation, by the gleam of marble altars sleeping in everlasting sanctity, oftentimes in dreams did I and the Dark Interpreter cleave the watery veil that divided us from her streets. We looked into the belfries, where the pendulous bells were waiting in vain for the summons which should awaken their marriage peals; together we touched the mighty organ-keys, that sang no *jubilates* for the ear of heaven, that sang no requiems for the ear of human sorrow; together we searched the silent nurseries, where the children were all asleep, and *had* been asleep through five generations. "They are waiting for the heavenly dawn," whispered the Interpreter to himself: "and, when *that* comes, the bells and the organs will utter a *jubilate* repeated by the echoes of Paradise." Then, turning to me, he said,—"This is sad, this is piteous; but less would not have sufficed for the purpose of God. Look here. Put into a Roman clepsydra one hundred drops of water; let these run out as the sands in an hour-glass, every drop measuring the hundredth part of a second, so that each shall represent but the three-hundred-and-sixty-thousandth part of an hour. Now, count the drops as they race along; and, when the fiftieth of the hundred is passing, behold! forty-nine are not, because already they have perished, and fifty are not, because they are yet to come. You see, therefore, how narrow, how incalculably narrow, is the true and actual present. Of that time which we call the present, hardly a hundredth part but belongs either to a past which has fled, or to a future which is still on the wing. It has perished, or it is not born. It was, or it is not. Yet even this approximation to the truth is *infinitely* false. For again subdivide that solitary drop, which only was found to represent the present, into a lower series of similar fractions, and the actual present which you arrest measures now but the thirty-sixth-millionth of an hour; and so by infinite declensions the true and very present, in which only we live and enjoy, will vanish into a mote of a mote, distinguishable only by a heavenly vision. Therefore the present, which only man possesses, offers less capacity for his footing than the slenderest film that ever spider twisted from her womb. Therefore, also, even this incalculable shadow from the narrowest pencil of moonlight is more transitory than geometry can measure, or thought of angel can overtake. The time which *is* contracts into a mathematic point; and even that point perishes a thousand times before we can utter its birth. All is finite in the present; and even that finite is infinite in its velocity of flight towards death. But in God there is nothing finite; but in God there is nothing transitory; but in God there *can* be nothing that tends to death. Therefore it follows that for God there can be no present. The future is the present of God, and to the future it is that he sacrifices the human present. Therefore it is that he works by earthquake. Therefore it is that he works by grief. O, deep is the ploughing of earthquake! O, deep"—(and his voice swelled like a *sanctus* rising from the choir of a cathedral)—" O, deep is the ploughing of grief! But oftentimes less would not suffice for the agriculture of God. Upon a night of earthquake he builds a thousand years of pleasant habitations for man. Upon the sorrow of an infant he raises oftentimes from human intellects glorious vintages that could not else have been. Less than these fierce ploughshares would not have stirred the stubborn soil. The one is needed for Earth, our planet,—for Earth itself as the dwelling-place of man; but the other is needed yet oftener for God's mightiest instrument,—yes" (and he looked solemnly at myself), "is needed for the mysterious children of the Earth!"

LEVANA AND OUR LADIES OF SORROW[1]

Oftentimes at Oxford I saw Levana in my dreams. I knew her by her Roman symbols. Who is Levana? Reader, that do not pretend to have leisure for very much scholarship, you will not be angry with me for telling you. Levana was the Roman goddess that performed for the newborn infant the earliest office of ennobling kindness,—typical, by its mode, of that grandeur which belongs to man everywhere, and of that benignity in powers invisible which even in Pagan worlds sometimes descends to sustain it. At the very moment of birth, just as the infant tasted for the first time the atmosphere of our troubled planet, it was laid on the ground. *That* might bear different interpretations. But immediately, lest so grand a creature should grovel there for more than one instant, either the paternal hand, as proxy for the goddess Levana, or some near kinsman, as proxy for the father, raised it upright, bade it look erect as the king of all this world, and presented its forehead to the stars, saying, perhaps, in his heart, "Behold what is greater than yourselves!" This symbolic act represented the function of Levana. And that mysterious lady, who never revealed her face (except to me in dreams), but always acted by delegation, had her name from the Latin verb (as still it is the Italian verb) *levare*, to raise aloft.

This is the explanation of Levana. And hence it has arisen that some people have understood by Levana the tutelary power that controls the education of the nursery. She, that would not suffer at his birth even a prefigurative or mimic degradation for her awful ward, far less could be supposed to suffer the real degradation attaching to the non-

---

[1] One reason for putting this piece last is that De Quincey himself calls attention to it as furnishing a key to the whole scheme of his SUSPIRIA DE PROFUNDIS had he been able to complete the series. See appended footnote at the end. Another reason, however, is that this little paper is perhaps, all in all, the finest thing that De Quincey ever wrote. It is certainly the most perfect specimen he has left us of his peculiar art of English prose-poetry, and certainly also one of the most magnificent pieces of prose in the English or in any other language.—M.

development of his powers. She therefore watches over human education. Now, the word *edŭco*, with the penultimate short, was derived (by a process often exemplified in the crystallisation of languages) from the word *edūco*, with the penultimate long. Whatsoever *educes*, or develops, *educates*. By the education of Levana, therefore, is meant,— not the poor machinery that moves by spelling-books and grammars, but by that mighty system of central forces hidden in the deep bosom of human life, which by passion, by strife, by temptation, by the energies of resistance, works for ever upon children,—resting not day or night, any more than the mighty wheel of day and night themselves, whose moments, like restless spokes, are glimmering[1] for ever as they revolve.

If, then, *these* are the ministries by which Levana works, how profoundly must she reverence the agencies of grief! But you, reader, think that children generally are not liable to grief such as mine. There are two senses in the word *generally*,—the sense of Euclid, where it means *universally* (or in the whole extent of the *genus*), and a foolish sense of this world, where it means *usually*. Now, I am far from saying that children universally are capable of grief like mine. But there are more than you ever heard of who die of grief in this island of ours. I will tell you a common case. The rules of Eton require that a boy on the *foundation* should be there twelve years: he is superannuated at eighteen; consequently he must come at six. Children torn away from mothers and sisters at that age not unfrequently die. I speak

---

[1] As I have never allowed myself to covet any man's ox nor his ass, nor anything that is his, still less would it become a philosopher to covet other people's images or metaphors. Here, therefore, I restore to Mr. Wordsworth this fine image of the revolving wheel and the glimmering spokes, as applied by him to the flying successions of day and night. I borrowed it for one moment in order to point my own sentence; which being done, the reader is witness that I now pay it back instantly by a note made for that sole purpose. On the same principle I often borrow their seals from young ladies, when closing my letters, because there is sure to be some tender sentiment upon them about "memory," or "hope," or "roses," or "reunion," and my correspondent must be a sad brute who is not touched by the eloquence of the seal, even if his taste is so bad that he remains deaf to mine.

of what I know. The complaint is not entered by the registrar as grief; but *that* it is. Grief of that sort, and at that age, has killed more than ever have been counted amongst its martyrs.

Therefore it is that Levana often communes with the powers that shake man's heart; therefore it is that she dotes upon grief. "These ladies," said I softly to myself, on seeing the ministers with whom Levana was conversing, "these are the Sorrows; and they are three in number: as the *Graces* are three, who dress man's life with beauty; the *Parcæ* are three, who weave the dark arras of man's life in their mysterious loom always with colours sad in part, sometimes angry with tragic crimson and black; the *Furies* are three, who visit with retributions called from the other side of the grave offences that walk upon this; and once even the *Muses* were but three, who fit the harp, the trumpet, or the lute, to the great burdens of man's impassioned creations. These are the Sorrows; all three of whom I know." The last words I say *now*; but in Oxford I said, "one of whom I know, and the others too surely I *shall* know." For already, in my fervent youth, I saw (dimly relieved upon the dark background of my dreams) the imperfect lineaments of the awful Sisters.

These Sisters—by what name shall we call them? If I say simply "The Sorrows," there will be a chance of mistaking the term; it might be understood of individual sorrow,—separate cases of sorrow,—whereas I want a term expressing the mighty abstractions that incarnate themselves in all individual sufferings of man's heart, and I wish to have these abstractions presented as impersonations,—that is, as clothed with human attributes of life, and with functions pointing to flesh. Let us call them, therefore, *Our Ladies of Sorrow*.

I know them thoroughly, and have walked in all their kingdoms. Three sisters they are, of one mysterious household; and their paths are wide apart; but of their dominion there is no end. Them I saw often conversing with Levana, and sometimes about myself. Do they talk, then? O no! Mighty phantoms like these disdain the infirmities of language. They may utter voices through the organs of man when they dwell in human hearts, but amongst themselves is no voice nor sound; eternal silence reigns in *their* kingdoms. They spoke not as they talked with Levana; they whispered not; they sang not; though oftentimes methought they *might* have sung: for I upon earth had heard their mysteries oftentimes deciphered by harp and timbrel, by dulcimer and organ. Like God, whose servants they are, they utter their pleasure not by sounds that perish, or by words that go astray, but by signs in heaven, by changes on earth, by pulses in secret rivers, heraldries painted on darkness, and hieroglyphics written on the tablets of the brain. *They* wheeled in mazes; *I* spelled the steps. *They* telegraphed from afar; *I* read the signals. *They* conspired together; and on the mirrors of darkness *my* eye traced the plots. *Theirs* were the symbols; *mine* are the words.

What is it the Sisters are? What is it that they do? Let me describe their form and their presence, if form it were that still fluctuated in its outline, or presence it were that for ever advanced to the front or for ever receded amongst shades.

The eldest of the three is named *Mater Lachrymarum*, Our Lady of Tears. She it is that night and day raves and moans, calling for vanished faces. She stood in Rama, where a voice was heard of lamentation,—Rachel weeping for her children, and refusing to be comforted. She it was that stood in Bethlehem on the night when Herod's sword swept its nurseries of Innocents, and the little feet were stiffened for ever which, heard at times as they trotted along floors overhead, woke pulses of love in household hearts that were not unmarked in heaven. Her eyes are sweet and subtle, wild and sleepy, by turns; oftentimes rising to the clouds, oftentimes challenging the heavens. She wears a diadem round her head. And I knew by childish memories that she could go abroad upon the winds, when she heard the sobbing of litanies, or the thundering of organs, and when she beheld the mustering of summer clouds. This Sister, the elder, it is that carries keys more than papal at her girdle, which open every cottage and every palace. She, to my knowledge, sat all last summer by the bedside of the blind beggar, him that so often and so gladly I talked with, whose pious daughter, eight years old, with the sunny countenance, resisted the temptations of play and village mirth, to travel all day long on dusty roads with her afflicted father. For this did God send her a great reward. In the spring time of the year, and whilst yet her own spring was budding, He recalled her to himself. But her blind father mourns for ever over *her*: still he dreams at midnight that the little guiding hand is locked within his own; and still he wakens to a darkness that is *now* within a second and a deeper darkness. This *Mater Lachrymarum* also has been sitting all this winter of 1844-5 within the bedchamber of the Czar, bringing before his eyes a daughter (not less pious) that vanished to God not less suddenly, and left behind her a darkness not less profound. By the power of the keys it is that Our Lady of Tears glides, a ghostly intruder, into the chambers of sleepless men, sleepless women, sleepless children, from Ganges to the Nile, from Nile to Mississippi. And her, because she is the first-born of her house, and has the widest empire, let us honour with the title of "Madonna."

The second Sister is called *Mater Suspiriorum*, Our Lady of Sighs. She never scales the clouds, nor walks abroad upon the winds. She wears no diadem. And her eyes, if they were ever seen, would be neither sweet nor subtle; no man could read their story; they would be found filled with perishing dreams, and with wrecks of forgotten delirium. But she raises not her eyes; her head, on which sits a dilapidated turban, droops for ever, for ever fastens on the dust. She weeps not. She groans not. But she sighs inaudibly at intervals. Her sister, Madonna, is oftentimes stormy and frantic, raging in the highest against heaven, and demanding back her darlings. But Our Lady of Sighs never clamours, never defies, dreams not of rebellious aspirations. She is humble to abjectness. Hers is the meekness that belongs to the hopeless. Murmur she may, but it is in her sleep. Whisper she may, but it is to herself in the twilight. Mutter she does at times, but it is in solitary places that are desolate as she is desolate, in ruined cities, and when the sun has gone down to his rest. This Sister is the visitor of the Pariah, of the Jew, of the bondsman to the oar in the Mediterranean galleys; of the English criminal in Norfolk Island, blotted out from the books of remembrance in sweet far-off England; of the baffled penitent reverting his eyes for ever upon a solitary grave, which to him seems the altar overthrown of some past and bloody sacrifice, on which altar no oblations can now be availing, whether towards pardon that he might implore, or towards reparation that he might attempt. Every slave that at noonday looks up to the tropical sun with timid reproach, as he points with one hand to the earth, our general mother, but for *him* a stepmother, as he points with the other hand to the Bible, our general teacher, but against *him* sealed and sequestered[1]; every woman sitting in darkness, without love to shelter her head, or hope to illumine her solitude, because the heaven-born instincts kindling in her nature germs of holy affections, which God implanted in her womanly bosom, having been stifled by social necessities, now burn sullenly to waste, like sepulchral lamps amongst the ancients; every nun defrauded of her unreturning May-time by wicked kinsman, whom God will judge; every captive in every dungeon; all that are betrayed, and all that are rejected; outcasts by traditionary law, and children of *hereditary* disgrace: all these walk with Our Lady of Sighs. She also carries a key; but she needs it little. For her kingdom is chiefly amongst the tents of Shem, and the houseless vagrant of every clime. Yet in the very highest ranks of man she finds chapels of her own; and even in glorious England there are some that, to the world, carry their heads as proudly as the reindeer, who yet secretly have received her mark upon their foreheads.

But the third Sister, who is also the youngest——! Hush! whisper whilst we talk of *her!* Her kingdom is not large, or else no flesh should live; but within that kingdom all power is hers. Her head, turreted like that of Cybele, rises almost beyond the reach of sight. She droops not; and her eyes, rising so high, *might* be hidden by distance. But, being what they are, they cannot be hidden: through the treble veil of crape which she wears the fierce light of a blazing misery, that rests not for matins or for vespers, for noon

---

[1] This, the reader will be aware, applies chiefly to the cotton and tobacco States of North America; but not to them only: on which account I have not scrupled to figure the sun which looks down upon slavery as *tropical,*—no matter if strictly within the tropics, or simply so near to them as to produce a similar climate.

of day or noon of night, for ebbing or for flowing tide, may be read from the very ground. She is the defier of God. She also is the mother of lunacies, and the suggestress of suicides. Deep lie the roots of her power; but narrow is the nation that she rules. For she can approach only those in whom a profound nature has been upheaved by central convulsions; in whom the heart trembles and the brain rocks under conspiracies of tempest from without and tempest from within. Madonna moves with uncertain steps, fast or slow, but still with tragic grace. Our Lady of Sighs creeps timidly and stealthily. But this youngest Sister moves with incalculable motions, bounding, and with tiger's leaps. She carries no key; for, though coming rarely amongst men, she storms all doors at which she is permitted to enter at all. And *her* name is *Mater Tenebrarum,*—our Lady of Darkness.

These were the *Semnai Theai* or Sublime Goddesses,[1] these were the *Eumenides* or Gracious Ladies (so called by antiquity in shuddering propitiation), of my Oxford dreams. Madonna spoke. She spoke by her mysterious hand. Touching my head, she beckoned to Our Lady of Sighs; and *what* she spoke, translated out of the signs which (except in dreams) no man reads, was this:—

"Lo! here is he whom in childhood I dedicated to my altars. This is he that once I made my darling. Him I led astray, him I beguiled; and from heaven I stole away his young heart to mine. Through me did he become idolatrous; and through me it was, by languishing desires, that he worshipped the worm, and prayed to the wormy grave. Holy was the grave to him; lovely was its darkness; saintly its corruption. Him, this young idolater, I have seasoned for thee, dear gentle Sister of Sighs! Do thou take him now to *thy* heart, and season him for our dreadful sister. And thou,"—turning to the *Mater Tenebrarum,* she said,— "wicked sister, that temptest and hatest, do thou take him from *her.* See that thy sceptre lie heavy on his head. Suffer not woman and her tenderness to sit near him in his

---

[1] "*Sublime Goddesses*":—The word σεμνός is usually rendered *venerable* in dictionaries,—not a very flattering epithet for females. But I am disposed to think that it comes nearest to our idea of the *sublime*, —as near as a Greek word *could* come.

darkness. Banish the frailties of hope; wither the relenting of love; scorch the fountains of tears; curse him as only *thou* canst curse. So shall he be accomplished in the furnace; so shall he see the things that ought *not* to be seen, sights that are abominable, and secrets that are unutterable. So shall he read elder truths, sad truths, grand truths, fearful truths. So shall he rise again *before* he dies. And so shall our commission be accomplished which from God we had,— to plague his heart until we had unfolded the capacities of his spirit."[1]

[1] To LEVANA AND OUR LADIES OF SORROW as originally printed in *Blackwood* of June 1845 De Quincey subjoined this important note:— "The reader who wishes at all to understand the course of these Confessions ought not to pass over this dream-legend. There is no great wonder that a vision which occupied my waking thoughts in those years should reappear in my dreams. It was, in fact, a legend recurring in sleep, most of which I had myself silently written or sculptured in my daylight reveries. But its importance to the present Confessions is this,—that it rehearses or prefigures their course. This FIRST Part belongs to Madonna. The THIRD belongs to the 'Mater Suspiriorum,' and will be entitled *The Pariah Worlds*. The FOURTH, which terminates the work, belongs to the 'Mater Tenebrarum,' and will be entitled *The Kingdom of Darkness*. As to the SECOND, it is an interpolation requisite to the effect of the others, and will be explained in its proper place."—Such was De Quincey's prefiguration in 1845 of the course of those SUSPIRIA DE PROFUNDIS papers, then only begun, which, when completed, were to be offered by him in his old age as a second, and more profoundly conceived, set of his CONFESSIONS OF AN ENGLISH OPIUM-EATER. I detect signs in the footnote of a mere momentary attempt to forecast the probable nature and range of a series of papers yet unborn for the most part, and to bespeak a plausible principle for their classification when they should all be in existence. It was a mere extempore scheme, very hazy in the gap between the finished Part I., which the *Mater Lachrymarum* was supposed already to own, and the projected Parts III and IV, which were to belong to the *Mater Suspiriorum* and the *Mater Tenebrarum* respectively; and I doubt whether the scheme could, in any circumstances, have been consistently and acceptably carried out. In fact, as has been explained in our Introduction to these SUSPIRIA, it broke down. What is most interesting in the words just quoted is the evidence they afford of the value which De Quincey himself attached, and partly for autobiographical reasons, to his mythological conception of "The Three Ladies of Sorrow" and of the diverse realms and functions of those three sister-goddesses in the world of mankind.—M.

MISCELLANEA

DANISH ORIGIN OF THE LAKE-COUNTRY DIALECT[1]

It was in the hottest part of a very hot day of August in the year 1812 or 1813 that I happened, in the course of a

[1] Appeared originally as the main portion of a series of four articles (on languages generally and the Lake dialect in particular) contributed by De Quincey to the columns of *The Westmorland Gazette* for 13th November and 4th and 18th December 1819, and 8th January 1820; and taken here from the copy in Mr Charles Pollitt's very interesting pamphlet recently printed at Kendal (1890) under the title "De Quincey's Editorship of the *Westmorland Gazette*: July 1818 to November 1819." Mr. Pollitt, having access to the files of the old newspaper and to the minutes of the meetings of its proprietors during De Quincey's memorable connexion with it, has been able to clear up in this pamphlet much that has hitherto been obscure in this portion of De Quincey's biography; and he has increased the interest of his narrative by giving numerous extracts from De Quincey's leading articles in the paper, his curious notices to correspondents, &c., in addition to those printed in 1877 in the first edition of Dr. Japp's Life of De Quincey. Most of these extracts are on current topics of general or local politics—illustrating De Quincey's peculiar conceptions of the duty of a Tory provincial editor in those days, and his fighting relations with the editor of the rival Whig newspaper at Kendal, but Mr. Pollitt quotes also specimens of the literary articles, and the occasional bits of scholarship and philosophy, with which De Quincey sought to enlighten and edify his north-country readers. The longest and liveliest of the literary articles so quoted, and the only one suitable for reproduction here, is that which we have selected. As De Quincey's actual editorship of the paper ceased, however, Mr. Pollitt tells us, on the 5th of November 1819, and as his four articles on the Lake Dialect were published in the paper during the next two months, they were really contributions from him as ex-editor, and may be regarded as spillings-over from his editorship in the shape of promised or already prepared matter.—M.

long walk, to find myself in a sequestered valley of Westmorland. Retired from the high road at some little distance I saw a respectable farmhouse, towards which I turned and begged permission to rest myself within doors for the sake of obtaining a short respite from the oppressive heat of the sun. This being immediately granted with the cheerful courtesy of a Westmorland 'statesman, I stepped in and took a seat. Whilst the master of the house was conversing with me upon Bonaparte, Marshal Blucher, the National Debt, and other like pastoral subjects, I observed, in the furthest corner of the house, a fine young woman sitting with an infant in her lap, and busily engaged in playing with it. So entirely was she taken up with her child that I am afraid she paid very little attention to the wisdom with which we settled the affairs of Europe, and that even the full and clear payment of the National Debt up to the last sixpence without defrauding a single creditor failed to give her that satisfaction which at another time no doubt it would have done. Indeed, to say the truth, the loveliness of the youthful mother and child, whose joint ages, I imagine, would not have made eighteen years—their innocent happiness and the perfect love which appeared to connect them—combined to make up a picture so touching and beautiful that even I, Stoic as I profess myself, could not contemplate it wholly unmoved. My attention being thus drawn to them, I could not fail to hear something of what the mother addressed to her child; and, though all passed in an under voice, little above a whisper, I was struck by the words "No more patten," repeated two or three times, and accompanied with a playful gesture as though defending her bosom from the busy little hands of the laughing infant. This word "*patten*" arrested my notice; for I remembered that "*patte*"—a dissyllable, the *e* final pronounced as the *a* in *sopha*, or the *e* in the French article *le*,—is the Danish word for a woman's breast. The plural of this word is "*patten*" pronounced exactly as it is in Westmorland; and the proper expression (indeed the only expression) in Danish for weaning a child is "*at vænner et barn fra patten*" (lit. *to wean a child from the breasts*); in which sentence, as the initial letter in "*vænner*" is pronounced like a *w*, a Westmorland man would be at a loss to know whether to call it English or Danish. To be sure that I had heard the word accurately, I took the liberty of asking the young woman what was the meaning of the word "*patten*," which, if I was not mistaken, she had addressed to her child. Hereupon the old 'statesman burst out a-laughing; but his grand-daughter (as I found she was) blushed, and evaded my question by saying that it was only a word used to children. I apologised for my freedom by explaining its object; and from the old man I learned that my conjecture was right, and since then I have had it frequently confirmed.

Such was the occasion of my first coming to perceive the Danish origin of the Westmorland dialect; and I have since met with further cases of the same fact in such abundance as would furnish matter for a small dictionary. Some few of the most striking instances which rest upon my memory I will here adduce.

Walking near Ambleside, I heard an old woman exclaim "I'll *skyander* him if he comes here again." I stepped up to her and conjured her, as she valued the interests of Philology and the further progress of Etymology, that she would expound to me that venerable word (as I doubted not it would prove) which she had just used. "Why," said she, "I'll give him a *serrogle.*" This was "*ignotum per ignotius*" with a vengeance. However, I remembered the Danish word *skiender* meant to *scold*, to *rate*, etc.; and, on cross-questioning the old woman, it appeared that such was the meaning which it still bore in Westmorland.—"Didn't thee blaspheme my name, and shake thy *neif* in my face at Keswick on Pie Saturday?" said a man at a country fair to another with whom he was wrangling. "*Næv*" (pronounced *neif*) is the Danish word for *fist*. But this word is found south of Westmorland; for it is used by Shakspere.[1] —"Master," said a Cumberland girl to me, "is I to sweep the *attercops* off them books?" By *attercops* (as I need scarcely tell your readers) she meant cobwebs: in Danish "*edderkop*" is a spider.[2]

* * * * * * *

[1] It is a common Scottish word.—M.
[2] This also is a common Scottish word,—in the form *ettercap.*—M.

1. The Danish origin of the Cumbrian dialect shows itself not merely in a very extensive list of words radically distinct from such as belong to the universal English, and wholly unintelligible to a Southern Englishman, but also in the peculiar pronunciation of many words common to the Cumbrian and the classical English. *E.g.* For a '*drunken* man' the Cumbrians say a '*drukken* man'; for 'wrong' —'wrang'; for 'long'—'lang' (as in *Langdale*);—all of which, though commonly ascribed to provincial mispronunciation, are good Danish.—Again, for '*sneeze*' the Cumbrians say '*neeze*'—which is the Danish '*nyse*'; for '*home*' they say '*yame*'; at least *that* comes as near the sound as I can express:—now '*yame*' is the true pronunciation of the Danish word '*hiem*' (home). So entirely, indeed, does the Danish pronunciation survive in some words that I have remarked (and I have heard others remark) among even well-educated people of Darlington, Stockton, and other places in Durham, the Danish practice of sounding the *k* in words beginning with *kn*; as, *e.g.*, in '*knife*' (Danish '*kniv*'), '*knee*' (Danish '*knæ*'), '*kneel*' (Danish '*knæle*'), '*knitting*' (Danish '*knytting*'): in all of which words the people of Stockton, &c., sound the *k*; and I think I have remarked the same practice in some persons of education from Penrith (though possibly brought up in Durham).[1] Now this practice is clearly Danish, and so abhorrent to the general usage of England that from the earliest times it has been customary to accommodate to the English pronunciation all Danish names beginning with *kn* by intercalating an *a* between the *k* and the *n*. On this principle we say 'King *Canute*,' whereas the Danish historians call him '*Konge Knud*'; which was his real name: and therefore it is that our Selden, whose monstrous erudition had mastered every language, ancient as well as modern, from the Euphrates to the Severn, never mentioned him by any other name than King *Knout*. Why not King *Knud*? The reader will see below.

2. So richly indeed is our northern vernacular speech interveined with Danish peculiarities that even the grossest

[1] This *kn* sound is also common in Scotland,—as are *drucken* for *drunken*, *lang* for *long*, &c.—M.

vulgarisms and barbarisms (as we are apt to consider them) cannot safely be condemned for such until the Danish and its sister-dialects have confirmed the verdict. What greater vulgarism, for instance, is there—according to the general feeling of well-educated persons—than the common substitute of 'I *mun*' for 'I *must*'? Yet this is good Icelandic, if not good English, and in earlier times was used by many tribes of those who were called Danes. 'Duo defectiva; *eg mun* et *eg skal* (i.e. *I mun* and *I shall*), in constructione cum aliis verbis, efficiunt orationis structuram non absimilem illi quam habet Græcorum MELLO: ut *eg mun giðra* vel *eg skal giora*, Faciam vel Facturus sum.' *Ionæ Gram. Island.*, p. 109.—Upon which passage the learned Hickes observes—'*Mun* apud septentrionales Anglos et Scotos gerundivam vim habet, conjunctum cum aliis verbis: ut *I mun go*, Abeundum est mihi.'—Again, to give another instance, I remember that a young woman from Lancashire who attended me in my infancy was accustomed, on any sudden surprise, to exclaim '*Odd rabbet it!*' and I think I have seen the same exclamation in some work of l'Estrange's or Tom Brown's. As English this expression has no meaning: read, therefore, on my authority '*Udraabet it*,' i.e. literally '*Cry out upon it*'—'*Curse it!*' '*Raaben*' in Danish is *to cry* or *ejaculate*, und '*ud*' is the preposition *out*: whence, by the way, '*Outlaw*' in law Latin is '*Utlegatus*'; whence also, for analogy's sake, Selden chose to Anglicize King *Knud* into King *Knout*.

3. Hitherto I have been indebted for my specimens of Danish to the men of Hawkshead, Ambleside, Bowness, &c.; that is, to the Cis-Alpines—as they may be called by those who live on the Windermere side of Kirkstone. But these tribes, though speaking very tolerable Danish for people that have had no Danish schoolmasters during the last eight hundred years, are mere novices in that language compared with the natives of the Trans-Alpine regions of Patterdale, Matterdale, Martindale, &c. There it is that the Danish is spoken in its purity: there lies our Westmorland Copenhagen. Amongst the Cis-Alpines are found Danish words in abundance: but in the Trans-Alpine vales the very nerves and sinews of the dialect are Danish. The particles

of most common use, the very joints for binding the parts of
a sentence together, are Danish. They say *at* for the participle *to*; as, for instance, 'I tell'd him *at* gang yame' for 'I
told him *to* go home.' They say '*til*' for the preposition *to*;
as 'He came *til* me' for 'He came *to* me.' They say '*fra*'
for *from*.[1] They say '*titter*' for *sooner*. They say '*over*' for
too, which indeed is common to all Westmorland,—as in
the two first lines of a song with which I heard a nurse
singing a child to sleep:—

> Bee-bo, Baby-lo! Babies are bonny:
> Two in a bed's enough—three's *over* many.[2]

All are Danish, except, perhaps, that '*titter*' comes nearer
to the Icelandic. In the early Metrical Romances, by the
bye, the positive degree '*tyte*,' quick, or soon, is used as commonly as the comparative '*titter*' is in Martindale.

I come now to say a few words on the topographical
nomenclature of the Lake District.

In a sublime and very philosophical sonnet Mr. Wordsworth has apostrophised the power of twilight as performing for the external world, as the object of sense, a
process analogous to that which he has attributed to the
imagination in respect to the world, external or internal,
as the objects of thought. Now, let us suppose a
spectator placed upon the summit of Helvellyn, and that
by some process of abstraction '*Day's mutable distinctions*'
have been gradually withdrawn from the spectacle below,
and only the immutabilities of the scenery preserved: on
such a supposition he will have before him a scene the very
same which heretofore the ancient Briton or the Dane may
have beheld under the same circumstances—

> Those mighty barriers, and the gulf between;
> The flood, the stars,—a spectacle as old
> As the beginning of the heavens and earth.

Whatsoever, then, under such circumstances the spectator
would see he may expect to find bearing a British or else
a Danish name. The grand barriers of the principal moun-

---

[1] *Til* for *to* and *frae* for *from* are also Scotch.—M.
[2] Scotch also, in the form *ower*.—M.

tains, the great chambers of the valleys which they enclose, the lakes, the streams which feed them at the head and by which they issue at the foot: all these may be expected to bear ancient names; for these are the ancient features of the scenery,—'the same yesterday, to-day, and for ever.' But the subordinate incidents of the landscape, which belong to the hand of man, and are measured as to duration by his years,—such as woods, and the subdivision of lands, roads, and houses,—will naturally have names coeval with their own origin; and, even where that origin ascends to a very high antiquity, it will sometimes happen with respect to houses and inclosures that the pride of ownership has superseded the ancient name by one more modern, especially where they have been acquired by purchase. Houses, therefore, and inclosures cannot in general be expected to bear Danish names. But to this rule there occur to me at this moment two cases of exception. First, it must be recollected that many houses, as well as towns, borrow from the localities the same prerogative of immortality which the laws of England attribute to the King: they never die. Like Sir Francis Drake's ship, which had been so often repaired that not one of the original timbers remained, there are many houses and towns at this day of which, whilst the materials have perished or been dilapidated, the form has been maintained by successive repairs. Wheresoever indeed the site of a house or town is peremptorily determined by the relation in which it stands to water or shelter, we may presume the house or the town to be the modern representative of more ancient structures. And it will present a still stronger ground for presuming this if we find reason for believing that second-rate situations were so occupied. If Aa, Ab, Ac, Ad, etc., be a series of homesteads of which the worst is better than the best of the series Ba, Bb, Bc, Bd, then will it be some reason for presuming all the first series to have been occupied in ancient times if we have sufficient evidence that some of the second series were then occupied. Now, this evidence is satisfactorily conveyed in the Danish name which to this day clings to certain houses or homesteads of that description. Here, then, is one case in which the words of man may, in respect to the perpetuity of their names, share in the privilege usually appropriated to the grandest works of nature,—viz. by approaching to nature in her immortality. But there is a second case of exception in which there is no need for supposing any such immortality. Whosoever is acquainted with the pastoral nomenclature will know that no figure of speech is of larger influence or more tends to disturb the accuracy of its use and its application than the common figure of synecdoche, by which a part is put for the whole or the whole for a part. Very often the name which in popular usage is understood to denote a mountain or even a range of mountains will be restricted amongst learned shepherds to a single point or eminence (just as the name *Holland*, by a natural usurpation over the names of the six confederate states, came to denote all the seven). And, *vice versa*, the name of a whole mountain (or even of a cluster of separate heights) will be found in some cases to have settled upon an individual estate or field, and thence upon the house of which they form the little domain.

Having premised these general remarks, I will now come more directly to the point. And, first, I will examine the *Appellatives* of topography (*i.e.* the general terms of classification under which we arrange the various elements of natural scenery), and, secondly, a few of the proper names.

Fells, the most comprehensive designation of mountainous grounds, under which as the *genus* are classed the various species of *How*, *Scar*, *Crag*, &c. I used to derive it from the German '*Fels*,' a rock ; but, perhaps, it may come from the Danish word '*Feld*,' a hill or mountain.

Dale, from the Danish '*Dal*,' a valley ; and that originally meant a *division* ; whence the Danish word '*Dæle*,' a plank, *i.e.* one of the divisions into which a cubic piece of wood was sawed up ; and thence our *Deal*, which, from denoting the shape and relation, has come to denote the species of timber ; though I believe that timber merchants still say *Deals* for *Planks*.

Mere, a Lake : I know of no Danish word to which it comes so near as the German word '*Meer*,' a Lake.

Beck, a Brook or Rivulet : Danish '*Bæk*,' a Brook.

Holm, applied to some of the small islands in Windermere: Danish '*Holme*,' an Islet. But this word is perhaps a classical English word, and not merely provincial: thus, two very remarkable islands in the British Channel are called *The Holms*.

Hawse, any depression or remarkable sinking in a mountainous ridge which allows a road to be carried over it. Thus, between Grasmere and Patterdale there is a communication by means of a bridle-road carried over a dip at the intersection of Seat-Sandal and Fairfield, either of which mountains at any other point would be almost impracticable. This is called *Grisdale Hawse*. Another lies between Little Langdale and Eskdale, Borrowdale and Wastdale, Ennerdale and Buttermere, Long Sleddale and Mardale (at the head of Hawswater), &c. &c. The word is manifestly the word '*Hals*,'—which both in Danish and German means *a neck*: the mountainous pass being imaged under the relation of a neck to the body or main mountain. The work '*Hals*,' by the way, is common in the old English Metrical Romances under its literal meaning,—though never used figuratively as in the Cumbrian. And, again, in a whimsical poem entitled '*The Garment of Good Ladies*,' by Robert Henrysoun, a Scotch Poet of the fifteenth century (written, as Lord Hailes had suggested, by way of expanding 1st Tim. chap. 2, verses 9, 11), in which he has dressed a young lady out of an allegorical wardrobe:—

> Her hat should be of fair *having* (*i.e.* demeanour),
> And her tippet of truth;
> Her patelet of good *pansing* (*i.e.* thinking),
> Her HALS-ribbon of ruth.

In which stanza, by the bye, the word '*Patelet*,'—which the critics have been unable to explain,—may mean her *tucker*: from the Danish '*Patte*,' a woman's breast, which I had occasion to cite before. I need scarcely add that the dropping of *l* in *Hals*, as we do in Cumberland, is agreeable to the analogy of most languages in the same case: thus '*fa's*' and '*ca's*' is common in the old Scotch ballads for *falls* and *calls*: '*fause*' is used for *false*: in French '*douce*,' sweet, from *dulcis*: the *Malvern* Hills we call *Mawvern*: *Malham*, near the Yorkshire caves, is called *Mawn*: *Belvoir* Castle, *Bever* Castle.

Tarn, a small lake usually lying above the level of the large Lakes and the inhabited dales.—In order to justify the derivation which I am going to suggest for this word I must call the reader's attention to a nearer scrutiny of an exact definition. That which I have given above is agreeable to the popular usage and meets the case of most tarns as they actually exist; but, if a hair-splitter of logical niceties were to cavil at it, I know not that it would be strictly tenable. To be *above* some dales is to be *on a level with* others, seeing that their levels are at such various elevations in respect to the sea: and, moreover, neither of the conditions expressed in the definition is strictly a *sine qua non*; for I presume that, if a lake were much above the neighbouring lakes, it would be called a tarn, even though it were not very small; and again I presume that, if a lake were a very small one, it would be called a tarn, even though it were not above the level of the neighbouring lakes. Indeed, this latter presumption is realized in the case of Blellam Tarn, a small lake between Ambleside and Hawkshead, and also in that between Carlisle and Hesketh. Thus, then, it appears that the definition cannot be a good one, because it does not reciprocate with the thing defined; for, though every small lake above other lakes is a tarn, yet every tarn is not a small lake above others. But, though it is not impregnable as a definition, it may answer pretty well as a description of the general circumstances which combine to constitute a tarn; and it will answer still better if to these we add one other, which was pointed out to me by Mr. Wordsworth. That gentleman, whose severe accuracy of logic is well known to those who have the honour of his acquaintance, once remarked to me in conversation that, whereas lakes have always one main feeder, of tarns on the contrary it is characteristic that they are fed by a multitude of small independent rills, all apparently equal in importance, or (it may be added) having only a transient pre-eminence according to the accidental inequalities in the distribution of mountain showers (which are often confined to spots of a few square yards) and of snow, both in respect to the very various dimensions of the areas which melt into any one rill, and also to the very different accumulations of it by driftings, as governed by the wind and the circumstances of the ground. Thus discriminated, then, a tarn will be rather a deposition or settling of waters from the little rain-rills converging from the steep banks immediately adjacent, whilst a lake will be the disemboguing of a river after it has collected many inferior streams into a spacious bed or area not necessarily surrounded by precipitous banks. With this preface I shall now venture to derive the word Tarn from the Danish word *Taaren*, a trickling or a gradual deposition.[1]

[1] See *ante*, p. 128 n, and Vol. IV, p. 118 n.

HISTORICO-CRITICAL INQUIRY

INTO THE ORIGIN OF THE

ROSICRUCIANS AND THE FREE-MASONS[1]

THERE is a large body of outstanding problems in history, great and little, some relating to persons, some to things, some to usages, some to words, &c., which furnish occasion, beyond any other form of historical researches, for the display of extensive reading and critical acumen. 1. In reference to *persons*: as those which regard whole nations :—*e.g.* What became of the ten tribes of Israel? Did Brennus and his Gauls penetrate into Greece? Who and what are the Gypsies? or those, far more in number, which regard individuals,—as the case of the Knights Templars, of Mary Stuart, of the Ruthvens (the Gowrie Conspiracy). Who was the man in the Iron Mask? Was the unhappy Lady of the Haystack, who in our own days slept out of doors or in barns up and down Somersetshire, a daughter of the Emperor of Germany? Was Perkin Warbeck three centuries ago the true Plantagenet?[2] 2. In reference to *things*; as—Who first discovered the sources of the Nile? Who built Stonehenge? Who discovered the compass? What was the

---

[1] Appeared originally in the *London Magazine* for January, February, March, and June 1824: not included by De Quincey himself in his Collective Edition; but reprinted in 1871 in the second of the two supplementary volumes published by Messrs. Black in their re-issue of that edition —M.

[2] There can be no doubt that he was. But I mention it as a question which most people suppose to be yet *sub judice*.

Golden Fleece? Was the Siege of Troy a romance or a grave historic fact? Was the Iliad the work of one mind, or (on the Wolfian hypothesis) of many? What is to be thought of the Thundering Legion? of the miraculous dispersion of the Emperor Julian's labourers before Jerusalem? of the burning of the Alexandrian library? &c. Who wrote Εἰκὼν Βασιλικὴ? Who wrote the letters of Junius? Was the Fluxional Calculus discovered simultaneously by Leibnitz and Newton; or did Leibnitz derive the first hint of it from the letter of Newton? 3. In reference to *usages*; as the May-pole and May-day dances—the Morris dancers—the practice (not yet extinct amongst uneducated people) of saying "God bless you!" on hearing a person sneeze, and thousands of others. 4. In reference to *words*; as whence came the mysterious *Labarum* of Constantine? &c.

Among the problems of the first class there are not many more irritating to the curiosity than that which concerns the well-known order of Free-masons. In our own language I am not aware of any work which has treated this question with much learning. I have therefore abstracted, rearranged, and in some respects, I shall not scruple to say, have improved, the German work on this subject, of Professor J. G. Buhle. This work is an expansion of a Latin Dissertation read by the Professor in the year 1803 to the Philosophical Society of Göttingen; and, in respect to the particular sort of merit looked for in a work of this kind, has (I believe) satisfied the most competent judges. Coming after a crowd of other learned works on the Rosicrucians, and those of Lessing and Nicolai on the Free-masons, it could not well fail to embody what was most important in their elaborate researches, and to benefit by the whole. Implicitly, therefore, it may be looked upon as containing the whole learning of the case as accumulated by all former writers, in addition to that contributed by the Professor himself; which, to do him justice, seems to be extensive and accurate. But the Professor's *peculiar* claims to distinction in this inquiry are grounded upon the solution which he first has given in a satisfactory way to the main problem of the case —What is the *origin* of Free-masonry? For, as to the *secret* of Free-masonry, and its occult doctrines, there is a readier and more certain way of getting at those than through any Professor's book. To a hoax played off by a young man of extraordinary talents in the beginning of the seventeenth century (*i.e.* about 1610-14), but for a more elevated purpose than most hoaxes involve, the reader will find that the whole mysteries of Free-masonry, as now existing all over the civilized world after a lapse of more than two centuries, are here distinctly traced. such is the power of a grand and capacious aspiration of philosophic benevolence to embalm even the idlest levities, as amber enshrines straws and insects!

Any reader who should find himself satisfied with the Professor's solution and its proof would probably be willing to overlook his other defects: his learning and his felicity of conjecture may pass as sufficient and redeeming merits in a Gottingen Professor. Else, and if these merits were set aside, I must say that I have rarely met with a more fatiguing person than Professor Buhle. That his essay is readable at all, if it *be* readable, the reader must understand that he owes to me. Mr. Buhle is celebrated as the historian of philosophy, and as a logic-professor at a great German University.[1] But a more illogical work than his as to the conduct of the question, or one more confused in its arrangement, I have not often seen. It is doubtless a rare thing to meet with minds sufficiently stern in their logic to keep a question steadily and immovably before them, without ever being thrown out of their track by verbal delusions: and for my own part I must say that I never was present in my life at one of those after-dinner disputations by which social pleasure is poisoned (except in the higher and more refined classes) where the course of argument did not within ten minutes quit the question upon which it had first started, and all upon the seduction of some equivocal word, or of some theme which bore affinity to the main theme but was

---

[1] I believe that he is also the editor of the Bipont Aristotle; but, not possessing that edition of Aristotle myself, I cannot pretend to speak of its value. His *History of Philosophy* I have; it is probably as good as such works usually are; and, alas!—no better. [Johann Gottlieb Buhle, 1763-1821, Professor of Philosophy at Gottingen from 1787 to 1804; author of two works on the History of Philosophy. His essay on the Rosicrucians and Freemasons was published at Gottingen in 1804 —M.]

not that main theme itself, or still oftener of some purely verbal transition. All this is common; but the eternal see-sawing, weaving and counter-weaving, flux and reflux, of Professor Buhle's course of argument is *not* common by any means, but very *un*common, and worthy of a place in any cabinet of natural curiosities. There is an everlasting confusion in the worthy man's mind between the two questions —What is the *origin* of Free-masonry? and What is the *nature* and *essence* of Free-masonry? The consequence is that, one idea always exciting the other, they constantly come out shouldering and elbowing each other for precedency —every sentence is charged with a double commission—the Professor gets angry with himself, begins to splutter unintelligibly, and finds on looking round him that he has wheeled about to a point of the argument considerably in the rear of that which he had reached perhaps 150 pages before. I have done what I could to remedy these infirmities of the book; and upon the whole it is a good deal less paralytic than it was. But, having begun my task on the assumption that the first chapter should naturally come before the second, the second before the third, and so on, I find now (when the mischief is irreparable) that I made a great mistake in that assumption,—which perhaps is not applicable to Gottingen books,—and that, if I had read the book on the Hebrew principle, or Βουστροφηδον, or had tacked and traversed or done anything but sail on a straight line, I could not have failed to improve the arrangement of my materials. But, after all, I have so whitewashed the Professor that nothing but a life of gratitude on his part, and free admission to his logic lectures for ever, can possibly repay me for my services.[1]

---

[1] The purport of this paragraph has to be remembered by the reader throughout the rest of the paper. While the *matter* of the paper is Buhle's, and the whole is therefore a kind of translation from Buhle, it is a translation after De Quincey's peculiar notion of what might sometimes be necessary in a translation. In other words it is a "De Quinceyfied" translation,—even the *matter* owing a good deal to De Quincey's digestion of it, while the *manner* is still more obviously here and there De Quincey's own. The reader will observe more particularly the lightening of the text at several points by little gleams of fun thrown in at Buhle's expense.—M.

The three most triumphant dissertations existing upon the class of historico-critical problems which I have described above are :—1, Bentley's upon the spurious Epistles ascribed to Phalaris ; 2, Malcolm Laing's upon Perkin Warbeck (published by Dr. Henry in his *History of Great Britain*) ; 3, Mr. Taylor's upon the Letters of Junius. All three are loaded with a superfetation of evidence, and conclusive beyond what the mind altogether wishes. For it is pleasant to have the graver part of one's understanding satisfied, and yet to have its capricious part left in possession of some miserable fragment of a scruple upon which it may indulge itself with an occasional speculation in support of the old error. In fact, coercion is not pleasant in any cases ; and, though reasons be as plenty as blackberries, one would not either give or believe them "on compulsion." In the present work the reader will perhaps not find himself under this unpleasant sense of coercion, but left more to the free exercise of his own judgment. Yet, upon the whole, I think he will give his final award in behalf of Professor Buhle's hypothesis.

CHAPTER I

Of the Essential Characteristics of the Orders of the Rosicrucians and the Free-masons

I deem it an indispensable condition of any investigation into the origin of the Rosicrucians and Free-masons that both orders should be surveyed comprehensively and in the whole compass of their relations and characteristic marks,—not with reference to this or that mythos, symbol, usage, or form ; and to the neglect of this condition, I believe, we must impute the unsuccessful issue which has hitherto attended the essays on this subject. First of all, therefore, I will assign those distinguishing features of these orders which appear to me universal and essential ; and these I shall divide into *internal* and *external*, accordingly as they respect the personal relations and the purposes of their members, or simply the outward form of the institutions.

The universal and essential characteristics of the two orders which come under the head of *internal* are these which follow :—

I. As their fundamental maxim they assume—*Entire equality of personal rights amongst their members in relation to their final object.* All distinctions of social rank are annihilated. In the character of masons the prince and the lowest citizen behave reciprocally as free men, standing to each other in no relation of civic inequality. This is a feature of masonry in which it resembles the Church; projecting itself, like *that*, from the body of the State, and in *idea* opposing itself to the State, though not in fact,—for, on the contrary, the ties of social obligation are strengthened and sanctioned by the masonic doctrines. It is true that these orders have *degrees*—many or few according to the constitution of the several mother-lodges. These, however, express no subordination in rank or power: they imply simply a more or less intimate connexion with the concerns and purposes of the institution. A gradation of this sort, corresponding to the different stages of knowledge and initiation in the mysteries of the order, was indispensable to the objects which they had in view. It could not be advisable to admit a young man, inexperienced and untried, to the full participation of their secrets: he must first be educated and moulded for the ends of the society. Even elder men it was found necessary to subject to the probation of the lower degrees before they were admitted to the higher. Without such a regulation dangerous persons might sometimes have crept into the councils of the society; which, in fact, happened occasionally in spite of all provisions to the contrary. It may be alleged that this feature of personal equality amongst the members in relation to their private object is not exclusively the characteristic of Rosicrucians and Free-masons. True; it belongs no less to all the secret societies which have arisen in modern times. But, notwithstanding *that*, it is indisputable that to them was due the original scheme of an institution having neither an ecclesiastic nor a political tendency, and built on the personal equality of all the individuals who composed it.

II. *Women, children, those who were not in the full possession of civic freedom, Jews, Anti-Christians generally, and* (according to undoubted historic documents), in the early days of these orders, *Roman Catholics, were excluded from the Society.* For what reason women were excluded I suppose it can hardly be necessary to say. The absurd spirit of curiosity, talkativeness, and levity, which distinguishes that unhappy sex was obviously incompatible with the grave purposes of the Rosicrucians and Masons,—not to mention that the familiar intercourse which co-membership in these societies brings along with it would probably have led to some disorders in a promiscuous assemblage of both sexes, such as might have tainted the good fame or even threatened the existence of the order. More remarkable is the exclusion of *persons* not *wholly free*, of *Jews*, and of *Anti-Christians*; and, indeed, it throws an important light upon the origin and character of the institutions. By *persons not free* we are to understand not merely slaves and vassals, but also those who were in the service of others, and, generally, all who had not an independent livelihood. Even freeborn persons are comprehended in this designation so long as they continued in the state of minority. Masonry presumes in all its members the devotion of their knowledge and powers to the objects of the institution. Now, what services could be rendered by vassals, menial servants, day-labourers, journeymen, with the limited means at their disposal as to wealth or knowledge, and in their state of dependency upon others? Besides, with the prejudices of birth and rank prevalent in that age, any admission of plebeian members would have immediately ruined the scheme. Indeed, we have great reason to wonder that an idea so bold for those times as the union of nobles and burghers under a law of perfect equality could ever have been realised. And, in fact, amongst any other people than the English, with their national habits of thinking and other favourable circumstances, it could *not* have been realised. *Minors* were rejected unless when the consent of their guardians was obtained; for otherwise the order would have exposed itself to the suspicion of tampering with young people in an illegal way: to say nothing of the want of free-agency in minors. That lay-brothers were admitted for the performance of servile offices is not to be taken as any departure from the general rule; for it was matter of necessity that persons of lower rank should fill the menial offices attached to the society; and these persons, be it observed, were always chosen from amongst those who had an independent property, however small. As to the exclusion of Anti-Christians, especially of Jews, this may seem at first sight inconsistent with the cosmopolitical tendency of Masonry. But had it that tendency at its first establishment? Be this as it may, we need not be surprised at such a regulation in an age so little impressed with the virtue of toleration, and indeed so little able—from political circumstances—to practise it. Besides, it was necessary for their own security. The Free-masons themselves were exposed to a suspicion of atheism and sorcery; and this suspicion would have been confirmed by the indiscriminate admission of persons hostile to Christianity. For the Jews in particular, there was a further reason for rejecting them, founded on the deep degradation of the national character. With respect to the Roman Catholics, I need not at this point anticipate the historic data which favour their exclusion. The fact is certain; but, I add, only for the earlier periods of Free-masonry. Further on, the cosmopolitical constitution of the order had cleared it of all such religious tests; and at this day I believe that in the lodges of London and Paris there would be no hesitation in receiving as a brother any upright Mahometan or Jew. Even in smaller cities, where lingering prejudices would still cleave with more bigotry to the old exclusions, greater stress is laid upon the natural religion of the candidate—his belief in God and his sense of moral obligation—than upon his positive confession of faith. In saying this, however, I would not be understood to speak of certain individual sects amongst the Rosicrucians, whose mysticism leads them to demand special religious qualities in their proselytes which are dispensed with by common Free-masonry.

III. *The orders make pretensions to mysteries.* These relate partly to ends and partly to means, and are derived from the East, whence they profess to derive an occult wisdom not revealed to the profane. This striving after hidden knowledge it was that specially distinguished these societies from others that pursued unknown objects. And, because their main object was a mystery, and that it might remain such, an oath of secrecy was demanded of every member on his admission. Nothing of this mystery could ever be discovered by a visit from the police; for, when such an event happens,

—and naturally it has happened many times,—the business is at an end and the lodge *ipso facto* dissolved; besides that all the acts of the members are symbolic, and unintelligible to all but the initiated. Meantime no government can complain of this exclusion from the mysteries, as every governor has it at his own option to make himself fully acquainted with them by procuring his own adoption into the society. This it is which in most countries has gradually reconciled the supreme authorities to Masonic Societies, hard as the persecution was which they experienced at first. Princes and prelates made themselves brothers of the order as the condition of admission to the mysteries. And, think what they would of these mysteries in other respects, they found nothing in them which could justify any hostility on the part of the State.

In an examination of Masonic and Rosicrucian Societies the weightiest question is that which regards the nature of these mysteries. To this question we must seek for a key in the spirit of that age when the societies themselves originated. We shall thus learn, first of all, whether these societies do in reality cherish any mystery as the final object of their researches; and, secondly, perhaps we shall thus come to understand the extraordinary fact that the Rosicrucian and Masonic secret should not long ago have been betrayed in spite of the treachery which we must suppose in a certain proportion of those who were parties to that secret in every age.

IV. *These orders have a general system of signs* (*e.g.* that of recognition), *usages, symbols, mythi, and festivals.* In this place it may be sufficient to say generally that even that part of the ritual and mythology which is already known to the public[1] will be found to confirm the conclusions drawn from other historical data as to the origin and purpose of the institution. Thus, for instance, we may be assured beforehand that the original Free-masons must have had some reason for appropriating to themselves the attributes and emblems of

---

[1] We must not forget, however, that the Rosicrucian and Masonic orders were not originally at all points what they now are: they have passed through many changes and modifications, and no inconsiderable part of their symbolic system, etc., has been the product of successive generations.

real handicraft Masons: which part of their ritual they are so far from concealing that in London they often parade on solemn occasions attired in full costume. As little can it be imagined that the selection of the feast of St. John (Midsummer-day) as their own chief festival was at first arbitrary and without a significant import.

Of the *external* characteristics—or those which the society itself announces to the world—the main is the *public profession of beneficence*; not to the brothers only, though of course to them more especially, but also to strangers. And it cannot be denied by those who are least favourably disposed to the order of Free-masons that many states in Europe, where lodges have formerly existed or do still exist, are indebted to them for the original establishment of many salutary institutions having for their object the mitigation of human suffering. The other external characteristics are properly negative, and are these:—

I. *Masonry is compatible with every form of civil constitution;* which cosmopolitical relation of the order to every mode and form of social arrangements has secured the possibility of its reception amongst all nations, however widely separated in policy and laws.

II. *It does not impose celibacy;* and this is the criterion that distinguishes it from the religious orders, and from many of the old knightly orders, in which celibacy was an indispensable law, or still is so.

III. *It enjoins no peculiar dress* (except indeed in the official assemblages of the lodges, for the purpose of marking the different degrees), *no marks of distinction in the ordinary commerce of life, and no abstinence from civil offices and business.* Here again is a remarkable distinction from the religious and knightly orders.

IV. *It grants to every member a full liberty to dissolve his connection with the order at any time, and without even acquainting the superiors of the lodge:* though of course he cannot release himself from the obligation of his vow of secrecy. Nay, even after many years of voluntary separation from the order, a return to it is always allowed. In the religious and knightly orders the members have not the powers, excepting under certain circumstances, of leaving them; and, under *no* circumstances, of returning. This last was a politic regulation; for, whilst on one hand the society was sufficiently secured by the oath of secrecy, on the other hand by the easiness of the yoke which it imposed it could the more readily attract members. A young man might enter the order, satisfy himself as to the advantages that were to be expected from it, and leave it upon further experience or any revolution in his own way of thinking.

In thus assigning the internal and external characteristics of the Rosicrucians and Free-masons, I have purposely said nothing of the distinctions between the two orders themselves; for this would have presupposed that historical inquiry which is now to follow. That the above characteristics, however, were common to both is not to be doubted. Rosicrucianism, it is true, is not Free-masonry; but the latter borrowed its form from the first. He that gives himself out for a Rosicrucian without knowing the general ritual of masonry is unquestionably an impostor. Some peculiar sects there are which adopt certain follies and chimeras of the Rosicrucians (as gold-making); and to these he may belong; but a legitimate Rosicrucian, in the original sense and spirit of the order, he cannot be.

Chapter II

Upon the Earliest Historical Traces of the Rosicrucian and Masonic Orders

The accredited records of these orders do not ascend beyond the two last centuries. On the other hand, it is alleged by many that they have existed for eighteen hundred years. He who adopts this latter hypothesis,—which even as a hypothesis seems to me scarcely endurable for a moment, —is bound to show, in the first place, in what respect the deduction of these orders from modern history is at all unsatisfactory; and, secondly, upon his own assumption of a far elder origin, to explain how it happened that for sixteen entire centuries no writers contemporary with the different periods of these orders have made any allusion to them. If he replies by alleging the secrecy of their proceedings, I rejoin that this might have secured their doctrines and mysteries from being divulged, but not the mere fact of their existence. My view of their origin will perhaps be granted with relation to Western Europe; but I shall be referred to the east for the *incunabula* of the order. At one time Greece, at another Egypt, or different countries of Asia, are alleged as the cradle of the Rosicrucians and the Free-masons. Let us take a cursory survey of the several hypotheses.

1. In the earlier records of GREECE we meet with nothing which bears any resemblance to these institutions but the Orphic and Eleusinian mysteries. Here, however, the word *mysteries* implied not any occult problem or science sought for, but simply sensuous[1] and dramatic representations of religious ideas—which could not otherwise be communicated to the people in the existing state of intellectual culture, and which (as often happens), having been once established, were afterwards retained in a more advanced state of the national mind. In the Grecian mysteries there were degrees of initiation amongst the members, but with purposes wholly distinct from those of the masonic degrees. The Grecian mysteries were not to be profaned; but *that* was on religious accounts. Lastly, the Grecian mysteries were a part of the popular religion acknowledged and authorised by the state. The whole resemblance, in short, rests upon nothing, and serves only to prove an utter ignorance of Grecian antiquities in those who have alleged it.[2]

2. Neither in the history of EGYPT is any trace to be found of the Rosicrucian and Masonic characteristics. It is true that the meaning of the Egyptian religious symbols and usages was kept secret from the people and from strangers; and in that sense Egypt may be said to have had mysteries; but these mysteries involved nothing more than the essential points of the popular religion.[3] As to the writings attributed

[1] The word *sensuous* is a Miltonic word, and is, moreover, a word that cannot be dispensed with.

[2] See the German essay of Meiners upon the Mysteries of the Ancients, especially the Eleusinian Mysteries, in the third part of his Miscellaneous Philosophical Works. Collate with this the work of Ste. Croix entitled *Mémoires pour servir à l'Histoire de la Réligion secrète des Anciens Peuples*. Paris, 1784.

[3] On the principle and meaning of the popular religion in Egypt,

to Hermes Trismegistus, they are now known to be spurious; and their pretensions could never have imposed upon any person who had examined them by the light of such knowledge as we still possess of the ancient Egyptian history and religion: indeed, the gross syncretism in these writings of Egyptian doctrines with those of the later Platonists too manifestly betrays them as a forgery from the schools of Alexandria. Forgery apart, however, the substance of the Hermetic writings disconnects them wholly from masonic objects: it consists of a romantic Theology and Theurgy; and the whole is very intelligible, and far from mysterious. What is true of these Hermetic books is true *a fortiori* of all later writings that profess to deliver the traditional wisdom of ancient Egypt.

3. If we look to ancient CHALDÆA and PERSIA for the origin of these orders, we shall be as much disappointed. The vaunted knowledge of the Chaldæans extended only to Astrology, the interpretation of dreams, and the common arts of jugglers. As to the Persian Magi, as well before as after the introduction of the doctrine of Zoroaster, they were simply the depositaries of religious ideas and traditions, and the organs of the public worship. Moreover, they composed no secret order, but rather constituted the highest *caste* or rank in the nation, and were recognised by the government as an essential part of the body-politic. In succeeding ages the religion of the Magi passed over to many great nations, and has supported itself up to our days. Anquetil du Perron has collected and published the holy books in which it is contained. But no doctrine of the Zendavesta is presented as a mystery; nor could any of those doctrines, from their very nature, have been presented as such. Undoubtedly amongst the Rosicrucian titles of honour we find that of Magus; but with them it simply designates a man of rare

---

and the hieroglyphics connected with it, consult Gatterer's essay *De Theogonia Aegyptiorum* in the 7th vol., and his essay *De metempsychosi, immortalitatis animorum symbolo Aegyptio*, in the 9th vol., of the Gottingen Transactions. The path opened by Gatterer has been since pursued with success by Dornedden in his *Amenophis* and in his new theory for the explanation of the Grecian Mythology: 1802. Consult also Vogel's Essay on the Religion of the ancient Egyptians and the Greeks: 4to. Nuremberg: 1793.

knowledge in physics—*i.e.* especially in Alchemy. That the ancient Magi in the age immediately before and after the birth of Christ attempted the transmutation of metals is highly improbable : that idea, there is reason to believe, first began to influence the course of chemical pursuits amongst the Arabian students of natural philosophy and medicine.

4. The pretensions of the DERVISHES and BRAHMINS of Asia, especially of Hindostan, to be the fathers of the two orders, need no examination, as they are still more groundless than those which have been just noticed.

5. A little before and after the birth of Christ there arose in Egypt and Palestine a Jewish religious sect which split into two divisions — the ESSENES and the THERAPEUTÆ. Their history and an account of their principles may be found in Josephus and more fully in Philo, who probably himself belonged to the Therapeutæ. The difference between the two sects consisted in this—that the Essenes looked upon practical morality and religion as the main business of life, whereas the Therapeutæ attached themselves more to philosophic speculations, and placed the essence of religion in the contemplation and reverence of the deity. They dwelt in hermitages, gardens, villages, and cottages, shunning the uproar of crowds and cities. With them arose the idea of monkish life ; which has subsisted to this day, though it has received a mortal shock in our revolutionary times. To these two sects have been traced the Rosicrucians and Freemasons. Now, without entering minutely into their history, it is sufficient for the overthrow of such a hypothesis to cite the following principles common to both the Essenes and the Therapeutæ. First, they rejected as morally unlawful all distinction of ranks in civil society. Secondly, they made no mystery of their doctrines. Thirdly, they admitted to their communion persons of either sex. Fourthly, though not peremptorily enjoining celibacy, they held it to be a more holy state than that of marriage. Fifthly, they disallowed of oaths. Sixthly, they had nothing symbolic in their worship or ritual. If it should be objected that the Free-masons talk much of the rebuilding of Solomon's temple, and refer some of their legends to this speculation, I answer that the

Essenes and Therapeutæ either were Christians or continued Jews until by little and little their sects expired. Now, to the Christians the rebuilding of the Temple must have been an object of perfect indifference; and to the Jews it must have been an important object in the literal sense. But with the Free-masons it is a mere figure under which is represented the secret purpose of the society: why this image was selected will be satisfactorily accounted for further on.[1]

6. The ARABS, who step forth upon the stage of History in the seventh century after Christ, have as little concern with the origin of these orders. They were originally a nomadic people that rapidly became a conquering nation not less from the weakness of their neighbours than their own courage and religious fanaticism. They advanced not less rapidly in their intellectual conquests; and these they owed chiefly to their Grecian masters, who had themselves at that time greatly degenerated from the refinement of their ancestors. The sciences in which the Arabs made original discoveries, and in which, next after the Greeks, they have been the instructors of the moderns, were Mathematics, Astronomy, Astrology, Medicine, Materia Medica, and Chemistry. Now, it is very possible that from the Arabs may have originally proceeded the conceit of physical mysteries without aid of magic, such as the art of gold-making, the invention of a panacea, the philosopher's stone, and other chimæras of alchemy which afterwards haunted the heads of the Rosicrucians and the elder Free-masons. But of Cabbalism and Theosophy, which occupied both sects in their early period, the Arabs as Mahometans could know nothing. And, if those sects had been derived from an Arabian stock, how comes it that at this day in most parts of Europe (and until lately everywhere) a Mahometan candidate would be rejected by both of them? And how comes it that in no Mahometan country at this time are there any remains of either?

In general, then, I affirm as a fact established upon historical research that before the beginning of the seven-

[1] With this paragraph compare De Quincey's own opinions about the Essenes and Therapeutæ, *ante*, Vol. VII, pp 101-172, and pp. 230-246.—M.

teenth century no traces are to be met with of the Rosicrucian or Masonic orders. And I challenge any antiquarian to contradict me. Of course, I do not speak of individual and insulated Adepts, Cabbalists, Theosophists, etc.; who doubtless existed much earlier. Nay, I do not deny that in elder writings mention is made of the *rose* and the *cross* as symbols of Alchemy and Cabbalism. Indeed it is notorious that in the sixteenth century Martin Luther used both symbols on his seal; and many Protestant divines have imitated him in this. Semler, it is true, has brought together a great body of data from which he deduces the conclusion that the Rosicrucians were of very high antiquity.[1] But all of them prove nothing more than what I willingly concede: Alchemists, Cabbalists, and dealers in the Black Art there were unquestionably before the seventeenth century; *but not Rosicrucians and Free-masons connected into a secret society and distinguished by those characteristics which I have assigned in the first chapter.*

One fact has been alleged from Ecclesiastical History as pointing to the order of the Rosicrucians. In 1586 the *Militia Crucifera Evangelica* assembled at Lunenburg. The persons composing this body have been represented as Rosicrucians; but in fact they were nothing more than a Protestant sect heated by apocalyptic dreams; and the object of the assemblage appears to have been exclusively connected with religion. Our chief knowledge of it is derived from the work of Simon Studion, a mystic and Theosophist, entitled *Naometria*, and written about the year 1604. The author was born at Urach, a little town of Wirtemberg; in 1565 he received the degree of Master of Arts at Tubingen; and soon after he settled at Marbach, not far from Louisburg, in the capacity of teacher. His labours in Alchemy brought him into great embarrassment, and his heretical novelties into all kinds of trouble. His *Naometria*,[2] which is a tissue of

[1] See Solomon Semler's *Impartial Collections for the History of the Rosicrucians.* In Four Parts, 8vo. Leipzig: 1786-8.

[2] The full title of this unprinted and curious book is this "NAOMETRIA, seu Nuda et Prima libri intus et foris scripti per clavem Davidis et calamum (virgæ similem) Apertio; in quo non tantum ad cognoscenda tam S Scripturæ totius quam Naturæ quoque Universæ mysteria brevis fit Introductio, verum etiam Prognosticis

dreams and allegories relating to the cardinal events of the world and to the mysteries of scripture, as well as of external nature from its creation to its impending destruction, contains a great deal of mysticism and prophecy about the *rose* and the *cross*. But the whole has a religious meaning; and the *fundus* of his ideas and his imagery is manifestly the Apocalypse of St. John. Nor is there any passage or phrase in his work upon which an argument can be built for connecting him with the Rosicrucians which would not equally apply to Philo the Alexandrian, to John Picus of Mirandula, to Reuchlin, to George of Venice, to Francis Patrick, and to all other Cabbalists, Theosophists, Magicians, and Alchemists.

Of the alleged connexion between the Templars and the Rosicrucians, or more properly with the Free-masons,—which connexion, if established, would undoubtedly assign a much earlier date to the origin of both orders,—I shall have occasion to speak in another part of my inquiry.

Chapter III

Of the circumstances which gave the first occasion to the rise of the Rosicrucian Order, and of the Earliest Authentic Records of History which relate to it.

Towards the end of the sixteenth century, Cabbalism, Theosophy, and Alchemy had overspread the whole of

(stellæ illius matutinæ anno Domini 1572 conspectæ ductu) demonstratur Adventus ille Christi ante diem novissimum Secundus per quem, Homine Peccati (Papa) cum filio suo perditionis (Mahometo) divinitus devastato, ipse Ecclesiam Suam et Principatus Mundi restaurabit, ut in iis posthac sit cum ovili pastor unus. In *Cruciferæ Militiæ Evangelicæ* gratiam. Authore Simone Studione inter Scorpiones. Anno 1604." An anonymous writer on the Rosicrucians in the *Wirtemberg Magazine* (No. 3, p. 523) and the learned Von Murr in his treatise upon the true origin of the Rosicrucians and Free-masons, printed at Sulzbach in the year 1803, have confounded the word Naometria (Ναομετρια), *Temple-measuring*, with Neometria (Νεομετρια), *New art of measuring*, as though Studion had written a new geometry. By the Temple, inner and outer, Studion means the Holy Scriptures and Nature; the *liber intus et foris scriptus* of which St. John says in the Revelations—"I saw on the right of him who sat upon the throne a book written within and without, and guarded with seven seals," etc.

Western Europe and especially of Germany. To this mania, which infected all classes—high and low, learned and unlearned—no writer had contributed so much as Theophrastus Paracelsus. How general was the diffusion, and how great the influence, of the writings of this extraordinary man (for such, amidst all his follies, he must ever be accounted in the annals of the human mind), may be seen in the life of Jacob Behmen. Of the many Cabbalistic conceits drawn from the Prophetic books of the Old Testament and still more from the Revelations, one of the principal and most interesting was this—that in the seventeenth century a great and general reformation was believed to be impending over the human race as a necessary forerunner to the Day of Judgment. What connects this very general belief with the present inquiry is the circumstance of Paracelsus having represented the comet which appeared in 1572 as the sign and harbinger of the approaching revolution, and thus fixed upon it the expectation and desire of a world of fanatics. Another prophecy of Paracelsus, which created an equal interest, was that soon after the decease of the Emperor Rudolph there would be found three treasures that had never been revealed before that time. Now, in the year 1610 or thereabouts there were published simultaneously three books, the substance of which it is important in this place to examine, because these books in a very strange way led to the foundation of the Rosicrucian order as a distinct society.

The first is so far worthy of notice as it was connected with the two others, and furnished something like an introduction to them. It is entitled *Universal Reformation of the whole wide World*, and is a tale not without some wit and humour. The Seven Wise Men of Greece, together with M. Cato and Seneca, and a secretary named Mazzonius, are summoned to Delphi by Apollo at the desire of the Emperor Justinian, and there deliberate on the best mode of redressing human misery. All sorts of strange schemes are proposed. Thales advises to cut a hole in every man's breast and place a little window in it; by which means it would become possible to look into the heart, to detect hypocrisy and vice, and thus to extinguish it. Solon proposes an equal partition of all possessions and wealth. Chilo's opinion is that the readiest way to the end in view would be to banish out of the world the two infamous and rascally metals, gold and silver. Kleobulus steps forward as the apologist of gold and silver, but thinks that iron ought to be prohibited, because in that case no more wars could be carried on amongst men. Pittacus insists upon more rigorous laws, which should make virtue and merit the sole passports to honour; to which, however, Periander objects that there had never been any scarcity of such laws nor of princes to execute them, but scarcity enough of subjects conformable to good laws. The conceit of Bias is that nations should be kept apart from each other, and each confined to its own home, and for this purpose that all bridges should be demolished, mountains rendered insurmountable, and navigation totally forbidden. Cato, who seems to be the wisest of the party, wishes that God in his mercy would be pleased to wash away all women from the earth by a new deluge, and at the same time to introduce some new arrangement [1] for the continuation of the excellent male sex without female help. Upon this pleasing and sensible proposal the whole company manifest the greatest displeasure, and deem it so abominable that they unanimously prostrate themselves on the ground and devoutly pray to God "that he would graciously vouchsafe to preserve the lovely race of woman" (what absurdity!) "and to save the world from a second deluge." At length, after a long debate, the counsel of Seneca prevails; which counsel is this.—That out of all ranks a society should be composed having for its object the general welfare of mankind, and pursuing it in secret. This counsel is adopted; though without much hope on the part of the deputation, on account of the desperate condition of "the Age"; who appears before them in person and describes his own wretched state of health.

[1] In which wish he seems to have anticipated the Miltonic Adam:

O why did God,
Creator wise, that peopled highest Heaven
With spirits masculine, create at last
This novelty on earth, this fair defect
Of nature, and not fill the world at once
With Men, as Angels, without feminine;
Or find some other way to generate
Mankind?   *P. L.*, Book x.

The second work gives an account of such a society as already established: this is the celebrated work entitled *Fama Fraternitatis of the meritorious Order of the Rosy Cross, addressed to the learned in general and the Governors of Europe;* and here we are presented with the following narrative:—Christian Rosycross, of noble descent, having upon his travels into the East and into Africa learned great mysteries from Arabians, Chaldeans, etc., upon his return to Germany established, in some place not mentioned, a secret society composed at first of four—afterwards of eight—members, who dwelt together in a building (called the House of the Holy Ghost) erected by him: to these persons, under a vow of fidelity and secrecy, he communicated his mysteries. After they had been instructed, the society dispersed agreeably to their destination, with the exception of two members, who remained alternately with the founder. The rules of the order were these · "The members were to cure the sick "without fee or reward. No member to wear a peculiar "habit, but to dress after the fashion of the country. On a "certain day in every year all the members to assemble in "the House of the Holy Ghost, or to account for their "absence. Every member to appoint some person with the "proper qualifications to succeed him at his own decease. "The word *Rosy-Cross* to be their seal, watch-word, and "characteristic mark. The association to be kept unrevealed "for a hundred years." Christian Rosycross died at the age of 106 years. His death was known to the society, but not his grave: for it was a maxim of the first Rosicrucians to conceal their burial-places even from each other. New masters were continually elected into the House of the Holy Ghost; and the society had now lasted 120 years. At the end of this period a door was discovered in the house, and upon the opening of this door a sepulchral vault. Upon the door was this inscription: *One hundred and twenty years hence I shall open (Post CXX annos patebo).* The vault was a heptagon. Every side was five feet broad and eight feet high. It was illuminated by an artificial sun. In the centre was placed, instead of a grave-stone, a circular altar, with a little plate of brass whereon these words were inscribed: *This grave, an abstract of the whole world, I made for myself whilst yet living (A. C. R. C. Hoc Universi compendium vivus mihi sepulchrum feci).* About the margin was—*To me Jesus is all in all (Jesus mihi omnia)* In the centre were four figures enclosed in a circle by this revolving legend: *Nequaquam vacuum legis jugum. Libertas Evangelii. Dei gloria intacta.* (The empty yoke of the Law is made void. The Liberty of the Gospel. The unsullied glory of God.) Each of the seven sides of the vault had a door opening into a chest; which chest, besides the secret books of the order and the *Vocabularium* of Paracelsus, contained also mirrors, little bells, burning lamps, marvellous mechanisms of music, etc., all so contrived that after the lapse of many centuries, if the whole order should have perished, it might be re-established by means of this vault. Under the altar, upon raising the brazen tablet, the brothers found the body of Rosycross, without taint or corruption. The right hand held a book written upon vellum with golden letters: this book, which is called T., has since become the most precious jewel of the society next after the Bible; and at the end stand subscribed the names of the eight brethren, arranged in two separate circles, who were present at the death and burial of Father Rosycross. Immediately after the above narrative follows a declaration of their mysteries addressed by the society to the whole world. They profess themselves to be of the Protestant faith; that they honour the Emperor and the laws of the Empire; and that the art of gold-making is but a slight object with them, and a mere πάρεργον. The whole work ends with these words:—" Our House of the Holy Ghost, " though a hundred thousand men should have looked upon " it, is yet destined to remain untouched, imperturbable, out of " sight, and unrevealed to the whole godless world for ever."

The third book,—which originally appeared in Latin with the title *Confessio Fraternitatis Roseæ Crucis ad Eruditos Europæ*—contains nothing more than general explanations upon the object and spirit of the order. It is added that the order has different degrees; that not only princes, men of rank, rich men, and learned men, but also mean and inconsiderable persons, are admitted to their communion, provided they have pure and disinterested purposes, and are able and willing to exert themselves for the ends of the institution; that the order has a peculiar language; that it is possessed of more gold and silver than the whole world beside could yield; that it is not this, however, but true philosophy, which is the object of their labours.

The first question, which arises on these three [1] works,—the *Universal Reformation*, the *Fama Fraternitatis*, and the *Confessio Fraternitatis*,—is this: from what quarter do they proceed? The reputed author was John Valentine Andreä, a celebrated theologian of Wirtemberg, known also as a satirist and a poet, and in our days revived into notice by the late illustrious Herder. Others have disputed his claim to these works; and Burke has excluded them from his catalogue of Andreä's writings. I shall attempt, however, to prove that he was the true author.

Andreä was born in 1586 at Herrenberg, a little town of Wirtemberg, and was the grandson of the Chancellor Jacob Andrea, so deservedly celebrated for his services to the church of Wirtemberg. From his father, the Abbot of Königsbronn, he received an excellent education, which his own extraordinary thirst for knowledge led him to turn to the best account. Besides Hebrew, Greek, and Latin (in which languages he was distinguished for the elegance of his style), he made himself master of the French, Italian, and

[1] The earliest edition of these works which I have seen is that of 1614, printed at Cassel, in 8vo, which is in the Wolfenbuttel library; but in this the *Confessio* is wanting. From a passage in this edition it appears that the *Fama Fraternitatis* had been received in the Tyrol as early as 1610,—in *manuscript*, as the passage alleges; but the words seem to imply that printed copies were in existence even before 1610.—In the year 1615 appeared "Secretioris Philosophiæ Consideratio à Philippo à Gabella, Philosophiæ studioso, conscripta, et nunc primum, una cum Confessione Fraternitatis Ros Crucis, in lucem edita. Cassellis: excud. G. Wesselius, A. 1615." In the very same year, at Frankfurt-on-the-Mayne, was printed by John Berner an edition of all the three works—the *Confessio* in a German translation. In this year also appeared a Dutch translation of all three: a copy of which is in the Gottingen library. The second Frankfurt edition was followed by a third in 1616, enlarged by the addition of some letters addressed to the brotherhood of the R. Cross. Other editions followed in the years immediately succeeding; but these it is unnecessary to notice. In the title-page of the third Frankfurt edit. stands—*First printed at Cassel in the year* 1616. But the four first words apply to the original edition, the four last to this.

Spanish: he was well versed in Mathematics, Natural and Civil History, Geography, and Historical Genealogy, without at all neglecting his professional study of divinity. Very early in life he seems to have had a deep sense of the evils and abuses of the times—not so much the political abuses as those in philosophy, morals, and religion. These it seems that he sought to redress by the agency of secret societies: on what motives and arguments he has not told us in the record of his own life which he left behind him in MS.[1] But the fact is certain: for as early as his sixteenth year he had written his *Chemical Nuptials of Christian Rosycross*, his *Julius, sive de Politia,* his *Condemnation of Astrology*, with other works of the same tendency.

Between the years 1607 and 1612 Andrea travelled extensively in south and west Germany, in Switzerland, France, and Italy.[2] In the succeeding years he made short excursions almost annually: after the opening of the Thirty Years' War he still continued this practice; and in the very midst of that great storm of wretchedness and confusion which then swept over Germany he exerted himself, in a way which is truly astonishing, to heal the "sorrow of the times," by establishing schools and religious worship, and by propagating the Lutheran faith, through Bohemia, Moravia, Carinthia, etc. Even to this day his country owes to his restless activity and enlightened patriotism many great blessings. At Stuttgart, where he was at length appointed chaplain to the court, he met with so much thwarting and persecution that, with his infirm constitution of body and dejection of mind from witnessing the desolation of Germany, it is not to be wondered that he became weary of life and sank into deep despondency and misanthropy. In this condition he requested leave in 1646 to resign his office. This was at first refused, with many testimonies of respect, by Eberhard, the then Duke of Wirtemberg; but on

[1] This is written in Latin. A German translation will be found in the second book of Seybold's Autobiographies of Celebrated Men.

[2] Travelling was not at that time so expensive for learned men as it now is. Many scholars travelled on the same plan as is now pursued by the journeymen artisans of Germany—exercising their professional knowledge at every stage of their journey, and thus gaining a respectable livelihood.

the urgent repetition of his request he was removed to the Abbey of Bebenhausen, and shortly afterwards was made Abbot of Adelberg. In the year 1654, after a long and painful sickness, he departed this life. On the day of his death he dictated a letter to his friend and benefactor, Augustus, Duke of Brunswick-Wolfenbuttel. He made an effort to sign it; wrote the two first letters of his name; and in the act of writing the third he expired.

From a close review of his life and opinions, I am not only satisfied that Andrea wrote the three works which laid the foundation of Rosicrucianism, but I see clearly *why* he wrote them. The evils of Germany were then enormous; and the necessity of some great reform was universally admitted. As a young man without experience, Andrea imagined that this reform would be easily accomplished. He had the example of Luther before him,—the heroic reformer of the preceding century whose memory was yet fresh in Germany, and whose labours seemed on the point of perishing unless supported by corresponding efforts in the existing generation. To organise these efforts and direct them to proper objects, he projected a society,—composed of the noble, the intellectual, the enlightened, and the learned, —which he hoped to see moving, as under the influence of one soul, towards the redressing of public evils. Under this hope it was that he travelled so much,—seeking everywhere, no doubt, for the coadjutors and instruments of his designs. These designs he presented originally in the shape of a project for a Rosicrucian Society; and in this particular project he intermingled some features that were at variance with its gravity and really elevated purposes. Young as he was at that time, Andrea knew that men of various tempers and characters could not be brought to co-operate steadily for any object so purely disinterested as the elevation of human nature: he therefore addressed them through the common foible of their age, by holding out promises of occult knowledge which should invest its possessor with authority over the powers of nature, should lengthen his life, or raise him from the dust of poverty to wealth and high station. In an age of Theosophy, Cabbalism, and Alchemy, he knew that the popular ear would be caught by an account, issuing nobody knew whence, of a secret society that professed to be the depositary of Oriental mysteries, and to have lasted for two centuries. Many would seek to connect themselves with such a society: from these candidates he might gradually select the members of that real society which he projected. The pretensions of the ostensible society were indeed illusions; but, before they could be detected as such by the new proselytes, those proselytes would become connected with himself and (as he hoped) moulded to nobler aspirations. On this view of Andrea's real intentions, we understand at once the ground of the contradictory language which he held about astrology and the transmutation of metals. His satirical works show that he looked through the follies of his age with a penetrating eye. He speaks with toleration there of these follies, as an exotic concession to the age; he condemns them in his own esoteric character as a religious philosopher. Wishing to conciliate prejudices, he does not forbear to bait his schemes with these delusions; but he is careful to let us know that they are with his society mere πάρεργα or collateral pursuits, the direct and main one being true philosophy and religion.

Meantime, in opposition to the claims of Andrea, it has been asked why he did not avow the three books as his own composition. I answer that to have done so at first would have defeated the scheme. Afterwards he had still better reasons for disavowing them. In whatever way he meant to have published the works, it is clear that they were in fact printed without his consent. An uproar of hostility and suspicion followed the publication, which made it necessary for the author to lie hid. If he would not risk his own safety, and make it impossible for his projects to succeed under any other shape, the author was called on to disown them. Andrea did so; and, as a suspected person, he even joined in public the party of those who ridiculed the whole as a chimera.[1] More privately, however, and in his posthu-

[1] In the midst of his ridicule, however, it is easy to discover the tone of a writer who is laughing not *with* the laughers but *at* them. Andrea laughed at those follies of the scheme which he well knew that the general folly of the age had compelled him to interweave with it against his own better judgment.

mous memoirs of himself, we find that he nowhere disavows the works. Indeed the bare fact of his being confessedly the author of the *Chemical Nuptials of Christian Rosycross* — a hero never before heard of—is alone sufficient to vindicate his claim. But, further, if Andrea were not the author, who was? Heidegger in his *Historia Vitæ Jo. Ludov. Fabricii* maintains that Jung, the celebrated mathematician of Hamburg, founded the sect of Rosicrucians and wrote the *Fama*: but on what ground? Simply on the authority of Albert Fabricius, who reported the story in casual conversation as derived from a secretary of the court of Heidelberg. (See the *Acta Eruditorum Lipsiensia*, 1698, p. 172.) Others have brought forward a claim for Giles Gutmann, supported by no other argument than that he was a distinguished mystic in that age of mysticism.

Morhof (*Polyhist.* i. p. 131, ed. Lubecæ, 1732) has a remark which, if true, might leave Andrea in possession of the authorship without therefore ascribing to him any influence in the formation of the Rosicrucian order: "*Fuere*," says he, "*non priscis tantum seculis collegia talia occulta, sed et superiori seculo* (i.e. *sexto-decimo*) *de Fraternitate Roseæ Crucis fama percrebuit.*" According to this remark,[1] the order existed in the sixteenth century,—that is, before the year 1600: now, if so, the three books in question are not to be considered as an anticipation of the order, but as its history. Here then the question arises — Was the brotherhood of Rosicrucians, as described in these books, an historical matter of fact or a romance? That it was a pure romantic fiction might be shown by arguments far more than I can admit. The *Universal Reformation* (the first of the three works) was borrowed from the "*Generale Riforma dell' Universo dai sette Savii della Grecia e da altri Letterati, publicata di ordine di Apollo,*" which occurs in the *Raguaglio di Parnasso* of Boccalini. It is true that the earliest edition of the *Raguaglio* which I have seen bears the date of 1615 (*in Milano*); but there was an edition of the first *Centuria* in 1612. Indeed

[1] Which has been adopted by many of the learned: see Arnold's *Hist. of the Church and of Heretics*, book ii. p. 245; Bruckeri *Hist. Crit. Philosophiæ*, tom. IV. p. 735, sq.; Nicolai, *On the charges against the Templars*, part I. p. 164; Herder's *Letters on Nicolai's Work* in the *German Mercury* for 1782.

Boccalini himself was cudgelled to death in 1613 (see *Mazzuchelli—Scrittori d'Italia*, vol. ii. p. iii. p. 1378). As to the *Fama*, which properly contains the pretended history of the order, it teems with internal arguments against itself. The House of the Holy Ghost exists for two centuries, and is seen by nobody. Father Rosycross dies, and none of the order even knew where he is buried, and yet afterwards it appears that eight brothers witnessed his death and his burial. He builds himself a magnificent sepulchre, with elaborate symbolic decorations; and yet for 120 years it remains undiscovered. The society offers its treasures and its mysteries to the world; and yet no reference to place or person is assigned to direct the inquiries of applicants. Finally, to say nothing of the *Vocabularium* of Paracelsus, which must have been put into the grave before it existed, the Rosicrucians are said to be Protestants, though founded upwards of a century before the Reformation. In short, the fiction is monstrous, and betrays itself in every circumstance. Whosoever was its author must be looked upon as the founder in effect of the Rosicrucian order, inasmuch as this fiction was the accidental occasion of such an order's being really founded. That Andrea was that author I shall now prove by one final argument: it is a presumptive argument, but in my opinion conclusive. *The armorial bearings of Andrea's family were a St. Andrew's Cross and four Roses.* By the order of the Rosy-cross he means therefore an order founded by himself.[1]

Chapter IV

Of the Immediate Results of the Fama *and the* Confessio *in Germany.*

The sensation which was produced throughout Germany by the works in question is sufficiently evidenced by the

---

[1] Nicolai supposes that the *rose* was assumed as the symbol of secrecy, and the *cross* to express the solemnity of the oath by which the vow of secrecy was ratified. Such an allegoric meaning is not inconsistent with that which I have assigned, and may have been a secondary purpose of Andrea. Some authors have insisted on the words *Sub Umbra Alarum tuarum Jehova*,—which stand at the end of the *Fama Fraternitatis*—as furnishing the initial letters of *Johannes Val. Andrea, Stipendiata Tubingensis*. But on this I have not thought it necessary to lay much stress.

repeated editions of them which appeared between 1614 and
1617, but still more by the prodigious commotion which
followed in the literary world. In the library at Gottingen
there is a body of letters addressed to the imaginary order of
Father Rosycross from 1614 to 1617 by persons offering
themselves as members. These letters are filled with com-
plimentary expressions and testimonies of the highest respect,
and are all printed—the writers alleging that, being unacquainted with the address of the society (as well they
might), they could not send them through any other than a
public channel. As certificates of their qualifications, most
of the candidates have inclosed specimens of their skill in
alchemy and cabbalism. Some of the letters are signed with
initials only, or with fictitious names, but assign real places
of address. Many other literary persons there were at that
day who forbore to write letters to the society, but threw out
small pamphlets containing their opinions of the order, and
of its place of residence. Each successive writer pretended
to be better informed on that point than all his predecessors.
Quarrels arose ; partisans started up on all sides ; the uproar
and confusion became indescribable ; cries of heresy and
atheism resounded from every corner ; some were for calling
in the secular power ; and, the more coyly the invisible
society retreated from the public advances, so much the more
eager and amorous were its admirers, and so much the more
bloodthirsty its antagonists Meantime there were some who
from the beginning had escaped the general delusion ; and
there were many who had gradually recovered from it. It was
remarked that of the many printed letters to the society,
though courteously and often learnedly written, none had
been answered ; and all attempts to penetrate the darkness in
which the order was shrouded by its unknown memorialist
were successively baffled. Hence arose a suspicion that some
bad designs lurked under the ostensible purposes of these
mysterious publications : a suspicion which was naturally
strengthened by what now began to follow. Many vile
impostors arose who gave themselves out for members of the
Rosicrucian order, and, upon the credit which they thus
obtained for a season, cheated numbers of their money by
alchemy, or of their health by panaceas. Three in particular

made a great noise,—at Wetzlar, at Nuremberg, and at Augsburg: all were punished by the magistracy; one lost his ears in running the gauntlet, and one was hanged. At this crisis stepped forward a powerful writer, who attacked the supposed order with much scorn and homely good sense: this was Andrew Libau. He exposed the impracticability of the meditated reformation, the incredibility of the legend of Father Rosycross, and the hollowness of the pretended sciences which they professed. He pointed the attention of governments to the confusions which these impostures were producing, and predicted from them a renewal of the scenes which had attended the fanaticism of the Anabaptists. These writings (of which two were Latin, Frankfurt, 1615, folio, one in German, Erfurt, 1616, 8vo), added to others of the same tendency, would possibly have laid the storm by causing the suppression of all the Rosicrucian books and pretensions; but this termination of the *mania* was defeated by two circumstances. The first was the conduct of the Paracelsists. With frantic eagerness they had sought to press into the imaginary order; but, finding themselves lamentably repulsed in all their efforts, at length they paused; and, turning suddenly round, they said to one another—" What need to court this perverse order any longer? We are ourselves Rosicrucians as to all the essential marks laid down in the three books. We also are holy persons of great knowledge; we also make gold, or shall make it · we also, no doubt, give us but time, shall reform the world: external ceremonies are nothing: substantially it is clear that we are the Rosicrucian Order." Upon this, they went on in numerous books and pamphlets to assert that they were the very identical order instituted by Father Rosycross and described in the *Fama Fraternitatis*. The public mind was now perfectly distracted; no man knew what to think; and the uproar became greater than ever. The other circumstance which defeated the tendency of Libau's exertions was the conduct of Andrea and his friends. Clear it is that Andrea enjoyed the scene of confusion, until he began to be sensible that he had called up an apparition which it was beyond his art to lay. Well knowing that, in all that great crowd of aspirants who were knocking clamorously for admittance into the airy college of Father Rosycross, though one and all pretended to be enamoured of that mystic wisdom he had promised, yet by far the majority were in fact enamoured of that *gold* which he had hinted at,—it is evident that his satirical [1] propensities were violently tickled : and he was willing to keep up the hubbub of delusion by flinging out a couple of pamphlets amongst the hungry crowd, which tended to amuse them. These were, 1. *Epistola ad Reverendam Fraternitatem R. Crucis. Francof.* 1613 ; 2. *Assertio Fraternitatis R. C. a quodam Fratern. ejus Socio Carmine Expressa,* Franc. 1614 : which last was translated into German in 1616, and again, in 1618, into German rhyme under the title of *Ara Fœderis Therapici,* or Altar of the *Healing* Fraternity (the most general abstraction of the pretensions made for the Rosicrucians being that they healed both the body and the mind). All this, in a young man and a professed satirist, was natural and excusable. But in a few years Andrea was shocked to find that the delusion had taken firm root in the public mind. Of the many authors who wrote with a sincere design to countenance the notion of a pretended Rosicrucian society I shall here mention a few of the most memorable : — 1. A writer calling himself *Julianus a Campis* wrote expressly to account for the Rosicrucians not revealing themselves and not answering the letters addressed to them. He was himself, he said, a member of the order ; but in all his travels he had met but three other members,—there being (as he presumed) no more persons on the earth worthy of being entrusted with its mysteries. The Rosicrucian wisdom was to be more exten-

[1] I have no doubt that Andrea alludes to his own high diversion on this occasion in the following passage of a later work (*Mythologia Christiana*) which he printed at Strasburg in 1619. It is *Truth* (*die Alethia*) who is speaking : " *Planissime nihil cum hac Fraternitate (sc. Ros. Crucis) commune habeo. Nam, cum paullo ante lusum quendam ingeniosiorem personatus aliquis* (no doubt himself) *in literario foro agere vellet, nihil motus sum libellis inter se conflictantibus, sed velut in scena prodeuntes histriones non sine voluptate spectari* "—Like *Miss in her Teens* (in the excellent farce of Garrick), who so much enjoys the prospect of a battle between her two lovers, Andrea, instead of calming the tumult which he had caused, was disposed at first to cry out to the angry polemics—" Stick him, Captain Flash ; do stick him, Captain Flash."

sively diffused in future, but still not to be hawked about in market-places.—2. Julius Sperber, of Anhalt-Dessau (according to common repute), wrote [1] the "*Echo of the divinely illuminated fraternity of the admirable order of the R. C.*" In this there is a passage which I recommend to the especial notice of Free-masons:—Having maintained the probability of the Rosicrucian pretensions on the ground that such *magnalia Dei* had from the creation downwards been confided to the keeping of a few individuals,—agreeably to which he affirms that Adam was the first Rosicrucian of the Old Testament and Simeon the last,—he goes on to ask whether the Gospel put an end to the secret tradition? By no means, he answers: Christ established a new "college of magic" amongst his disciples, and the greater mysteries were revealed to St. John and St. Paul. In this passage, which I shall notice farther on, we find the Grand-Master and the St. John of Masonry.—3. Radtich Brotoffer was not so much a Cabbalist, like Julius Sperber, as an Alchemist. He understood the three Rosicrucian books not in a literal or historical sense, but allegorically as a description of the art of making gold and finding the philosopher's stone. He even favoured the public with an interpretation of it; so that both "*materia et præparatio lapidis aurei*" was laid bare to the profane. With this practical test of his own pretensions, it might have been supposed that Brotoffer would have exposed himself as an impostor; but on the contrary his works sold well, and were several times reprinted.—4. A far more important person in the history of Rosicrucianism was Michael Maier. He it was that first transplanted it into England, where (as we shall see) it led ultimately to more lasting effects than in Germany. He was born in Holstein, and was physician to the Emperor Rudolph II; who, being possessed by the mystical frenzy of the age, sent for him to Prague. In 1622 he died at Magdeburg, having previously travelled extensively and particularly to England. His works are among the

---

[1] This was printed at Dantzig in 1616. Nicolai, however, cites an edition printed in 1615. Whether Sperber was the author is a point not quite settled. Katzauer, in his *Dissert. de Rosæcrucianis*, p. 38, takes him for the same person as Julianus a Campis: but from internal grounds this is very improbable.

rarities of bibliography, and fetch very high prices. The first of them which concerns our present inquiry is that entitled *Jocus Severus: Francof.* 1617. It is addressed (in a dedication written on his road from England to Bohemia), "*omnibus Veræ Chymiæ amantibus per Germaniam,*" and amongst them more especially "*illi ordini adhuc delitescenti, ut Fama Fraternitatis et Confessione sua admiranda et probabili manifestato.*" This work, it appears, had been written in England. On his return to Germany he became acquainted with the fierce controversy on the Rosicrucian sect; and, as he firmly believed in the existence of such a sect, he sought to introduce himself to its notice; but, finding this impossible, he set himself to establish such an order by his own efforts; and in his future writings he spoke of it as already existing,—going so far even as to publish its laws (which indeed had previously been done by the author of the *Echo*). From the principal work which he wrote on this subject, entitled *Silentium post Clamores*,[1] I shall make an extract, because in this work it is that we meet with the first traces of Masonry. "Nature is yet but half unveiled. What we "want is chiefly experiment and tentative inquiry. Great, "therefore, are our obligations to the Rosicrucians for labour-"ing to supply this want. Their weightiest mystery is a "Universal Medicine. Such a Catholicon lies hid in nature. "It is, however, no simple, but a very compound, medicine. "For out of the meanest pebbles and weeds medicine, *and* "*even gold*, is to be extracted."—"He that doubts the exist-"ence of the R. C. should recollect that the Greeks, "Egyptians, Arabians, etc., had such secret societies; where, "then, is the absurdity in their existing at this day? Their "maxims of self-discipline are these—To honour and fear "God above all things; to do all the good in their power to "their fellow-men;" and so on.—"What is contained in the "*Fama* and *Confessio* is true. It is a very childish objection "that the brotherhood have promised so much and per-

---

[1] "Silentium post Clamores, h. e. Tractatus Apologeticus, quo causæ non solum *Clamorum* (seu revelationum) Fraternitatis Germanicæ de R. C., sed et *Silentii* (seu non redditæ ad singulorum vota responsionis) traduntur et demonstrantur. Autore Michaele Maiero, Imp. Consist. Comite, et Med. Doct. Francof. 1617."

"formed so little. With them, as elsewhere, many are
called, but few chosen. The masters of the order hold out
the rose as a remote prize, but they impose the cross on
those who are entering."[1]—"Like the Pythagoreans and
Egyptians, the Rosicrucians exact vows of silence and
secrecy. Ignorant men have treated the whole as a fiction;
but this has arisen from the five years' probation to which
they subject even well-qualified novices before they are
admitted to the higher mysteries: within this period they
are to learn how to govern their tongues."—In the same
year with this book he published a work of Robert Fludd's
(with whom he had lived on friendly terms in England), *De
Vita, Morte, et Resurrectione*.[2] Of other works, which he
published afterwards, I shall here say nothing: neither
shall I detain my reader with any account of his fellow-
labourers in this path — Theophilus Schweighart of Con-
stance, Josephus Stellatus, or Giles Gutmann.

The books I have mentioned were enough to convince
Andreä that his romance had succeeded in a way which he
had never designed. The public had accredited the *charlatanerie* of his books, but gave no welcome to that for the sake
of which this *charlatanerie* was adopted as a vehicle. The
Alchemy had been approved, the moral and religious scheme
slighted. And societies were forming even amongst the
learned upon the basis of all that was false in the system, to
the exclusion of all that was true. This was a spectacle
which could no longer be viewed in the light of a joke: the
folly was becoming too serious; and Andreä set himself to
counteract it with all his powers. For this purpose he now
published his *Chemical Nuptials of Christian Rosycross*, which
he had written in 1601-2 (when only in his sixteenth year),
but not printed. This is a comic romance of extraordinary
talent, the covert purpose of it being a refined and delicate
banter of the Pedants, Theosophists, Goldmakers, and En-
thusiasts of every class, with whom Germany at that time
swarmed. In his former works he had treated the Paracelsists with forbearance, hoping by such treatment to have

---

[1] Ecce innumeri adsunt ex vocatis, seseque offerunt: at non audiuntur a magistris R. Crucis, qui rosas ostentant, at crucem exhibent. P. 77.   [2] Robert Fludd, 1574-1637.—M.

won them over to his own elevated designs; but in this they were invested with the cap and bells. Unfortunately for the purpose of Andrea, however, even this romance was swallowed by the public as true and serious history. Upon this, in the following year, he published a collection of satirical dialogues under the title of *Menippus; sive Dial. Satyricorum Centuria, inanitatum nostratium Speculum.* In this he more openly unveils his true design—revolution of method in the arts and sciences, and a general religious reformation. The efforts of Andrea were seconded by those of his friends, especially of Irenæus, Agnostus, and of Joh. Val. Alberti under the name of Menapius. Both wrote with great energy against the Rosicrucians: the former, indeed, from having ironically styled himself "an unworthy clerk of the Fraternity of the R. C.," has been classed by some learned writers on the Rosicrucians as one of that sect; but it is impossible to read his writings without detecting the lurking satire. Soon after these writers a learned foreigner placed the Rosicrucian pretensions in a still more ludicrous light: this was the celebrated Thomas Campanella. In his work upon the Spanish Monarchy, which was translated into German, published, and universally read in Germany some time [1] before the original work appeared, the Italian philosopher—speaking of the follies of the age—thus expresses himself of the R. C.: "That the whole of
"Christendom teems with such heads (viz. Reformation-
"jobbers) we have one proof more than was wanted in
"the Fraternity of the R. C. For scarcely was that
"absurdity hatched when—notwithstanding it was many
"times declared to be nothing more than a *lusus ingenii*
"*nimium lascivientis*, a mere hoax of some man of wit
"troubled with a superfluity of youthful spirits—yet, be-
"cause it dealt in reformations and in pretences to mystical
"arts, straightway from every country in Christendom pious
"and learned men, passively surrendering themselves dupes
"to this delusion, made offers of their good wishes and

[1] It was published in 1620,—at which time Campanella was confined in prison at Naples. The publishers had obtained the original copy either from some traveller or during their own residence in Italy.

"services: some by name; others anonymously, but con-
"stantly maintaining that the brothers of the R. C.
"could easily discover their names by Solomon's mirror
"or other cabbalistic means. Nay, to such a pass of ab-
"surdity did they advance that they represented the first of
"the three Rosicrucian books (the *Universal Reformation*) as
"a high mystery, and expounded it in a chemical sense as
"if it had contained a cryptical account of the art of gold-
"making, whereas it is nothing more than a literal trans-
"lation, word for word, of the Parnasso of Boccalini."
The effect of all this ridicule and satire was that in Germany, as there is the best reason to believe, no regular lodge of Rosicrucians was ever established. Des Cartes, who had heard a great deal of talk about them in 1619, during his residence at Frankfort-on-the-Maine, sought to connect himself with some lodge (for which he was afterwards exposed to the ridicule of his enemies); but the impossibility of finding any body of them formally connected together, and a perusal of the Rosicrucian writings, satisfied him in the end that no such order was in existence. Many years after, Leibnitz came to the same conclusion. He was actually connected in early life with a soi-disant society of the R. C. in Nuremberg,—for even at this day there is obviously nothing to prevent any society in any place from assuming that or any other title; but that they were not connected traditionally with the alleged society of Father Rosycross Leibnitz was convinced. "Il me paroit," says he, in a letter to a friend published by Feller in the *Otium Hannoveranum* (p. 222), "il me paroit que tout ce que l'on "a dit des Freres de la Croix de la Rose est une pure in-
"vention de quelque personne ingenieuse." And again, so late as the year 1696, he says in another letter—"Fratres
"Roseæ Crucis fictitios fuisse suspicor; quod et Helmontius
"mihi confirmavit." Adepts there were here and there, it is true, and even whole clubs of swindlers, who called themselves Rosicrucians: thus Ludov. Conr. Orvius, in his *Occulta Philosophia, sive Cœlum Sapientum et Vexatio Stultorum*, tells a lamentable tale of such a society, pretending to deduce themselves from Father Rosycross, who were settled at the Hague in 1622, and, after swindling him out of his

own and his wife's fortune, amounting to eleven thousand dollars, kicked him out of the order, with the assurance that they would murder him if he revealed their secrets: "which secrets," says he, "I have faithfully kept, and for "the same reason that women keep secrets—viz. because I "have none to reveal; for their knavery is no secret." There is a well-known story also in Voltaire's Diction. Philosoph., Art. *Alchimiste,* of a rogue who cheated the Duke of Bouillon of 40,000 dollars under the masque of Rosicrucianism. But these were cases for the police-office, and the gross impostures of jail-birds. As the aberration of learned men, and as a case for the satirist, Rosicrucianism received a shock from the writings of its accidental father, Andrea, and others, such as in Germany[1] it never recovered. And hence it has happened that, whatever number there may have been of individual mystics calling themselves Rosicrucians, no collective body of Rosicrucians acting in conjunction was ever matured and actually established in Germany. In England the case was otherwise; for there, as I shall show, the order still subsists under a different name. But this will furnish matter for a separate chapter. Meantime one word remains to be said of Andrea's labours with respect to the Rosicrucians He was not content with opposing gravely and satirically the erroneous societies which

---

[1] In France it never had even a momentary success. It was met by the ridicule of P. Garasse and of Gabriel Naudé in his *Instruction à la France sur la verité de l'histoire des Frères de la Rose-Croix*: Paris, 1623; and in *Le Mascurat,* a rare work printed in 1624, and of which the second edition, 1650, is still rarer. Independently of these works, France was at that time the rival of Italy in science, and had greatly the start of Germany and England in general illumination. She was thus sufficiently protected from such a delusion.—Thus far Professor Buhle. But, *pace tua,* worthy Professor, I—the translator of your book—affirm that France had *not* the start of England, nor wanted then or since the ignobler elements of credulity, as the history of Animal Magnetism and many other fantastic follies before *that* have sufficiently shown. But she has always wanted the nobler (*i.e.* the imaginative) elements of credulity. On this account the French have always been an irreligious people. And the scheme of Father Rosycross was too much connected with religious feelings, and moved too much under a religious impulse, to recommend itself to the French. This reason apart, however, accident had much to do with the ill fortune of Rosicrucianism in France.

learned men were attempting to found upon his own romance of the *Fama Fraternitatis*, but laboured more earnestly than ever to mature and to establish that genuine society for the propagation of truth which had been the real though misinterpreted object of his romance and indeed of his whole life. Such a society he lived to see accomplished: and, in order to mark upon what foundation he placed all hopes of any great improvement in the condition of human nature, he called it by the name of *The Christian Fraternity*. This fact I have recorded in order to complete the account of Andrea's history in relation to Rosicrucianism; but I shall not further pursue the history of *The Christian Fraternity*,[1] as it is no ways connected with the subject of my present inquiry.

Chapter V

Of the Origin of Free-masonry in England

Thus I have traced the history of Rosicrucianism from its birth in Germany; and I have ended with showing that, from the energetic opposition and ridicule which it latterly incurred, no college or lodge of Rosicrucian brethren, professing occult knowledge and communicating it under solemn forms and vows of secrecy, can be shown from historical records to have been ever established in Germany. I shall now undertake to prove that Rosicrucianism was transplanted to England, where it flourished under a new name, under which name it has been since re-exported to us in common with the other countries of Christendom. For I affirm, as the main thesis of my concluding labours, THAT FREE-MASONRY IS NEITHER MORE NOR LESS THAN ROSICRUCIANISM AS MODIFIED BY THOSE WHO TRANSPLANTED IT INTO ENGLAND.

At the beginning of the seventeenth century many learned heads in England were occupied with Theosophy, Cabbalism, and Alchemy: amongst the proofs of this (for many of which

---

[1] See the *Invitatio Fraternitatis Christi ad Sacri Amoris candidatos*, Argentor. 1617; the *Christianæ Societatis Idea*, Tubingæ, 1624; the *Veræ Unionis in Christo Jesu Specimen*, Norimb. 1628; and other works on the same subject. A list of the members composing this Christian Brotherhood, which continued its labours after Andrea's death, is still preserved.

see the *Athenæ Oxonienses*) may be cited the works of John Pordage, of Norbert, of Thomas and Samuel Norton, but above all (in reference to our present inquiry) of Robert Fludd.[1] Fludd it was, or whosoever was the author of the *Summum Bonum*, 1629, that must be considered as the immediate father of Free-masonry, as Andrea was its remote father. What was the particular occasion of his own first acquaintance with Rosicrucianism is not recorded: all the books of Alchemy or other occult knowledge published in Germany were at that time immediately carried over to England—provided they were written in Latin; and, if written in German, were soon translated for the benefit of English students. He may therefore have gained his knowledge immediately from the three Rosicrucian books. But it is more probable that he acquired his knowledge on this head from his friend Maier (mentioned in the preceding chapter), who was intimate with Fludd during his stay in England, and corresponded with him after he left it. At all events he must have been initiated into Rosicrucianism at an early period, having published his *Apology*[2] for it in the year 1617. This indeed is denied to be his work, though ascribed to him in the title-page: but, be that as it may, it was at any rate the work of the same author who wrote the *Summum Bonum*,[3] being expressly claimed by him at p. 39. If not Fludd's, it was the work of a friend of Fludd's; and, as the name is of no importance, I shall continue to refer to it as Fludd's—having once apprised my reader that I mean by Fludd the author, be he who he may, of those two works. Now, the first question which arises is this: For what reason did Fludd drop the name of Rosicrucians? The reason was briefly

---

[1] John Pordage, 1625-1698; Robert Fludd (Latinised as "De Fluctibus"), 1574-1637.

[2] Tractatus Apologeticus, integritatem Societatis de Rosea Cruce defendens Authore Roberto De Fluctibus, Anglo, M D.L. Lugd. Bat. 1617.

[3] This work was disavowed by Fludd. But, as the principles, the style, the animosity towards Mersenne, the publisher, and the year, were severally the same in this as in the *Sophiæ cum Moria Certamen* —which Fludd acknowledged,—there cannot be much reason to doubt that it was his. Consult the "Catalogue of some Rare Books," by G Serpilius, No. II. p. 238.

this: His Apology for the Rosicrucians was attacked by the celebrated Father Mersenne. To this Fludd replied, under the name of Joachim Fritz, in two witty but coarse books entitled *Summum Bonum* and *Sophiæ cum Moria Certamen*; in the first of which, to the question—"Where the Rosicrucians resided?" he replied thus—"In the houses of God, where Christ is the corner-stone"; and he explained the symbols of the Rose and Cross in a new sense, as meaning "the Cross sprinkled with the rosy blood of Christ." Mersenne being obviously no match for Fludd either in learning or in polemic wit, Gassendi stepped forward into his place and published (in 1630) an excellent rejoinder to Fludd in his *Exercitatio Epistolica*, which analysed and ridiculed the principles of Fludd in general, and in particular reproached him with his belief in the romantic legend of the Rosicrucians. Upon this, Fludd, finding himself hard pressed under his conscious inability to assign their place of abode, evades the question, in his answer to Gassendi (published in 1633), by formally withdrawing the name *Rosicrucians*: for, having occasion to speak of them, he calls them "*Fratres R. C. olim sic dicti, quos nos hodie Sapientes (Sophos) vocamus; omisso illo nomine, tanquam odioso miseris mortalibus velo ignorantiæ obductis, et in oblivione hominum jam fere sepulto.*" Here then we have the negative question answered—why and when they ceased to be called Rosicrucians. But now comes a second, or affirmative question—why and when they began to be called Free-masons. In 1633 we have seen that the old name was abolished, but as yet no new name was substituted; in default of such a name, they were styled *ad interim* by the general term *Wise Men*. This, however, being too vague an appellation for men who wished to form themselves into a separate and exclusive society, a new one was to be devised, bearing a more special allusion to their characteristic objects. Now, the immediate hint for the name Masons was derived from the legend, contained in the *Fama Fraternitatis*, of the "House of the Holy Ghost." Where and what was that house? This had been a subject of much speculation in Germany; and many had been simple enough to understand the expression of a literal house, and had inquired after it up and down the Empire. But

Andreä had himself made it impossible to understand it in any other than an allegoric sense, by describing it as a building that would remain "invisible to the godless world for ever." Theophilus Schweighart also had spoken of it thus: "It is a building," says he, "a great "building, *carens fenestris et foribus*,—a princely, nay an "imperial palace,—everywhere visible, and yet not seen by "the eyes of man." This building in fact represented the purpose or object of the Rosicrucians. And what was that? It was the secret wisdom, or in their language *magic*—(viz. 1. Philosophy of Nature, or occult knowledge of the works of God; 2. Theology, or the occult knowledge of God himself; 3. Religion, or God's occult intercourse with the spirit of man)—which they imagined to have been transmitted from Adam through the Cabbalists to themselves. But they distinguished between a carnal and a spiritual knowledge of this magic. The spiritual knowledge is the business of Christianity, and is symbolised by Christ himself as a rock, and as a building of which he is the head and the foundation. What rock, and what building? says Fludd. A spiritual rock, and a building of human nature, in which men are the stones and Christ the corner-stone.[1] But how shall stones move and arrange themselves into a building? They must become living stones: "*Transmutemini, transmutemini*," says Fludd, "*de lapidibus mortuis in lapides vivos philosophicos.*" But what is a living stone? A living stone is a *mason* who builds himself up into the wall as a part of the temple of human nature: "*Viam hujusmodi transmutationis nos docet Apostolus dum ait — Eadem mens sit in vobis quæ est in Jesu.*" In these passages we see the rise of the allegoric name *masons* upon the extinction of the former name. But Fludd expresses this allegory still more plainly

---

[1] *Summum Bonum*, p. 37. "*Concludimus igitur quod Jesus sit templi humani lapis angularis; atque ita ex mortuis lapides vivi facti sunt homines pii; idque transmutatione reali ab Adami lapsi statu in statum suæ innocentiæ et perfectionis*—i.e. *a vili et leprosa plumbi conditione in auri purissimi perfectionem.*" Masonic readers will remember a ceremony used on the introduction of a new member which turns upon this distinction between lead and gold as the symbol of transition from the lost state of Adam to the original condition of innocence and perfection.

elsewhere: "*Denique*," says he, "*qualiter debent operari Fratres ad gemmæ istiusmodi* (meaning *magic*) *inquisitionem nos docet pagina sacra.*" How, then? *Nos docet Apostolus ad mysterii perfectionem vel sub Agricolæ vel Architecti typo pertingere*";— either under the image of a husbandman who cultivates a field, or of an architect who builds a house: and, had the former type been adopted, we should have had *Free-husbandmen*, instead of *Free-masons*. Again, in another place, he says, "*Atque sub istiusmodi Architecti typo nos monet Propheta ut ædificemus Domum Sapientiæ.*" The society was therefore to be a *masonic* society, in order to represent typically that temple of the Holy Spirit which it was their business to erect in the spirit of man. This temple was the abstract of the doctrine of Christ, who was the Grand-Master: hence the light from the *East*, of which so much is said in Rosicrucian and Masonic books. St. John was the beloved disciple of Christ: hence the solemn celebration of his festival. Having, moreover, once adopted the attributes of masonry as the figurative expression of their objects, they were led to attend more minutely to the legends and history of that art; and in these again they found an occult analogy with their own relations to the Christian Wisdom. The first great event in the art of Masonry was the building of the Tower of Babel: this expressed figuratively the attempt of some unknown Mason to build up the temple of the Holy Ghost in anticipation of Christianity,—which attempt, however, had been confounded by the vanity of the builders. The building of Solomon's Temple, the second great incident in the art, had an obvious meaning as a prefiguration of Christianity. Hiram,[1] simply the architect of this temple to the real professors of the art of building, was to the English Rosicrucians a type of Christ; and the legend of Masons, which represented this Hiram as having been murdered by his fellow-workmen, made the type still more striking. The two pillars also, *Jachin* and *Boaz*[2] (strength and power),

---

[1] The name of Hiram was understood by the elder Free-masons as an anagram. H I. R. A. M meant Homo Jesus Redemptor AnimaruM Others explained the name Homo Jesus Rex Altissimus Mundi Others added a C to the Hiram, in order to make it CHristus Jesus, etc.

[2] See the account of these pillars in the 1st Book of Kings, vii. 14-22, where it is said—"And there stood upon the pillars as it were

which are amongst the memorable singularities in Solomon's Temple, have an occult meaning to the Free-masons; which, however, I shall not undertake publicly to explain. This symbolic interest to the English Rosicrucians in the attributes, incidents, and legends of the art exercised by the literal Masons of real life naturally brought the two orders into some connexion with each other. They were thus enabled to realise to their eyes the symbols of their own allegories; and the same building which accommodated the guild of builders in their professional meetings offered a desirable means of secret assemblies to the early Free-masons. An apparatus of implements and utensils, such as were presented in the fabulous sepulchre of Father Rosycross, were here actually brought together. And, accordingly, it is upon record that the first formal and solemn lodge of Free-masons, —on occasion of which the very name of Free-masons was first publicly made known,—was held in Mason's Hall, Mason's Alley, Basinghall Street, London, in the year 1646. Into this lodge it was that Ashmole the antiquary was admitted. Private meetings there may doubtless have been before; and one at Warrington (half-way between Liverpool and Manchester) is expressly mentioned in the life of Ashmole; but the name of a Free-mason's Lodge, with all the insignia, attributes, and circumstances of a lodge, first came forward in the page of history on the occasion I have mentioned. It is perhaps in requital of the services at that time rendered in the loan of their hall, etc., that the guild of Masons as a body, and where they are not individually objectionable, enjoy a precedency of all orders of men in the right to admission, and pay only half-fees. Ashmole, by the way, whom I have just mentioned as one of the earliest Free-masons, appears from his writings to have been a zealous Rosicrucian.[1] Other members of the lodge were Thomas

Roses." This may be taken as a free translation of the first passage in verse 20. Compare 2d Book of Chron. iii. 17.

[1] When Ashmole [Elias Ashmole, 1617-1692.—M.] speaks of the antiquity of Free-masonry, he is to be understood either as confounding the order of philosophic masons with that of the handicraft masons (as many have done), or simply as speaking the language of Rosicrucians, who (as we have shown) carry up their traditional pretensions to Adam as the first professor of the secret wisdom. In Florence,

Wharton, a physician, George Wharton, Oughtred the mathematician, Dr. Hewitt, Dr. Pearson the divine, and William Lilly, the principal astrologer of the day.[1] All the members, it must be observed, had annually assembled to hold a festival of astrologers *before* they were connected into a lodge bearing the title of Free-masons. This previous connexion had no doubt paved the way for the latter.

I shall now sum up the results of my inquiry into the origin and nature of Free-masonry, and shall then conclude with a brief notice of one or two collateral questions growing out of popular errors on the main one.

I. The original Free-masons were a society that arose out of the Rosicrucian mania, certainly within the thirteen years from 1633 to 1646, and probably between 1633 and 1640. Their object was *magic* in the cabbalistic sense: *i.e* the *occult wisdom* transmitted from the beginning of the world, and matured by Christ; to communicate this when they had it, to search for it when they had it not; and both under an oath of secrecy.

II. This object of Free-masonry was represented under the form of Solomon's Temple—as a type of the true Church, whose corner-stone is Christ. This Temple is to be built of men, or living stones; and the true method and art of building with men it is the province of *magic* to teach. Hence it is that all the masonic symbols either refer to Solomon's Temple or are figurative modes of expressing the ideas and doctrines of *magic* in the sense of the Rosicrucians and their mystical predecessors in general.

III. The Free-masons, having once adopted symbols, etc., from the art of masonry, to which they were led by the language of Scripture, went on to connect themselves in a certain degree with the order itself of handicraft masons, and adopted their distribution of members into apprentices, journeymen, and masters.—Christ is the Grand-Master, and was put to death whilst laying the foundation of the temple of human nature.

about the year 1512, there were two societies (the *Compagnia della Cazzuola* and the *Compagnia del Pajuolo*) who assumed the mason's hammer as their sign; but these were merely convivial clubs. See the life of J. F. Rustici in Vasari—*Vite dei Pittori*, etc. Roma· 1760, p. 76

[1] Thomas Wharton, M.D., 1610-1673; Sir George Wharton, 1617-1681; Oughtred, 1574-1660; Dr. John Hewitt, ——1658; Pearson, 1613-1686; William Lilly, 1602-1682.—M.

IV. The Jews were particularly excluded from the original lodges of Free-masons as being the great enemies of the Grand-Master. For the same reason, in a less degree, were excluded Mohamedans and Pagans.—The reasons for excluding Roman Catholics were these:—First, the original Free-masons were Protestants in an age when Protestants were in the liveliest hostility to Papists, and in a country which had suffered deeply from Popish cruelty. They could not therefore be expected to view popery with the languid eyes of modern indifference. Secondly, the Papists were excluded prudentially, on account of their intolerance: for it was a distinguishing feature of the Rosicrucians and Free-masons that *they* first [1] conceived the idea of a society which should

[1] It is well known that until the latter end of the seventeenth century all churches and the best men discountenanced the doctrine of religious toleration in fact they rejected it with horror, as a deliberate act of compromise with error: they were intolerant on principle, and persecuted on conscientious grounds It is among the glories of Jeremy Taylor and Milton that, in so intolerant an age, they fearlessly advocated the necessity of mutual toleration as a Christian duty. Jeremy Taylor in particular is generally supposed to have been the very earliest champion of toleration in his *Liberty of Prophesying*, first published in 1647, and the present Bishop of Calcutta has lately asserted in his life of that great man (prefixed to the collected edition of his works, 1822) that "*The Liberty of Prophesying* is the *first* attempt on record to conciliate the minds of Christians to the reception of a doctrine which was then by every sect alike regarded as a perilous and portentous novelty" (p xxvii.); and again (at p. ccxi) his lordship calls it "the *first* work perhaps, since the earliest days of Christianity, to teach the art of differing harmlessly." Now, in the place where this assertion is made, —*i.e.* in the life of Jeremy Taylor—perhaps it is virtually a just assertion: for it cannot affect the claims of Jeremy Taylor that he was anticipated by authors whom in all probability he never read No doubt he owed the doctrine to his own comprehensive intellect and the Christian magnanimity of his nature. Yet, in a history of the doctrine itself, it should not be overlooked that the *Summum Bonum* preceded the *Liberty of Prophesying* by eighteen years [A doctrine of Toleration far more absolute than that of Jeremy Taylor had been promulgated in tracts of the English Baptists from 1611 onwards, and had been preached, with memorable energy and eloquence, for the instruction of both sides of the Atlantic, by the Americanised Welshman, Roger Williams (founder of the state of Rhode Island) in his *Bloudy Tenent of Persecution for Cause of Conscience*, published in London in 1644 To this day there has been no advocacy of toleration so bold and exceptionless as that of Roger Williams, himself a fervid evangelical Puritan.—M.]

act on the principle of religious toleration, wishing that nothing should interfere with the most extensive co-operation in their plans except such differences about the essentials of religion as must make all sincere co-operation impossible. This fact is so little known, and is so eminently honourable to the spirit of Free-masonry, that I shall trouble the reader with a longer quotation in proof of it than I should otherwise have allowed myself. Fludd, in his *Summum Bonum* (Epilog p. 53), says:—" Quod, si quæratur cujus sint reli-
" gionis qui mystica ista Scripturarum interpretatione pollent,
" —viz. an Romanæ, Lutheranæ, Calvinianæ, etc.,—vel
" habeantne ipsi religionem aliquam sibi ipsis peculiarem et
" ab aliis divisam—facillimum erit ipsis respondere. Nam,
" cum omnes Christiani, cujuscunque religionis, tendant ad
" unam eandem metam (viz. ipsum Christum, qui est sola
" veritas), in hoc quidem unanimi consensu illæ omnes reli-
" giones conveniunt. At verò, quatenus religiones istæ in
" ceremoniis Ecclesiæ externis, humanis nempe inventionibus
" (cujusmodi sunt habitus varii Monachorum et Pontificum,
" crucis adoratio, imaginum approbatio vel abnegatio, luminum
" de nocte accensio, et infinita alia), discrepare videntur,—
" hæ quidem disceptationes sunt *præter* essentiales veræ
" Sapientiæ Mysticæ leges." [1]

V. Free-masonry, as it honoured all forms of Christianity, deeming them approximations more or less remote to the ideal truth, so it abstracted from all forms of civil polity as alien from its own objects—which, according to their briefest expressions, are 1. The Glory of God ; 2. The Service of Men.

[1] "But, if it is asked of what religion those are who excel in that
" mystical interpretation of the Scriptures—whether the Roman, the
" Lutheran, the Calvinian, &c., or whether they have some religion
" peculiar to themselves and distinct from others,—the answer is very
" easy. For, since all Christians, of whatsoever religion, tend to one
" and the same goal (viz Christ himself, who is the sole Truth) in this
" with unanimous consent all those religions meet. But, so far as
" those religions seem to differ in external church-ceremonies of human
" invention (of which sort are the various habits of monks and priests,
" the adoration of the Cross, the use or abnegation of images, the
" burning of lights at night, and endless other things),—these differ-
" ences are beyond the essential laws of the true mystical wisdom."
— M.

VI. There is nothing in the imagery, myths, ritual, or purposes of the elder Free-masonry which may not be traced to the romances of Father Rosycross, as given in the *Fama Fraternitatis*.

APPENDIX

[IN REFUTATION OF CERTAIN SPECULATIONS]

I. *That the object of the elder Free-masons was not to build Lord Bacon's imaginary temple of Solomon :—*

This was one of the hypotheses advanced by Nicolai. The House of Solomon, which Lord Bacon had sketched in his romantic fiction of the island of Bensalem (New Atlantis), Nicolai supposed that the elder Free-masons had sought to realise, and that forty years afterwards they had changed the Baconian house of Solomon into the Scriptural type of Solomon's Temple.—Whoever has read the *New Atlantis* of Bacon, and is otherwise acquainted with the relations in which this great man stood to the literature of his own times, will discover in this romance a gigantic sketch from the hand of a mighty scientific intellect, that had soared far above his age, and sometimes, on the heights to which he had attained, indulged in a dream of what might be accomplished by a rich state under a wise governor for the advancement of the arts and sciences. This sketch, agreeably to the taste of his century, he delivered in the form of an allegory, and feigned an island of Bensalem, upon which a society, composed on his model, had existed for a thousand years under the name of Solomon's House ; for the lawgiver of this island, who was also the founder of the society, had been indebted to Solomon for his wisdom. The object of this society was the extension of physical science ; on which account it was called the College of the Work of Six Days. Romance as all this was, it led to very beneficial results ; for it occasioned in the end the establishment of the Royal Society of London, which for nearly two centuries has continued to merit immortal honour in the department of physics. Allegory, however, it contains none, except in its idea and name. The House of Solomon is neither more nor less than a great academy of learned men, authorised and supported by the state, and endowed with a liberality approaching to profusion for all purposes of experiment and research. Beneficence, education of the young, support of the sick, cosmopolitism, are not the objects of this institution. The society is divided into classes according to the different objects of their studies; but it has no higher and lower degrees. None but learned men can be members; not, as in the masonic societies, every decent workman who is *sui juris*. Only the exoteric knowledge of nature, not the esoteric, is pursued by the House of Solomon. The Book of the Six Days is studied as a book that lies open before every man's eyes; by the Free-masons it was studied as a mystery which was to be illuminated by the light out of the East. Had the Free-masons designed to represent or to imitate the House of Solomon in their society, they would certainly have adopted the forms, constitution, costume, and attributes of that house as described by Bacon. They would have exerted themselves to produce or to procure a philosophical apparatus such as that house is represented as possessing; or would at least have delineated this apparatus upon their carpets by way of symbols. But nothing of all this was ever done. No mile-deep cellars, no mile-high towers, no lakes, marshes, or fountains, no botanic or kitchen gardens, no modelling-houses, perspective-houses, collections of minerals and jewels, etc., were ever formed by them, either literal or figurative. Universally the eldest Free-masonry was indifferent with respect to all profane sciences and all exoteric knowledge of nature. Its business was with a secret wisdom in which learned and unlearned were alike capable of initiation. And, in fact, the *exoterici*, at whose head Bacon stood, and who afterwards composed the Royal Society of London, were the antagonist party of the Theosophists, Cabbalists, and Alchemists, at the head of whom stood Fludd, and from whom Free-masonry took its rise.[1]

[1] There is besides in this hypothesis of Nicolai's a complete confusion of the *end* of the society with the *persons* composing it. The Free-masons wished to build the Temple of Solomon. But Lord Bacon's House of Solomon did not typify the *object* of his society: it was simply the *name* of it, and means no more than what is understood at present by an academy, i.e. a circle of learned men united for a common purpose. It would be just as absurd to say of the Academicians of Berlin—not that they composed or formed an Academy, but that they proposed, as their secret object, to build one.

II. *That the object of the elder Free-masons and the origin of the master's degree had no connexion with the restoration of Charles II:*—

This is another of the hypotheses advanced by Nicolai, and not more happy than that which we have just examined. He postulates that the elder Free-masons pretended to no mystery; and the more so because very soon after their first origin they were really engaged in a secret transaction, which made it in the highest degree necessary that their assemblies should wear no appearance of concealment, but should seem to be a plain and undisguised club of inquirers into natural philosophy. What was this secret transaction according to Mr Nicolai? Nothing less than the restoration of the Prince of Wales, afterwards King Charles II, to the throne of England. The members of the Masonic union, says he, were hostile to the Parliament and to Cromwell, and friendly to the Royal family. After the death of Charles I (1649) several people of rank united themselves with the Free-masons, because under this mask they could assemble and determine on their future measures. They found means to establish within this society a "secret conclave" which held meetings apart from the general meetings. This conclave adopted secret signs expressive of its grief for its murdered master, of its hopes to revenge him on his murderers, and of its search for the lost word or logos (the son) and its design to re-establish him on his father's throne. As faithful adherents of the Royal family, whose head the Queen had now become, they called themselves *Sons of the Widow*. In this way a secret connexion was established amongst all persons attached to the Royal family, as well in Great Britain and Ireland as in France and the Netherlands, which subsisted until after the death of Cromwell, and had the well-known issue for the royal cause. The analogies alleged by Nicolai between the historical events in the first period of Free-masonry and the symbols and mythi of the masonic degree of master are certainly very extraordinary; and one might easily be led to suppose that the higher object of masonry had passed into a political object, and that the present master's degree was nothing more than a figurative memorial of this event. Meantime the weightiest historical reasons are so entirely opposed to this hypothesis that it must evidently be pronounced a mere conceit of Mr. Nicolai's:—

1. *History mentions nothing at all of any participation of the Free-masons in the transactions of those times.* We have the most accurate and minute accounts of all the other political parties—the Presbyterians, the Independents, the Levellers, etc. etc.; but no historian of this period has so much as mentioned the Free-masons. Is it credible that a society which is represented as the centre of the counter-revolutionary faction should have escaped the jealous eyes of Cromwell, who had brought the system of *espionage* to perfection, and who carried his vigilance so far as to seize the *Oceana* of Harrington at the press? He must have been well assured that Free-masonry was harmless; or he would not have wanted means to destroy it, with all its pretensions and mysteries. Moreover, it is a pure fancy of Nicolai's that the elder Free-masons were all favourably disposed to the royal cause. English clubs, I admit, are accustomed to harmonise in their political principles; but the society of Free-masons, whose true object abstracted from all politics, must have made an exception to this rule then as certainly as they do now.

2. *The Masonic Degree of Master, and indeed Free-masonry in general, is in direct contradiction to this hypothesis of Nicolai.* It must be granted to me, by those who maintain this hypothesis, that the order of the Free-masons had attained some consistence in 1646 (in which year Ashmole was admitted a member), consequently about three years before the execution of Charles I. It follows, therefore, upon this hypothesis, that it must have existed for some years without any ground or object of its existence. It pretended as yet to no mystery, according to Nicolai (though I have shown that at its very earliest formation it made such a pretension): it pursued neither science, art, nor trade; social pleasure was not its object: it "masoned" mysteriously with closed doors in its hall in London; and no man can guess at *what* it "masoned." It constituted a "mystery" (a guild) — with this contradiction *in adjecto*, that it consisted not of masters, journeymen, and apprentices; for the master's degree, according to Nicolai, was first devised by the conclave after the

execution of Charles I. Thus far the inconsistencies of this hypothesis are palpable; but in what follows it will appear that there are still more striking ones. For, if the master's degree arose first after the execution of Charles I. and symbolically imported vengeance on the murderers of their master and restoration of his son to the royal dignity, in that case, during the two Protectorates, and for a long time after the abdication of Richard, the mythus connected with that degree might indeed have spoken of a murdered master, but not also (as it does) of a master risen again, living, and triumphant; for as yet matters had not been brought thus far. If to this it be replied that perhaps in fact the case was really so, and that the mythus of the restored master might have been added to that of the slain master after the Restoration, there will still be this difficulty,—that in the masonic mythus the two masters are one and the same person who is first slain and then restored to life: yet Charles I, who was slain, did not arise again from the dead; and Charles II, though he was restored to his throne, was yet never slain, and therefore could not even metaphorically be said to rise again.[1] Suiting therefore to neither of these kings, the mythus of the masonic master's degree does not adapt itself to this part of history. Besides, as Herder has justly remarked, what a childish part would the Free-masons be playing *after* the Restoration! With this event their object was accomplished: to what purpose, then, any further mysteries? The very ground of the mysteries had thus fallen away; and, according to all analogy of experience, the mysteries themselves should have ceased at the same time.

But the Free-masons called themselves at that time *Sons of the Widow* (*i.e.*, as it is alleged, of Henrietta Maria, the wife of the murdered king); and they were in search of the lost

[1] Begging Professor Buhle's pardon, he is wrong in this particular argument—though no doubt right in the main point he is urging against Nicolai. The mere passion of the case would very naturally express the identity of interest in any father and son by attributing identity to their persons, as though the father lived again and triumphed in the triumph of his son. But in the case of an English king, who never dies *quoad* his office, there is not only a pathos, but a philosophic accuracy and fidelity to the constitutional doctrine, in this way of symbolising the story.

Word (the Prince of Wales). This, it is argued, has too near an agreement with the history of that period to be altogether a fiction. I answer that we must not allow ourselves to be duped by specious resemblances The elder Free-masons called themselves *Sons of the Widow* because the working masons called and still call themselves by that name agreeably to their legend. In the 1st Book of Kings, vii. 13, are these words :—" And King Solomon sent and fetched Hiram of Tyre, a widow's son of the tribe of Naphtali." Hiram, therefore, the eldest mason of whom anything is known, was a widow's son. Hence, therefore, the masons of the seventeenth century, who were familiar with the Bible, styled themselves in memory of their founder *Sons of the Widow*; and the Free-masons borrowed this designation from them as they did the rest of their external constitution. Moreover, the masonic expression *Sons of the Widow* has the closest connexion with the building of Solomon's Temple.

Just as little did the Free-masons mean by *the lost word* which they sought the Prince of Wales. That great personage was not lost; so that there could be no occasion for seeking him. The Royal party knew as well where he was to be found as in our days the French Royalists have always known the residence of the emigrant Bourbons. The question was not—where to find him, but how to replace him on his throne. Besides, though a most majestic person in his political relations, a Prince of Wales makes no especial pretensions to sanctity of character ; and, familiar as scriptural allusions were in that age, I doubt whether he could have been denominated *the logos* or *word* without offence to the scrupulous austerity of that age in matters of religion. What was it, then, that the Free-masons really *did* mean by the lost word ? Manifestly the masonic mystery itself, the secret wisdom delivered to us under a figurative veil through Moses, Solomon, the Prophets, the grand-master Christ, and his confidential disciples. Briefly, they meant the lost word of God in the Cabbalistic sense ; and therefore it was that long *after* the Restoration they continued to seek it, and are still seeking it to this day.

III. *That Cromwell was not the founder of Free-masonry :—*
As Nicolai has chosen to represent the elder Free-masons

as zealous Royalists, so, on the contrary, others have thought fit to describe them as furious democrats. According to this fiction, Cromwell, with some confidential friends (*e.g.* Ireton, Algernon Sidney, Neville, Martin Wildman, Harrington, etc.), founded the order of 1645—ostensibly, on the part of Cromwell, for the purpose of reconciling the contending parties in religion and politics, but really with a view to his own ambitious projects. To this statement I oppose the following arguments :—

First, it contradicts the internal character and spirit of Free-masonry—which is free from all political tendency, and is wholly unintelligible on this hypothesis.

Secondly, though it is unquestionable that Cromwell established and supported many secret connexions, yet the best English historians record nothing of any connexion which he had with the Free-masons. *Divide et impera* was the Machiavelian maxim which Cromwell derived, not from Machiavel, but from his own native political sagacity ; and, with such an object before him, it is very little likely that he would have sought to connect himself with a society that aims at a general harmony amongst men.

Thirdly, how came it—if the order of Free-masons were the instrument of the Cromwellian revolution—that the Royalists did not exert themselves after the restoration of Charles II to suppress it ?

But the fact is that this origin of Free-masonry has been forged for the purpose of making it hateful and an object of suspicion to monarchical states. See for example " *The Freemasons Annihilated, or Prosecution of the detected Order of Free-masons,*" Frankfort and Leipzig, 1746. The first part of this work, which is a translation from the French, appeared under the title of " Free-masonry exposed," etc., Leipz. 1745.

IV. *That the Scotch degree, as it is called, did not arise from the intrigues for the restoration of Charles II :—*

I have no intention to enter upon the tangled web of the modern higher masonry ; though, from an impartial study of the historical documents, I could perhaps bring more light, order, and connexion into this subject than at present it exhibits. Many personal considerations move me to let the curtain drop on the history of the modern higher masonry, or at most to allow myself only a few general hints, which may be pursued by those amongst my readers who may be interested in such a research. One only of the higher masonic degrees—viz. the Scotch degree, which is the most familiarly known and is adopted by most lodges, I must notice more circumstantially—because, upon some statements which have been made, it might seem to have been connected with the elder Free-masonry. Nicolai's account of this matter is as follows:—

"After the death of Cromwell and the deposition of his "son, the government of England fell into the hands of a "violent but weak and disunited faction. In such hands, "as every patriot saw, the government could not be durable, "and the sole means for delivering the country was to "restore the kingly authority. But in this there was the "greatest difficulty; for the principal officers of the army in "England, though otherwise in disagreement with each "other, were yet unanimous in their hostility to the king. "Under these circumstances the eyes of all parties were "turned upon the English army in Scotland, at that time "under the command of Monk, who was privately well "affected to the royal cause; and the secret society of the "king's friends in London, who placed all their hopes on "him, saw the necessity in such a critical period of going "warily and mysteriously to work. It strengthened their "sense of this necessity that one of their own members, Sir "Richard Willis, became suspected of treachery; and there-"fore out of the bosom of their 'secret conclave' (the "masonic master's degree) they resolved to form a still "narrower conclave, to whom the Scotch, *i.e.* the most "secret, affairs should be confided. They chose new sym-"bols, adapted to their own extremely critical situation. "These symbols imported that, in the business of this "interior conclave, wisdom, obedience, courage, self-sacrifice, "and moderation were necessary. Their motto was— "*Wisdom above thee*. For greater security they altered their "signs, and reminded each other in their tottering condition "not to stumble and *break the arm.*"

I do not deny that there is much plausibility in this

hypothesis of Nicolai's; but, upon examination, it will appear that it is all pure delusion, without any basis of historical truth.

1. Its validity rests upon the previous assumption that the interpretation of the master's degree, as connected with the political interests of the Stuarts between the death of Charles I. and the restoration of his son, is correct. it is therefore a *petitio principii*; and what is the value of the *principium* we have already seen.

2. Of any participation on the part of a secret society of Free-masons in the counsels and expedition of Gen. Monk history tells us absolutely nothing. Even Skinner[1] preserves a profound silence on this head. Now, if the fact were so, to suppose that this accurate biographer should not have known it is absurd; and, knowing it, that he should designedly suppress a fact so curious and so honourable to the Free-masons amongst the Royal party is inexplicable.

3. Nicolai himself maintains, and even proves, that Monk was not himself a Free-mason. In what way then could the society gain any influence over his measures. My sagacious friend justly applauds the politic mistrust of Monk (who would not confide his intentions even to his own brother), his secrecy, and the mysterious wisdom of his conduct; and in the very same breath he describes him as surrendering himself to the guidance of a society with which he was not even connected as a member. How is all this to be reconciled?

Undoubtedly there existed at that time in London a secret party of Royalists, known in history under the name of the Secret Conclave; but we are acquainted with its members, and there were but some few Free-masons amongst them. Nicolai alleges the testimony of Ramsay—"that the restoration of Charles II to the English throne was first concerted in a society of Free-masons; because Gen. Monk was a member of it." But in this assertion of Ramsay's there is at any rate one manifest untruth on Nicolai's own showing; for Monk, according to Nicolai, was not a Free-

[1] *The Life of General Monk*, by Thomas Skinner, M.D.: London, 1723.—M.

mason. The man who begins with such an error in his premises must naturally err in his conclusions.[1]

4. The Scotch degree,—nay, the very name of Scotch masonry,—does not once come forward in the elder Freemasonry throughout the whole of the seventeenth century; as it must inevitably have done if it had borne any relation to the restoration of Charles II. Indeed it is doubtful whether the Scotch degree was known even in Scotland or in England before the third decennium of the eighteenth century.

But how then did this degree arise? What is its meaning and object? The answer to these questions does not belong to this place. It is enough on the present occasion to have shown how it did *not* arise, and what were *not* its meaning and object. I am here treating of the origin and history of the elder and legitimate masonry, not of an indecent pretender who crept at a later period into the order, and, by the side of the Lion, the Pelican, and the Dove, introduced the Ape and the Fox.

V. *The Free-masons are not derived from the order of the Knights Templars:*—

No hypothesis upon the origin and primitive tendency of the Free-masons has obtained more credit in modern times than this—that they were derived from the order of Knights Templars so cruelly persecuted and ruined under Pope Clement V and Philip the Fair of France, and had no other

---

[1] Andrew Michael Ramsay [1686-1743—M.] was a Scotchman by birth, but lived chiefly in France (where he became a Catholic), and is well known as the author of *The Travels of Cyrus*, and other works. His dissertation on the Free-masons contains the old legend that Free-masonry dated its origin from a guild of working masons who resided during the crusades in the Holy Land for the purpose of rebuilding the Christian churches destroyed by the Saracens, and were afterwards summoned by a king of England to his own dominions. As tutor to the two sons of the Pretender, for whose use he wrote *The Travels of Cyrus*, Ramsay is a distinguished person in the history of the later Free-masonry. Of all that part of its history which lay half a century before his own time he was, however, very ill informed. On this he gives us nothing but the cant of the later English lodges, who had lost the kernel in the shell—the original essence and object of masonry in its form—as early as the beginning of the eighteenth century.

secret purpose on their first appearance than the re-establishment of that injured order. So much influence has this opinion had in France that in the first half of the eighteenth century it led to the amalgamation of the external forms and ritual of the Templars with those of the Free-masons; and some of the higher degrees of French masonry have undoubtedly proceeded from this amalgamation. In Germany it was Lessing who, if not first, yet chiefly, gave to the learned world an interest in this hypothesis by some allusions to it scattered through his masterly dialogues for Free-masons. With many it became a favourite hypothesis; for it assigned an honourable origin to the Masonic order, and flattered the vanity of its members. The Templars were one of the most celebrated knightly orders during the Crusades: their whole institution, acts, and tragical fate are attractive to the feelings and the fancy: how natural therefore it was that the modern masons should seize with enthusiasm upon the conjectures thrown out by Lessing! Some modern English writers have also adopted this mode of explaining the origin of Free-masonry; not so much on the authority of any historical documents as because they found in the French lodges degrees which had a manifest reference to the Templar institutions, and which they naturally attributed to the elder Free-masonry, being ignorant that they had been purposely introduced at a later period to serve an hypothesis. In fact the French degrees had been originally derived from the hypothesis; and now the hypothesis was in turn derived from the French degrees. If in all this there were any word of truth, it would follow that I had written this whole book of 418 pages to no purpose: and what a shocking thing would that be![1] Knowing therefore the importance to myself of this question, it may be presumed that I have examined it not negligently before I ventured to bring forward my own deduction of the Free-masons from the Rosicrucians. This is not the place for a full critique upon all the idle prattle about the Templars and the Free-masons; but an impartial review of the arguments for and against the Templar hypothesis may reasonably be demanded of me as a negative attestation of my own hypothesis. In

[1] De Quincey's interjection, doubtless!—M.

doing this I must presume in my reader a general acquaintance with the constitution and history of the Templars, which it will be very easy for any one not already in possession of it to gain.

1. It is alleged that the masonic mystical allegory represented nothing else in its capital features than the persecution and overthrow of the Templars, especially the dreadful death of the innocent grand-master James Burg de Mollay. Some knights, together with Aumont, it is said, made their escape in the dress of masons to Scotland, and, for the sake of disguise, exercised the trade of masons. This was the reason that they adopted symbols from that trade, and, to avoid detection, gave them the semblance of moral purposes. They called themselves *Franc Maçons*: as well in memory of the Templars, who in Palestine were always called Franks by the Saracens, as with a view to distinguish themselves from the common working masons. The Temple of Solomon, which they professed to build, together with all the masonic attributes, pointed collectively to the grand purpose of the society—the restoration of the Templar order. At first the society was confined to the descendants of its founders; but within the last 150 years the Scotch masters have communicated their hereditary right to others, in order to extend their own power; and from this period, it is said, begins the *public* history of Free-masonry.[1]

Such is the legend; which is afterwards supported by the general analogy between the ritual and external characteristics of both orders. The *three* degrees of masonry (the holy masonic number) are compared with the triple office of general amongst the Templars. The masonic dress is alleged to be copied from that of the Templars. The signs of Free-masonry are the same with those used in Palestine by the Templars. The rights of initiation, as practised on the admission of a novice, especially on admission to the master's degree, and the symbolic object of this very degree, are all

---

[1] See "The Use and Abuse of Free-masonry by Captain George Smith, Inspector of the Royal Military School at Woolwich, &c. &c., London, 1783." See also, "Scotch Masonry compared with the three Vows of the Order and with the Mystery of the Knights Templars: from the French of Nicolas de Bonneville."

connected with the persecution of the Templars, with the trial of the knights, and the execution of the grand-master. To this grand-master (James *B*urg) the letters I and B, which no longer mean Jachin and Boaz, are said to point. Even the holiest masonic name of Hiram has no other allusion than to the murdered grand-master of the Templars. With regard to these analogies in general, it may be sufficient to say that some of them are accidental, some very forced and far-sought, and some altogether fictitious. Thus, for instance, it is said that the name *Franc Maçon* was chosen in allusion to the connexion of the Templars with Palestine. And thus we are required to believe that the eldest Free-masons of Great Britain styled themselves at first Frank Masons: as if this had any warrant from History, or, supposing even that it had, as if a name adopted on such a ground could ever have been dropped. The simple fact is that the French were the people who first introduced the seeming allusion to Franks by translating the English name *Free-mason* into *Franc Maçon*; which they did because the word *libre* would not so easily blend into composition with the word Maçon. So also the late Mr. Von Born, having occasion to express the word Free-masons in Latin, rendered it Franco-murarii. Not to detain the reader, however, with a separate examination of each particular allegation, I will content myself with observing that the capital mythus of the masonic master's degree tallies but in one half with the execution of the Grand-Master of the Templars, or even of the Sub-Prior of Montfaucon (Charles de Monte Carmel). The grand-master was indeed murdered, as the grand-master of the Free-masons is described to have been; but not, as the latter, by treacherous journeymen: moreover, the latter rose from the grave, still lives, and triumphs; which will hardly be said of James Burg de Mollay. Two arguments, however, remain to be noticed, both out of respect to the literary eminence of those who have alleged them, and also because they seem intrinsically of some weight.

2. *The English word masony.*—This word, or (as it ought in that case to be written) the word *masony*, is derived, according to Lessing, from the Anglo-Saxon word *massoney*, a secret commensal society; which last word again comes

from *mase*, a table. Such table societies and compotuses were very common amongst our forefathers, especially amongst the princes and knights of the middle ages: the weightiest affairs were there transacted, and peculiar buildings were appropriated to their use. In particular, the *masonies* of the Knights Templars were highly celebrated in the thirteenth century. One of them was still subsisting in London at the end of the 17th century,—at which period, according to Lessing, the public history of the Free-masons first commences. This society had its house of meeting near St. Paul's Cathedral; which was then rebuilding. Sir Christopher Wren, the architect, was one of its members. For thirty years, during the building of the cathedral, he continued to frequent it. From this circumstance the people, who had forgotten the true meaning of the word *massoney*, took it for a society of architects with whom Sir Christopher consulted on any difficulties which arose in the progress of the work. This mistake Wren turned to account. He had formerly assisted in planning a society which should make speculative truths more useful for purposes of common life. The very converse of this idea now occurred to him,—viz. the idea of a society which should raise itself from the praxis of civil life to speculation. "In the former," thought he, "would be examined all that was useful amongst the true; in this all that is true amongst the useful. How if I should make some principles of the *masony* exoteric? How if I should disguise that which cannot be made exoteric under the hieroglyphics and symbols of *masonry*, as the people pronounce the word, and extend this masonry into a Freemasonry in which all may take a share?" In this way, according to Lessing, did Wren scheme; and in this way did Free-masonry arise. Afterwards, however, from a conversation which he had with Nicolai, it appears that Lessing had thus far changed his first opinion (as given in the *Ernst und Falk*)—that he no longer supposed Sir Christopher simply to have modified a *massoney*, or society of Knights Templars, which had subsisted secretly for many centuries, and to have translated their doctrines into an exoteric shape, but rather to have himself first established such a *massoney*—upon some basis of analogy, however, with the elder *massoneys*.

To an attentive examiner of this conjecture of Lessing's it will appear that it rests entirely upon the presumed identity of meaning between the word *massoney* and the word *masony* (or *masonry*, as it afterwards became, according to the allegation, through a popular mistake of the meaning). But the very meaning and etymology ascribed to *massoney* (viz. a secret club or *compotus*, from *mase*, a table) are open to much doubt. Nicolai, a friend of Lessing's, professes as little to know any authority for such an explanation as myself, and is disposed to derive the word *massoney* from *massonya*: which in the Latin of the middle age meant first a club (*clava*, in French *massue*); secondly, a key (*clavis*), and a secret society (a club). For my part I think both the etymologies false. *Massoney* is doubtless originally the same word with *maison* and *magione*; and the primitive etymon of all three words is clearly the Latin word *mansio*, in the sense of the middle ages. It means simply a residence or place of abode, and was naturally applied to the dwelling-houses of the Templars. Their meetings were held *in mansione Templariorum*, *i.e.* in the massoney of the Templars. On the suppression of the order, their buildings still remained, and preserved the names of temples, templar-mansions, &c., just as at this day we find many *convents* in Hanover, though they are no longer occupied by monks or nuns; and in Italy there are even yet churches to be found which are denominated *de la Mason*; which Paciaudi properly explains by *della Magione*—these churches having been attached to the dwellings of the Knights Templars. It is therefore very possible that a Templar *Massoney* may have subsisted in London, in the neighbourhood of St. Paul's church, up to the end of the seventeenth century. Some notice of such a fact Lessing perhaps stumbled on in the course of his reading. He mistook the building for a secret society of Templars that still retained a traditional knowledge of the principles peculiar to the ancient order of Knights Templars; next he found that Sir Christopher Wren had been a frequenter of this *massoney*. He therefore was a Knight Templar, but he was also an architect; and by him the Templar doctrines had been moulded into a symbolic conformity with his own art, and had been fitted for diffusion amongst the people!

Such is the way in which a learned hypothesis arises ; and on this particular hypothesis may be pronounced what Lessing said of many an older one—Dust ! and nothing but dust !— In conclusion, I may add what Nicolai had already observed, that Lessing was wholly misinformed as to the history and chronology of Free-masonry. So far from arising out of the ashes of the Templar traditions at the end of the seventeenth century, we have seen that it was fully matured in the forty-sixth year of that century, and therefore long before the rebuilding of St. Paul's. In fact Sir Christopher Wren was himself elected Deputy Grand-master of the Free-masons in 1666 ; and in less than twenty years after (viz. in 1685) he became Grand-master.

3. *Baphomet.*—But, says Mr. Nicolai, the Templars had a secret, and the Free-masons have a secret ; and the secrets agree in this, that no uninitiated person has succeeded in discovering either. Does not this imply some connexion originally between the two orders ; more especially if it can be shown that the two secrets are identical ? Sorry I am, my venerable friend, to answer—No. Sorry I am, in your old days, to be under the necessity of knocking on the head a darling hypothesis of yours, which has cost you, I doubt not, much labour of study and research, much thought, and, I fear also, many many pounds of candles. But it is my duty to do so ; and indeed, considering Mr. Nicolai's old age and his great merits in regard to German Literature, it would be my duty to show him no mercy, but to lash him with the utmost severity for his rotten hypothesis,—if my time would allow it. But to come to business. The Templars, says old Nicolai, had a secret. They had so ; but what was it ? According to Nicolai, it consisted in the denial of the Trinity, and in a scheme of natural religion opposed to the dominant Popish Catholicism. Hence it was that the Templars sought to make themselves independent of the other Catholic clergy : the novices were required to abjure the divinity of Christ, and even to spit upon a crucifix and trample it under foot. Their Anti-Trinitarianism Mr. Nicolai ascribes to their connexion with the Saracens, who always made the doctrine of the Trinity a matter of reproach to the Franks. He supposes that, during periods of truce or in captivity, many

Templars had, by communication with learned Mohammedans, become enlightened to the errors and the tyranny of Popery; but at the same time, strengthening their convictions of the falsehood of Mohammedanism, they had retained nothing of their religious doctrines but Monotheism. These heterodoxies, however, under the existing power of the hierarchy and the universal superstition then prevalent, they had the strongest reasons for communicating to none but those who were admitted into the highest degree of their order,—and to them only symbolically. From these data,—which may be received as tolerably probable and conformable to the depositions of the witnesses on the trial of the Templars,—old Mr. Nicolai flatters himself that he can unriddle the mystery of mysteries: viz. Baphomet (Baffomet, Baphemet, or Baffometus); which was the main symbol of the Knights Templars in the highest degrees. This Baphomet was a figure representing a human bust, but sometimes of monstrous and caricature appearance, which symbolized the highest object of the Templars; and therefore upon the meaning of Baphomet hinges the explanation of the great Templar mystery.

First, then, Mr. Nicolai tells us what Baphomet was *not* It was not Mohammed. According to the genius of the Arabic language, out of *Mohammed* might be made *Mahomet* or *Bahomet* but not *Baphomet*. In some Latin historians about the period of the Crusades Bahomet is certainly used for Mahomet, and in one writer perhaps Baphomet (viz. in the *Epistola Anselmi de Ribodimonte ad Manassem Archiepiscopum Remensem*, of the year 1099, in Dachery's *Spicilegium*, tom. ii. p. 431. — "Sequenti die aurora apparente altis " vocibus *Baphomet* invocaverunt; et nos, Deum nostrum in " cordibus nostris deprecantes, impetum fecimus in eos, et de " muris civitatis omnes expulimus." Nicolai, supposing that the cry of the Saracens was in this case addressed to their own prophet, concludes that *Baphomet* is an error of the press for *Bahomet*, and that this is put for *Mahomet*. But it is possible that *Baphomet* may be the true reading; for it may not have been used in devotion for Mohammed, but scoffingly as the known watchword of the Templars). But it contradicts the whole history of the Templars to suppose that they had introduced into their order the worship of an image of Mohammed. In fact, from all the records of their trial and persecution, it results that no such charge was brought against them by their enemies. And, moreover, Mohammedanism itself rejects all worship of images.

Secondly, not being Mahomet, what *was* it? It was, says Mr. Nicolai, Βαφὴ μήτους: *i.e.* as he interprets it, the word *Baphomet* meant the *baptism of wisdom*; and the image so called represented God, the universal father,—*i.e.* expressed the *unity* of the divine being. By using this sign therefore under this name, which partook much of a Gnostic and Cabbalistic spirit, the Templars indicated their dedication to the truths of natural religion.

Now, in answer to this learned conceit of Mr. Nicolai's, I would wish to ask him—

First, in an age so barbarous as that of the twelfth and thirteenth centuries, when not to be able to read or write was no disgrace, how came a body of rude warriors like the Templars to descend into the depths of Gnosticism?

Secondly, if by the image called Baphomet they meant to represent the unity of God, how came they to designate it by a name which expresses no attribute of the Deity, but simply a mystical ceremony amongst themselves (viz. the baptism of wisdom)?

Thirdly, I will put a home question to Mr. Nicolai; and let him parry it if he can: How many heads had Baphomet? His own conscience will reply—Two. Indeed a whole length of Baphomet is recorded which has also four feet; but, supposing these to be disputed, Mr. Nicolai can never dispute away the two heads. Now, what sort of a symbol would a two-headed image have been for the expression of unity of being? Answer me that, Mr. Nicolai. Surely the rudest skulls of the twelfth century could have expressed their meaning better.

Having thus upset my learned brother's hypothesis, I now come forward with my own. Through the illumination which some of the Templars gained in the east as to the relations in which they stood to the Pope and Romish Church, but still more perhaps from the suggestions of their own great power and wealth opposed to so rapacious and potent a supremacy, there gradually arose a separate Templar interest, no less hostile to the Pope and Clergy of Rome than to Mohammed. To this separate interest they adapted an appropriate scheme of theology: but neither the one nor the other could be communicated with safety except to their own superior members; and thus it became a mystery of the order. Now, this mystery was symbolically expressed by a two-headed figure of *Baphomet*, — *i.e.* of the Pope and Mohammed together. So long as the Templars continued orthodox, the watchword of their undivided hostility was *Mahomet*; but, as soon as the Pope became an object of jealousy and hatred to them, they devised a new watchword, which should covertly express their double-headed enmity by intertwisting the name of the Pope with that of Mohammed.[1] This they effected by cutting off the two first letters of *Mahomet* and substituting *Bap* or *Pup*—the first syllable of *Papa*. Thus arose the compound word *Baphomet*; and hence it was that the image of Baphomet was figured with two heads, and was otherwise monstrous in appearance. When a Templar was initiated into the highest degree of the order, he was shown this image of Baphomet, and received a girdle with certain ceremonies which referred to that figure. At sight of this figure in the general chapters of the order, the knights expressed their independence of the Church and the Church creed, by testifying their abhorrence of the crucifix, and by worshipping the sole God of heaven and earth. Hence they called a newly initiated member a "friend of God, who could now speak with God if he chose," *i.e.* without the intermediation of the Pope and the Church. Upon this explanation of Baphomet, it becomes sufficiently plain why the secret was looked upon as so inviolable that even upon the rack it could not be extorted from them. By such a confession the order would have exposed itself to a still more cruel persecution, and a more inevitable destruction. On the other hand, upon Mr. Nicolai's explanation, it is difficult to conceive why, under

---

[1] Those who are acquainted with the German Protestant writers about the epoch of the Reformation will remember the many fanciful combinations extracted from the names Pabst (Pope) and Mohammed by all manner of dislocations and inversions of their component letters.

such extremities, the accused should not have confessed the truth. In all probability the Court of Rome had good information of the secret tendency of the Templar doctrines; and hence no doubt it was that Pope Clement V proceeded so furiously against them.

Now then I come to my conclusion; which is this:—If the Knights Templars had no other secret than one relating to a *political* interest which placed them in opposition to the Pope and the claims of the Roman Catholic clergy on the one hand, and to Mohammed on the other,—then it is impossible that there can have been any affinity or resemblance whatsoever between them and the Free-masons; for the Free-masons have never in any age troubled themselves about either Mohammed or the Pope. Popery[1] and Mohammedanism are alike indifferent to the Free-masons, and always have been. And, in general, the object of the Free-masons is not political. Finally, it is in the highest degree probable that the secret of the Knights Templars perished with their order: for it is making too heavy a demand on our credulity to suppose that a secret society never once coming within the light of history can have propagated itself through a period of four centuries—*i.e.* from the thirteenth to the seventeenth century; in which century it has been shown that Free-masonry first arose.

[1] In rejecting Roman Catholic candidates for admission into their order the reader must remember that the Free-masons objected to them not *as* Roman Catholics, but as persons of intolerant principles.—*Translator.*

END OF VOL. XIII

Printed by R. & R. CLARK, LIMITED, *Edinburgh.*

www.ingramcontent.com/pod-product-compliance
Lightning Source LLC
Chambersburg PA
CBHW022140300426
44115CB00006B/278